FINANCIAL DATA ANALYSIS USING PYTHON

FINANCIAL DATA ANALYSIS USING PYTHON

Dmytro Zherlitsyn

MERCURY LEARNING AND INFORMATION
Boston, Massachusetts

Publisher: David Pallai
MERCURY LEARNING AND INFORMATION
121 High Street, 3rd Floor
Boston, MA 02110
info@merclearning.com
www.merclearning.com
800-232-0223

D. Zherlitsyn. *Financial Data Analysis Using Python.*
ISBN: 978-1-50152-386-1

Library of Congress Control Number: 2024948825

242526321   This book is printed on acid-free paper in the United States of America.

Our titles are available for adoption, license, or bulk purchase by institutions, corporations, etc. For additional information, please contact the Customer Service Dept. at 800-232-0223(toll free).

CONTENTS

PREFACE

Financial markets are complex systems involving many participants, interconnected entities, as well as models, methods and technologies. In recent years, the financial sector has experienced an "explosion" due to the catastrophic growth in information volumes. Classical methods of financial data analysis need to gain competitive ground. Therefore, financial analysts increasingly use IT technologies, particularly Python programming tools, for quick decision-making and profit generation.

Python, a high-level programming language, has become a staple in various fields, including finance. Its straightforward syntax, vast user community, and extensive range of libraries and tools make it a practical and powerful tool for financial data analysis. This book utilizes key Python libraries such as Pandas, NumPy, SciPy, Statsmodels, Matplotlib, Seaborn, Scikit-learn, Prophet, and others, empowering you with the tools you need to excel in financial analysis.

This book introduces fundamental concepts for analyzing financial markets and supporting investment decisions. These concepts, including time-series analysis, graphical analysis, technical and fundamental analysis, asset pricing, portfolio theory, investment and trading strategies, risk assessment, and the basics of financial machine learning, are more than just theoretical. We bring them to life with real-world examples of analyzing financial market dynamics, forecasting future trends, optimizing investment portfolios, assessing strategies, and managing financial risks, making the content engaging and applicable to your work.

With this book, you will gain Python programming basics, its primary libraries for data analysis, and their integration with the core financial concepts.

Chapter 1: Getting Started with Python for Finance - explains foundational knowledge of Python's role in finance and its advantages over other programming languages. The installation and configuration of Python on local computers or using the Google Colab cloud platform are described. This chapter provides an overview of the top libraries for solving financial problems with Python. It also illustrates the fundamentals of the Python programming language, including syntax, operators, and basic data structures, including those related to financial data analysis.

Chapter 2: Python Tools for Data Analysis: Primer to Pandas and NumPy - presents an overview of the essential Python control and data structures operations, built-in functions, and primary libraries for financial data analysis (NumPy and Pandas). The chapter provides practical examples close to actual financial data to explore foundational tools and operations crucial for such manipulation. Learn to create and manage arrays with NumPy and handle tabular data effortlessly with Pandas, gearing you to derive insightful outcomes from the financial data analyses.

Chapter 3: Financial Data Manipulation with Python - covers the foundational concepts of financial data, explores various open data sources, and investigates their role in finance. The practical skills with Python will be expanded while collecting real-world financial datasets by importing and structuring information. In the chapter, explain how to use the benefits of yfinance, pandas_datareader, quandl and other Python libraries, as well as CSV and Excel data files, APIs, and web-scraping tools. The practical results create datasets for analyzing financial data and making informed decisions using Python.

Chapter 4: Exploratory Data Analysis for Finance - allows the reader to learn essential exploratory data analysis skills for finance. The data-transforming processes and patterns used to inspect and clean financial data and related mathematical operations are described. The chapter provides hands-on experience in data visualization using Matplotlib and Seaborn, as well as understanding the descriptive statistics metrics and moving average data to determine financial trends. Investment returns and risk statistics, as well as explanatory, visual, and correlation analysis tools, are explored. This skill set helps to make informed, data-driven investment decisions and prepares for the typical analytical stages.

Chapter 5: Investment and Trading Strategies - gives special attention to investment, analytical and trading strategies, with the ability to integrate technical, fundamental, and graphical analysis into your trading strategy. The chapter delves into core investment principles and metrics, offering practical insights and advanced candlestick chart techniques. Utilizing Python's visualization tools, financial market data is brought to life, highlighting significant patterns and interpreting market indicators. Essential graphical and technical analysis tools are covered, enabling the generation and testing of trading strategies. Real-world market data is used to solidify understanding, preparing readers to navigate the dynamic nature of trading with a thorough grasp of risk and return dynamics and equipping them to make informed decisions using sophisticated analytical tools.

Chapter 6: Asset Pricing and Portfolio Management - details Python tools for estimating investment portfolio parameters and regression model parameters. The basics of modern portfolio theory are covered to inform long-term investment strategies. Foundational portfolio theories, such as Markowitz's model and the Sharpe Ratio criteria, are examined. Statistical tools and regression models are used to quantify the risk-return ratio for making investment decisions. The power of Python statistical libraries, such as Statsmodels and SciPy, is highlighted for regression analysis and to find optimum solutions mathematically.

Chapter 7: Time Series Analysis and Financial Data Forecasting - applies traditional time series analysis in financial forecasting with Python, pointing out the core limitations of these models. Various forecasting techniques are explored, from exponential smoothing to advanced SARIMAX models, revealing the challenges faced in volatile financial markets. The chapter describes why the Mean Absolute Percentage Error (MAPE) metric can sometimes yield better results with actual financial time series data variations. This insight is pivotal for applying more robust and adaptive forecasting techniques, including machine learning.

Chapter 8: Risk Assessment and Volatility Modelling – explains sophisticated principles of probability theory with executable Python code, leading to a deep understanding of financial risk and volatility principles. Proficiency is gained in applying Python's computational capabilities to financial risk assessment and volatility modelling. Understanding how to use Python tools with key probabilistic distributions is achieved through the computation of VaR and aVaR. The power of Monte Carlo simulations is used by applying randomizing or stochastic methods to real-world examples of option price prediction and VaR estimation. By comprehensively exploring ARCH and GARCH models, the ability to anticipate and model financial volatility is developed.

Chapter 9: Machine Learning and Deep Learning in Finance – touches the ML world as it applies to the financial sector. An understanding of fundamental theories, models, and steps for applying machine learning to analyze and predict financial data is provided. The chapter focuses on the practical utility of the scikit-learn library, demonstrating how to implement machine learning models such as clustering and regression and employ feature engineering to enhance model performance. Description of the scikit-learn, XGBoost, and lightGBM libraries and evaluation of the basic machine learning models using appropriate tools for financial applications are covered. The chapter lays the foundation for applying skills in using Python-based regression and clustering techniques, understanding the importance of cross-validation, and performing hyperparameter tuning to improve model accuracy.

Chapter 10: Time Series Analysis and Forecasting with FB Prophet Library – describes the FB Prophet library for advanced time series analysis and forecasting in finance. This chapter provides a detailed understanding of Prophet's functionalities, from executing basic operations to exploiting advanced features for more accurate forecasting. Techniques for applying Prophet to various financial datasets are covered, enabling the forecasting of market trends, evaluation of investment risks, and making well-informed financial decisions. The tools are provided to construct, assess, and refine complex forecasting models, employ cross-validation techniques, tune hyperparameters, and combine Prophet with machine learning methods for enhanced financial decision-making.

Appendix A: Python Code Examples for Finance – includes the main code examples from this book.

Appendix B: Glossary – outlines the meaning of keywords and definitions.

Appendix C: Valuable Resources – describes key resources for future development of new Python programming and self-development

Companion Files Code samples and figures from the text are available for downloading from the publisher by writing to info@merclearning.com.

ACKNOWLEDGMENTS

I want to express my deepest gratitude to my family and friends for their unwavering support and encouragement throughout the writing of this book, especially my wife Darya.

I am also profoundly grateful to BPB Publications for their unwavering guidance and expertise. Their role in bringing the original book to fruition has been invaluable. The journey of revising this book was made possible by the valuable participation and collaboration of reviewers, technical experts, and editors.

I would also like to acknowledge the valuable contributions of my colleagues and students. They have taught me so much and provided valuable feedback on my results.

Finally, I would like to thank all the readers who have taken an interest in my book and for their support in making it a reality.

ABOUT THE AUTHOR

Dmytro Zherlitsyn, a Professor and Doctor of Science, has dedicated over 20 years to university teaching, business training, financial consulting, scientific research, and data analysis. He has authored over 250 academic publications (e-learning courses, textbooks, scientific papers, and monographs) in Economics, Finance, Data Science, System Analysis and Software Engineering. Dmytro headed the Economic Cybernetics department and co-led several data science and business improvement projects. His current roles include: researcher at the University of National and World Economy in Bulgaria and professor at the Technical University "Metinvest Polytechnic" in Ukraine. His teaching comprises pioneering courses in Python for Data Analysis and Applied Statistics, aligning with his professional focus on using Python to drive financial insights and innovations. His work encompasses the development of predictive models for business and market analysis, including advanced regression, simulation and machine learning methods for financial sectors and the cryptocurrency market.

REVIEWERS

Dheerendra Panwar is a seasoned professional in the field of Edge, IoT, and Machine Learning with over ten years of experience. He earned his master's degree in embedded electrical and computer systems from San Francisco State University, further fortifying his expertise in the domain. Throughout his career, he has contributed significantly to various IoT projects, ranging from manufacturing and smart cities to the retail and energy sectors. Having worked in large organizations and startups, he has a comprehensive understanding of the intricacies of IoT/edge technologies and their practical applications.

Yash Yennam is an experienced data scientist and ML engineer with a robust background in developing data-driven solutions and comprehensive ML models. He excels in transforming complex datasets into actionable insights, particularly within the domains of geographic information systems, credit risk and market risk. His expertise encompasses various ML frameworks such as TensorFlow, Scikit-Learn, and PyTorch, in addition to proficiency in big data tools like Spark and Hadoop.

Yash has led projects involving data orchestration pipelines, model deployment, and real-time data processing. His contributions have been instrumental in driving business impact through innovative solutions and operational efficiencies. He possesses a strong foundation in computer science and maintains a passion for continuous learning. Yash is dedicated to advancing the fields of AI and ML, with a keen interest in the latest developments and their practical applications. Beyond his professional endeavors, he is an avid reader of science fiction and non-fiction, and he enjoys playing the guitar. A technology enthusiast, Yash continually explores the fields of astrophysics, engineering, and stock markets.

Suryakant is a distinguished expert in the fields of ML, deep learning, and AI. With a wealth of experience and proven proficiency in these cutting-edge disciplines, Suryakant leads pioneering efforts in generative AI solutions. His extensive knowledge and expertise are instrumental in exploring the transformative potential of this burgeoning technology.

Having authored several research papers and a seminal book on hyperautomation, Suryakant's contributions to the field are widely recognized. With a steadfast commitment to pushing the boundaries of AI innovation, he is dedicated to harnessing the power of generative AI to drive creativity and innovation. Positioned as a key influencer in the realm of generative AI, Suryakant's relentless pursuit of excellence and passion for leveraging data-driven insights exemplify his status as a prominent figure in this dynamic and rapidly evolving domain.

1

GETTING STARTED WITH PYTHON FOR FINANCE

INTRODUCTION

In the constantly evolving field of finance, professionals and enthusiasts must stay up to date with the latest tools and methodologies. One such tool that has gained substantial traction in finance is the Python programming language. This chapter will introduce the dynamic world of Python and its potential in finance and financial data analysis. Initially conceived in the late 1980s for students' software engineering skills training, Python has become an impressive part of the world of finance and FinTech as one of the most popular analytical tools. With its simplicity and expansive ecosystem of libraries, the tool has become an indispensable asset for financial analysts, quantitative researchers, and investment bankers. This might prompt the following questions:

- What makes Python different from other programming languages for finance and data analysis aims?
- Why have major financial institutions and individual investors applied Python tools at the core of their data analytics and financial modeling?

We will learn more about the Python programming language's core principles for data analysis and finance sector decision-making to answer these questions. We will also compare and show Python's advantages as an analysis tool with other major programming languages, such as Java, Julia, and R. Furthermore, to ensure that we are well equipped to use Python, we will explore the essentials of Python installation and the intricacies of setting up *integrated development environments (IDEs)* for Python coding. We will also introduce the pivotal packages and libraries for finance and data analysis. Python is well known for its friendly syntaxes. This chapter will describe the essential principles of syntax, basic operations, control flow, and data types.

So, whether you are a seasoned finance professional looking to enhance your analytical toolkit or a programming enthusiast keen on financial data analysis, this chapter promises to be an enlightening starting point for your journey into the world of Python for finance, a combination that has revolutionized the financial world.

STRUCTURE

This chapter covers the following topics:

- Finance principles and contemporary trends in data analysis
- Comparison of analytical tools for various programming languages
- Installing Python and using IDEs for financial data analysis
- Overview of the main Python libraries for finance
- Python essentials: Syntax, basic operations, control flow, and data types

OBJECTIVES

By the end of this chapter, you will have a foundational knowledge of Python's role in finance and its advantages over other programming languages. You will investigate installing and configuring Python on local computers or using the Google Colab cloud platform. This chapter provides an overview of the top libraries for solving financial problems with Python. It also illustrates the fundamentals of the Python programming language, including syntax, operators, and basic data structures, including those related to financial data analysis.

FINANCE PRINCIPLES AND CONTEMPORARY TRENDS IN DATA ANALYSIS

The emergence of the notion of finance is intertwined with the inception of the earliest states and the nascent trading and market relations. The contemporary, practical meaning of finance, however, relates to managing financial assets. Hence, the paramount objective of financial management is maximizing potential returns and profits from utilizing these assets.

Therefore, the term *finance* often refers to operations in the financial markets, particularly transactions involving the profitability bay or sale of financial assets (stocks, bonds, derivatives, cryptocurrencies, etc.). This book will explore the primary analytical algorithms that use the Python programming language in this domain. Nonetheless, most of the analytical or managerial tools discussed can be used for other financial tasks, such as individual or corporate budget planning, risk assessment and forecasting, and formulating analytical reports to make financial decisions. For those unacquainted with the details of finance, this book will describe the essential principles of managerial decisions on financial markets and core terms relating to financial assets. It delves into the world of financial information and computation.

Inherently quantitative entities, finance invariably involves the numerical representation of outcomes: stock price, profits, turnovers, or past losses. This intrinsic quantitativeness positions finance near the modern world of *information technology (IT)*. In some respects, the valuation of financial assets is dictated by informational factors. For instance, the global financial crisis of 2008–2009 was instigated by discernible fundamental factors. This crisis's precursors, or the weak signals, manifested well before its peak, however. Individual investors and financial institutions that astutely identified these informational cues either minimized their losses or even capitalized on the repercussions of the crisis. The cinematic depiction of this in *The Big Short* (2015) is a recommended reference for an insightful exploration of this theme. The film artistically demonstrates examples of the informational aspects of finance and might even inspire risky financial instincts.

The simultaneous development of innovations in the field of finance and IT technologies has led to a sharp increase in the volume of data, including financial data, which requires the adoption of advanced data processing methodologies. According to data from Statista.com, by 2025, the volume of data created, captured, copied, and consumed globally is projected to double compared to 2021, reaching 181 zettabytes (*source*: Statista, *https://www.statista.com/statistics/871513/worldwide-data-created/*). Thus, a mere momentary lapse in financial decision-making could translate to substantial losses or foregone profits in this high-velocity digital age. Even a slight delay or a small mistake when making financial decisions can lead to lost profits or significant financial losses. Consequently, using tools offered by modern high-level programming languages (R, Python, Java, etc.) has become indispensable for finance, and even parts of most analytical software products.

A conceptual view of gaining profit from investing in financial assets using Python (the general logic of the topic of this book) is illustrated in *Figure 1.1*:

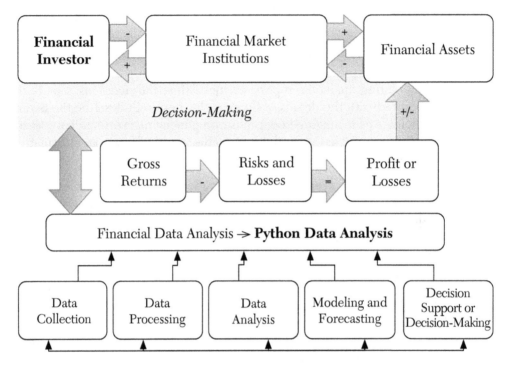

FIGURE 1.1 Outcomes workflow for Python for finance

Figure 1.1 depicts both the participants in the financial markets and the tools utilized for decision-making in the management of the portfolio of financial assets. These will be discussed in more detail in the following subsections.

Financial Investor

This refers to a participant in financial relations with liquidity (financial assets that can easily be exchanged for other assets or services, such as cash). Think of Bob, a software developer who just received his year-end bonus. He is an individual investor looking to grow that bonus by investing in the financial market. An investor can be an individual or a financial institution making a profit in financial markets. The distinguishing characteristic of an investor in the turnover process of financial assets is that they are the owner of the initial capital for investment. Active investors might decide to conduct all financial calculations and forecasts to manage their financial investment portfolios using all analytical tools, including financial data analysis tools from Python.

Passive investors delegate some or all analytical and decision-making functions to financial institutions. Both, however, use financial data analysis tools to maximize profit and minimize losses.

Financial Market Institutions

This category comprises financial and service (consulting) institutions offering diverse services to access financial market opportunities. These institutions include financial asset traders, stock exchanges, consulting firms, analytical bureaus, and rating agencies. Let us understand each, one by one:

- *Exchange institutions*: All financial markets (stock market, bond market, options, or cryptocurrency) need an institution that provides legal compliance and a certain level of investor protection. For example, imagine a busy market where buyers and sellers come to exchange goods. Without the market administration, police, and even cleaners, this market could not exist. Likewise, the exchange institution (usually an exchange) helps financial investors buy, sell, or exchange financial assets. Modern financial exchanges (stock, foreign exchange, cryptocurrency, etc.) have expanded their role. They can also provide consulting and trading services. The primary function, however, of the financial exchange institution remains to fulfill clients' orders and conduct settlement transactions.

- *Financial market traders*: These are individuals or entities who actively trade in the financial markets, either for themselves or on clients' (individual and corporate investors) behalf. Imagine someone at multiple computer screens, watching the numbers and graphs move, deciding when to buy or sell—that is a trader in action. They bring liquidity (supply and demand) to the markets, ensuring that securities can be bought or sold anytime. Thanks to traders, we can be sure that the valuable assets that we have in our possession can be sold to someone. Traders use various investment strategies based on analytical calculations and the preferences of their clients.

- *Consulting institutes*: These include rating and information agencies, trust companies, and mutual funds, which are key players in the financial sector. They offer various services, from one-time consultations for purchase and sale decisions to comprehensive management of investment portfolios. These institutes serve as financial guides, advising clients on their financial tasks and problems. Rating agencies show the creditworthiness of various organizations, from corporations to governments. News agencies provide essential analytical data for informed trading. Trust companies and mutual funds are responsible for professionally financial-assessing and managing investors' resources. They devise and execute priority investment strategies for maximum profit. In essence, these institutes combine consulting, trading, and exchange functions.

Intertwining the needs of financial institutions and investors ensures a dynamic and fluid financial market. Therefore, analytical skills are critical for all participants in financial relations.

Two Critical Finance Categories

For finance, as illustrated in *Figure 1.1*, two critical categories emerge: return (profit, revenue) and risk (potential losses). Imagine setting out on a sea voyage. The *returns* are the treasures you hope to find, and the *risks* are the turbulent waters and pirates you might encounter on the way. These twin pillars are the basis of any financial analysis.

When an analyst forecasts high returns based on financial computations and constructs a portfolio of financial assets without adequately accounting for risk, potential losses may culminate in eventual deficits. Conversely, the net investment profit will likely approximate zero if an investor's strategy is singularly oriented toward risk minimization. Further, when inflation's impact is not considered, this may even result in a capital reduction. Hence, the deployment of analytical tools, both within this book and in broader financial practice, usually aims at gauging and prognosticating return metrics from the utilization of financial assets and potential associated losses.

These categories, however, can be assessed using various metrics or indicators. This significantly increases the volume of financial information and other data used in making management decisions in finance. Going back to our sea voyage example, imagine a dashboard full of dials, each representing indicators such as speed, direction, and weather conditions. All the dashboard data is essential to reaching your destination port successfully. Financial indicators often include qualitative and quantitative measures—for example, knowledge of past market sentiment, prices, and trading volumes. They can be compared to a ship's compass (quantitative) and a sailor's intuition based on experience (qualitative). Balancing risk and return is the cornerstone of sound financial management. After all, the pursuit of profits can lead to bankruptcy. It is as if we are going around the reefs, trying to reach our destination port with the treasure faster than our competitors, but successfully.

Financial Data Analysis

The last segment in *Figure 1.1* pertains to financial data analysis. Consider this analogous to a master chef preparing a gourmet meal. Every step is critical, from selecting the freshest ingredients to presenting the dish beautifully. Contemporary data analysis is mainly grounded in five foundational processes, though it is not confined to these alone:

- *Data collection* is a critical step that forms the basis for effective financial data analysis. It involves collecting relevant information from various sources (stock exchanges, financial statements, economic indicators, news, and many others). For example, an investor might regularly check news sites to understand how geopolitical events may affect stock prices. The speed, accuracy, and relevance of data collection are paramount to actionable analysis.

- *Data processing* means that data must be cleaned, organized, and converted into a format suitable for the further application of models and analysis methods. For example, suppose an analyst discovers that a source's prices for a particular stock are erroneously recorded in cents rather than dollars. In that case, this requires transformation and the application of appropriate data processing algorithms. This step may include data normalization, handling missing values, data type conversion, and other *extract, transform, and load (ETL)* instruments. Advanced Python tools primarily focus on making this process easier and automated.

NOTE *ETL is a core part of the financial data analysis process, particularly in data preparation. In fact, ETL can be viewed as a subset or specific implementation of the data collection and data processing stages described in the financial data analysis workflow.*

- *Data analysis* involves analyzing processed data to identify patterns, correlations, or other information useful for decision-making. For example, discovering a correlation between rising oil prices and falling airline stocks can help guide future investments. It mainly includes *exploratory data analysis (EDA)* techniques such as statistical, trend, and regression analyses.

NOTE *EDA is an important step in the data analysis process. EDA involves basic data exploration to discover patterns, identify anomalies, and test hypotheses and assumptions using statistical graphs and information tables. The purpose* *of EDA is to understand and structure data, obtain valuable information, and prepare data for the subsequent application of modeling and forecasting methods.*

- *Modeling and forecasting* is the application of existing financial or statistical models (which will be discussed in detail later in this book in *Chapters 4 to 10*) to study complex patterns in financial data and make informed investment decisions. Imagine an algorithm predicting a boom in electric vehicle stock prices due to breakthroughs in new battery technology, or a crash in automaker stock prices due to the depletion of oil reserves. This is mainly aimed at optimizing returns and losses. Classical and modern implementations of statistical models typically provide *templates* for the required estimates. This includes assessing the impact of dynamic factors, predicting average returns, assessing the detrimental effects of risk, and formulating machine learning and neural network models.

- *Decision-making and support* are perhaps the most important aspects of any practice. Typically, an investor or financial institution manager uses the full range of modeling, forecasting, and analytical results to decide to buy, sell, or take other actions. Modern algorithmic trading tools, however, including those based on the Python programming language, can autonomously determine the realization of profits/losses without human intervention. This significantly increases the speed of decision-making, but it can increase the likelihood of losses in complex scenarios. In general, this stage is associated with implementing the chosen investment strategy.

In essence, leveraging modern IT and programming language analytical tools in finance is necessary to promptly respond to the rapidly shifting conditions of the external environment. At the very least, financial investors or institutions forego alternative benefits by not making use of these opportunities.

COMPARING ANALYTICAL TOOLS FOR VARIOUS PROGRAMMING LANGUAGES

There are a lot of different programming languages in the sphere of analytical tools for financial data analysis, each with pros and cons. Each language has strengths, tailored libraries, and particular niches where it shines brightest. Python has rapidly become prominent in financial research and data analysis.

According to *IEEE Spectrum's 10th annual ranking of the top programming languages*[1], Python stands out as the top-ranked language based on a combined grade. Java follows closely in the 2nd position. Notably, R and Julia, commonly used for data analysis, occupy the 11th and 30th positions, respectively.

In DataCamp's ranking of the *Top Programming Languages for Data Scientists in 2023*[2], Python retains its dominant position. R, Java, and Julia, however, have risen to the 2nd, 4th, and 5th positions, respectively. This suggests that while Python remains a leader, other dominators exist in the market of analytical programming languages.

What distinguishes Python in the competitive landscape of financial data analysis? In the following table, we will look at a comparative analysis of the functions and capabilities of various programming languages, including Python. To discern the differences between Python, Java, Julia, and R, especially regarding their applicability in financial data analysis and decision-making, refer to *Table 1.1*:

TABLE 1.1 Critical differences between Python, Java, Swift, and R for finance

Language/ Feature	Python	Java	R	Julia
Readability for data analysis	**High** Simplicity and clear syntax	**Moderate** More verbose syntax	**Very high** Designed for statistics and data analysis	**Moderate** Although inspired by Python, it has its own unique syntax
Performance	**Moderate** Can be integrated with Cython for enhanced performance	**High** Compiled language known for its speed	**Moderate** Optimized for statistics but can sometimes be slower	**High** Just-in-time compiled, making it particularly fast
Learning curve	**Easy** Beginner-friendly	**Moderate to hard**	**Easy** Especially for statisticians	**Moderate** Has its learning nuances, but manageable
Community support	**Vast** Python has a broad and active community	**Large** Java has been around for a long time with an active community	**Dedicated** R has a focused community around statistics	**Growing** Julia is relatively new but has an enthusiastic community

(Continued)

---

[1]*Source: https://spectrum.ieee.org/the-top-programming-languages-2023*
[2]*Source: https://www.datacamp.com/blog/top-programming-languages-for-data-scientists-in-2022*

Language/ Feature	Python	Java	R	Julia
Integration	**Extensive** Can integrate with various databases, tools, and platforms	**Extensive** Widely used in enterprise solutions	**Moderate** Can integrate with C, C++, and Fortran code	**Good** Can integrate with C, Fortran, and Python
Ecosystem for data analysis	**Extensive** A wide range of packages for different analytical tasks	**Moderate** Mainly oriented toward enterprise applications	**Extensive** A wide range of packages for different analytical tasks	**Growing** Several packages for data manipulation and statistics
Ecosystem for finance	**Excellent** A lot of libraries, such as pandas, NumPy, mplfinance, and QuantLib	**Good** Libraries such as JQuantLib	**Excellent** quantmod, PerformanceAnalytics, and other dedicated packages	**Good** Growing ecosystem with packages such as JuliaFin
Library stability	**High** Stable core libraries with frequent updates, a lot of decentralized solutions	**Very high** Enterprise-grade stability	**Moderate** Stable core libraries, some decentralized packages lack maintenance	**Moderate** Growing ecosystem, some libraries still maturing

Let us summarize the results of the comparative analysis (*Table 1.1*):

- *Java* has made significant strides in data science, especially in enterprise-grade financial applications. It leverages amazing performance, extensive libraries, and robust integration capabilities to deliver scalable and efficient solutions. Notable, however, is that major new methods and innovative solutions in data analysis are supported by Java late and often require rewriting the code. Therefore, this programming language is usually unsuitable for junior data analytics or beginners in finance.

- *R* is the top choice of many data scientists. It is specifically designed for academic research and advanced statistical analysis. Most of the world's leading scientific publications are based on R. This programming language quickly considers new data analysis and financial analysis developments. Many libraries are, however, still in the development stage and aren't yet suited to working with big data. Also, R does not allow you to create competitive end solutions (software applications, analytical modules, and analytical trading tools). Therefore, this programming language, although easy to learn and implement, is rarely used by practicing financiers.

- *Julia*, propelled by its computational prowess, is rapidly establishing itself in scientific computing and cutting-edge research projects. Its potential to become an effective solution for many data analysis and decision-making areas is immense. The current low prevalence of this programming language, however, might limit its widespread use, which could be a point of consideration for potential users.

- *Python* currently holds the best advantages for data analysis and use in various fields: a simple and intuitive interface, a huge ecosystem, and computer support. It also quickly implements innovative methods and is widely adopted. Thus, Python consistently stands out as the best choice for both beginners and experts.

Python Programming Language Advantages

Let us detail the critical advantages of the Python programming language as a tool for finance:

- *Readability and easy syntax*: Python's design philosophy emphasizes code readability. Its clean and expressive syntax makes writing, understanding, and maintaining code easier. This readability facilitates a smoother transition into programming for finance professionals, many of whom may not have a strict coding background.

- *Vast community*: Python boasts one of the largest and most active programming communities, especially for data analysts. This means many resources, tutorials, and forums are available for troubleshooting and learning. Additionally, whenever there is a new trend or technology in finance, someone in the Python community will likely already be working on it or have developed a library to handle it.

- *Extensive libraries for finance*: Python offers a large ecosystem of libraries specifically designed for data analysis and financial tasks. Libraries such as *pandas* for tabular data manipulation (DataFrames), *NumPy* for matrix and array numerical calculations, and *mplfinance* for quantitative and graphical analysis in finance make modeling easier and decision-making more efficient.

- *Platform independence*: Python is platform-independent, meaning it can run on various operating systems without modification (macOS, Windows, Linux, x86-compatible or ARM CPUs, etc.). This is crucial for finance, as it may need to be deployed across different server architectures or platforms.

- *Flexibility and integration*: Python can integrate with other languages, such as C or Java. This makes it versatile for creating competitive software solutions for complex financial problems, where Python can be used for high-level logic and high-performance tasks can be translated into other languages.

- *Cost-effective*: Python and its basic libraries have open-source licenses (mainly distributed under the Python Software Foundation, GNU General Public Licenses, Berkeley Software Distribution, and other licenses), providing a cost-effective solution for financial analysis. Organizations can invest less in permits to use and deploy Python-based applications.

- *Adaptability*: Python tools' versatility means that they are not limited to finance or data analysis; they are widely used in Web and desktop application development, machine learning, artificial intelligence, and other fields. This adaptability ensures that finance professionals using Python have skills that can be applied in many fields.

Python for finance is a relatively simple, robust community with a broad arsenal of data analysis tools. The language's adaptability and cost-effectiveness further cement its place as a top contender in the financial world.

The Role of Python in Finance

Python has carved a niche in finance, and its utility is far-reaching. Let us look at a brief overview of the roles it plays in finance:

- *Automation*: Time is money, especially in finance. Automate mundane tasks such as data collection with Python so that you can focus on more critical tasks.

- *Quantitative analysis*: Python libraries such as NumPy, SciPy, and pandas can perform complex calculations quickly. Let us consider a real-life example. Have you ever heard of the *Black-Scholes* model for option pricing? Python can help you compute it in less than 10 lines of code!

- *Data analysis and visualization*: These are crucial components of decision-making. The pandas library facilitates the efficient manipulation and analysis of this vital resource. While the pandas tools help to refine this raw data, Matplotlib, Seaborn, and mplfinance serve as your canvases for crafting compelling data stories. Many professional financial institutions and individual investors use Python to visualize trends and make valuable decisions.

- *Portfolio management*: If your goal is to manage a financial portfolio someday, Python—in particular SciPy—can help you construct optimized portfolios.

- *Regression and forecasting*: In finance, regression and ARIMA models are powerful tools for modeling financial processes and forecasting time-series data, especially for predicting stock prices or other economic indicators. Libraries such as statsmodels and sklearn are the basis for assessing the relationship between financial indicators. Utilizing Python libraries such as statsmodels, you can easily fit an ARIMA model to your data. This is a crucial skill for making informed financial decisions.

- *Risk management*: Picture yourself as a bank loan officer evaluating a startup's creditworthiness. Python's robust risk management financial libraries include credit and market processes. With specialized models such as GARCH (from the arch Python library), you can rigorously assess market volatility, enhancing your risk evaluation toolkit. Basic Python tools will also allow you to estimate the *value at risk* (*VaR*) and the probability of losses. Thus, Python is an indispensable resource for financial institutions to make risk-adjusted decisions.

- *Financial machine learning*: Python is a critical player in financial machine learning, thanks to libraries such as scikit-learn. If predicting stock prices is on your agenda, take notice of the Prophet library. With Prophet, forecasting future stock prices can be done in just a few lines of code.

- *Technical analysis*: Python offers general-purpose statistical libraries and specialized libraries for technical analysis, such as TA-Lib. These libraries make it easy to identify statistical patterns, calculate moving averages, and use other indicators to assess market trends and make informed investment choices.

- *Derivatives pricing and options valuation*: Python helps beginner finance analysts who want to dive deeper to understand the principles of financial derivatives pricing. Libraries such as QuantLib and yfinance can be best for this.

- *Integration*: Python's beauty is its versatility and integration. It interoperates well with other systems and products, databases, and languages, making it a valuable knowledge asset for any financial specialist and financial IT environment.

Many other financial tasks can be solved using Python programming language instruments.

PYTHON INSTRUMENTS ARE READY FOR DATA ANALYSIS

After understanding the essence of finance and developing a keen interest in profiting from the financial markets, it is only logical to lean into the advantages of the Python programming language. Before you can begin, however, you must first grasp how Python functions.

Working with Python is more complex than using traditional office software with installation files or available via app stores. For instance, once you have installed Microsoft Excel or OpenOffice Calc, you are instantly greeted with a familiar spreadsheet interface. Most users are accustomed to the concept of having a direct, user-friendly interface immediately after installation. With Python, however, as *Figure 1.2* shows, the situation is slightly complicated. Fear not, though; persistence makes it manageable in no time.

As illustrated in *Figure 1.2*, working in Python entails three primary components: the Python interpreter, an IDE, and various extension modules sourced from diverse repositories. Let us break down each component:

- The *Python interpreter* essentially bridges human-readable Python code and machine-executable commands. Given Python's syntax, which resembles plain English, it needs to be translated into machine-level instructions. This is the interpreter's primary role. Many modern operating systems come pre-equipped with a Python interpreter version, so there is no pressing need for a fresh installation. Installing the latest interpreter is advisable, however, to exert complete control over your analytical endeavors and harness all modern functionalities. As *Figure 1.2* indicates, there are two primary sources for Python interpreter installation:

  - *python.org*: The official Web site for Python provides the core interpreter, suitable for general-purpose programming.

  - *anaconda.org*: There are no fundamental differences between this and the previous installation source. Targeted toward data analysts, however, Anaconda offers a Python interpreter and incorporates several other analytical tools and libraries. This makes it a convenient solution for those who want to dive deeply into data analysis methods without considering installing and configuring additional packages. On the other hand, *python.org* provides a basic version of the Python interpreter. This makes it suitable for those who want to learn Python natively. The ability to install specific analytical libraries, however, is similar to Anaconda. Please refer to the following figure:

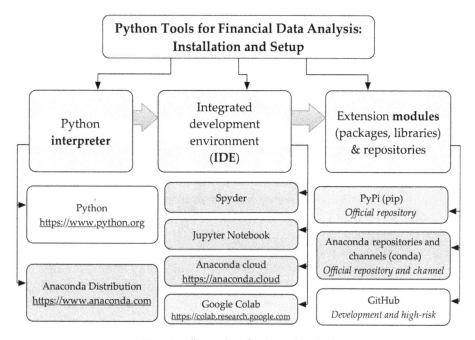

FIGURE 1.2 Installing and configuring Python for finance

- An IDE provides tools for writing, debugging, and running programs. It often comes with features such as syntax highlighting, code and error suggestions, integrated documentation, and interactive help. Visualize it as your one-stop shop for coding, equipped with everything you might need to craft your software masterpiece. After the interpreter's installation, there would not be any apparent changes to your user interface. The newly installed interpreter discreetly resides within your system files, accessible via terminal or CMD windows. Several IDEs have been developed to enhance user engagement and efficiency. These IDEs offer a platform where users can easily input commands or code.

- *Extension modules* are indispensable if it is necessary to implement models and methods from specific areas of data analysis, e.g., finance, data analysis, machine learning, etc. That functionality is not included in the basic Python interpreter installation package. Imagine this: you're trying to make a delicious sandwich, but instead of making every ingredient from scratch, you use pre-made sauces and toppings. This is where extension modules (packages or libraries) come into play. Extension modules complement the basic functionality by adding new tools and features. Instead of rewriting standard functions, these modules can tap into the Python community's or specific developers' collective knowledge and leverage their expertise.

- *Library repositories* can be thought of as large libraries with shelves filled with books on various topics. Now, replace these books with extension modules or code libraries and we have a library repository. It is a centralized file server where developers share and distribute code libraries. In Python, these repositories contain libraries for everything from data analysis and visualization to machine learning and neural network models. *PyPI* and `conda` are the two primary sources in this space. In fact, these are servers with a vast archive of software solutions from the community and individual professionals, where Python enthusiasts can save, publish, and find a tool for almost any task. Let us also not forget about GitHub—it is not just a repository but a vibrant community hub where developers collaborate, contribute, and develop open-source projects. GitHub is a risky repository, however; anyone can change it, and it is not recommended for new Python programmers.

Having understood this information, let us dive into the nuances of installing Python interpreters, importing libraries, and running simple code.

INSTALLING PYTHON ON A LOCAL PC

As we discussed earlier, working with Python requires the installation of a Python interpreter, an IDE, and essential libraries. Two primary ways to set up Python are installing the necessary software locally and utilizing cloud-based services.

Here, we will guide you through the steps for local installation using the Anaconda distribution—a package tailored for data analysts that includes the most necessary tools.

Installation Procedure

Install Python using the following steps:

1. *Navigate to Anaconda's Web site*: Go to the Anaconda distribution download page in your Web browser.

2. *Select the distribution*: You will be prompted to choose the distribution that fits your operating system and version of Python 3. Then, click on the Download button.

3. *Execute the installer*: Once the installer is downloaded, run it and follow the on-screen instructions to set up Python 3.

We are ready to code!

NOTE   *Although Python 2 is still available for download, it is generally not recommended. If you have never worked with Python 2, you will likely not need it. Modern financial data analysis packages are adapted to Python 3.*

Post-Installation Setup and Configuration

Upon completing the installation, your system will have the current version of the Python interpreter and the default IDE and libraries for data analysis. You will also have access to the Anaconda prompt terminal with a Start button for Windows users. The central hub for managing your installed software is Anaconda Navigator. Look for its green icon and launch it to access its features (refer to *Figure 1.3*):

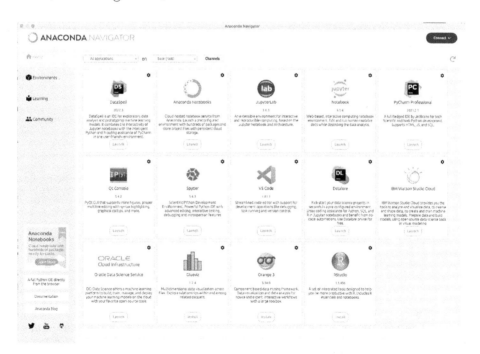

FIGURE 1.3 Interface of Anaconda Navigator

The Anaconda Navigator interface may vary slightly depending on your installed version. The core functionalities remain the same, however.

The Home tab, located on the left side of Anaconda Navigator, serves as the primary window for initiating Python workflows. In this view, installed applications are marked with a blue Launch button at the bottom (e.g., Jupyter Notebook). Conversely, applications available for installation are indicated by a green Install button (e.g., RStudio).

The Environments tab, also on the left but typically inactive, provides an overview of all packages available within the Anaconda distribution. This panel offers graphical control for adding, deleting, and updating packages (see *Figure 1.4*). Furthermore, you can manage virtual environments, often abbreviated as *venv*. A base environment is named *base(root)* by default. Utilizing the buttons at the bottom of the panel, you can create, clone, import, back up, and remove virtual environments.

NOTE *A virtual environment (venv) for Python programming tasks isolates the current workspace, allowing it to manage dependencies specific to each project without touching the Python general system dependencies and packages. This helps to avoid further conflicts between individual projects.*

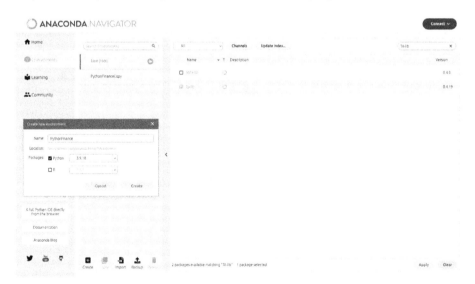

FIGURE 1.4 Window view for environment management in Anaconda Navigator

You can manage the installed packages in each virtual environment—that is, add, delete, or update them. For example, to install the TA-Lib package, type its name in the Search Package field, select the package using the checkmark icon (indicated by a downward green arrow), and then click the green Apply button.

Managing Non-Standard Packages

Some packages are not included in the standard Anaconda repository (for example, Prophet). To install these, you will need to connect to other channels. This option is visible at the top of the screen in *Figure 1.4*. In the dialog box that appears, click Add... and enter the name of the alternative channel, such as `conda-forge`, followed by Update channels. After doing this, you can see the packages you need when searching for them (such as `fbprophet` or Prophet).

Not all libraries, however, are available in the standard repositories. If you need to install non-standard packages, refer to the installation instructions.

Anaconda Navigator is a graphical application and package management interface for the Python Anaconda distribution. The command-line (terminal) tools `pip` and `conda` can be used, however. For more details, see the resources *https://docs.conda.io* and *https://pypi.org*.

Thus, we can use tools to graphically configure and manage package dependencies and specialized virtual environments for each project. Remember to experiment with these tools, as visual tools may change over time. The principles remain the same, however.

PYTHON IDES

So, where exactly should you input commands or code in Python? To answer this, you need to be familiar with IDEs. These should be well known to any programmer. IDEs provide a graphical interface for executing programs. Broadly speaking, Python IDEs can be categorized into two types. First, there are script-based IDEs, such as *Scientific Python Development Environment* (*Spyder*), Visual Studio Code, and PyCharm, among many others. Second, interactive IDEs may operate in a request (command)-response (result) manner within cells; Jupyter Notebook and its various adaptations are prime examples of this category.

The choice of IDE ultimately remains a matter of user preference. Interactive solutions allow you to get immediate results, quickly identify and fix errors, execute code in parts, and debug code on the fly. Script-based (entirely code) IDEs, however, are used to automate repetitive processes without constant user intervention, such as creating an algorithmic trading robot, writing an analytical product, or creating a monitoring module. Overall, both approaches have similarities. They can control errors, monitor the execution process, inspect variable values, and display results on the screen or export them to other sources.

Spyder

Spyder is an open-source IDE designed specifically for scientific computing and data analysis in Python. It offers a powerful editor with syntax highlighting, real-time code analysis, and advanced debugging features. One of its standout features is the *Variable Explorer*, which allows you to inspect the variables defined during a program's execution.

Its interface features (refer to *Figure 1.5*) are as follows:

- A multi-tabbed editor with features such as code folding, automatic indenting, and smart code completion
- An integrated *Interactive Python* (*IPython*) terminal for running and debugging scripts
- A Variable Explorer panel for real-time variables, arrays, and DataFrame inspection
- A dedicated Plots panel to view graphs and plots generated by your code
- A Help panel to access Python and library documentation

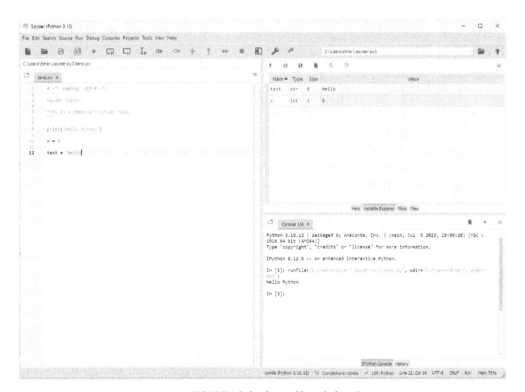

FIGURE 1.5 Spyder working window view

Jupyter Notebook

Jupyter Notebook and JupyterLab are other widely used open-source IDEs that are popular among data scientists and researchers. Unlike Spyder, they follow a Web-based interface that facilitates the creation of documents containing live code, equations, visualizations, and explanatory text.

Their interface features (refer to *Figure 1.6*) are as follows:

- Code and text are organized into cells, which can be run individually.
- The Markdown language for advanced text formatting is supported. It allows the inclusion of formatted text, HTML links, and LaTeX equations for the resulting documentation, such as a final analytical report.
- In-line plotting and visualization are displayed directly below the code cells that produced them.
- There is a debugging mode for real-time variables and DataFrame inspection.
- Interactive widgets support sliders, buttons, and other widgets to manipulate and visualize data dynamically.

FIGURE 1.6 Jupyter Notebook (JupyterLab version) working window view

EASY START WITH PYTHON IN THE CLOUD

If you do not want to install software on your computer but want to immediately start analyzing financial data, you can use ready-made cloud solutions. Cloud-based Python environments such as Anaconda Cloud and Google Colab offer various features that streamline the data science workflow, from code development to data analysis and machine learning.

Anaconda Cloud (*https://anaconda.cloud*) distributes libraries, notebooks, and environments for data scientists and analysts online. It also facilitates sharing and collaboration among team members both free of charge and through paid plans. Like other online platforms, Anaconda Cloud provides a user-friendly interface for uploading, downloading, and managing all your Python resources and serves as an integration with Anaconda Navigator, giving users a more cohesive experience. In the initial stages of exploring Python's capabilities, however, Google's solution is a more helpful and easy-to-start-with platform.

Google Colab, or just Colab (*https://colab.research.google.com*), is a free cloud service based on Jupyter Notebook interface principles and is particularly suitable for machine learning and data analysis. Google Colab provides a platform for writing and executing Python code, with the added benefit of free access to GPUs and TPUs for faster computation. It also offers real-time collaboration and is integrated with other Google infrastructure, e.g., Google Drive. The Colab IDE offers a range of Markdown hypertext-like coding, Python code cells, and output display cells. Those features allow you to insert form fields and make your notebooks interactive.

NOTE   *Choosing between Anaconda Cloud and Google Colab takes work. It may hinge on specific project needs, the team's collaboration, computational resource requirements, developing and analytical costs, etc. Thus, it is desirable to have parallel versions of these IDEs to improve the efficiency of decision-making results in various conditions and tasks.*

Utilizing these cloud-based resources provides an all-in-one solution that includes a Python interpreter, an IDE, and access to additional libraries and packages. The advantage of this approach is that you do not have to allocate space on your local computer; all resources are hosted on remote servers. While this service is often free for basic functionalities, some premium features may require a subscription fee, especially for larger projects. Refer to the pricing section of the respective service Web sites for more details.

PYTHON LIBRARIES FOR FINANCE

The Python programming language offers an expansive ecosystem of libraries specifically designed for various applications in finance. Python has many libraries for finance data analysis, statistical modeling, machine learning, portfolio management, and so on. The most significant Python libraries for financial tasks are listed in *Table 1*.2:

TABLE 1.2 Comparing Python libraries for finance

Package name	Primary purpose	Application to tasks in finance	Additional notes
Data manipulation and transformation			
pandas	Data manipulation	Time-series analysis, financial data aggregation	Ideal for working with time-series and tabular data
NumPy	Numerical computations	Option pricing, risk assessment	Core library for numerical array computations
openpyxl	Excel file manipulation	Financial reporting, Excel-based financial models	Enables advanced read/write operations for Excel files (`.xlsx`)
Statistical analysis			
SciPy	Scientific computing	Statistical analysis, optimization models	Integrates with NumPy; provides advanced math functions and tools
statsmodels	Statistical models	Econometric analysis, hypothesis testing	Uses for estimating and interpreting models for many types of statistical data
pmdarima	Time-series forecasting	Predicting future financial indices	Provides automatic parameter defining for SARIMAX prediction models
arch	Econometric analysis	Volatility modeling, VaR calculations	Uses for econometric and statistical evaluation of financial risks
Data visualizations			
Matplotlib	Data visualization	Plotting stock trends, financial indicators	Provides a powerful plotting framework
Seaborn	Data visualization	Heatmaps of portfolio correlations, financial analytics visualization	Integrates with Matplotlib; provides a high-level, easier-to-use interface
Bokeh	Interactive visualization	Real-time financial dashboards	Allows for elegant and interactive Web-based data visualization
Plotly	Interactive visualization	Interactive financial reports, 3D plots	Supports a wide range of charts, interactive and high-quality visualizations

(Continued)

Package name	Primary purpose	Application to tasks in finance	Additional notes
Machine learning			
Scikit-learn	Machine learning	Risk assessment, fraud detection, stock price prediction, algorithmic trading, etc.	Provides simple and efficient tools for data analysis
XGBoost	Machine learning		Handle complex data, improve model accuracy, and reduce overfitting
LightGBM	Machine learning		High speed, accuracy, and ability to handle imbalanced data
Prophet	Forecasting and machine learning	Stock price prediction, demand forecasting	Allows easy time-series forecasting tools in financial markets
Data acquisition			
pandas-datareader	Accessing and fetching data from various sources	Market and economic research, various indices analysis	Universal and simplified data collection process for financial analysis
Quandl	Fetching financial data	Market research, economic indicators analysis	Allows easy access to numerous free and premium financial datasets
yfinance	Fetching data from Yahoo Finance	Market research, analysis of historical and current financial data	Easy to use with pandas to fetch data from Yahoo Finance
Specific finance tasks			
mplfinance	Financial data visualization	Advanced financial time-series charts (technical and graphical analysis)	Generates high-quality candlestick charts, volume bars, and other financial data visualizations
QuantLib	Quantitative finance	Options pricing, risk management	Provides a wide range of tools for quantitative finance
TA-Lib	Technical analysis	Moving averages, oscillators, trend identification	Provides tools for the technical analysis of the market

Table 1.2 compares the most used Python libraries in finance, categorizing them based on their primary purposes—data manipulation and transformation, statistical analysis, data visualization, machine learning, data acquisition, and specific finance tasks. The table also shows how each library is commonly deployed in finance-related tasks and offers additional notes for each library. Let us describe the libraries:

- *Data manipulation libraries*: The pandas library is a basic and universal tool for aggregating financial data, analyzing and manipulating it, and working with time series. An advantage of it is that it is good for working with two-dimensional tables. NumPy is another important library that offers many functions for numerical calculations, which are critical in finance (option pricing, risk assessment, etc.). Excel-related libraries such as openpyxl provide an advanced interface for managing Excel files, which is important in finance and making informed decisions.

- *Statistical analysis libraries*: There are many solutions available in Python for statistical analysis purposes. statsmodels and SciPy, however, are often the preferred libraries. statsmodels functions implement the classical statistical models necessary for econometric analysis and hypothesis testing (descriptive statistics, regression analysis, ANOVA, etc.). It highlights the tools for creating forecasting models for time-series data—ARIMA and SARIMAX models. pmdarima is a library that extends the evaluation capabilities of SARIMAX models. It allows us to automatically search for optimal model parameters—an analog of cross-validation for machine learning. SciPy offers various advanced mathematical and statistical functions. It is beneficial for optimization modeling tasks. The **arch** library specializes in econometric and statistical financial risk modeling, which is ideal for volatility modeling, the GARCH model, and VaR analysis.

- *Data visualization libraries*: Data visualization is central to decision-making in finance. Matplotlib offers universal tools for plotting data with any complexity. Although these graphs are universal by default, fine-tuning the parameters allows you to build specific plots, e.g., candles and bars, for price dynamic analysis. Seaborn extends Matplotlib's capabilities by providing an easy-to-use interface for building classic statistical visualizations but has less customization ability. Bokeh and Plotly are excellent choices for more interactive and Web-based data visualizations. Both offer interactive features and visualizations that assist in constantly monitoring information in financial markets.

- *Machine learning libraries*: Machine learning and neural network models have been rapidly integrated into the financial sector. Libraries such as scikit-learn, XGBoost, LightGBM, and Prophet are invaluable. Scikit-learn offers general-purpose, end-to-end machine learning tools. The library implements algorithms for classification, regression, clustering, and dimensionality reduction, as well as utilities for sampling sets, evaluation, and data pre-processing. A unified interface makes it easy to operate with various models and algorithms. XGBoost and LightGBM are powerful machine learning libraries similar in functionality and interface to scikit-learn. They only implement gradient boosting algorithms, optimizing for speed and performance. Prophet is a forecasting tool developed by Facebook. It is specifically designed for time-series forecasting with elements of machine learning. Prophet's functions are user-friendly and require minimal data pre-processing. Its ability to account for seasonality, holidays, and changing trends makes it especially valuable when working with financial data. All these libraries provide a comprehensive set of tools for accomplishing virtually any financial task. Using machine learning methods, however, requires more effort from the user than classical approaches.

- *Data acquisition libraries*: Pandas-datareader, Quandl, and yfinance are the best and most useful libraries for data acquisition in finance. The unified libraries pandas-datareader and Quandl allow the retrieval of financial data directly into a pandas DataFrame. They support fetching data from many sources, such as Yahoo Finance, Google Finance, and *Federal Reserve Economic Data (FRED)*. The specialized yfinance library lets users get historical data from the Yahoo Finance server. It is widely used to obtain option and stock pricing data, including prices, dividends, and splits. These libraries are useful for providing time-series analysis and forecasting, technical analysis, and portfolio management tasks.

- *Libraries for specific finance tasks*: The mplfinance, QuantLib, and TA-Lib libraries are designed to solve specific financial problems. mplfinance's tools are used for the visualization and graphical analysis of financial data. mplfinance can be used to generate candlestick charts, volume bars, and other financial data visualizations. TA-Lib specializes in technical analysis tasks. It offers many functions for calculating moving averages, oscillators, and trend identification indicators. Those libraries help financial analysts and traders visualize and estimate market data and identify trends over time. QuantLib is a comprehensive library for quantitative finance. It includes tools for options pricing, risk management, and other quantitative financial tasks. Together, these and other financial libraries provide the ability to solve specific financial problems. This simplifies the processes of program analytics and the operational use of innovative financial methods.

Installation of Essential Libraries for Data Manipulation and Data Analysis

As we have already said, the most significant distributions and Python IDEs for data analysis are the Anaconda distribution (with Jupyter Notebook, Spyder, and Visual Studio Code IDEs) and Google Colab. Many foundational libraries required for data analysis are already pre-installed in those solutions. Some specialized packages, however, necessitate additional installation steps. This section will demonstrate how to set up a dedicated virtual environment—PythonFinance—to address general financial tasks.

NOTE *Some extension packages may have conflicting dependencies or require non-stable and third-party libraries. Therefore, it is recommended that you create a virtual environment for each project when you start working with Python. This isolation makes it easier to follow the examples and exercises in later chapters without affecting the default Python settings.*

Follow these detailed steps to establish a virtual environment on Unix-based systems such as Linux, macOS, Microsoft Windows, and Google Colab cloud-based systems:

1. For an Anaconda Python distribution, execute the following command-line script to install the necessary packages:

```
1. conda create --name PythonFinance

2. conda activate PythonFinance

3. conda install -c conda-forge -c defaults python=3.9
   numpy pandas openpyxl matplotlib seaborn plotly
   bokeh scipy statsmodels scikit-learn ta-lib
   mplfinance lightgbm xgboost pandas-datareader
   quandl yfinance mplfinance arch-py prophet pmdarima
   beautifulsoup4 requests
```

This script (for Bash, CMD, or other command-line interpreters) will create a new `conda` environment named `PythonFinance` (line *1*), activate it (line *2*), and then install the specified libraries using the `conda-forge` and `defaults` channels (line *3*). These libraries (described in *Table 1.2*) include core, required packages for financial data analysis, visualization, machine learning, and financial analysis. We are using two library sources for Python `conda` libraries and installing Python version 3.9. You may, however, use another, more up-to-date Python version or other sources for the required libraries.

2. To easily install the prerequired Python finance packages (as mentioned earlier) for the Anaconda Python distribution, we can also use the `PythonFinanceConda.yml` script file and then execute the `conda` one-line script as follows:

```
1. conda env create -f [path_to_file]
   PythonFinanceConda.yml

2. conda activate finance
```

The `yml-file` may have the following, or similar to the following, contents:

```
name: PythonFinance
channels:
  - conda-forge
  - defaults
dependencies:
  - python=3.9
  - numpy
  - pandas
  - openpyxl
  - matplotlib
  - seaborn
  - plotly
  - bokeh
  - scipy
  - statsmodels
  - scikit-learn
  - ta-lib
  - mplfinance
  - lightgbm
  - xgboost
  - pandas-datareader
  - quandl
  - yfinance
  - mplfinance
  - arch-py
  - prophet
  - pmdarima
  - beautifulsoup4
  - requests
```

Installing and using essential Python finance libraries in *Google Colab* is relatively straightforward:

a. First, a lot of the libraries mentioned previously (refer to *Table 1.2*) are already available in the virtual environment of Google Colab, and you simply need to import them as the following Python code:

```
1.  # Import built-in libraries
2.  import numpy as np
3.  import pandas as pd
4.  import openpyxl
5.  import matplotlib.pyplot as plt
6.  import seaborn as sns
7.  import plotly.express as px
8.  import bokeh
9.  import scipy
10. import statsmodels.api as sm
11. import sklearn
12. import lightgbm as lgb
13. import xgboost as xgb
14. import pandas_datareader as pdr
15. import yfinance as yf
16. from prophet import Prophet
17. from bs4 import BeautifulSoup
18. import requests
```

b. Second, you can quickly run shell commands (in a virtual terminal) by prefixing them with an exclamation mark, !, in a Colab notebook. The pip install command installs a library from the standard PyPI repository (*https://pypi.org*). For example, to install the particular libraries previously listed in *Table 1.2*, we may use the following Python code:

```
1. # Install and import non-standard for the Google
   Colab libraries
2. !pip install ta-lib-bin mplfinance quandl arch
   pmdarima
3. import talib
4. import mplfinance as mpf
5. import quandl
6. import arch
7. import pmdarima as pm
```

NOTE *Using Google Colab's cloud-based solution is highly recommended for studying the materials in this book. This avoids the need for complex local operating system configurations. Once you have tested and found your preferred tools, you can transition to automated processes using scripting and local IDEs (Spyder, Visual Studio Code, etc.).*

After installing the preceding libraries, you can run all the examples in this book. The development of new packages and libraries is ongoing, however. There is a large community and robust repositories where you can search for the solutions you need. Note, however, that the principles of installing and configuring new packages and libraries remain the same.

PYTHON ESSENTIALS

Renowned for its readability and ease of use, Python's syntax allows developers to express concepts in fewer lines of code than C or Java. Before further consideration of specialized tools, such as for data preparation and analysis, modeling, forecasting, or machine learning, it is essential to have a strong understanding of Python's essential principles as well as its structure, syntax, and operator features. We will provide a concise yet comprehensive overview of these elements to give you a solid foundation for the short Python programming examples that follow in this book. To improve your Python programming skills, practice more and look into other resources. Some are provided at the end of the chapter.

Syntax Principles and Python Code Style

The main features of the language are as follows:

▪ *Whitespace and indentation*: Unlike many programming languages that rely on braces, {}, to define code blocks, Python uses whitespace and indentation. The indentation level is crucial for determining the scope of loops, functions, classes, and more. It makes the code easier to read and enforces a consistent layout. An example is shown in the following code:

```
1. for i in range(5):  # The colon signifies the start
   of a block
2.     print(i)  # This line is indented, so it's part
   of the loop
```

▪ *Single-line comments*: In Python, single-line comments are preceded by a hash symbol (#). Anything that comes after the # on that line is considered a comment and is ignored by Python's interpreter. An example is shown in the following code:

```
1. # This is a single-line comment
```

▪ *Multiple-line comments*: For multiple-line comments, you can use triple quotes, although this is typically reserved for docstrings in functions or classes. An example is shown in the following code block:

```
1. '''
2. This is a multi-line comment
3. or a docstring
4. '''
```

■ *Variables and naming conventions*: Variables in Python are case-sensitive and should be named in a way that conveys their purpose. The convention is to use lowercase for variables and to separate words with underscores (my_variable). Constant variables are often defined in all caps (MY_CONSTANT). An example is shown in the following code:

```
1. my_variable = 10   # Integer
2. another_variable = "Hello"   # String
```

We can use understandable words for the variables or read PEP 8—the style guide for the Python code standard (*https://pep8.org*)—carefully.

NOTE   *PEP 8 is the Python Enhancement Proposal that describes the style guide for writing code in Python. It covers naming conventions, line length, indentation, and other formatting aspects. Following PEP 8 guidelines is highly recommended for maintaining readability and consistency across your codebase.*

■ *Importing modules (libraries, packages)*: As we learned before, Python has a rich library and functionality extensions, and you can import modules or packages to extend its functionality very simply if you know the module name and/or function name. An example is shown in the following code:

```
1. import math
2. from math import sqrt
3. import pandas as pd
4. import numpy as np
```

Basic Operators

The basic operators in Python facilitate mathematical and logical operations with variables and values. Let us describe these operators available in the Python language:

■ *Arithmetic operators*: Python includes standard arithmetic operators, such as addition (+), subtraction (-), multiplication (*), division (/), and modulus (%). An example is shown in the following code:

```
1. result = 10 + 20   # result is 30
```

■ *Comparison operators*: These operators are used to compare two values. These include equality (==), inequality (!=), greater than (>), less than (<), greater than or equal to (>=), and less than or equal to (<=). An example is shown in the following code:

```
1. is_equal = (10 == 20)   # Evaluates to False
```

■ *Logical operators*: Python includes the logical operators and, or, and not. An example is shown in the following code:

```
1. result = True and False   # Evaluates to False
```

■ *Assignment operators*: Besides the primary assignment operator, =, Python also includes compound assignment operators such as +=, -=, *=, and /=. An example is shown in the following code:

```
1. x = 10
2. x += 20   # Equivalent to x = x + 20
```

Control Flow and Simple Output

Control flow refers to the order in which the analytical programming processes' individual statements, instructions, or functions are executed or evaluated. The main control flow Python tools are as follows:

■ Python uses if, elif, and else for *conditional statements*. An example is shown in the following code:

```
1. x = int(input())
2. if x > 10:
3.     print("x is greater than 10")
4. elif x == 10:
5.     print("x is 10")
6. else:
7.     print("x is less than 10")
```

■ Python includes `for` and `while` loops for iterative tasks. An example is shown in the following code:

```
1.  for i in range(3):
2.      print(i)
3.
4.  for j in [1, 5, 7, 9]:
5.      print(j)
6.
7.  count = 0
8.  while count < 3:
9.      print(count)
10.     count += 1
```

■ The Python `print()` function simply outputs the results and debug information. Here are some examples of using `print()`:

```
1.  # Output the text or other variable:
2.  variable = 42
3.  print("The value of the variable is:")
```

```
4.  print(variable)
5.  # Output:
6.  # The value of the variable is:
7.  # 42
8.
9.  # Formatted String:
10. # allows for embedded Python expressions within a
    string.
11. print(f"The value of the variable is:
    {variable}")
12. # Output: The value of the variable is: 42
13.
14. # New Line symbol:
15. # outputs a new line inside the text line.
16. print(f"\nText with variable is:\n{variable}")
17. # Output:
18. # Text with variable is:
19. # 42
```

These are just a few of the important principles of the Python workflow. To work effectively with Python, it is crucial to deeply understand the syntax requirements, operators, and how functions are applied. Writing *clean code*, however, requires complex knowledge and practical skills, which can only be achieved by solving specific problems.

Python Basic Data Structures

Understanding data structures and types is also crucial to effectively solving data analysis problems in Python. Basic structures help store and manipulate data efficiently and form the basis for using more complex structures (arrays and tables). Let us briefly review Python's basic structures and data types.

The basic atomic data structures in Python language are as follows:

- *Integers* are whole numbers and can be positive or negative. An example is shown in the following code:

```
1. my_int = 10
```

- *Floating-point numbers* are decimal numbers and can also be expressed in scientific notation. An example is shown in the following code:

```
1. my_float = 20.5
2. my_sci_float = 2.5e3   # Represents 2500.0
```

- *Boolean* values represent one of two states: true or false. An example is shown in the following code:

```
1. is_true = True
2. is_false = False
```

- *Strings* are sequences of Unicode characters and are enclosed in single or double quotes. An example is shown in the following code:

```
1. my_str = "Hello, World!"
2. my_str = 'Hello, World!' # the same !!!
```

Types for Data Analysis

The essential data structures for data analysis, which may be applied to vector, matrix, or table data in Python, are described as follows:

- *List*: This is a *mutable, ordered* data collection containing *multiple data types*. An example is shown in the following code:

```
1. my_list = [1, 2.5, "data", True]
```

List operations mainly allow functionalities such as:

- *Indexing and slicing*: Retrieve elements by their index:

```
1. my_list[1]   # Output: 2.5
```

- *Appending*: Add elements using append():

```
1. my_list.append("new data")
2. # my_list becomes [1, 2.5, "data", True, "new
   data"]
```

- *Tuple*: This is an *immutable, ordered* collection of *multiple data type* elements. An example is shown in the following code:

```
1. my_tuple = (1, 2.5, "data", True)
```

Tuple operations primarily facilitate:

- *Indexing and slicing*: Similar to the *list* (see the previous set of bullet points).
- *Unpacking*: Assign elements to variables:

```
1. a, b, c, d = my_tuple
2. # a=1, b=2.5, c="data", d=True
```

- *Dictionary*: This is an *unordered mutable* collection of *key-value pairs*:

```
1. my_dict = {'key1': 'value1', 'key2': 'value2'}
```

Dictionary operations mainly focus on:

▦ *Accessing*: Retrieve a value by its key:

```
1. value = my_dict['key1']   # Output: 'value1'
```

▦ *Adding*: Add new key-value pairs:

```
1. my_dict['key3'] = 'value3'
2. # my_dict becomes {'key1': 'value1', 'key2':
   'value2',
                      'key3': 'value3'}
```

▦ *Set*: This is an *unordered* collection of *unique* elements, primarily used for logical operations and collecting unique items. This data structure is rarely used in finance. It can, however, be useful in certain scenarios, which will be outlined in future chapters.

Understanding these basic data structures and types is the cornerstone for data analysis in Python. These elements offer flexibility and functionality, from basic mathematical calculations to storing complex data structures.

The following chapters will build on this foundation and expand Python's capabilities. Data structures for working with arrays and data tables will be presented in *Chapter 2, Python Tools for Data Analysis: Primer to Pandas and NumPy*; tools for working with the file system and open data in *Chapter 3, Financial Data Manipulation with Python*; and graphical analysis capabilities in *Chapter 4, Exploratory Data Analysis for Finance*.

CONCLUSION

The combination of finance and IT is a powerful force that has led to remarkable results. Using modern information technologies in the big data world lets you quickly assess current financial problems and evaluate solutions. There are many consumers of management information, from individual investors to large financial intermediaries. This is why learning analytical programming tools or automation methods for working with data provides a critical competitive advantage.

Despite its minor speed disadvantages compared to other programming languages, Python is a leader in data analysis. Its wide distribution and huge community offer many extension libraries tailored to various aspects of data analysis and specific financial tasks. Today, knowledge of Python is not just a hard skill; it is a tool that empowers modern financial specialists, giving them a competitive edge in the industry.

Setting up Python, its IDE, and specialized libraries on your local computer can be daunting, requiring time and local PC resources. Cloud-based solutions such as Google Colab or Anaconda, however, can provide a smoother learning experience and a faster onboarding process. These solutions take the burden off your shoulders, allowing you to focus more on analytical tasks rather than troubleshooting problems or conflicts between packages.

The basic principles and algorithms for working with Python are similar to most other programming languages. Although the Python syntax, data structures, and control flows are relatively simple and universal, they have crucial points that must be understood before getting started. For a more detailed understanding of analytical code and searching for possible errors, however, constant practice and study of special materials on Python programming are required. To do this, each chapter of the book is accompanied by recommended references and extensive examples.

QUESTIONS

1. What are the fundamental principles of finance that are important for data analysis?

2. How do financial investors and market institutions use financial data analysis to get profit?

3. What are the two critical categories in finance for maximizing the outcome?

4. Why is Python the preferred language for financial data analysis over other programming languages?

5. What are the key advantages of using Python for financial tasks?

6. What are the steps involved in installing Python on a local PC?

7. What does the virtual environment in Python programming do?

8. How do you manage non-standard packages in Python?

9. What is the significance of Spyder and Jupyter Notebook in Python development?

10. How do you create and run a virtual environment for essential data analysis with the Anaconda distribution?

11. How can you get started with Python in the cloud, and why might you have to use it?

12. What Python libraries are essential for finance?

13. What Python essentials must one understand before diving into financial analysis?

14. What is control flow, and why is it essential in Python for financial analysis?

15. What data structures in Python are particularly useful for data analysis in finance?

KEY TERMS

- *Financial assets* are any resources that provide store value and produce income (income potential) through interest, dividends, capital gains, or other outcomes. These assets range from stocks and bonds to derivatives and cryptocurrencies. Acquiring financial assets leads to preserving and accumulating wealth over time.

- *Investment* is using an asset's potential to make a profit in the future. Thus, investing aims to increase short-term or long-term wealth and achieve other specific financial goals over time.

- A *financial investor* is an individual or institution that invests primarily in financial assets.

- An *investment portfolio* (portfolio of financial assets, for financial investors) combines various assets the investor owns. It is usually designed to balance returns and risk according to the investor's financial goals.

- *Return*, or outcome, refers to the profits or losses generated by an investment over a specified period, usually expressed as a percentage of the asset's original cost.

- The *percentage change* (*pct change*) of income is a mathematical expression of the return indicator. It is calculated as the relative increase in income or the dividing profit or loss by the value of the investment in the previous or base (initial) period.

- *Risk*, in terms of investment risk, refers to the degree of uncertainty associated with future losses from an investment or the possibility of suffering losses greater than the predicted results. *Financial losses* are monetary reductions that occur when an investment performs negatively. Risk goes hand in hand with the possibility of loss, and understanding both is critical to making informed financial decisions. *Risk assessment* usually involves calculating the probability of losses exceeding a certain level.

- The *extract, transform, and load* (*ETL*) process involves collecting data from various sources, converting it into a format suitable for further analysis, and cleaning it. ETL processes are the first and most time-consuming stage for preparing large datasets for analytical tasks in financial data analysis.

- The *exploratory data analysis* (*EDA*) process is an approach in statistics and machine learning that analytically and visually examines datasets to understand their underlying characteristics, features, and other crucial dependencies.

REFERENCES

- *Hilpisch, Y. (2021). Financial Theory with Python. O'Reilly Media, Inc.*
- *Guleria, P. (2020). Basics of Python Programming. [Paperback]. BPB Publications.*
- *Lutz, M. (2014). Python Pocket Reference (5th ed.). O'Reilly Media, Inc.*

2

PYTHON TOOLS FOR DATA ANALYSIS: PRIMER TO PANDAS AND NUMPY

INTRODUCTION

This chapter explores the core Python operations for working with data structures, highlighting its strengths in collection, tabular, and array-based analyses and focusing on the tools within the NumPy and pandas libraries. We will delve into Python's basic structures for effective data management and processing. The built-in Python functions and custom functions that enhance routine tasks will be described. Exploring the capabilities of the NumPy library, we will explain how it is designed to manage and manipulate large datasets. pandas' prowess in handling, processing, and applying arithmetic operations and transforming table-like structures makes it indispensable for anyone interested in extracting meaningful insights from structured data. We will uncover the details of essential tools for sorting, filtering, and grouping table data with pandas and lay the groundwork for the further analysis of financial markets.

In this chapter, we not only explore Python tools and functions but also apply the philosophy of software engineering to financial data analysis.

STRUCTURE

This chapter covers the following topics:

- The creation and manipulation of Python data structures
- Defining custom functions for data analysis
- NumPy for data analysis
- Working with pandas for data analysis

OBJECTIVES

By the end of this chapter, we will know how to use Python's essential control and data structures, built-in functions, and primary libraries for financial data analysis (NumPy and pandas). We will use examples that simulate actual financial data to explore foundational tools and operations crucial for such manipulation. You will learn how to create and manage arrays with NumPy and handle tabular data effortlessly with pandas, gearing you to derive insightful outcomes from financial data analyses.

THE CREATION AND MANIPULATION OF PYTHON DATA STRUCTURES

As we know from *Chapter 1, Getting Started with Python for Finance*, Python's primary nonatomic data structures are lists, sets, and tuples, each offering a unique set of functionalities and instruments for various aspects of data analysis. All these types of variables have specific applications in data analysis tasks. For instance, while *lists* and *tuples* are sequences of mutable and immutable values, *sets* support some original mathematical operations, such as union and intersection. Knowing when to use them can significantly optimize the data analysis process, which is a precious skill in financial analytics. That is, having an understanding of the crucial tasks for creating, manipulating, and analyzing data using these structures to solve commonly used financial algorithms is incredibly valuable. Whether for generating a new list with calculated data derived from daily stock prices or employing dictionaries to represent single tables effectively, this section will guide you through common tasks with illustrative examples rooted in real-world financial scenarios.

Basic Data Manipulations and Computations Within Python Built-In Data Structures

With its built-in data structures, Python offers a robust framework for handling complex tasks for finance data analysis. We will use the daily stock price dynamics of a prominent company, such as Apple Inc., as a reference point. Look at the following table:

TABLE 2.1 Daily stock price data for Apple Inc. (August 2023) [1]

Date	Open	High	Low	Close	Volume
2023-08-01	196.2400	196.7300	195.2800	195.6100	35,175,100
2023-08-02	195.0400	195.1800	191.8500	192.5800	50,389,300
2023-08-03	191.5700	192.3700	190.6900	191.1700	61,235,200
2023-08-04	185.5200	187.3800	181.9200	181.9900	115,799,700
2023-08-07	182.1300	183.1300	177.3500	178.8500	97,576,100
2023-08-08	179.6900	180.2700	177.5800	179.8000	67,823,000
2023-08-09	180.8700	180.9300	177.0100	178.1900	60,378,500
2023-08-10	179.4800	180.7500	177.6000	177.9700	54,686,900

Let us delve into the fundamental data manipulation processes:

1. *Finding tasks for data analysis* involves locating specific items, values, or patterns within the collection. For instance, we could find all days when the price exceeded 180. Execute the following code:

```
1. dates = [
2.     "2023-08-01", "2023-08-02", "2023-08-03", "2023-08-04",
3.     "2023-08-07", "2023-08-08", "2023-08-09", "2023-08-10"
4. ]
5. closing_prices = [
6.     195.6100, 192.5800, 191.1700, 181.9900,
7.     178.8500, 179.8000, 178.1900, 177.9700
8. ]
9. # Find all prices and dates in closing_prices
   which is greater than 180
10. for i in closing_prices:
11.     if i > 180:
12.         print(f"The price was {i} on
   {dates[closing_prices.index(i)]}")
```

[1]*Source: https://finance.yahoo.com/quote/AAPL/history?period1=1659312000&period2=16953 40800&interval=1d&filter=history&frequency=1d&includeAdjustedClose=true*

The results of the code are:

```
The price was 195.61 on 2023-08-01

The price was 192.58 on 2023-08-02

The price was 191.17 on 2023-08-03

The price was 181.99 on 2023-08-04
```

2. *Filtering tasks for data analysis* reduce the dataset to a subset that meets specific criteria or creates collections within the dataset. For example, we can create `new_closing_prices` using values from `closing_prices` that are greater than 180. Execute the following code:

```
1. # Create a new list
2. new_closing_prices = [i for i in closing_prices
   if i > 180]
3. print("The list of values > 180:\n",
   new_closing_prices)
4.
5. # Find the closing prices where they were either
   greater than 190 or less than 180
6. selected_closing_prices = [i for i in closing_
   prices if i > 190 or i < 180]
7.
8. print("The list of values > 190 or values
   < 180:\n", selected_closing_prices)
```

The results of the code are:

```
The list of values > 180:
 [195.61, 192.58, 191.17, 181.99]
The list of values > 190 or values < 180:
 [195.61, 192.58, 191.17, 178.85, 179.8, 178.19,
177.97]
```

Calculating Operations for Data Analysis and Rate of Returns

Calculating operations provides insights into the data, facilitates the extraction of meaningful patterns, and guides decision-making processes. The most useful calculated metric for financial data analysis is the *rate of returns (RoR)*.

The RoR is the growth rate of the daily (monthly, annually, etc.) price. This value provides insights into the stock's price momentum, revealing whether it is on an upward trend, remains stable, or is declining.

The RoR, often referred to as the return, is a finance performance measure used to evaluate the profit or loss made on an investment over some period. The formula for the RoR is:

$$RoR = ((Current\ price - Previous\ price) / Previous\ price) \times 100$$

We can use the list, tuple, and dictionary data structures to calculate Apple Inc.'s daily stock price returns using data from eight observations (refer to *Table 2.1*).

The *list-of-tuples structure* provides pairs of dates and closing prices in one construction. We can use this structure to analyze related data, in particular, to sort by the first value of the tuple. The .sort() method arranges elements in a list in a specific order, which is ascending by default.

Use the following code:

```
1.  %%time
2.  data_tuples = [
3.      ("2023-08-08", 179.8000), ("2023-08-01",
        195.6100),
4.      ("2023-08-02", 192.5800), ("2023-08-03",
        191.1700),
5.      ("2023-08-04", 181.9900), ("2023-08-07",
        178.8500),
6.      ("2023-08-09", 178.1900), ("2023-08-10",
        177.9700) ]
7.  # Sort the data by date (by the first elements of
        each tuple)
```

```
 8.  data_tuples.sort()
 9.  # Calculate RoR with looping list creating syntax
10.  returns_tuples = [(data_tuples[i][1] - data_
     tuples[i-1][1]) /
11.                    data_tuples[i-1][1]
12.                    for i in range(1,
     len(data_tuples))]
13.  # Show the RoR by the days
14.  for i in range(len(returns_tuples)):
15.      print(f"Return on {data_tuples[i+1][0]} is
     {returns_tuples[i]*100:.2f}%")
```

The results of the code are:

```
Return on 2023-08-02 is -1.55%
Return on 2023-08-03 is -0.73%
Return on 2023-08-04 is -4.80%
Return on 2023-08-07 is -1.73%
Return on 2023-08-08 is 0.53%
Return on 2023-08-09 is -0.90%
Return on 2023-08-10 is -0.12%
CPU times: user 975 µs, sys: 0 ns, total: 975 µs
Wall time: 2.56 ms
```

When applied to a list of tuples such as data_tuples.sort(), the method will, by default, use the data from the first element of each tuple as the basis for sorting. This is because tuples are ordered collections, and the .sort() method respects this order when rearranging them. A key=fuction argument, however, should be employed if dealing with more untypical data structures (as showcased in subsequent examples). This allows us to specify which values from the collection should be considered for sorting, giving us greater control over the process.

NOTE   *The range() and len() functions are frequently used in statements to determine the number of loop iterations. When provided with arguments such as 1 and 10, the range() function creates a sequence of numbers starting from 1 up to, but not including, 10. The len() function, on the other hand, returns the number of items in a list or any other data collection.*

An example of a *list-of-dictionaries structure* is as follows:

```
1.  %%time
2.  data_dicts = [
3.      {"date": "2023-08-01", "open": 196.2400,
        "close": 195.6100},
4.      {"date": "2023-08-02", "open": 195.0400,
        "close": 192.5800},
5.      {"date": "2023-08-03", "open": 191.5700,
        "close": 191.1700},
6.      {"date": "2023-08-04", "open": 185.5200,
        "close": 181.9900},
7.      {"date": "2023-08-07", "open": 182.1300,
        "close": 178.8500},
8.      {"date": "2023-08-08", "open": 179.6900,
        "close": 179.8000},
9.      {"date": "2023-08-09", "open": 180.8700,
        "close": 178.1900},
10.     {"date": "2023-08-10", "open": 179.4800,
        "close": 177.9700} ]
11. # Sort the data by date key
12. data_dicts.sort(key=lambda x: x["date"])
13. # Calculate RoR for Close prices
14. returns_dicts = [(data_dicts[i]["close"] - data_
    dicts[i-1]["close"]) /
15.                 data_dicts[i-1]["close"]
16.                 for i in range(1,
    len(data_dicts))]
17. # Show the RoR by the days
18. for i in range(len(returns_dicts)):
```

```
19.      d = data_dicts[i+1]['date']
20.      r = returns_dicts[i]
21.      print(f"Return on {d} for Close prices is
         {r*100:.2f}%")
```

The results of the code are:

```
Return on 2023-08-02 for Close prices is -1.55%

Return on 2023-08-03 for Close prices is -0.73%

Return on 2023-08-04 for Close prices is -4.80%

Return on 2023-08-07 for Close prices is -1.73%

Return on 2023-08-08 for Close prices is 0.53%

Return on 2023-08-09 for Close prices is -0.90%

Return on 2023-08-10 for Close prices is -0.12%

CPU times: user 2.95 ms, sys: 0 ns, total: 2.95 ms

Wall time: 3.34 ms
```

Each dictionary represents a single day's worth of stock data, containing the date, open price, and close price.

NOTE *The key argument of the .sort() method is set to a lambda function, which takes each dictionary, x, as its input and returns the value of the date key. This ensures that the list is sorted by date key from each dictionary from the list.*

When executing the provided examples in Jupyter Notebook or Google Colab, the magic commands `%%time` and `%timeit` are utilized. These commands print the time in seconds (milliseconds or microseconds) to execute various operations. It can be observed that all the presented collections take approximately the same time to perform calculations for small data sizes. Some advantages can be noticed with the simpler data structures (tuple and list). These performance differences become particularly noticeable with large datasets. Therefore, specialized data structures for data analysis, such as NumPy arrays and pandas DataFrames, have been developed.

DEFINING CUSTOM FUNCTIONS FOR DATA ANALYSIS

Data analysis and decision-making processes often lead to situations that require custom computation solutions or repetitive tasks. With Python, we can define custom functions to address these needs and streamline analytical code. The user-defined functions allow us to encapsulate a block of reusable code that can be executed whenever required.

A custom function in Python is defined using the `def` keyword, followed by the function name, a pair of parentheses that may house parameters, and a colon.

Let us dive into some examples and describe the significance of custom functions.

The syntax for a simple function is as follows:

```
1. def is_positive(x):
2.     return (x > 0)
3. print(is_positive(-1))
4. print(is_positive(0.1))
```

The results of the code are:

```
False
True
```

This function, named `is_positive()`, takes a single argument, x, and checks whether the given value is greater than 0. It returns `True` if the condition is satisfied and `False` otherwise. When executed, the function is called twice with the values `-1` and `0.1`, and the results are printed. The function is a basic demonstration of conditional checks within a function.

Two essential statistical metrics for data analysis are the average and standard deviation (mean deviation from the mean value). While many Python libraries provide corresponding functions, we can create custom functions with specific features, such as trim max and min values.

The syntax for a function with multiple arguments and outputs is as follows:

```
1.  def mean_for_list(data:list, rnd = 2, sd = False)
    -> float:
2.    mean_value = sum(data)/len(data)
3.    if sd:
4.        sd_value = ( sum([(x - mean_value)**2 for x
    in data]) /
5.                      len(data) ) ** 0.5
6.        return (round(mean_value, rnd),
7.                round(sd_value, rnd) )
8.    else:
9.        return round(mean_value, rnd)
10. print(mean_for_list(closing_prices, rnd=1))
11. mean, sd = mean_for_list(closing_prices, sd=True)
12. print(f"Mean: {mean:.2f}, Standart Deviation:
    {sd:.2f}")
```

The results of the code are:

```
184.52
```

The function `mean_for_list()` calculates the average (mean) of a given list of numbers with the default argument `sd`. It has three parameters: `data`, which is a list of numbers; `rnd=2`, an integer that defaults to 2; and `sd=False`, a Boolean indicator. This more structured approach allows for more explicit expectations and better documentation.

NOTE *The sum() function in Python calculates all the elements in the list data. The round() function rounds off the resulting mean to n decimal places.*

The `mean_for_list()` function with the argument `sd=True` returns two vital statistics, the mean and standard deviation. It efficiently utilizes tuple packing to encapsulate these metrics, and through tuple unpacking, users can seamlessly extract individual values for further analysis.

Lambda functions, a type of anonymous function, are small, single-use functions in Python. Usually, this is a function without a name. They are often used for short, repetitive tasks—for example, in this chapter, when sorting a dictionary by the `date` key. The basic syntax of a lambda function is as follows:

```
1. lambda arguments: expression
```

Here, the arguments are the inputs to the function, and the expression is a single output expression. Using the lambda function to determine the non-negativity of a number as in previous examples would look as follows:

```
1. print((lambda x: x > 0)(-1))   # Output: False
2. print((lambda x: x > 0)(0.1))  # Output: True
```

Lambda functions are limited to a single expression and are mainly used as a utility tool, but they are very powerful.

NUMPY FOR DATA ANALYSIS

NumPy, short for Numerical Python, is one of Python's most ubiquitous numerical computation libraries. It supports large, multi-dimensional arrays, matrices, and various functions to operate on these data structures efficiently. NumPy arrays combine the advantages of the *list* and *set* data structures and have tools for manipulating big datasets.

To use the NumPy library, we must first connect it to the current workflow. This is usually done with the following command line: `import numpy as np`. The `numpy` part here is the library's name, and `np` is the pseudonym for the quick function calls indicated.

Creating NumPy Arrays

At the heart of NumPy is an array object. Arrays are like lists in Python, but every item in an array must be the same type, for example, a numeric type such as `float` or `int`. Execute the following code to create and manipulate NumPy arrays:

```
1. import numpy as np
2. # 1D NumPy array
```

```
3.  dates = np.array([
4.      "2023-08-01",
5.      "2023-08-09", # This date is out of place by
    date sorting
6.      "2023-08-02", "2023-08-03", "2023-08-04",
7.      "2023-08-07", "2023-08-08", "2023-08-10",
8.  ])
9.  print("The NumPy array for observation dates \n",
    dates)
10. # 2D NumPy array. Format: [Open, High, Low,
    Close]
11. apple_ohlc = np.array([
12.      [196.24, 198.00, 195.00, 195.61],  # 1st Aug
13.      [180.87, 182.00, 178.50, 178.19],  # 9th Aug !
14.      [195.04, 197.50, 193.00, 192.58],  # 2nd Aug
15.      [191.57, 192.50, 190.00, 191.17],  # 3rd Aug
16.      [185.52, 188.00, 184.50, 181.99],  # 4th Aug
17.      [182.13, 183.40, 178.00, 178.85],  # 7th Aug
18.      [179.69, 181.50, 178.80, 179.80],  # 8th Aug
19.      [179.48, 181.00, 177.00, 177.97],]) # 10th
    Aug
20. print("2D NumPy array for OHLC data \n",
    apple_ohlc)
21. # Fetching specific data points using direct
    indexing
22. print(dates[1])
23. print(apple_ohlc[1, 3])
24. # Accessing non-consecutive dates and their
    entire OHLC data using list-based indexing
```

```
25.  print(dates[[0, 7, 3]])
26.  print(apple_ohlc[[0, 7, 3],:])
27.  # Extracting specific high prices using a
     combination of row and column indices
28.  print(apple_ohlc[[0, 7, 3],[1]])
29.  # Storing and utilizing indices through a list
     for reusability and clarity
30.  indices = [0, 3, 7]
31.  print(dates[indices])
32.  print(apple_ohlc[indices])
33.  print(apple_ohlc[indices, 0])
34.  print(apple_ohlc[indices, 3])
```

The results of the code are:

```
2023-08-09
178.19
['2023-08-01' '2023-08-10' '2023-08-03']
[[196.24 198.    195.    195.61]
 [179.48 181.    177.    177.97]
 [191.57 192.5  190.    191.17]]
[198.   181.   192.5]
['2023-08-01' '2023-08-03' '2023-08-10']
[[196.24 198.    195.    195.61]
 [191.57 192.5  190.    191.17]
 [179.48 181.    177.    177.97]]
[196.24 191.57 179.48]
[195.61 191.17 177.97]
```

We apply direct and list-based indexing to access specific or multiple elements in these examples. The concept is consistent with Python's zero-based indexing system. Be aware of when you need to extract individual data points or slices; in NumPy (as in Python lists), the index starts from 0, ensuring a systematic and predictable data access mechanism.

NOTE *The OHLC acronym stands for open, high, low, and close, representing the four key data points in a trading period for any assets' prices (as shown in the example).*

Sorting and Sorting by Arguments

In data analysis, especially when working with time-series data, sorting datasets based on specific criteria is indispensable. Fortunately, NumPy provides a range of utilities to facilitate sorting, making this task intuitive and efficient. The methods `np.sort()` and `np.argsort()` stand out as the primary tools for this purpose.

Let us explore sorting functionalities in depth using the following code:

```
1. sorted_dates = np.sort(dates)
2. print("Dates sorted in ascending order:\n",
   sorted_dates)
3. sorted_date_indices = np.argsort(dates)
4. print("Indices that would sort 'dates':\n",
   sorted_date_indices)
5. apple_ohlc_sorted_by_date =
   apple_ohlc[sorted_date_indices]
6. print("OHLC data sorted by 'dates':\n",
   apple_ohlc_sorted_by_date)
7. sorted_close_price_indices = np.argsort(apple_
   ohlc[:, 3])
8. dates_sorted_by_close_price =
   dates[sorted_close_price_indices]
9. print("Dates sorted by Close prices:\n",
   dates_sorted_by_close_price)
```

The results are as follows:

```
Dates sorted in ascending order:
 ['2023-08-01' '2023-08-02' '2023-08-03' '2023-08-04'
 '2023-08-07'

 '2023-08-08' '2023-08-09' '2023-08-10']
Indices that would sort 'dates':
 [0 2 3 4 5 6 1 7]
OHLC data sorted by 'dates':
 [[196.24 198.    195.    195.61]

 [195.04 197.5  193.    192.58]

 [191.57 192.5  190.    191.17]

 [185.52 188.    184.5  181.99]

 [182.13 183.4  178.    178.85]

 [179.69 181.5  178.8  179.8 ]

 [180.87 182.    178.5  178.19]

 [179.48 181.    177.    177.97]]
Dates sorted by Close prices:
 ['2023-08-10' '2023-08-09' '2023-08-07' '2023-08-08'
 '2023-08-04'

 '2023-08-03' '2023-08-02' '2023-08-01']
```

In the examples, the emphasis is on sorting and arranging datasets based on another dataset. The `np.argsort` function gives us the indices that can be used to reorder multiple arrays coherently. In the case of stock market analysis, it is common to manage date and OHLC data separately, making these techniques invaluable for maintaining consistency and coherence in the datasets. The `np.array` data structure also has a built-in `.sort` method— `dates.sort()`. The peculiarity of its application is that the data array itself is sorted, and this method is more often applied to independent arrays.

Adding and Removing Data

When analyzing and processing data, there might be situations where we need to add new observations or remove existing ones. Despite being a fixed size by default, NumPy arrays can be reshaped and modified using a set of functions. Let us delve into methods for adding and removing data in NumPy arrays by using the following code:

```
1.  # Appending new data
2.  new_date = np.array(["2023-08-11"])
3.  new_ohlc = np.array([[180.50, 183.00, 179.50,
    182.40]])
4.  sorted_dates = np.append(sorted_dates, new_date)
5.  apple_ohlc_sorted_by_date = np.append(apple_ohlc_
    sorted_by_date, new_ohlc, axis=0)
6.  # Inserting data at the third position (Index 2)
7.  insert_date = np.array(["2023-08-05"])
8.  insert_ohlc = np.array([[184.20, 185.50, 182.90,
    183.30]])
9.  sorted_dates = np.insert(sorted_dates, 2,
    insert_date)
10. apple_ohlc_sorted_by_date = np.insert(apple_ohlc_
    sorted_by_date, 2, insert_ohlc, axis=0)
11. # Deleting data for the date "2023-08-04"
    (which is now at Index 3 after insertion)
12. sorted_dates = np.delete(sorted_dates, 3)
13. apple_ohlc_sorted_by_date = np.delete(apple_ohlc_
    sorted_by_date, 3, axis=0)
14. print("Modified Dates Array:\n", sorted_dates)
15. print("\nModified OHLC Data:\n", apple_ohlc_
    sorted_by_date)
```

The results of the code are:

```
Modified Dates Array:
 ['2023-08-01' '2023-08-02' '2023-08-05' '2023-08-04'
 '2023-08-07'
 '2023-08-08' '2023-08-09' '2023-08-10' '2023-08-11']
Modified OHLC Data:
 [[196.24 198.   195.   195.61]
 [195.04 197.5  193.   192.58]
 [184.2  185.5  182.9  183.3 ]
 [185.52 188.   184.5  181.99]
 [182.13 183.4  178.   178.85]
 [179.69 181.5  178.8  179.8 ]
 [180.87 182.   178.5  178.19]
 [179.48 181.   177.   177.97]
 [180.5  183.   179.5  182.4 ]]
```

As we can see, the key modifying operations are as follows:

- Appending allows us to add new data at the end of an array. The `np.append()` function serves this purpose.
- Insertion lets us add data at a specific position. The `np.insert()` function can achieve this.
- To remove specific observations based on their indices, we can employ the `np.delete()` function.

NOTE *The axis parameter is applied to the 2D array. To append or insert rows, use axis=0; to append or insert columns, use axis=1.*

Array Shape Manipulation

Manipulating the shape or structure of a NumPy array is often required during data processing. Whether changing the dimensions, merging arrays, or even dividing them, NumPy provides an arsenal of functions to efficiently transform arrays without altering the underlying data.

- np.concatenate(): Join two or more arrays along an existing axis.
- np.split(): Split an array into multiple subarrays.
- np.reshape(): Alter the dimensions of an array without changing its data.
- np.transpose() or array.T: Reverse or permute the axes of an array.
- np.hstack(): Stack arrays in sequence horizontally (column-wise).
- np.vstack(): Stack arrays in sequence vertically (row-wise).

Let us demonstrate these operations using some NumPy arrays:

```
1.  transposed_ohlc = apple_ohlc_sorted_by_date.T
2.  print("Transposed OHLC Data:\n", transposed_ohlc)
3.  split_arrays = np.split(transposed_ohlc, 4,
    axis=0)
4.  print("\nSplitted array is \n", split_arrays)
5.  for idx, arr in enumerate(split_arrays):
6.      print(f"\nSplit {idx + 1}:\n", arr)
7.  concatenated_data = np.concatenate(split_arrays,
    axis=1)
8.  print("\nConcatenated Data:\n", concatenated_
    data)
9.  horizontal_stack = np.hstack(split_arrays[0])
10. print("\nHorizontally Stacked Open Price
    Data:\n", horizontal_stack)
11. vertical_stack = np.vstack(split_arrays)
12. print("\nVertically Stacked Data:\n",
    vertical_stack)
13. reshaped_dates_3x3 = sorted_dates.reshape(3, 3)
14. print("\nReshaped Dates (3x3):\n", reshaped_
    dates_3x3)
15. reshaped_dates_col = sorted_dates.reshape(9, 1)
16. print("\nReshaped Dates (9x1):\n", reshaped_
    dates_col)
```

The results of the code are:

Transposed OHLC Data:

```
[[196.24 195.04 184.2  185.52 182.13 179.69 180.87 179.48
180.5 ]

[198.   197.5  185.5  188.   183.4  181.5  182.   181.
183.  ]

[195.   193.   182.9  184.5  178.   178.8  178.5  177.
179.5 ]

[195.61 192.58 183.3  181.99 178.85 179.8  178.19 177.97
182.4 ]]
```

Splitted array is

```
[array([[196.24, 195.04, 184.2 , 185.52, 182.13, 179.69,
180.87, 179.48, 180.5 ]]), array([[198. , 197.5, 185.5,
188. , 183.4, 181.5, 182. , 181. , 183. ]]), array([[195.
, 193. , 182.9, 184.5, 178. , 178.8, 178.5, 177. ,
179.5]]), array([[195.61, 192.58, 183.3 , 181.99, 178.85,
179.8 , 178.19, 177.97, 182.4 ]])]
```

Split 1:

```
[[196.24 195.04 184.2  185.52 182.13 179.69 180.87 179.48
180.5 ]]
```

Split 2:

```
[[198.   197.5 185.5 188.   183.4 181.5 182.   181.   183. ]]
```

Split 3:

```
[[195.   193.   182.9 184.5 178.   178.8 178.5 177.   179.5]]
```

Split 4:

```
[[195.61 192.58 183.3  181.99 178.85 179.8  178.19 177.97
182.4 ]]
```

Concatenated Data:

```
[[196.24 195.04 184.2  185.52 182.13 179.69 180.87 179.48
180.5  198. 197.5  185.5  188.   183.4  181.5  182.
181.   183.  195.   193. 182.9  184.5  178.   178.8
```

```
  178.5   177.    179.5   195.61 192.58 183.3 181.99 178.85
  179.8   178.19 177.97 182.4 ]]
```

Horizontally Stacked Open Price Data:

```
 [196.24 195.04 184.2   185.52 182.13 179.69 180.87 179.48
 180.5 ]
```

Vertically Stacked Data:

```
 [[196.24 195.04 184.2   185.52 182.13 179.69 180.87 179.48
 180.5 ]

 [198.    197.5  185.5  188.    183.4  181.5  182.    181.
 183.  ]

 [195.    193.   182.9  184.5  178.    178.8  178.5  177.
 179.5 ]

 [195.61 192.58 183.3   181.99 178.85 179.8   178.19 177.97
 182.4 ]]
```

Reshaped Dates (3x3):

```
 [['2023-08-01' '2023-08-02' '2023-08-05']

 ['2023-08-04' '2023-08-07' '2023-08-08']

 ['2023-08-09' '2023-08-10' '2023-08-11']]
```

Reshaped Dates (9x1):

```
 [['2023-08-01']

 ['2023-08-02']

 ['2023-08-05']

 ['2023-08-04']

 ['2023-08-07']

 ['2023-08-08']

 ['2023-08-09']

 ['2023-08-10']

 ['2023-08-11']]
```

This code captures the essence of shape manipulations in NumPy, illustrating the library's versatility in restructuring data arrays. Whether the aim is to pivot data's orientation, segment it, or aggregate segments, these operations provide the tools to achieve those structural transformations efficiently. Please investigate the results for further application.

Find Values and Filtering Operations

NumPy offers an extensive suite of tools to query and filter arrays. Here, we will delve into the techniques for finding and filtering data using our reference datasets: the sorted dates and OHLC price arrays. Execute the following code:

```
1.  date_index = np.where((sorted_dates == "2023-08-04") |
2.                         (sorted_dates == "2023-08-01"))[0]
3.  print("\n Date index for 2023-08-04 or
    2023-08-01:")
4.  print(date_index)
5.  ohlc_on_specific_date = apple_ohlc_sorted_
    by_date[date_index]
6.  print("\n OHLC data for the specific date:")
7.  print(ohlc_on_specific_date)
8.  highest_close_index = np.argmax(apple_ohlc_
    sorted_by_date[:, 3])
9.  date_with_highest_close = sorted_dates
    [highest_close_index]
10. print("\n Date with the highest close price:")
11. print(date_with_highest_close)
12. above_threshold_dates = sorted_dates[apple_ohlc_
    sorted_by_date[:, 3] > 190]
13. print("\n Dates with close prices above 190:")
14. print(above_threshold_dates)
```

```
15. between_threshold_dates = sorted_dates[(apple_
    ohlc_sorted_by_date[:, 0] < 190) &
16.                                       (apple_
    ohlc_sorted_by_date[:, 0] > 180)]
17. print("\n Dates with open prices between 180 and
    190:")
18. print(between_threshold_dates)
```

The results of the code are:

```
Date index for 2023-08-04 or 2023-08-01:
[0 3]
 OHLC data for the specific date:
[[196.24 198.   195.   195.61]
 [185.52 188.   184.5  181.99]]
 Date with the highest close price:
2023-08-01
 Dates with close prices above 190:
['2023-08-01' '2023-08-02']
 Dates with open prices between 180 and 190:
['2023-08-05' '2023-08-04' '2023-08-07' '2023-08-09'
 '2023-08-11']
```

The code searches for a specific trading date using NumPy's np.where function. This is often the first step in financial analysis, where an analyst wants to extract price information for a particular date. The found index is then used to retrieve the OHLC prices for that specific date. Moving forward, the np.argmax functions help identify the trading day with the highest closing price. Such information is crucial for traders and analysts to spot significant peaks in a price series. Similarly, one could use np.argmin to spot the lowest values. Lastly, the code demonstrates filtering techniques. Using conditional statements (> and <, or others such as ==, >=, and <=), we can quickly filter out trading dates based on specific price thresholds. This can be used to search for bullish or bearish trading days based on the closing price.

Therefore, with just a few lines, we can pinpoint specific trading days, remove relevant price information, and filter out data based on price thresholds. This suite of capabilities makes NumPy an indispensable tool for data analysis.

Arithmetical and Statistical Operations

Numerical computing is a foundational aspect of financial data and quantitative analysis. NumPy libraries for mathematical operations in Python are packed with functions that allow for complex numerical computations on arrays and matrices. The given examples underscore the ease and efficiency with which such calculations can be executed.

Use the following code:

```
1.  # Combining results into a single array for
    display
2.  stats_array = np.array([
3.      apple_ohlc_sorted_by_date.mean(axis=0),
4.      np.median(apple_ohlc_sorted_by_date, axis=0),
5.      np.var(apple_ohlc_sorted_by_date, axis=0),
6.      np.std(apple_ohlc_sorted_by_date, axis=0)])
7.  print("Statistical measures for OHLC data:\n",
    stats_array.T)
8.  # Rate of Return calculation
9.  ror_ohlc = (apple_ohlc_sorted_by_date[1:]
    - apple_ohlc_sorted_by_date[:-1]) /
    apple_ohlc_sorted_by_date[:-1]
10. print("Rate of Return for each day:\n", ror_ohlc)
11. # Logarithmic version of the Rate of Return
    calculation
12. ror_ohlc_log = np.log(apple_ohlc_sorted_by_
    date[1:] / apple_ohlc_sorted_by_date[:-1])
13. print("Logarithmic version of the Rate of Return
    for each day:\n", ror_ohlc_log)
```

The results of the code are:

```
Statistical measures for OHLC data:
 [[184.85222222 182.13        36.8959284    6.07420187]
 [186.65555556 183.4         39.29358025   6.26845916]
 [183.02222222 179.5         39.71061728   6.30163608]
 [183.41       181.99        36.29391111   6.02444281]]
Rate of Return for each day:
 [[-0.00611496 -0.00252525 -0.01025641 -0.01549001]
 [-0.05557834 -0.06075949 -0.05233161 -0.04818777]
 [ 0.00716612  0.01347709  0.00874795 -0.00714675]
 [-0.01827296 -0.02446809 -0.03523035 -0.0172537 ]
 [-0.01339702 -0.01035987  0.00449438  0.00531171]
 [ 0.00656687  0.00275482 -0.00167785 -0.00895439]
 [-0.00768508 -0.00549451 -0.00840336 -0.00123464]
 [ 0.00568308  0.01104972  0.01412429  0.02489184]]
Logarithmic version of the Rate of Return for each day:
 [[-0.00613373 -0.00252845 -0.01030937 -0.01561123]
 [-0.05718254 -0.0626837  -0.05375063 -0.0493875 ]
 [ 0.00714057  0.01338708  0.00870991 -0.00717241]
 [-0.01844198 -0.0247724  -0.03586591 -0.01740427]
 [-0.01348757 -0.01041391  0.00448431  0.00529766]
 [ 0.0065454   0.00275103 -0.00167926 -0.00899473]
 [-0.00771476 -0.00550966 -0.00843887 -0.0012354 ]
 [ 0.005667    0.01098912  0.01402548  0.02458708]]
```

The first operation is directed toward understanding the central tendency of stock market data by using core statistical metrics on the OHLC data for Apple Inc.

The following are the statistical measures:

- `np.mean()`: This computes the average value of array elements along a specified axis.
- `np.median()`: This finds the median or middle value of the sorted array along the specified axis.
- `np.var()`: This calculates the variance of array elements, which is a measure of the spread between numbers (individual values are squared to remove the influence of the sign of the difference).
- `np.std`: This computes the standard deviation, indicating the amount of variation or square root of variance.

The NumPy library has many more similar functions, as shown in the following table:

TABLE 2.2 Main functions of the NumPy library for performing mathematical and statistical operations on arrays

Function	Description
Mathematical functions	
`np.sum(x)`	Sum of all elements in x
`np.prod(x)`	Product of all elements in x
`np.cumsum(x)`	Cumulative sum of each element along x
`np.cumprod(x)`	Cumulative product of each element along x
`np.sqrt(x)`	Square root of each element in x
`np.power(x, n)`	Raise each element in x to the power n
`np.exp(x)`	Exponential of each element in x
`np.log(x)`	Natural logarithm of each element in x
`np.log10(x)`	Base-10 logarithm of each element in x
`np.log1p(x)`	Natural logarithm of 1 plus each element in x (applied for small or zero growth)
`np.expm1(x)`	Calculate exp(x) – 1 of each element in x (applied for small or zero growth)

Statistical functions	
`np.mean(x)`	Compute the arithmetic mean of x
`np.median(x)`	Compute the median of x
`np.std(x)`	Compute the standard deviation of x
`np.var(x)`	Compute the variance of x
`np.min(x)`	Find the minimum value in x
`np.max(x)`	Find the maximum value in x
`np.percentile(x, p)`	Compute the p-th percentile of x
`np.quantile(x, q)`	Compute the q-th quantile of x

With the argument `axis=0`, we perform the desired statistical measure for each OHLC value of the `apple_ohlc_sorted_by_date` array.

The second and third operations are used to calculate the RoR and logarithmic RoR.

The *logarithmic RoR*, or continuously compounded return, is often used because of its properties that simplify time aggregation. The formula is as follows:

LogReturns = LogRoR = ln (Current price / Previous price)

The logarithmic RoR is approximately equal to the RoR. It is, however, considered a continuous estimate of price dynamics. Both versions of this metric are applied in practical analysis.

In the context of the code:

- `apple_ohlc_sorted_by_date[1:]` selects all rows from the second row to the OHLC data's last row. This corresponds to the *current price* subarray in our formula.
- `apple_ohlc_sorted_by_date[:-1]` selects all rows from the first row up to (but not including) the last row of the OHLC data. This represents the *previous price* subarray in our formula.

When using lists or dictionaries, we applied a relatively large amount of code and additional loops to calculate the RoR. With the NumPy library, this calculation was done in one line for all prices in the period. This is the magic of array-based operations. To better understand matrix operations, you can experiment with individual parts of the code and the resulting structures.

NOTE *A custom function can be converted into a NumPy vectorized form using np.vectorize().*

For example, let's consider applying a custom function to the `ror_ohlc` array, using `is_positive()`, which was defined earlier, as in the following code:

```
1. is_positive_v = np.vectorize(is_positive)
2. print(is_positive_v(ror_ohlc))
```

The results of the code are:

```
[[False False False False]
 [False False False False]
 [ True  True  True False]
 [False False False False]
 [False False  True  True]
 [ True  True False False]
 [False False False False]
 [ True  True  True  True]]
```

Though NumPy is the go-to library for processing large data arrays, it has some limitations; for instance, a NumPy array cannot use different data types within structures and assign names to rows and columns. Therefore, the powerful pandas library was developed to address these issues.

WORKING WITH PANDAS FOR DATA ANALYSIS

pandas is a powerful Python library tailored for data manipulation and analysis. At the heart of pandas are its two primary data structures: *Series* and *DataFrames*. A Series is akin to a one-dimensional array that can hold any data type with its name and specific indexes of the rows. A DataFrame is a two-dimensional and size-mutable tabular data structure with labeled axes (rows and columns). Think of a DataFrame as an in-memory spreadsheet, like Excel, where we can perform operations easily.

When working with pandas, using specific import aliases is a common convention. As with NumPy, where the standard alias is np, pandas is typically imported under the alias pd. Here is how you can do it:

```
1. import numpy as np
2. import pandas as pd
```

Creating a Series and DataFrame

A Series and DataFrame allow for flexible and efficient data manipulation. Let us explore how to create and work with Series and DataFrame structures using data from *Table 2.1* (based on the NumPy arrays dates and apple_ohlc). Use the following code:

```
1. dates = np.array([
2.     "2023-08-01", "2023-08-09", "2023-08-02",
3.     "2023-08-03", "2023-08-04", "2023-08-07",
4.     "2023-08-08", "2023-08-10",
5. ])
6.
7. apple_ohlc = np.array([
8.     [196.24, 198.00, 195.00, 195.61],   # 1st Aug
9.     [180.87, 182.00, 178.50, 178.19],   # 9th Aug !
10.    [195.04, 197.50, 193.00, 192.58],   # 2nd Aug
11.    [191.57, 192.50, 190.00, 191.17],   # 3rd Aug
12.    [185.52, 188.00, 184.50, 181.99],   # 4th Aug
13.    [182.13, 183.40, 178.00, 178.85],   # 7th Aug
14.    [179.69, 181.50, 178.80, 179.80],   # 8th Aug
15.    [179.48, 181.00, 177.00, 177.97],   # 10th Aug
```

```
16.  ])
17.
18.  ds = pd.Series(apple_ohlc[:,3], index=dates,
     name='Close Prices')
19.  print("Series is \n", ds)
20.
21.  df = pd.DataFrame(apple_ohlc, index=dates,
22.                    columns=["Open", "High", "Low",
     "Close"])
23.  print("\nDataFrame is \n", df)
```

The results of the code are:

```
Series is
 2023-08-01    195.61
2023-08-09     178.19
2023-08-02     192.58
2023-08-03     191.17
2023-08-04     181.99
2023-08-07     178.85
2023-08-08     179.80
2023-08-10     177.97
Name: Close Prices, dtype: float64

DataFrame is
             Open   High    Low   Close
2023-08-01  196.24  198.0  195.0  195.61
2023-08-09  180.87  182.0  178.5  178.19
```

```
2023-08-02   195.04   197.5   193.0   192.58
2023-08-03   191.57   192.5   190.0   191.17
2023-08-04   185.52   188.0   184.5   181.99
2023-08-07   182.13   183.4   178.0   178.85
2023-08-08   179.69   181.5   178.8   179.80
2023-08-10   179.48   181.0   177.0   177.97
```

As seen in the example, the structures of pandas resemble tables, complete with headers and row labels.

Indexing, Finding, and Filtering Data

When working with pandas, one of the fundamental steps in data manipulation is retrieving specific portions of the dataset, which includes indexing, finding, and filtering the data effectively. pandas provides powerful and user-friendly methods to perform these operations on Series and DataFrames, allowing for precise data extraction and manipulation based on specific conditions or criteria.

Selecting Values and Slicing Datasets

To get values in a Series and DataFrame by indexes, we can use the following code:

```
1.  # Series Selection
2.  print("The first element in the Series is: ",
3.        ds.iloc[0])
4.  print("\nThe elements from index 1 to 2 in the
        Series are: \n",
5.        ds[1:3])
6.  print("\nThe element in the Series at index
        '2023-08-02' is: ",
7.        ds["2023-08-02"])
8.  print("\nThe elements in the Series from '2023-
        08-09' to '2023-08-04' are: \n",
```

```
 9.          ds.loc["2023-08-09":"2023-08-04"])
10.  # DataFrame Selection
11.  print("The 'Open' column from the DataFrame is:
     \n",
12.          df["Open"])
13.  print("\nThe 'Open' and 'Close' columns from the
     DataFrame are: \n",
14.          df[["Open", "Close"]])
15.  print("\nThe 'Close' column values between
     indexes '2023-08-09' and '2023-08-04' are: \n",
16.          df.loc["2023-08-09":"2023-08-04", "Close"])
17.  print("\nAll column values between '2023-08-09'
     and '2023-08-04' are: \n",
18.          df.loc["2023-08-09":"2023-08-04", :])
19.  print("\nThe value at the second row and the
     third column is: ",
20.          df.iloc[1, 2])
21.  print("\nThe values from the second and fourth
     rows, excluding the last column, are: \n",
22.          df.iloc[[1, 3], :-1])
```

The results of the code are:

```
The first element in the Series is:  195.61

The elements from index 1 to 2 in the Series are:
 2023-08-09    178.19
2023-08-02    192.58
Name: Close Prices, dtype: float64
```

The element in the Series at index '2023-08-02' is:
192.58

The elements in the Series from '2023-08-09' to
'2023-08-04' are:

 2023-08-09   178.19

2023-08-02   192.58

2023-08-03   191.17

2023-08-04   181.99

Name: Close Prices, dtype: float64

The 'Open' column from the DataFrame is:

 2023-08-01   196.24

2023-08-09   180.87

2023-08-02   195.04

2023-08-03   191.57

2023-08-04   185.52

2023-08-07   182.13

2023-08-08   179.69

2023-08-10   179.48

Name: Open, dtype: float64

The 'Open' and 'Close' columns from the DataFrame are:

	Open	Close
2023-08-01	196.24	195.61
2023-08-09	180.87	178.19
2023-08-02	195.04	192.58
2023-08-03	191.57	191.17
2023-08-04	185.52	181.99

```
2023-08-07   182.13   178.85
2023-08-08   179.69   179.80
2023-08-10   179.48   177.97
```

The 'Close' column values between indexes '2023-08-09' and '2023-08-04' are:

```
 2023-08-09      178.19
2023-08-02      192.58
2023-08-03      191.17
2023-08-04      181.99
Name: Close, dtype: float64
```

All column values between '2023-08-09' and '2023-08-04' are:

	Open	High	Low	Close
2023-08-09	180.87	182.0	178.5	178.19
2023-08-02	195.04	197.5	193.0	192.58
2023-08-03	191.57	192.5	190.0	191.17
2023-08-04	185.52	188.0	184.5	181.99

The value at the second row and the third column is:
178.5

The values from the second and fourth rows, excluding the last column, are:

	Open	High	Low
2023-08-09	180.87	182.0	178.5
2023-08-03	191.57	192.5	190.0

This code example shows how to access and slice data within a pandas Series (`ds`) and a DataFrame (`df`) with the following statements:

- `[]`: Directly accesses elements of a Series or selects columns from a DataFrame (the functionality of treating keys as positions is deprecated).
- `loc[]`: Enables selection by index/label, which is useful for slicing a DataFrame and Series with a clear focus on utilizing index labels.
- `iloc[]`: Employs integer-location-based indexing for selection by position, allowing the slicing of a DataFrame and Series with positional integer indexes.
- `::` Acts as a slicer to select a range of values in a Series or DataFrame when used within `loc[]` or `iloc[]`.

As we can observe, the syntax for the basic data types in pandas closely resembles the classic spreadsheet navigation. This similarity is helpful to those familiar with spreadsheet software, making the transition to pandas smooth and intuitive.

Filtering Data

When working with datasets in pandas, we often used different mechanisms and methods provided by pandas to filter out, extract, or isolate parts of the data, ensuring focused and efficient analysis.

First, contemporary IDEs such as Jupyter Notebook and Google Colab offer tools to interact with DataFrames, which are like Excel tables (refer to *Figure 2.1*). If you run a cell with the `df` code, you will obtain a table as shown on the top left (screen 1). If you press the Calculator button, the view will change to what is shown on the top right (screen 2), allowing you to search for values by index or table element and filter in a convenient dialog mode (see screen 3 at the bottom):

df

	Open	High	Low	Close	
2023-08-01	196.24	198.0	195.0	195.61	
2023-08-09	180.87	182.0	178.5	178.19	
2023-08-02	195.04	197.5	193.0	192.58	
2023-08-03	191.57	192.5	190.0	191.17	
2023-08-04	185.52	188.0	184.5	181.99	
2023-08-07	182.13	183.4	178.0	178.85	
2023-08-08	179.69	181.5	178.8	179.80	
2023-08-10	179.48	181.0	177.0	177.97	

Screen 1

df

1 to 8 of 8 entries   Filter

index	Open	High	Low	Close
2023-08-01	196.24	198.0	195.0	195.61
2023-08-09	180.87	182.0	178.5	178.19
2023-08-02	195.04	197.5	193.0	192.58
2023-08-03	191.57	192.5	190.0	191.17
2023-08-04	185.52	188.0	184.5	181.99
2023-08-07	182.13	183.4	178.0	178.85
2023-08-08	179.69	181.5	178.8	179.8
2023-08-10	179.48	181.0	177.0	177.97

Screen 2

1 to 8 of 8 entries   Filter   ✕

index:
[   ]

Open:
[   ] to [   ]

High:
[   ] to [   ]

Low:
[   ] to [   ]

Close:
[   ] to [   ]

Search by all fields:
[   ]

index	Open	High	Low	Close
2023-08-01	196.24	198.0	195.0	195.61
2023-08-09	180.87	182.0	178.5	178.19
2023-08-02	195.04	197.5	193.0	192.58
2023-08-03	191.57	192.5	190.0	191.17
2023-08-04	185.52	188.0	184.5	181.99
2023-08-07	182.13	183.4	178.0	178.85
2023-08-08	179.69	181.5	178.8	179.8
2023-08-10	179.48	181.0	177.0	177.97

Screen 3

FIGURE 2.1 Visualization of a DataFrame as a table in Google Colab

pandas data structures also have powerful functions and methods for filtering datasets based on the *Boolean* (logical) indexing principle. Execute the following code to try it:

```
1.  # Dataset Filtering

2.  # Series

3.  print("Elements in Series > 190: \n",

4.      ds > 190)
```

```
5.  print("\nSeries where elements > 190: \n",
6.       ds[ds > 190])
7.  print("\nSeries element at index '2023-08-03':
    \n",
8.       ds[ds.index == "2023-08-03"])
9.  # DataFrame
10. print("\nDataFrame where 'Open' > 190 and 'Close'
    < 192: \n",
11.      df[(df['Open'] > 190) & (df['Close'] <
    192)])
12. print("\nDataFrame where 'Open' is greater than
    'Close': \n",
13.      df[df['Open'] > df['Close']])
14. print("\nDataFrame where 'Close' is in [192.58,
    178.19]: \n",
15.      df[df['Close'].isin([192.58, 178.19])])
16. print("\nDataFrame at index '2023-08-03': \n",
17.      df[df.index == "2023-08-03"])
18. print("\nDataFrame at indices ['2023-08-
    03','2023-08-09']: \n",
19.      df[df.index.isin(["2023-08-03",
    "2023-08-09"])])
20.
21. # Combining Conditions
22. print("\nDataFrame where 'Open' > 180, 'Open' <
    190, and 'Close' != 181.99: \n",
23.      df[(df['Open'] > 180) &
          (df['Open'] < 190) &
          (df['Close'] != 181.99)])
24.
```

```
25.  # Creating a sub-dataframe for the date range and
     applying the condition
26.  subset_df = df.loc["2023-08-01":"2023-08-08"]
27.  print("\nSubset DataFrame where 'Open' > 180,
     'Open' < 190, and 'Close' != 181.99: \n",
28.      subset_df[(subset_df['Open'] > 180) &
             (subset_df['Open'] < 190) &
             (subset_df['Close'] != 181.99)])
```

The results of the code are:

```
Elements in Series > 190:
2023-08-01     True
2023-08-09     False
2023-08-02     True
2023-08-03     True
2023-08-04     False
2023-08-07     False
2023-08-08     False
2023-08-10     False
Name: Close Prices, dtype: bool


Series where elements > 190:
 2023-08-01     195.61
2023-08-02     192.58
2023-08-03     191.17
Name: Close Prices, dtype: float64
```

```
Series element at index '2023-08-03':
 2023-08-03    191.17
Name: Close Prices, dtype: float64


DataFrame where 'Open' > 190 and 'Close' < 192:
              Open    High    Low    Close
2023-08-03  191.57  192.5  190.0  191.17


DataFrame where 'Open' is greater than 'Close':
              Open    High    Low    Close
2023-08-01  196.24  198.0  195.0  195.61
2023-08-09  180.87  182.0  178.5  178.19
2023-08-02  195.04  197.5  193.0  192.58
2023-08-03  191.57  192.5  190.0  191.17
2023-08-04  185.52  188.0  184.5  181.99
2023-08-07  182.13  183.4  178.0  178.85
2023-08-10  179.48  181.0  177.0  177.97


DataFrame where 'Close' is in [192.58, 178.19]:
              Open    High    Low    Close
2023-08-09  180.87  182.0  178.5  178.19
2023-08-02  195.04  197.5  193.0  192.58


DataFrame at index '2023-08-03':
              Open    High    Low    Close
2023-08-03  191.57  192.5  190.0  191.17
```

```
DataFrame at indices ['2023-08-03','2023-08-09']:
                Open    High    Low    Close
2023-08-09   180.87   182.0   178.5   178.19
2023-08-03   191.57   192.5   190.0   191.17
```

```
DataFrame where 'Open' > 180, 'Open' < 190, and 'Close' !=
181.99:
                Open    High    Low    Close
2023-08-09   180.87   182.0   178.5   178.19
2023-08-07   182.13   183.4   178.0   178.85
```

```
Subset DataFrame where 'Open' > 180, 'Open' < 190, and
'Close' != 181.99:
                Open    High    Low    Close
2023-08-09   180.87   182.0   178.5   178.19
2023-08-07   182.13   183.4   178.0   178.85
```

The preceding code example shows the use of essential data filtering tools, as follows:

- *Boolean indexing*: By utilizing comparison operators such as > and <, this tool filters rows of a DataFrame or Series, yielding rows where the condition is `True`. For example, `ds > 190` extracts values in the Series greater than 190.
- *Equality and inequality checks*: Based on the Boolean indexing principle, operators such as == and != perform equality and inequality checks within a DataFrame or Series, filtering rows where the conditions are met. For example, `df['Close'] != 181.99` retains rows where the `Close` value is not 181.99.
- *Combining conditions*: The & (AND) and | (OR) operators combine multiple conditions, facilitating intricate filtering based on several criteria.

When using &, every condition must be `True`, while for |, only one condition needs to be `True` for a row to be included.

▪ *Using the isin() method*: The `.isin([])` method is utilized for filtering based on multiple potential values for a column. For example, `df['Close'].isin([192.58,    178.19])` filters rows where the `Close` value is either `192.58` or `178.19`.

▪ *Index value filtering*: Using the `.index` attribute coupled with methods such as `.isin([])` or comparison operations allows filtering data based on the values of the index. For instance, `df[df.index.isin(["2023-08-03",   "2023-08-09"])]` returns rows where the index is either `"2023-08-03"` or `"2023-08-09"`.

This set of tools allows for the meticulous exploration and analysis of data in pandas, enabling the precise and flexible extraction of specific insights from the dataset.

Data Manipulation

Data manipulation with pandas includes changing values, reshaping datasets, sorting data in specific orders, and creating new features through calculations, each providing diverse ways to interact with and understand the dataset effectively.

Insertion and Deletion of Data

Let us execute some examples. Inserting new data, modifying existing data, and deleting specific entries or labels can be done in pandas as follows:

```
1. # For Series
2. ds_new = pd.Series(data=[177.79, 179.46],
3.                    index=["2023-08-11",
   "2023-08-14"],
4.                    name=ds.name)
5. ds = pd.concat([ds, ds_new]) # method is
   deprecated
6. print("Modified Series (showing last 3
   entries):\n", ds.tail(3))
```

```
 7.  ds["2023-08-11"] = 177.32
 8.  print("Series after value change (showing last 3
     entries):\n",
           ds.tail(3))
 9.
10.  ds = ds.drop(labels=["2023-08-11", "2023-08-14"])
11.  print("\nSeries after Deletion (showing last 3
     entries):\n",
           ds.tail(3))
12.
13.  # For DataFrame
14.  df.loc["2023-08-11"] = [177.32, 178.62, 176.55,
     177.79]
15.  print("\nModified DataFrame (showing last 3
     entries):\n",
           df.tail(3))
16.
17.  new_df = pd.DataFrame(data=[[177.32, 178.62,
     176.55, 177.79],
18.                             [177.97, 179.69,
     177.31, 179.46]],
19.                      index=["2023-08-11",
     "2023-08-14"],
20.                      columns=df.columns)
21.  df = pd.concat([df, new_df]) # method is
     deprecated
22.  print("\nModified DataFrame (showing last 5
     entries):\n", df.tail())
23.
24.  df = df.drop(labels=["2023-08-11"], axis=0)
```

```
25. print("\nDataFrame after Deletion (showing last 3
    entries):\n",
        df.tail(3))

26.

27. df.drop(labels=["2023-08-14"], axis=0,
    inplace=True)

28. print("\nDataFrame after Deletion (showing last 3
    entries):\n",
        df.tail(3))

29.

30. print("DataFrame after Deletion two Columns (the
    first 3 entries):",

31.     df.drop(labels=["High", "Low"], axis=1).
    head(3))
```

The examples given are based on the use of basic methods and functions, namely:

- The `.concat()` and `.append()` methods combine two or more pandas collections along a particular axis (`axis=0` by rows (as default) or `axis=1` by columns), efficiently enabling the extension of datasets.
- `.loc[]` adds a new row if the row index name does not exist.

NOTE *It is crucial to note that indexes in pandas can be non-unique, meaning that care must be taken when manipulating data to avoid unintended consequences due to multiple rows sharing the same index label.*

- `.drop()` is a tool for removing specified labels from the rows or columns of a DataFrame or Series. It deletes all occurrences of the specified labels, providing a convenient way to cleanse the datasets; for example, `ds.drop(labels=["2023-08-11", "2023-08-14"])` removes all occurrences of the specified row labels in the `ds` Series.
- Methods such as `.drop()` with the `inplace=True` parameter and direct value assignment allow for modifying the object directly without needing to create a new variable for storage, optimizing memory usage. By default (when `inplace=False`), the original DataFrame is usually left unchanged.

▪ The .name attribute for Series and the .columns attribute for DataFrames are fundamental for preserving the identity of objects. For example, when creating new objects, name=ds.name and columns=df.columns ensure the inheritance of names and column labels from existing objects, fostering consistent identification and structural coherence in the datasets.

▪ The .head() and .tail() methods provide a quick glimpse of the dataset. The .head(n) method displays the first n rows, and the .tail(n) method displays the last n rows of the DataFrame or Series, which is extremely useful for preliminary data examination and verification of manipulations. The default is n=5.

These tools allow you to manipulate the values of individual records. To change the order and structure of a DataFrame, however, NumPy statements are used, as follows:

```
1.  # Resetting and setting the index
2.  df_reset = df.reset_index()
3.  print("\nDataFrame after resetting the index:\n",
4.          df_reset.head(3))
5.  # Renaming the 'index' column to 'Date'
6.  df_reset = df_reset.rename(columns={'index':
    'Date'})
7.  print("\nDataFrame after renaming the 'index'
    column to 'Date':\n",
8.          df_reset.head(3))
9.  # Setting 'Date' as the index of the DataFrame
10. df_reset = df_reset.set_index('Date')
11. print("\nDataFrame after Reindexing with
    'Date':\n",
12.         df_reset.head(3))
13. # Preparing DataFrames for Join operation
```

```
14.    # Dropping rows with index '2023-08-10' and
       '2023-08-01'
15.    df_reset.drop(labels=["2023-08-10", "2023-08-01"],
                      axis=0, inplace=True)
16.
17.    # Dropping 'Open', 'High', 'Low' columns
18.    df_reset.drop(labels=["Open", "High", "Low"],
       axis=1, inplace=True)
19.    # Performing Join operations
20.    # Right join keeps every row from the right
       DataFrame, and drops the unmatched rows from the
       left DataFrame.
21.    print("\nDataFrame after Right Join:\n",
22.          df_reset.join(df, how="right",
                            lsuffix='_left',
       rsuffix='_right'))
23.    # Left join keeps every row from the left
       DataFrame, and drops the unmatched rows from the
       right DataFrame.
24.    print("\nDataFrame after Left Join:\n",
25.          df_reset.join(df, how="left",
                            lsuffix='_left',
       rsuffix='_right'))
26.    # Sort Operations
27.    # Sorting DataFrame by 'Open' column values in
       descending order
28.    df_sorted = df.sort_values(by='Open',
       ascending=False)
29.    print("\nDataFrame sorted by 'Open' values in
       descending order:\n",
30.          df_sorted.head(3))
```

```
31.  # Sorting DataFrame by Index in ascending order
     (default)
32.  df_sorted = df.sort_index()
33.  print("\nDataFrame sorted by Index in ascending
     order:\n",
34.         df_sorted.head(3))
```

The results of the code are:

```
DataFrame after resetting the index:
        index      Open   High    Low    Close
0   2023-08-01   196.24   198.0  195.0   195.61
1   2023-08-09   180.87   182.0  178.5   178.19
2   2023-08-02   195.04   197.5  193.0   192.58


DataFrame after renaming the 'index' column to 'Date':
         Date       Open   High    Low    Close
0   2023-08-01   196.24   198.0  195.0   195.61
1   2023-08-09   180.87   182.0  178.5   178.19
2   2023-08-02   195.04   197.5  193.0   192.58


DataFrame after Reindexing with 'Date':
               Open   High    Low    Close
Date
2023-08-01   196.24   198.0  195.0   195.61
2023-08-09   180.87   182.0  178.5   178.19
2023-08-02   195.04   197.5  193.0   192.58
```

DataFrame after Right Join:

	Close_left	Open	High	Low	Close_right
2023-08-01	NaN	196.24	198.0	195.0	195.61
2023-08-09	178.19	180.87	182.0	178.5	178.19
2023-08-02	192.58	195.04	197.5	193.0	192.58
2023-08-03	191.17	191.57	192.5	190.0	191.17
2023-08-04	181.99	185.52	188.0	184.5	181.99
2023-08-07	178.85	182.13	183.4	178.0	178.85
2023-08-08	179.80	179.69	181.5	178.8	179.80
2023-08-10	NaN	179.48	181.0	177.0	177.97

DataFrame after Left Join:

	Close_left	Open	High	Low	Close_right
Date					
2023-08-09	178.19	180.87	182.0	178.5	178.19
2023-08-02	192.58	195.04	197.5	193.0	192.58
2023-08-03	191.17	191.57	192.5	190.0	191.17
2023-08-04	181.99	185.52	188.0	184.5	181.99
2023-08-07	178.85	182.13	183.4	178.0	178.85
2023-08-08	179.80	179.69	181.5	178.8	179.80

DataFrame sorted by 'Open' values in descending order:

	Open	High	Low	Close
2023-08-01	196.24	198.0	195.0	195.61
2023-08-02	195.04	197.5	193.0	192.58
2023-08-03	191.57	192.5	190.0	191.17

```
DataFrame sorted by Index in ascending order:
              Open    High    Low    Close
2023-08-01   196.24   198.0   195.0   195.61
2023-08-02   195.04   197.5   193.0   192.58
2023-08-03   191.57   192.5   190.0   191.17
```

These code examples show basic techniques for manipulating various pandas objects and changing table structures, namely:

- `.reset_index()` resets the index of a DataFrame, providing an incremental default integer index. The previous index becomes a new column, offering a new structured sequence.
- `.set_index()` allows users to designate a column as the index, enhancing data accessibility and visibility.
- `.rename()` employs dictionary mapping to rename columns effectively, maintaining data consistency and clarifying data semantics.
- `.join()` merges DataFrames horizontally, using the index. The choice of left or right join affects which DataFrame's rows are retained. Suffixes distinguish between identically named columns in the joined DataFrames.

NOTE *The .join() method in pandas facilitates merging DataFrames based on their argument conditions.*

- *how='left': Keeps all rows from the left frame, adding matched ones from the right*
- *how='right': Retains all rows from the right frame, adding matched ones from the left*
- *how='inner': Includes only rows with matching indexes in both frames*
- *how='outer': Combines all rows from both, filling missing matches with NaN.*

New column names get suffixes, which are defined by the lsuffix and rsuffix arguments.

The `.sort_values()` and `.sort_index()` methods arrange the data based on either the values of a specific column or the index, allowing for expedited data retrieval and enhanced data comprehension. They offer flexibility with the ascending parameter to determine the sort order.

We have now reviewed the basic operations for creating and manipulating table data. Let us move on to a review of the most straightforward calculations.

Calculated Values and Creating New Features

In the previous examples, we employed the RoR and the logarithmic RoR to demonstrate essential calculation ability in Python. pandas offers similar, yet more streamlined, calculation tools akin to what can be accomplished in Excel and other spreadsheet software. In the subsequent examples, we will utilize the previously sorted dataset—the df_sorted DataFrame. Execute the following code:

```
1. df_sorted['Price_Diff'] = df_sorted['High']
   - df_sorted['Low']

2. df_sorted['Log_Close'] =
   np.log(df_sorted['Close'])

3. df_sorted['RoR'] = df_sorted['Close'].pct_
   change() * 100

4. df_sorted['Log_RoR'] = np.log(df_sorted['Close'] /
                           df_sorted['Close'].
   shift(1))

5. df_sorted['RoR_Status'] = df_sorted['RoR'].
   apply(is_positive)

6. df_sorted['Cum_Prod_RoR'] = ((1 + df_
   sorted['RoR'] / 100).cumprod() - 1)*100

7. df_sorted['Cum_Prod_Log_RoR'] = (1 + df_
   sorted['Log_RoR']).cumprod() - 1

8. print("\nDataFrame after calculating the
   Cumulative Product for RoR and Log_RoR:\n",

9.     df_sorted)
```

The results of the code are:

```
DataFrame after calculating the Cumulative Product for RoR
and Log_RoR:
                  Open   High    Low   Close   Price_Diff
Log_Close         RoR  \
2023-08-01  196.24  198.0  195.0  195.61       3.0
5.276123    NaN
2023-08-02  195.04  197.5  193.0  192.58       4.5
5.260512 -1.549001
2023-08-03  191.57  192.5  190.0  191.17       2.5
5.253163 -0.732163
2023-08-04  185.52  188.0  184.5  181.99       3.5
5.203952 -4.802009
2023-08-07  182.13  183.4  178.0  178.85       5.4
5.186547 -1.725370
2023-08-08  179.69  181.5  178.8  179.80       2.7
5.191845  0.531171
2023-08-09  180.87  182.0  178.5  178.19       3.5
5.182850 -0.895439
2023-08-10  179.48  181.0  177.0  177.97       4.0
5.181615 -0.123464
```

	Log_RoR	RoR_Status	Cum_Prod_RoR	Cum_Prod_Log_RoR
2023-08-01	NaN	False	NaN	NaN
2023-08-02	-0.015611	False	-1.549001	-0.015611
2023-08-03	-0.007349	False	-2.269823	-0.022845
2023-08-04	-0.049211	False	-6.962834	-0.070932
2023-08-07	-0.017404	False	-8.568069	-0.087102
2023-08-08	0.005298	True	-8.082409	-0.082266
2023-08-09	-0.008995	False	-8.905475	-0.090520
2023-08-10	-0.001235	False	-9.017944	-0.091644

By executing several lines of code (seven lines, to be precise), pandas enabled the calculation of numerous metrics that are vital for analyzing the price dynamics of Apple shares. These metrics include the market's maximum price fluctuations, the closing price logarithm, the RoR and its logarithmic form, a flag indicating positive RoR, and the accumulated RoR over the entire observation period. Let us detail these methods and calculations:

- *Calculation of new value (feature)*: The difference between high and low prices is `Price_Diff`. It is computed for each row and stored in a new column, called `Price_Diff`. This helps in analyzing the price volatility on a given day.

- *Array-based function application*: The natural logarithm of close prices is calculated and stored in the `Log_Close` column. This transformation can often help in normalizing the data distribution.

- *Application of a custom function*: The `is_positive()` function categorizes RoR values, and the categorized values are stored in a new column, called `RoR_Status`. It provides a quick overview of positive or negative returns.

- *RoR calculation*: The RoR column represents the daily RoR, calculated as the percentage change in close prices. It is essential for assessing the investment's profitability.

- *Logarithmic RoR calculation*: Using the `.shift()` method, the `Log_RoR` column is computed as the natural logarithm of the ratio of consecutive close prices, providing an alternative perspective on returns.

- *Cumulative values calculation*: The cumulative product `.cumprod()` and cumulative sum `.cumsum()` functions are the essential pandas methods for computing the ongoing product and sum of a sequence of numbers, respectively. It may help to understand the compounded or aggregated effects of the price or asset value changes over time. It is crucial in domains such as finance to evaluate accumulated profits, losses, or other measurable quantities.

We have explored examples of executing basic operations with pandas data structures. As we progress through this book, we will delve deeper into the details of using each tool. To fully understand the extensive functionality of pandas, however, continual practice and tackling non-standard problems are crucial.

CONCLUSION

Utilizing Python's built-in data structures, such as *list*, *tuple*, *set*, and *dictionary*, empowers users to undertake various simple analytical tasks. Combinations of these structures are used for storing parameters for other data structures and offering a complex understanding of Python's syntaxis principles and analytical functionality. Furthermore, custom Python functions are usually created to apply specific financial and statistical metrics and indicators that are not standard but are crucial for analyzing specific financial market instruments. These fundamental concepts of the Python language are vital to understand for the application of further data analysis tools.

The NumPy library was introduced, and you saw how it goes beyond mere analysis and touches on vectorized mathematical operations and manipulations, which are pivotal for handling matrices and multi-dimensional arrays. Such capabilities facilitate fast and comprehensive financial data analysis, allowing the application of computation operations on data arrays with just one statement. The array manipulations, efficient sorting algorithms, and other functionalities within NumPy are often applied in financial analytics.

pandas is a core package for managing and optimizing structured data analysis, analogous to spreadsheet software such as Excel. This library is indispensable for handling structured data efficiently through *Series* and *DataFrames*, allowing users to operate on tabular data easily and with various functionality. pandas tools serve numerous advanced manipulations, from nuanced data insertion and deletion to intricate calculations of new values and features, creating vast opportunities in the financial data analysis realm.

This chapter took us on a journey that included exploring theoretical concepts and running through a practical demonstration of the implementation and utility of Python data structures, NumPy, and pandas tools in the financial context. For a deeper study of manipulation and computation tools, however, it is necessary to refer to additional examples, many of which will be discussed in subsequent chapters.

QUESTIONS

1. How can Python's built-in structures facilitate fundamental financial calculations?

2. How can creating custom functions simplify user-specific financial analyses?

3. Why is NumPy crucial for performing numerical and statistical tasks in financial analysis?

4. How does NumPy manage multi-dimensional arrays for comprehensive financial analysis?

5. What are pandas' functionalities for managing and optimizing structured data analytics?

6. How does pandas compare to Excel in structured data analysis?

7. How are Python's data structures and libraries applied to explore various financial indices?

8. How can Python data structures be used to sort parameters and perform basic computations in finance?

9. How does integrating Python data structures, NumPy, and pandas apply theoretical financial knowledge to practical solutions?

KEY TERMS

- *Rate of return (RoR)* is a financial metric measuring the investment's returns (profits and losses) or performance changes over a certain period. It is calculated by subtracting the asset's previous price from its current price, then dividing the result by the previous price and multiplying this by 100. The result, usually expressed as a percentage, illustrates the overall gain or loss experienced by the investor. Mathematically, these are the percentage changes in the price of an asset.

- *Logarithmic rate of return (logarithmic RoR)* is a method to assess investment performance, emphasizing the continuous effect. It is derived by finding the natural logarithm of the price growth rate—divisions of the asset's current price by its previous price. The logarithmic RoR is approximately equal to the RoR and is used alongside the RoR calculation.

▦ *NumPy* is a Python library for numerical computations and advanced mathematical operations. It allows the operation of large, multi-dimensional arrays and matrices and a collection of mathematical functions.

▦ *Pandas* is a Python library for data manipulation and analysis. It offers data structures such as DataFrames and Series for tabular data (as in Excel data sheets), time-series analysis functions, and other tools for data manipulation, such as merging, reshaping, sorting, filtering, selecting, and data cleaning.

▦ *Series* are one-dimensional arrays with flexible indices in the pandas package (a Python library). They represent a single column of tabular data in a DataFrame.

▦ *DataFrames* are two-dimensional, size-mutable, potentially heterogeneous tabular data structures with labeled axes (rows and columns). In Python, they are supported by the pandas library.

REFERENCES

▦ *pandas data analysis library: https://pandas.pydata.org*

▦ *NumPy documentation: https://numpy.org/doc/stable/*

▦ *Dixit, R. (2022). Data Analysis with Python. [Paperback]. BPB Publications.*

▦ *Guleria, P. (2020). Basics of Python Programming. [Paperback]. BPB Publications.*

3

FINANCIAL DATA MANIPULATION WITH PYTHON

INTRODUCTION

This chapter highlights the principles of financial data, providing an overview of the primary financial data sources and metrics, as well as the data structure, in the global financial world. The chapter explores how information plays into financial decision-making today. The process of automatically obtaining Yahoo Finance open data using the yfinance library is detailed. Universal Python tools for manipulating data files in traditional structured formats, such as *comma-separated values (CSV)* and Excel, as well as *application programming interface (API)* concepts, will also be described. We will explore the most popular open data sources for financial analysis and describe the main Python libraries that allow automatic data collection. Examples of applying the tools from the Quandl and pandas_datareader libraries will be provided. In addition, we will explore API sourcing and transforming financial data from low-level APIs and Web-page-scraping Python tools. By the end of the chapter, you will have created the initial datasets needed to complete the main financial tasks and make an investment decision in this and future chapters. You will also easily be able to apply basic and advanced Python tools to collect data from various sources and transform it into valuable financial information.

STRUCTURE

This chapter covers the following topics:

- Financial data world: Sources and valuation aspects
- Yahoo Finance to access financial market data
- Working with diverse files and formats in financial data analysis
- Open data sources and Python library for getting data
- Low-level APIs and Web scraping

OBJECTIVES

By the end of this chapter, you will have understood the foundational concepts of financial data, as well as explored various open data sources and investigated their role in finance. Your practical skills with Python will be expanded through the use of real-world financial datasets to import and structure information. You will have learned about the benefits of *yfinance, pandas_datareader, Quandl,* and other Python libraries; CSV and Excel data files; APIs; and Web-scraping tools. Therefore, you will be ready to analyze financial data and make informed decisions using Python, setting a solid foundation for later chapters.

FINANCIAL DATA WORLD: SOURCES AND VALUATION ASPECTS

As we know from *Chapter 1, Getting Started with Python for Finance,* data volumes continually increase alongside experience. Financial data, and subsequently managerial information, is essential for the success of investment operations. This is precisely why we will attempt to understand this issue more. Refer to the diagram in *Figure 3.1:*

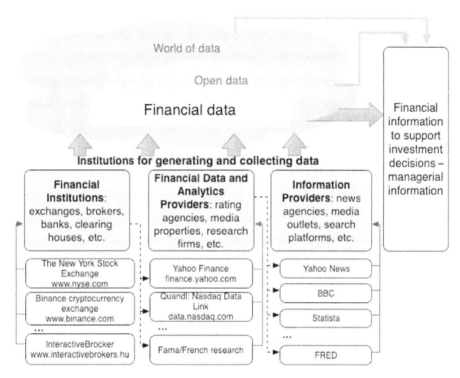

FIGURE 3.1 The sources and types of financial data for supporting investment decisions

While many financial operations extend beyond financial markets, we will focus primarily on the exchange markets. As depicted in *Figure 3.1*, the data required for making investment decisions in the financial market can be categorized into quantitative information from financial institutions directly related to trading outcomes; both quantitative and qualitative information associated with financial markets; and fundamental financial indicators from analytical results, news, etc.

From an institutional perspective, all sources of financial data are associated with the organizations that generate this data—exchanges, brokers, and the like, as well as analytical aggregators and news providers such as Yahoo, Google, BBC, and *Federal Reserve Economic Data* (*FRED*). Suppose our investment operations are tied to activities on unique trading platforms or broker services (such as the forex market or cryptocurrencies). In that case, it is more appropriate to source data directly from the primary source. Financial information from aggregator companies, however, also has its advantages: the data is pre-processed, grouped, and statistically harmonized, and it allows for quick access through Python extension libraries. This aggregated data is, however, less worthwhile for a short-term trading strategy (which will be discussed in *Chapter 5, Investment and Trading Strategies*).

Since most financial transactions occur in financial markets and related institutions, our primary focus will be this area. As illustrated in *Figure 3.1*, when investing in well-known companies' stocks (*blue chips*) listed on exchanges such as the New York Stock Exchange and possibly other famous trading platforms, we can confidently use data from aggregators such as Yahoo Finance. For active trading on lesser-known or specialized exchanges, however, especially cryptocurrency exchanges or forex market brokers, it is essential to monitor data directly from these institutions. Furthermore, for specific operations, such as arbitrage, it is crucial to continuously compare prices across different exchanges simultaneously. Theoretically, there exists a single global financial market (stock, currency, cryptocurrency, etc.), but an individual investor interacts with a specific broker or trading platform (paying bills, placing orders, etc.). Therefore, a comprehensive raw dataset is required to form a complete picture for investment decisions.

YAHOO FINANCE TO ACCESS FINANCIAL MARKET DATA

Yahoo Finance, a comprehensive financial news and data platform, has long been a trusted source for investors, analysts, and researchers seeking market insights, real-time stock quotes, and historical data for middle- and long-term trading strategies. Yahoo Finance is a media property with a vast financial data repository spanning various asset classes, including stocks, bonds, commodities, currencies, and cryptocurrencies. Go to the Yahoo Finance Web site, *https://finance.yahoo.com*, and search for a stock ticker. A stock exchange ticker is a short abbreviation that connects specific securities on a particular market. For example, the ticker TSLA is used for the stock of Tesla on the New York Stock Exchange (well-known securities have the same tickers on different exchange platforms). The result of the TSLA ticker search is presented in *Figure 3.2*. This figure depicts the following groups of data: summary information (the active view in *Figure 3.2*), chart, conversations, statistics, historical data (prices and volumes of security market), profile, financials, analysis, options, holders, and sustainability. Scrolling through the data on the Web page will show information regarding the TSLA security. Let us look at the data in the following figure more closely:

FIGURE 3.2 Common search results for a security with the ticker TSLA on Yahoo Finance

Yahoo Finance offers APIs and allows users to fetch financial data. An API is a set of rules and protocols that allows different software applications to communicate with each other. In Yahoo Finance, the API provides a gateway for users to retrieve financial data directly into their applications, scripts, or analytical tools without manual data entry, a copy-paste operation, or Web scraping. The Python library yfinance has been developed, which is based on Yahoo Finance.

Let us explore how to retrieve stock data for Tesla, Inc. (TSLA) using the yfinance library in Python and investigate its basic functionality.

```
1. import yfinance as yf
2. # Download TSLA stock data from Yahoo Finance
3. # for the specified date range and include
   corporate actions
4. df = yf.download('TSLA',
5.                  start='2022-08-22',
6.                  end='2023-09-01',
7.                  actions=True)
```

```
8.  # Display the info and 5 top rows of the
    DataFrame
9.  print(df.info(),'\n')
10. print(df.head(),'\n')
11. # Display the 'Close' column of the DataFrame
12. print(df['Close'],'\n')
13. # Display the 'Open' and 'Close' columns for the
    specified date range
14. print(df.loc['2023-08-25':'2023-09-05', ['Open',
    'Close']],'\n')
15. # Display rows where the 'Stock Splits' is
    carried out
16. print(df[(df['Stock Splits'] > 0)],'\n')
```

The results of the code are:

```
[**********************100%%*********************]  1 of 1
completed
<class 'pandas.core.frame.DataFrame'>
DatetimeIndex: 259 entries, 2022-08-22 to 2023-08-31
Data columns (total 8 columns):
 #   Column        Non-Null Count  Dtype
---  ------        --------------  -----
 0   Open          259 non-null    float64
 1   High          259 non-null    float64
 2   Low           259 non-null    float64
 3   Close         259 non-null    float64
 4   Adj Close     259 non-null    float64
 5   Volume        259 non-null    int64
 6   Dividends     259 non-null    float64
 7   Stock Splits  259 non-null    float64
```

```
dtypes: float64(7), int64(1)

memory usage: 18.2 KB

None
```

	Open	High	Low	Close	Adj Close \
Date					
2022-08-22	291.913330	292.399994	286.296661	289.913330	289.913330
2022-08-23	291.453339	298.826660	287.923340	296.453339	296.453339
2022-08-24	297.563324	303.646667	296.500000	297.096680	297.096680
2022-08-25	302.359985	302.959991	291.600006	296.070007	296.070007
2022-08-26	297.429993	302.000000	287.470001	288.089996	288.089996

	Volume	Dividends	Stock Splits
Date			
2022-08-22	55843200	0.0	0.0
2022-08-23	63984900	0.0	0.0
2022-08-24	57259800	0.0	0.0
2022-08-25	53230000	0.0	3.0
2022-08-26	57163900	0.0	0.0

```
Date
2022-08-22     289.913330
2022-08-23     296.453339
2022-08-24     297.096680
2022-08-25     296.070007
2022-08-26     288.089996
Name: Close, dtype: float64
```

```
                Open        Close

Date

2023-08-25   231.309998   238.589996

2023-08-28   242.580002   238.820007

2023-08-29   238.580002   257.179993

2023-08-30   254.199997   256.899994

2023-08-31   255.979996   258.079987



                Open         High         Low        Close     Adj Close \

Date

2022-08-25   302.359985   302.959991   291.600006   296.070007   296.070007



                Volume   Dividends   Stock Splits

Date

2022-08-25   53230000        0.0           3.0
```

As we can see from the results of running the analytical code, the df DataFrame has been generated with Tesla stock market data. The basic operations can be described as follows:

▪ The yf.download() function is used to get the stock data from Yahoo Finance. We specify the date range using the start and end parameters. The actions=True argument ensures that corporate actions such as dividends and stock splits are included in the data.

▪ df.info() and df.head() are data-inspecting and overview functions. They are applied to check the structure of the DataFrame and that the data was imported correctly. For example, all data is imported in numeric format, there is no missing data, and the table header has a one-line structure and an index column named Date.

▪ As was shown in *Chapter 2, Python Tools for Data Analysis: Primer to pandas and NumPy,* the .loc[] and .iloc[] methods and syntaxis structures for slicing operations with pandas by column name and data index value or range can be used.

NOTE *Dividends are payments a corporation makes to its shareholders, usually in cash or additional shares. The Yahoo Finance data shows dividends in the Dividends column. Stock splits are adjustments to the total number of available shares of a publicly traded company. Stock splits are captured in the Stock Splits column in the data. For example, in a 3-for-1 stock split (for TSLA on Aug 25, 2022), 2 additional shares are granted for each share held by a shareholder. Therefore, TSLA's close price should be 891.29004 (297.096680*3), but Yahoo's service adjusts all previous prices before being split to scale the dataset.*

Therefore, using the yfinance library function, investors and analysts can easily access and analyze financial data for middle- and long-term strategies. Furthermore, the New York Stock Exchange data and other Exchange platforms are updated almost on time.

The following analytical code works with financial data for three securities: Apple (AAPL), Microsoft (MSFT), and Tesla (TSLA). Please run it and investigate the results:

```
1.  # Download stock data for AAPL, MSFT, and TSLA
2.  # for the past 2 years with a monthly interval
3.  df = yf.download(tickers=['AAPL', 'MSFT',
    'TSLA'],
4.                        period='2y', interval='1mo',
5.                        actions=False)
6.  # Calculate and display the percentage change for
7.  # the stock data and display the first 5 rows
8.  print(df.sort_index().pct_change().head())
9.  # Display the 'Close' and 'Open' columns for the
    year 2022 for all securities
10. print(df.loc['2022', ['Close', 'Open']])
11. # Extract and display data specific to TSLA only
    across all columns
```

```
12. print(df.xs(key='TSLA', axis=1, level=1))
13. # Plot the percentage change of the 'Adj Close'
    column for all stocks
14. df['Adj Close'].pct_change().plot(figsize=(10,5))
```

The results (truncated) of the code are:

```
[**********************100%%*******************]  3 of 3 completed
         Adj Close                          Close
\
                AAPL       MSFT       TSLA      AAPL       MSFT       TSLA
Date
2021-11-01       NaN        NaN        NaN       NaN        NaN        NaN
2021-12-01  0.075796   0.019194  -0.076855  0.074229   0.017333  -0.076855
2022-01-01 -0.015712  -0.075345  -0.113609 -0.015712  -0.075345  -0.113609
2022-02-01 -0.055269  -0.039199  -0.070768 -0.055270  -0.039199  -0.070768
2022-03-01  0.058821   0.033995   0.238009  0.057473   0.031862   0.238009


              High                             Low                      \
                AAPL       MSFT       TSLA      AAPL       MSFT       TSLA
Date
2021-11-01       NaN        NaN        NaN       NaN        NaN        NaN
2021-12-01  0.099155  -0.015357  -0.056816  0.069976  -0.027944  -0.094502
2022-01-01  0.004447  -0.018298   0.029979 -0.019645  -0.129866  -0.106205
2022-02-01 -0.034383  -0.067692  -0.215422 -0.017453  -0.016410  -0.116173
2022-03-01  0.016756   0.002634   0.176203 -0.012500  -0.005598   0.080057
(...)
```

There are some things to note about the last code. As we can see, the DataFrame has a two-line header structure for three securities. Therefore, we use the .xs() method to extract data specific to TSLA. The key='TSLA' argument specifies the value for `axis=1` (applied to the header; if `axis=0`, to the row index) and `level=1` (apply the key argument value for the second row of the header), which contains the stock tickers. The results of the `Adj Close` column `pct_change()`, visualized by the `.plot()` method with the size adjusted with the `figsize=(10,5)` argument (more options for data visualization will be presented in *Chapter 4, Exploratory Data Analysis for Finance*), are shown in *Figure 3.3*:

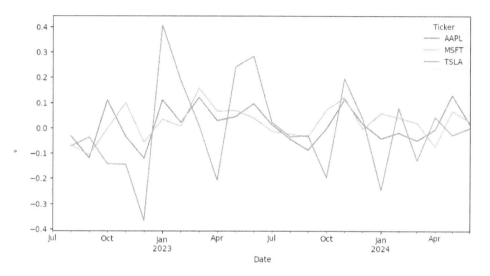

FIGURE 3.3 Percentage change in monthly Adj Close prices for three securities

Figure 3.3 depicts a line chart showing each security's price percentage change over time. Therefore, applying the benefits of the yfinance and pandas libraries can help with effortlessly analyzing and visualizing critical financial metrics with just a few lines of code.

When analyzing securities, looking beyond the historical price data is often beneficial. There are a lot of fundamental factors that contribute to understanding market trends. Yahoo Finance provides other historical data about a company. This includes general legislative information, news articles, and financial statements (see the tabs in *Figure 3.2*). Using the yfinance library in Python, we can easily access and analyze this data as follows:

```
1. # Initialize the Ticker object for TSLA
2. df_tsla = yf.Ticker("TSLA")
3. # Print general information about TSLA
4. print(df_tsla.info)
5. # Retrieve and display recent news articles related
       to TSLA
6. print(pd.DataFrame(df_tsla.news))
7. # Fetch and display the balance sheet of TSLA
8. print(pd.DataFrame(df_tsla.balance_sheet))
```

The results (truncated) of the code are:

```
{'address1': '1 Tesla Road', 'city': 'Austin', 'state':
'TX', 'zip': '78725', 'country': 'United States',
'phone': '512 516 8177', 'website': 'https://www.
tesla.com', 'industry': 'Auto Manufacturers', 'indus-
tryKey': 'auto-manufacturers', 'industryDisp': 'Auto
Manufacturers', 'sector': 'Consumer Cyclical', 'sec-
torKey': 'consumer-cyclical', 'sectorDisp': 'Consumer
Cyclical',
```

(...)

```
title  \

0  Elon Musk Wasn't A Superstar Genius Student As...

1  May Mobility is trying to solve self-driving —...

2  Tesla signs lease to open vast sales and servi...

3  Tesla Vs. BYD 2023: Tesla Rallies Despite Bad ...
```

(...)

```
                                    2022-12-31  \

Ordinary Shares Number              3164000000.0

Share Issued                        3164000000.0
```

(...)

```
Other Short Term Investments                          5932000000.0

Cash And Cash Equivalents                            22185000000.0


                                                    2021-12-31  \

Ordinary Shares Number                                3099000000.0

Share Issued                                          3099000000.0

(...)

Other Short Term Investments                           131000000.0

Cash And Cash Equivalents                            17576000000.0

(...)

[78 rows x 4 columns]
```

In the preceding code, we initialize a `Ticker` object for Tesla (TSLA) using `yf.Ticker()`. Then, we get information with the following attributes:

▪ The `.info` attribute provides a dictionary of various details about the company, such as its market cap, volume, and 52-week high/low.

▪ The `.news` attribute fetches recent news articles related to TSLA, which can be crucial for fundamental analysis.

▪ The `.balance_sheet` attribute gives us the company's balance sheet, offering insights into its financial health by showing assets, liabilities, and shareholder equity.

In addition to the indicators and variables in the example, the `yf.Ticker()` object allows us to obtain data on the following main attributes (the availability of these attributes must be checked individually since they may not be available for certain types of assets):

▪ `financials`: Provides an overview of the company's financial statements

▪ `sustainability`: Provides sustainability values

▪ `options`: Retrieves option expiry dates

▪ The `option_chain()` method: Provides option chain data for the specified expiry date

▨ `cashflow`: Provides the cash flow statement

▨ `earnings`: Retrieves earnings data

▨ `quarterly_balance_sheet`: Fetches the quarterly balance sheet

▨ `quarterly_cashflow`: Provides the quarterly cash flow statement

▨ `quarterly_earnings`: Retrieves quarterly earnings data

▨ `major_holders`: Gives information about major stakeholders

▨ `institutional_holders`: Provides details about institutional holders

▨ `mutualfund_holders`: Retrieves mutual fund holders' data

This is not a complete list of attributes and methods. Some of these attributes may have already been changed or updated in the development process of the yfinance module. The actual attributes can be found with the Python function `help(df_tsla)`. Using these attributes, however, investors can understand a company comprehensively, aiding in more informed decision-making.

WORKING WITH DIVERSE FILE FORMATS

Individual investors and other professionals frequently use plenty of data files in diverse formats. These files come from various sources. The pandas library provides functions tailored for working with different file formats commonly used in data analysis. Some of these functions for reading datasets include[1]:

▨ Microsoft Excel files (`.xlsx` or `.xls`): `pd.read_excel()`

▨ CSV files (`.csv`): `pd.read_csv()`

▨ *JavaScript Object Notation* (*JSON*) files (`.json`): `pd.read_json()`

▨ Tables from HTML files (`.html`): `pd.read_html()`

▨ Data from SQL databases: `pd.read_sql()`

▨ Stata files (`.dta`): `pd.read_stata()`

▨ SAS files: `pd.read_sas()`

▨ Data from the clipboard, which is useful for quickly importing tables from Web pages: `pd.read_clipboard()`

With these essential pandas functions, gathering and analyzing financial data becomes a relatively easy process, as previously. We will go deeper with some examples, focusing on the Microsoft Excel and CSV formats.

---

[1]*For more information, see the official documentation: IO tools (text, CSV, HDF5, …): https://pandas.pydata.org/docs/user_guide/io.html*

Excel Data File Format with pandas

Microsoft Excel is one of the most widely used tools in the financial world, offering many instruments for analyzing and visualizing data. Its native file formats, `.xls` and `.xlsx`, are widely used for investment decisions and data management. The pandas library provides a seamless way to interact with Excel files, making integrating and collecting Excel data into more advanced analytical workflows easier.

Let us explore how to read and write Excel files using Python:

```python
1.  # Download stock data
2.  df = yf.download(tickers=['AAPL', 'msft',
    'TSLA'],
3.                  period = '2y', interval = '1mo')
4.  # Save to Excel
5.  df.to_excel('stocks.xlsx',
6.              sheet_name = 'Stocks2y1mo')
7.  # Read from Excel with 'Date' as index and skip
    the 3th row
8.  df_xlsx = pd.read_excel('stocks.xlsx',
9.                  index_col=0, header=[0,
    1], skiprows=[2])
10. # Rename the index column to 'Date'
11. df_xlsx.index.name = 'Date'
12. # Convert the 'Close' column to float32 data type
13. df_TSLA_xlsx['Close'] = df_TSLA_xlsx['Close'].
    astype('float32')
14. # Display info and table head
15. print(df_xlsx.info())
16. print(df_xlsx.head())
```

The results (truncated) of the code are:

```
[*********************100%%**********************]  3 of 3 completed
<class 'pandas.core.frame.DataFrame'>
DatetimeIndex: 24 entries, 2021-11-01 to 2023-10-01
Data columns (total 18 columns):
 #   Column            Non-Null Count  Dtype
---  ------            --------------  -----
 0   (Adj Close, AAPL)  24 non-null     float64
 1   (Adj Close, MSFT)  24 non-null     float64
(...)
 16  (Volume, MSFT)     24 non-null     int64
 17  (Volume, TSLA)     24 non-null     int64
dtypes: float64(15), int64(3)
memory usage: 3.6 KB
None
              Adj Close                              Close
\
                    AAPL        MSFT        TSLA        AAPL        MSFT
Date
2021-11-01  163.409485  324.707336  381.586670  165.300003  330.589996
2021-12-01  175.795364  330.939758  352.260010  177.570007  336.320007
2022-01-01  173.033218  306.005127  312.239990  174.779999  310.980011
2022-02-01  163.469772  294.010162  290.143341  165.119995  298.790009
2022-03-01  173.085175  304.005157  359.200012  174.610001  308.309998
(...)
```

Please review this code and the resulting files carefully. Note that the column data has mostly been imported from Excel correctly. There may, however, be some missing data (this problem will be discussed in *Chapter 4, Exploratory Data Analysis for Finance*). Problems may also arise with data with a header extending beyond a one-line cell or merged cells. Also, for this example, the names of row indexes (date) are not restored correctly by default. Let us look at the code in more detail:

- *Saving data to Excel*: Once the data is fetched, it can be saved to an Excel file using the `to_excel()` method of the DataFrame. The `sheet_name` parameter allows us to specify the sheet's name where the data will be stored. In our case, the data is saved to the sheet named 'Stocks2y1mo'.
- *Reading data from Excel*: To read the data back into Python, we use `pd.read_excel()`. The `index_col` parameter is set to 0, indicating that the first column in the Excel file should be treated as the index of the DataFrame. The `header` parameter is set to [0, 1], meaning the first two Excel file rows are treated as multi-level column headers. The `skiprows` parameter is also set to [2] to skip the third row when reading the data.
- *Renaming the index column*: For clarity and ease of reference, the index column is renamed to `Date` using the `index.name` attribute.
- *Data type conversion*: Although the results are good, we are converting certain columns into a different data type to optimize memory usage. This is usually important to ensure the precision of the financial data. The `Close` column for TSLA is converted into the `float32` data type using the `astype()` method in the code (there is no need for this operation, but has been done to show this functionality).

Python can easily save data from a DataFrame to an Excel file type. The reverse process requires attention, especially with a complicated (multi-level) DataFrame header. While Python provides efficient data in Excel format, *remember to inspect data after each reading operation* by applying the `.info()` and `.head()` methods, at a minimum.

CSV Data File Format with pandas

The CSV format is one of the most common and versatile data storage formats. It is a simple text file. Each row is one observation, and data for the columns is often separated by dots (.). This format is widely used for transferring large amounts of structured data and is supported across leading platforms and programming languages. In the financial world, CSV files are often used to store and share large datasets, such as stock prices and trading volumes.

Let us describe how we can work with CSV files using pandas with the following examples:

```
1.  # Download stock data
2.  df = yf.download(tickers=['AAPL', 'MSFT', 'TSLA'],
3.                  period = '2y', interval = '1mo')
4.  # Create 1-row header
5.  # Join the multi-level columns and rename the
    columns
6.  df.columns = ['_'.join(col).strip() for col in
    df.columns.values]
7.  print(df.head())
8.  # Save the data to a CSV file
9.  df.to_csv(path_or_buf = 'stocks.csv',
10.             decimal = '.', sep=',', header=True)
11. # Save the data to a TSV file
12. df.to_csv(path_or_buf = 'stocks.tsv',
13.             decimal = '.', sep='\t', header=True)
14. # Read stock data from a CSV file with specified
    parameters
15. df_csv = pd.read_csv(filepath_or_buffer =
    'stocks.csv',
16.                     index_col = ['Date'],
17.                     parse_dates = True,
18.                     decimal = '.', sep = ',' )
19. # Display the info and first 5 rows of the
    dataframe
20. print(df_csv.info())
21. print(df_csv.head())
```

The results (truncated) of the code are:

```
[*********************100%%**********************]  3 of 3 completed
          Adj Close_AAPL  Adj Close_MSFT  Adj Close_TSLA  Close_AAPL  \
Date
2021-11-01      163.409500      324.707336      381.586670  165.300003
2021-12-01      175.795364      330.939758      352.260010  177.570007
2022-01-01      173.033234      306.005157      312.239990  174.779999
2022-02-01      163.469772      294.010162      290.143341  165.119995
2022-03-01      173.085159      304.005157      359.200012  174.610001
(...)


<class 'pandas.core.frame.DataFrame'>
DatetimeIndex: 24 entries, 2021-11-01 to 2023-10-01
Data columns (total 18 columns):
 #   Column          Non-Null Count  Dtype
---  ------          --------------  -----
 0   Adj Close_AAPL  24 non-null     float64
 1   Adj Close_MSFT  24 non-null     float64
(...)
 16  Volume_MSFT     24 non-null     int64
 17  Volume_TSLA     24 non-null     int64
dtypes: float64(15), int64(3)
memory usage: 3.6 KB
None


          Adj Close_AAPL  Adj Close_MSFT  Adj Close_TSLA  Close_AAPL  \
Date
2021-11-01      163.409500      324.707336      381.586670  165.300003
2021-12-01      175.795364      330.939758      352.260010  177.570007
```

2022-01-01	173.033234	306.005157	312.239990	174.779999
2022-02-01	163.469772	294.010162	290.143341	165.119995
2022-03-01	173.085159	304.005157	359.200012	174.610001

(...)

Usually, importing data from the CSV format is relatively easy. The main requirement of this format is that the table header should be represented by one row of data. As our last example shows, however, complex headings and indexes are common in financial data contexts.

Let us look at some basic notes on using the CSV format with pandas:

- *Reorganizing columns before exporting to CSV*: Multi-level columns should be joined and renamed to make the column names compatible with the CSV format. This step ensures the data has a single-level header, but some data manipulation must be applied (see *Chapter 2, Python Tools for Data Analysis: Primer to Pandas and NumPy*).

NOTE *If we want to leave the original two-row header, we can utilize the header=[] parameter with the pd.read_csv() and df.to_csv() functions. For instance, pd.read_csv('stocks.csv', index_col=0, parse_dates=[0], header=[0, 1]) reads the stocks.csv file, where the first column is designated as the index column for row data with dates formatted accordingly. Additionally, the table header comprises two rows: the first row for asset names and the second row for open, high, low, close, and volume data.*

- *Saving data with the pd.to_csv() function*: The DataFrame may be saved as different variants of the CSV format depending on the `decimal` and `sep` parameters defined. For TSV format, the separator is the tab symbol. For CSV2 format, the separator is ; and the decimal part is separated by , . In the example, two different files are generated: a CSV file (`stocks.csv`) and a *tab-separated values (TSV)* file (`stocks.tsv`).
- *Reading data from CSV to a DataFrame*: The data is read into a DataFrame using `pd.read_csv()`. The `index_col` parameter specifies that the `Date` column should be treated as the index. The `parse_dates` parameter ensures that the `Date` column is parsed as a date. As mentioned earlier, the `decimal` and `sep` parameters define the decimal point and separator, respectively, used in the various types of CSV files.

NOTE *Remember that all DataFrame methods for saving the data (such as df.to_ excel() and df.to_csv()) replace all existing files in the same location without additional confirmation. If we execute code with an export-to-file DataFrame method, the old version of the file with the same name is lost forever.*

The CSV format is limited in its requirements, which makes it more interoperable than, for example, the ever-changing and powerful Excel file data format. Therefore, many open data resources offer it for information exchange. If you have a choice of which format to store your row data for analysis, you should choose CSV.

In addition to obtaining data from a disk (local file system), pandas functions will allow you to fetch data within the framework of standard network protocols. We can specify the full path to the file name in the usual `pd.read_ csv()` function, and it will be possible to access network resources. Let us look at an example:

```python
1.  # Read TSLA stock data from Yahoo Finance URL
    into a DataFrame
2.  # The latest URL can be found on ynance.yahoo.com
    site (Historical data View)
3.  url = 'https://query1.finance.yahoo.com/v7/
    finance/download/TSLA?period1=1609459200&period2=
    1917216000&interval=1d&events=history&
    includeAdjustedClose=true'
4.  df_url = pd.read_csv(url, parse_dates = True,
    index_col=['Date'])
5.
6.  # Display the info of the DataFrame
7.  print(df_url.info())
8.
9.  # Display the first 5 rows of the DataFrame
10. print(df_url.head())
11.
12. # Save the DataFrame to a CSV file
13. df_url.to_csv('TSLA.csv')
```

The results (truncated) of the code are:

```
<class 'pandas.core.frame.DataFrame'>
DatetimeIndex: 695 entries, 2021-01-04 to 2023-10-06
Data columns (total 6 columns):
 #   Column        Non-Null Count   Dtype
---  ------        --------------   -----
 0   Open          695 non-null     float64
(...)
              Open        High         Low       Close    Adj Close   \
Date
2021-01-04  239.820007  248.163330  239.063339  243.256668  243.256668
2021-01-05  241.220001  246.946671  239.733337  245.036667  245.036667
2021-01-06  252.830002  258.000000  249.699997  251.993332  251.993332
2021-01-07  259.209991  272.329987  258.399994  272.013336  272.013336
2021-01-08  285.333344  294.829987  279.463318  293.339996  293.339996
(...)
```

Fetching data from the Internet can be done with `pd.read_csv()` by defining a URL as a file name parameter. The URL to the historical data of TSLA on Yahoo Finance can be found on the official Web site (refer to *Figure 3.2*). Right-click with the mouse on the Download button on the Historical Data tab and select the copy link. Other arguments have the same meanings as for local files.

NOTE *There are often Input/Output (I/O) errors when carrying out file operations. These errors can be attributed to invalid file paths or URLs, no permissions to read a file, network connectivity issues, file format discrepancies, corrupted files, etc. Handling these errors gracefully ensures smooth data processing, typically using try-except blocks.*

OPEN DATA SOURCES AND PYTHON LIBRARY FOR GETTING DATA

There are a lot of institutions and data resources (see *Figure 3.1*) for generating and delivering data to individual investors and financial professionals. As we noted earlier, an API is a set of protocols and tools that allows different software applications to communicate with each other. The best example of using the benefits of an API and Python is Yahoo Finance, but it is not the only one. A comparison of popular open-source libraries and APIs for finance data analysis is presented in *Table 3.1*:

TABLE 3.1 Top open-source APIs and Python libraries for fetching financial data

Name/site	Python library	Data types	Paid content
Yahoo Finance *finance.yahoo.com*	yfinance	Provides financial market data	Yes, for premium features
Quandl *data.nasdaq.com*	quandl, pandas_datareader	A platform for financial, economic, and alternative data	Yes, for premium datasets
FRED *fred.stlouisfed.org*	pandas_datareader	Federal Reserve Economic Data	No
Alpha Vantage *www.alphavantage.co*	alpha_vantage, pandas_datareader	Provides stocks, forex, and cryptocurrency data	Yes, for premium access
Fama/French *https://bit.ly/46xBts0*	famafrench, pandas_datareader	Data library maintained by Professors Fama and French	No
Tiingo *www.tiingo.com*	tiingo, pandas_datareader	Provides stock market data, news, and analysis	Yes, for premium access
IEX Cloud *www.iexcloud.io*	iexfinance, pandas_datareader	Provides real-time historical stock and market data	Yes, for premium access

Table 3.1 provides an overview of some data resources, but there are a lot more. As we can see, Yahoo Finance and Quandl are comprehensive platforms offering a wide range of financial market data. FRED and Fama/French are fully free resources. FRED focuses on official economic data, mainly for the USA but also globally. Fama/French, maintained by Professors Fama and French, provides academic-oriented financial data. Alpha Vantage, Tiingo, and IEX Cloud are versatile platforms offering various types of financial data, including stocks, forex, and cryptocurrency in the case of Alpha Vantage. These

platforms require an API ID for access and offer premium features for a fee (the API ID can usually be obtained after registering on the platform).

The Python community and the developers have created a lot of libraries for easy data access. Quandl, like Yahoo Finance, also uses its library for Python but can be used by the universal pandas_datareader. This universal module provides an interface for data access for various financial data resources (see *Table 3.1*). pandas_datareader is, however, a dynamic project and constantly changes. Thus, some functions may become deprecated or unsupported over time. Always check that your code is compatible with the latest version on the official site (*https://pandas-datareader.readthedocs.io/en/latest/*). Furthermore, the APIs update their endpoints or require specific authentication methods. Therefore, using the native library for each resource is often recommended for more stable and feature-rich data retrieval.

After installing all the required packages (see *Chapter 1, Getting Started with Python for Finance*), you can import them into your Python script or notebook and start fetching financial data.

```
1. # Importing libraries
2. import quandl
3. import pandas_datareader as pdr
4. # Set API Key
5. quandl.ApiConfig.api_key = 'Your API key'
```

This code example imports two Python libraries, Quandl and pandas_datareader, and defines an API key for further requests using `quandl.ApiConfig.api_key`. An API key is a unique identifier to authenticate a user, application, or service requesting an API. It is mainly used for paid content. Be careful, as the API key gives access to important resources on your profile and even the wallet. Take care of it as you would your credit card details. For the Quandl API, we can obtain the private key by registering on the Web site. Once you have the key, replace `Your API key` in the code with the key to authenticate the requests.

Let us look at a few examples:

NOTE   *It is better to use the official site on the Internet to obtain the feature or dataset names for the resources considered. For example, the Quandl official search site is https://data.nasdaq.com/search. Here, you can select the required data* *source. After selecting a dataset (feature, ticker, etc.), a hint is usually provided on how to use native libraries for data fetching with Python*

(https://data.nasdaq.com/data/HKEX-hong-kong exchange/usage/quickstart/python).

- Apply Quandl library functions to fetch data from the Hong Kong Stock Exchange:

```
1.  # Get Data from the Hong Kong Exchange
2.  # Lenovo Group (Ticker 00992)
3.  # Stock Prices for Lenovo Group from the Hong
    Kong Stock Exchange. Currency: HKD
4.  # https://data.nasdaq.com/data/
    HKEX/00992-lenovo-group-00992
5.  data = quandl.get('HKEX/00992',
    start_date='2022-08-01',
6.                      end_date='2023-10-10')
7.
8.  # Inspect and display Data
9.  print(data.info())
10. print(data.head())
```

The results (truncated) of the code are:

```
<class 'pandas.core.frame.DataFrame'>
DatetimeIndex: 292 entries, 2022-08-01 to 2023-10-06
Data columns (total 12 columns):
 #   Column          Non-Null Count   Dtype
---  ------          --------------   -----
 0   Nominal Price   292 non-null     float64
 1   Net Change      0 non-null       object
```

```
2    Change (%)           0 non-null      object
3    Bid                  292 non-null    float64
4    Ask                  292 non-null    float64
5    P/E(x)               0 non-null      object
6    High                 292 non-null    float64
7    Low                  292 non-null    float64
8    Previous Close       292 non-null    float64
9    Share Volume (000)   292 non-null    float64
10   Turnover (000)       292 non-null    float64
11   Lot Size             0 non-null      object
dtypes: float64(8), object(4)
memory usage: 29.7+ KB
None
```

```
            Nominal Price Net Change Change (%)   Bid   Ask P/E(x)  High \
Date
2022-08-01          7.15       None       None  7.14  7.15   None  7.39
2022-08-02          7.03       None       None  7.03  7.04   None  7.21
2022-08-03          6.90       None       None  6.89  6.90   None  7.14
2022-08-04          6.97       None       None  6.97  6.98   None  7.05
2022-08-05          7.15       None       None  7.15  7.16   None  7.19
```

```
            Low  Previous Close  Share Volume (000)  Turnover (000) Lot
Size
Date
2022-08-01 7.14            7.29             41330.0         297007.0
None
2022-08-02 7.00            7.15             31005.0         218483.0
None
2022-08-03 6.86            7.03             36637.0         255281.0
None
2022-08-04 6.91            6.90             29833.0         207655.0
None
2022-08-05 7.00            6.97             22385.0         159985.0
None
```

■ Apply Quandl library functions to fetch data from the Bombay Stock Exchange:

```
1.  # Get Data from the Bombay Stock Exchange
2.  # INFOSYS LTD. EOD Prices (Ticker BOM500209)
3.  # End of Day (EOD) prices and additional trading
    information for INFOSYS LTD.
4.  # https://data.nasdaq.com/data/BSE/BOM500209-
    infosys-ltd-eod-prices
5.  data = quandl.get('BSE/BOM500209',
    start_date='2022-08-01',
6.                       end_date='2023-10-10')
7.
8.  # Inspect and display Data
9.  print(data.info())
10. print(data.head())
```

The results (truncated) of the code are:

```
<class 'pandas.core.frame.DataFrame'>
DatetimeIndex: 270 entries, 2022-08-01 to 2023-09-01
Data columns (total 12 columns):
 #   Column          Non-Null Count   Dtype

---  ------          --------------   -----

 0   Open            270 non-null     float64
 1   High            270 non-null     float64
 2   Low             270 non-null     float64
 3   Close           270 non-null     float64
 4   WAP             270 non-null     float64
 5   No. of Shares   270 non-null     float64
```

```
6    No. of Trades                270 non-null     float64

7    Total Turnover               270 non-null     float64

8    Deliverable Quantity         269 non-null     float64

9    % Deli. Qty to Traded Qty    269 non-null     float64

10   Spread H-L                   270 non-null     float64

11   Spread C-O                   270 non-null     float64
dtypes: float64(12)
memory usage: 27.4 KB
None
```

	Open	High	Low	Close	WAP	No. of Shares \
Date						
2022-08-01	1570.0	1570.0	1537.70	1550.60	1549.71	4624163.0
2022-08-02	1549.0	1549.0	1528.65	1542.90	1536.35	77041.0
2022-08-03	1544.0	1570.0	1540.30	1565.15	1558.72	141963.0
2022-08-04	1583.0	1603.7	1574.90	1599.65	1592.16	230784.0
2022-08-05	1610.0	1625.6	1603.65	1616.55	1616.06	109383.0

	No. of Trades	Total Turnover	Deliverable Quantity \
Date			
2022-08-01	5411.0	7.166106e+09	4583058.0
2022-08-02	5527.0	1.183617e+08	31812.0
2022-08-03	7416.0	2.212807e+08	69999.0
2022-08-04	10165.0	3.674447e+08	73643.0
2022-08-05	7627.0	1.767698e+08	51686.0

	% Deli. Qty to Traded Qty	Spread H-L	Spread C-O
Date			
2022-08-01	99.11	32.30	-19.40
2022-08-02	41.29	20.35	-6.10
2022-08-03	49.31	29.70	21.15
2022-08-04	31.91	28.80	16.65
2022-08-05	47.25	21.95	6.55

▨ Apply the pandas_datareader library functions for different sources:

```
1.  import pandas_datareader as pdr
2.  # Fetching data from FRED (Federal Reserve
    Economic Data)
3.  # 10-Year Treasury Constant Maturity Minus 2-Year
    Treasury Constant Maturity
4.  # More details: https://fred.stlouisfed.org/tags/
    series
5.  data_t10y2y = pdr.get_data_fred('T10Y2Y')
6.  print("10-Year Treasury Constant Maturity Minus
    2-Year Treasury Constant Maturity:\n",
7.        data_t10y2y.head(), "\n")
8.  # Federal Funds Effective Rate
9.  # More details: https://fred.stlouisfed.org/
    series/FEDFUNDS
10. data_fedfunds = pdr.get_data_fred('FEDFUNDS')
11. print("Federal Funds Effective Rate:\n",
12.        data_fedfunds.head(), "\n")
13. # Fetching data using Alpha Vantage API source
14. # More details: https://www.alphavantage.co/
    documentation/
15. start_date = '2022-08-22'
16. data_av_tsla = pdr.get_data_alphavantage("TSLA",
17.                                  api_key='YourAPI1',
18.                                  start=start_date)
19. print(f"TSLA data from Alpha Vantage starting
    from: \n",
20.        data_av_tsla.head(), "\n")
21. # Using pandas_datareader.data to fetch data
```

```
22. import pandas_datareader.data as web
23. # Fetching daily data for TSLA from Alpha Vantage
24. data_web_av_tsla = web.DataReader("TSLA",
    "av-daily",
25.                                    api_key='ABC123',
26.                                    start=start_date)
27. print(f"Daily data for TSLA from Alpha Vantage
    starting from:\n",
28.       data_web_av_tsla[0:5], "\n")
29. # Fetching 5 Industry Portfolios data from Ken
    French's Data Library
30. # More details: https://mba.tuck.dartmouth.edu/
    pages/faculty/ken.french/data_library.html
31. data_industry = web.
    DataReader('5_Industry_Portfolios',
32.                                    'famafrench')
33. print("5 Industry Portfolios data from Ken
    French's Data Library")
34. for k in data_industry.keys():
35.   print(data_industry[k][0:5])
```

The results (truncated) of the code are:

```
10-Year Treasury Constant Maturity Minus 2-Year Treasury
Constant Maturity:

            T10Y2Y
DATE
2018-10-09    0.33
2018-10-10    0.34
2018-10-11    0.29
```

```
2018-10-12    0.30
2018-10-15    0.31
```

Federal Funds Effective Rate:

```
              FEDFUNDS
DATE
2018-11-01    2.20
2018-12-01    2.27
2019-01-01    2.40
2019-02-01    2.40
2019-03-01    2.41
```

TSLA data from Alpha Vantage starting from:

	open	high	low	close	volume
2022-08-22	875.74	877.2000	858.89	869.74	18614449
2022-08-23	874.36	896.4799	863.77	889.36	21328348
2022-08-24	892.69	910.9400	889.50	891.29	19086572
2022-08-25	302.36	302.9600	291.60	296.07	52827378
2022-08-26	297.43	302.0000	287.47	288.09	57163947

Daily data for TSLA from Alpha Vantage starting from:

	open	high	low	close	volume
2022-08-22	875.74	877.2000	858.89	869.74	18614449
2022-08-23	874.36	896.4799	863.77	889.36	21328348
2022-08-24	892.69	910.9400	889.50	891.29	19086572
2022-08-25	302.36	302.9600	291.60	296.07	52827378
2022-08-26	297.43	302.0000	287.47	288.09	57163947

5 Industry Portfolios data from Ken French's Data Library:

	Cnsmr	Manuf	HiTec	Hlth	Other
Date					
2018-10	-6.01	-8.65	-7.62	-8.79	-6.74
2018-11	2.08	2.47	-0.93	6.42	2.81
2018-12	-9.88	-9.06	-8.23	-8.25	-10.94
2019-01	8.10	8.96	8.70	5.32	9.80
2019-02	1.09	4.16	5.39	3.30	2.96

	Cnsmr	Manuf	HiTec	Hlth	Other
Date					
2018-10	-8.36	-11.62	-10.16	-14.50	-8.26
2018-11	-1.25	-1.91	0.59	-0.45	0.70
2018-12	-12.94	-14.08	-10.11	-18.41	-11.25
2019-01	12.25	14.16	15.41	18.35	11.05
2019-02	4.24	4.21	6.44	6.55	4.85

	Cnsmr	Manuf	HiTec	Hlth	Other
Date					
2018	-3.55	-11.27	-0.50	4.69	-10.12
2019	25.88	21.03	42.10	20.28	30.65
2020	37.95	-0.07	41.80	18.71	7.20
2021	20.64	27.35	26.68	13.72	27.45
2022	-25.12	5.40	-31.89	-5.68	-12.77

	Cnsmr	Manuf	HiTec	Hlth	Other
Date					
2018	-14.25	-22.04	-6.61	-22.48	-13.64
2019	17.47	12.04	27.65	25.96	26.37
2020	42.78	18.60	66.13	63.63	12.54

```
2021  36.13  42.26  17.92 -10.98  32.33
2022 -29.23  -3.68 -38.34 -42.11 -18.58
```

	Cnsmr	Manuf	HiTec	Hlth	Other
Date					
2018-10	499	599	658	635	1036
2018-11	496	593	655	631	1030
2018-12	493	591	647	628	1026
2019-01	491	589	642	626	1019
2019-02	491	585	634	624	1016

	Cnsmr	Manuf	HiTec	Hlth	Other
Date					
2018-10	9687.81	8603.35	13837.58	4814.64	7131.81
2018-11	9153.51	7871.26	12796.78	4407.25	6612.71
2018-12	9271.66	8059.38	12778.06	4699.31	6804.94
2019-01	8366.99	7330.71	11795.42	4314.54	6087.78
2019-02	9038.11	8013.78	12948.30	4535.67	6689.74

	Cnsmr	Manuf	HiTec	Hlth	Other
Date					
2018	0.22	0.39	0.22	0.19	0.49
2019	0.22	0.41	0.21	0.19	0.50
2020	0.22	0.48	0.19	0.18	0.61
2021	0.16	0.32	0.14	0.16	0.42
2022	0.21	0.36	0.20	0.22	0.53

	Cnsmr	Manuf	HiTec	Hlth	Other
Date					
2018	0.22	0.39	0.23	0.20	0.47
2019	0.24	0.45	0.26	0.21	0.56

```
2020    0.20    0.36    0.19    0.19    0.45

2021    0.19    0.41    0.16    0.17    0.52

2022    0.17    0.37    0.15    0.19    0.43

5 Ind
```

The code samples demonstrate fetching financial data using different libraries and sources. The first and second examples use Quandl to fetch stock data from the Hong Kong and Bombay Stock Exchanges. The data structures returned reflect the unique financial metrics provided by each exchange. In order to interpret the output, you need to read up on these metrics on the respective resource Web sites.

The third example uses pandas_datareader (`pdr`) to fetch data from multiple sources, such as FRED, Alpha Vantage, and Ken French's data source. We can use the `pandas_datareader` and `pandas_datareader.data` variants to fetch data for compatibility with previous code and receive different data types. The pandas_datareader tools return data in the DataFrame structure, which is more useful for further research. The library is a universal tool but may offer specialized features and options different from those of a dedicated library such as Quandl. The data fetched using `pdr` also highly varies in structure, depending on the source.

LOW-LEVEL APIS AND WEB SCRAPING

Low-level APIs are ones that provide the most detailed level of functionality. They are closer to the system hardware, allowing for detailed customization and control, but often require more code and a deeper understanding of the system to use effectively. Not all financial institutions, however, have an interface through pandas_datareader or native Python modules. Therefore, we must understand how to operate with low-level APIs and use common-use Python libraries, such as request, Beautiful Soup, and pandas (`read_json` or `read_html`).

Binance Cryptocurrency Exchange Example

Binance is one of the world's leading cryptocurrency exchanges, and it offers a low-level API for users who want to have granular control over their trading strategies and data analysis. To interact with Binance's low-level API, we can use a programming-specialized Python library such as python-binance. This library does, however, have some errors and does not fully support some versions of Anaconda. The Binance API allows you to access real-time open and private market data, make trade operations, and manage your account.

NOTE   *Be careful with the Binance API key and ID. They are tools to open your account in Binance and give access to your money.*

The Binance API is a good example of a low-level API because it provides detailed trading and data retrieval functions with detailed API documentation. To get started, familiarize yourself with the official Binance API documentation, which you can access at *https://www.binance.com/en/binance-api*. For the following examples, we will focus on the spot market, as detailed in the spot market API change log: *https://binance-docs.github.io/apidocs/spot/en/#change-log*.

The core steps of using low-level APIs with Binance are:

1. *Get API endpoints*: Binance offers five URLs to access the API. The primary one is *https://api.binance.com*.

2. *Investigate API commands*: The API documentation provides essential commands (requests) to retrieve data with specific options. In our example, we will use the `klines` request to obtain price and trading volume data for the ETHBTC currency pair.

3. *Generate a request string*: The request string is formed by combining the server address and the parameters of a specific request.

4. *Execute the request*: The request is then executed using basic pandas tools.

5. *Manipulate the request results data*: The received result is usually in the JSON data format. Analyzing the results and transforming the data into a more convenient DataFrame format is crucial.

NOTE   *It is important to note that working with low-level APIs can often lead to various types of errors. This can happen because there might be no network connection, the server may not respond, etc. For instance, Binance API requests are not executed by Google Colab virtual machines. So, the example provided here should be run from a local machine, and you must be vigilant for potential errors.*

Here is a simple example:

```
1.  # https://binance-docs.github.io/apidocs/spot/
    en/#kline-candlestick-data
2.  # Kline/candlestick bars for a symbol.
3.  # Klines are uniquely identified by their open
    time.
4.  # Parameters:
5.  # Name Type Mandatory Description
6.  # symbol STRING YES
7.  # interval ENUM YES
8.  # startTime LONG NO
9.  # endTime LONG NO
10. # limit INT NO Default 500; max 1000.
11. # Request: https://api.binance.com/api/v3/
    klines?interval=1d&limit=1000&symbol=<TICKER>
12.
13. url = 'https://api.binance.com/api/v1/
    klines?symbol=ETHBTC&interval=1d'
14. df = pd.read_json(url)
15. # Response:
16. #[
17. #   [
18. #     1499040000000,      // Kline open time
19. #     "0.01634790",       // Open price
20. #     "0.80000000",       // High price
21. #     "0.01575800",       // Low price
22. #     "0.01577100",       // Close price
23. #     "148976.11427815",  // Volume
24. #     1499644799999,      // Kline Close time
```

```
25. #     "2434.19055334",      // Quote asset volume
26. #     308,                  // Number of trades
27. #     "1756.87402397",      // Taker buy base asset
    volume
28. #     "28.46694368",        // Taker buy quote asset
    volume
29. #     "0"                   // Unused field, ignore.
30. #   ]
31. #]
32.
33. df.columns = ['date','open','high','low','close',
    'volume',
34.                   'close time','quote asset volume',
35.                   'number of trades','taker buy base
    asset volume',
36.                   'Taker buy quote asset
    volume','unused']
37. df['date'] = pd.to_datetime(df['date'], unit =
    'ms')
38. df.set_index('date',inplace=True)
39. print("Historical Candlestick Data (Last 5 Days):")
40. print(df.head())
```

The results (truncated) of the code are:

```
Historical Candlestick Data (Last 5 Days):
            open      high       low     close     volume  \
date
2022-05-27  0.061373  0.062325  0.059793  0.060334  246573.4627
2022-05-28  0.060334  0.062217  0.060159  0.061731  146078.3526
2022-05-29  0.061732  0.061962  0.061057  0.061541   90799.2918
```

```
2022-05-30   0.061541   0.063098   0.061441   0.062991   149815.4541

2022-05-31   0.062991   0.063269   0.060960   0.061062   157633.8933
```

```
                close time   quote asset volume   number of trades  \
date
2022-05-27   1653695999999           15024.382970             298316

2022-05-28   1653782399999            8953.503337             139847

2022-05-29   1653868799999            5589.875179              96868

2022-05-30   1653955199999            9329.637854             178438

2022-05-31   1654041599999            9762.035058             215453
```

```
                taker buy base asset volume   Taker buy quote asset volume   unused
date
2022-05-27                   123540.9160                      7529.397715        0

2022-05-28                    75939.0545                      4654.556964        0

2022-05-29                    44098.4113                      2715.291780        0

2022-05-30                    76939.3055                      4791.201970        0

2022-05-31                    78826.1248                      4880.643684        0
```

The code uses Python's pandas library to read JSON data with a generated request URL string. The URL contains query parameters such as `symbol` and `interval` to specify the trading pair and time frame. The fetched data includes the main fields for the OHLC data model. These fields are then renamed with names from the API documentation, and the date is converted into a readable format. Finally, the data is set to be indexed by the date.

The program code accompanying this book contains another example of this request based on the request library. This is a universal library for all GET requests in Python and can be used with various API options.

Web Scraping and the Beautiful Soup Python Library

While APIs are a clean and efficient way to retrieve data, not all Web sites or platforms offer an API. In such cases, data or Web scraping becomes a viable option. Beautiful Soup is a Python library that uses a relatively easy way of Web scraping to pull the data out of HTML and XML files. It creates a parse tree from page source code that can extract data in a hierarchical and more readable manner. Let us look at an example:

```python
1.  import requests
2.  from bs4 import BeautifulSoup
3.  url = "https://finance.yahoo.com/quote/TSLA/
    history?p=TSLA"
4.  headers = {"User-Agent": "Mozilla/5.0"}
5.  response = requests.get(url, headers=headers)
6.  soup = BeautifulSoup(response.content, 'html.
    parser')
7.  # Find the historical data table
8.  table = soup.find('table')
9.  rows = table.find_all('tr')
10. data = list()
11. for row in rows[1:]:  # Skip the header row
12.     columns = row.find_all('td')
13.     if len(columns) == 7: # Skip divedents and
    splits
14.         row_data = {'Date': columns[0].text,
15.                      'Open':columns[1].text,
16.                      'Close':columns[4].text,
17.                      'Volumes': columns[6].text}
18.     data.append(row_data)
19. print(pd.DataFrame(data))
```

The results (truncated) of the code are:

	Date	Open	Close	Volumes
0	Oct 06, 2023	253.98	260.53	117,947,000
1	Oct 05, 2023	260.00	260.05	119,159,200
2	Oct 04, 2023	248.14	261.16	129,721,600
3	Oct 03, 2023	248.61	246.53	101,985,300
4	Oct 02, 2023	244.81	251.60	123,810,400

This code opens the Yahoo Finance Web page on the Historical Data tab (see *Figure 3.2*) and finds the table with TSLA security data. The results will be the same as if we used `yf.download()`.

NOTE *Unfortunately, Web scraping is a volatile method. Success can depend on many factors, from the selected request headers parameter to changing the site structure. Therefore, if you cannot execute this example successfully, something has changed since this book was written on the official Yahoo Finance page.*

Thus, although low-level APIs and Web scraping are challenging programming procedures, they are better than copy-paste in complex data analysis situations.

CONCLUSION

This chapter has explored the fundamental principles underlying the global world of financial data. We began by outlining the various sources and types of financial data crucial for making informed investment decisions. Then, we emphasized that data sources and their value are contingent upon the strategy chosen for their utilization. For long-term conservative strategies, publicly available data with short time frames may suffice. If you trade within a single day or even an hour, however, access to data from specific trading platforms becomes indispensable. It is also important to remember that financial markets incorporate various information. Therefore, news can also be considered a source of financial data for making investment decisions.

Yahoo Finance is one of the most prominent, but not the only, financial data providers. The advantages of using this service are manifold. Not only does it offer trading performance metrics, but it also provides fundamental indicators that are crucial for comprehensive financial analysis. The highly functional Python library yfinance facilitates quick and relatively straightforward access to vast global financial market data. By leveraging the capabilities of this library, users can efficiently gather the information they need for a wide range of investment strategies and financial research.

The financial sector is undergoing rapid development, leading to an increase in various providers and suppliers of financial data and managerial information. We have explored the top primary open-source links and APIs for financial data analysis. The list of institutions that generate and collect data, however, is continually growing, and existing ones are expanding their functionalities through new data and services. The Python tools and libraries described can, however, reduce routine tasks, allowing investors to focus on generating profits.

The last section of this chapter presented critical examples for downloading real-world financial data and basic operations for manipulating it. Specifically, we discussed working with file formats such as CSV and XLS, interfacing with online resources via APIs and HTML, and Web scraping fundamentals. Having mastered these methods, investors and analysts can create a custom solution for data collection tasks of any complexity.

QUESTIONS

1. What are the primary sources of financial data?

2. How does the valuation aspect of financial data vary depending on the investment strategy?

3. What data inspection functions in pandas do you know?

4. What are the advantages of Yahoo Finance as a financial data provider?

5. What is the purpose of the Python library yfinance?

6. What file formats are commonly used for storing financial data, and how can they be manipulated using pandas?

7. What is a low-level API, and what problems could we have with it when importing data?

8. What is Web scraping, and how is the Beautiful Soup Python library used?

9. What are the critical parameters for fetching `kline`/candlestick data from Binance?

10. What are some open-source links and APIs for financial data analysis?

11. How can financial market news be considered a source of financial data for investment decisions?

12. What are the fundamental operations for manipulating real-world financial data?

KEY TERMS

- *Data* is usually understood as raw, unorganized facts and figures collected from various sources for analysis, computation, interpretation, or other purposes. Data may seem random and meaningless in its raw form, but once processed and interpreted, it gains context and becomes useful information.

- *Financial information* often refers to processed data used to make informed decisions—investments, for example. The information is usually derived from raw financial data, such as stock prices, market volumes, returns and rate of returns, risk estimation, and other financial metrics.

- *Financial instruments* are assets that can be traded or used for investment purposes. They represent a legal agreement that may hold monetary value, including the potential for price fluctuations, and can carry out other financial benefits.

- *Stocks*, also known as *shares* or *equities*, are financial instruments that confirm the right to a part (share) of a company's property, including the potential to receive profits in the form of dividends or equity growth.

- *Securities* are financial instruments in the broader sense that encompass a range of tradable assets, including stocks, bonds, and derivatives, as well as many others. Securities can produce income through interests, dividends, capital gains, and so on.

- *Open data sources* are publicly available datasets that anyone can freely use, modify, and share. This source offers not only free access but also easy access to well-structured data.

- An *API* is a set of rules and protocols that enable different applications to communicate using the same language. In the finance industry, APIs are used to retrieve data, access real-time information, and even automate trading processes.

REFERENCES

- *pandas data analysis library: https://pandas.pydata.org*
- *Panditrao, P. M. (2021) A Python Guide for Web Scraping [Paperback]. BPB Publications.*
- *Dixit, R. (2022). Data Analysis with Python. [Paperback]. BPB Publications.*

4

EXPLORATORY DATA ANALYSIS FOR FINANCE

INTRODUCTION

This chapter describes the tools and patterns of *exploratory data analysis (EDA)* for the financial sector. We start by discussing *extract, transform, and load (ETL)* data processes, focusing on inspecting and clearing datasets, transforming formats, etc. Here, we will detail mathematical and other transformations, such as the *rate of return (RoR)*, that are essential for financial data preparation. After that, we will learn how to handle missing data, duplicates, and errors. Then, we will move on to the basics of EDA, where we will get hands-on experience with data visualization. We will introduce you to basic descriptive statistics metrics and three fundamental statistical graphics using the *Matplotlib* and *Seaborn* libraries. Data windows and *moving averages (MAs)* will be described. They offer a crucial understanding of financial data trends. We will also delve into investment risk statistics with descriptive and correlation analytical tools. This gives us the ability to prepare and make informed investment decisions.

After finishing this chapter, you will have a robust understanding of EDA in finance and be well equipped with Python's financial data manipulation and analysis capabilities.

STRUCTURE

This chapter covers the following topics:

- Basic patterns in ETL financial data processes
- Exploring the basics of EDA for financial analysis
- Data visualization with the Matplotlib and Seaborn libraries
- Data windows and MA estimations
- Essentials of statistics and correlation analysis

OBJECTIVES

By the end of this chapter, you will have the essential skills to perform EDA for finance. You will have mastered data transforming processes and learned patterns to inspect and clean financial data, including related mathematical operations. Your toolkit will have expanded to include Python functions for handling missing data and data errors. You will have gained hands-on experience in data visualization using Matplotlib and Seaborn, as well as understood the descriptive statistics metrics and MA data to determine financial trends. Additionally, you will have explored investment risk statistics, applying the tools for descriptive, visual, and correlation analysis. This skill set will enable you to make informed, data-driven investment decisions and prepare you for the typical analytical stages.

BASIC PATTERNS FOR PROCESSING RAW FINANCIAL DATA

A practical financial data analysis should be based on clear and accurate information. For example, shares of different companies or various investment assets can differ widely, be evaluated in other currencies, etc. The information becomes distorted if equivalent statistical methods are applied to such data. As described in the previous chapters, Python has many tools for getting, collecting, and transforming data.

A crucial aspect of preparing data for analysis or converting it into managerial information is using ETL tools, which we discussed in the first three chapters. The good news is that most of the steps involved in preparing raw data for further analysis can be standardized. Well-defined operations and data processing patterns exist based on the ETL and EDA methodologies. For data obtained from stock or similar financial exchanges, the data processing patterns are as follows:

- *Import files*: Read all flat files from a folder or Web-based data into separate DataFrames, which takes care of I/O errors and so on.

- *Create, merge, or join DataFrames*: Organize the dataset structure, merge and combine table actions, and process OHLC data for each ticker.

- *Sort time-series data*: Ensure the DateTime index is sorted for all DataFrames.

- *Inspect dataset*: Perform initial data inspection for structure and quality.

- *Handle NaNs and duplicates and find errors*: Drop duplicate rows and fill in missing values. For example, if stock market data for Sundays and Mondays is unavailable, we can use the value from the preceding Friday.

- *Processing data validations*: Adjust historical data based on stock split events or other operations.

- *Calculate new features*: Use `pct_change()` to calculate daily percentage changes (RoR), calculate weight values, etc.

- *Grouping and data aggregation*: Group daily data by month, quarter, or year and calculate the mean and count.

- *Data backup*: Save the cleaned and transformed data to new files or a database.

Additional ETL procedures that may be combined with EDA techniques are:

- *Outlier detection*: Identify and handle outliers that could skew your analysis.

- *Data validation*: Ensure that each column's data types are appropriate for analysis.

- *Scaling and normalizing*: Scale numerical features into a comparative range.

- *Exploratory feature engineering*: Create new features (variables) that might be useful for analysis, such as MA or volatility measures.

- *Data annotation*: Add labels or flags to the data, such as marking significant financial events.

- *Time zone adjustment*: If the data comes from markets in different time zones, consider aligning them.

- *Data partitioning (splitting)*: If we use machine learning models, we can split the data into training, validation, and test sets.
- *Audit trail*: Note and comment on all the transformations when transforming datasets.

Using examples, let us look at the main patterns of processing raw financial data.

Importing Data and Structuring DataFrames

In *Chapter 3, Financial Data Manipulation with Python*, we discussed the various sources of financial information and the Python tools available for accessing them. While there are numerous options, gathering and updating data typically involves a set of standard functions. Let us consider an example that deals with processing files stored locally, specifically CSV files, which are provided in the appendix of this book. Moreover, in the code appendix for this chapter, you can find and execute code for importing and creating these CSV files from open resources.

Execute the following code and analyze its results:

```
1.  import os
2.  # Directory where your CSV files are stored
3.  # data_dir = "./data_folder" # for Unix-based
    operation systems
4.  # data_dir = r"C:\path\to\your\data_folder" # for
    Windows
5.  # data_dir = ".\\"  # Current folder for Windows-
    based operating systems
6.  data_dir = "."     # Current for Unix-based
    operation systems
7.  # Get the list of all files in the directory
8.  # all_files = os.listdir(data_dir)
9.  all_files = os.listdir() # from current location
10. # Filter out the action and OHLC files
```

```
11. action_files = [f for f in all_files if '_
    actions.csv' in f]
12. ohlc_files = [f for f in all_files if '_ohlc.csv'
    in f]
13. # Extract tickers from file names
14. tickers_from_actions_files = set(f.split('_')[0]
    for f in action_files)
15. tickers_from_ohlc_files = set(f.split('_')[0] for
    f in ohlc_files)
16. # Find tickers that are in both sets
    (intersection)
17. common_tickers = tickers_from_actions_files &
                    tickers_from_ohlc_files
18. # Find tickers that are only in the second set
    (difference)
19. tickers_only_in_ohlc = tickers_from_ohlc_files -
                    tickers_from_actions_files
20. # Find tickers that are in either set (union)
21. all_tickers = tickers_from_actions_files |
    tickers_from_ohlc_files
22.
23. # Initialize final DataFrame
24. final_df = pd.DataFrame()
25. # Loop through tickers common to both action and
    ohlc files
26. for ticker in common_tickers:
27.     # Load and filter action data
28.     action_df = pd.read_csv(f"{data_dir}/
    {ticker}_actions.csv", parse_dates=['Date'],
    index_col='Date')
```

```
29.     action_df = action_df[['Dividends','Stock
    Splits']]
30.     action_df.rename(columns={'Dividends':
    f"{ticker}_div",
                                    'Stock Splits':
    f"{ticker}_split"},
                                inplace=True)
31.     # Load and filter OHLC data
32.     ohlc_df = pd.read_csv(f"{data_dir}/{ticker}_
    ohlc.csv",
                            parse_dates=['Date'],
    index_col='Date')
33.     ohlc_df = ohlc_df[['close','volume']]
34.     ohlc_df.rename(columns={'close': f"{ticker}_
    close",
                                'volume': f"{ticker}_
    volume"},
                                inplace=True)
35.     # Merge action and OHLC data
36.     merged_df = action_df.join(ohlc_df,
    how='outer')
37.     # Update final DataFrame
38.     final_df = merged_df if final_df.empty
                            else final_df.join
    (merged_df,how='outer')
39.
40. # Loop through tickers only in OHLC files
41. for ticker in tickers_only_in_ohlc:
42.     # Load and filter ohlc data
43.     ohlc_df = pd.read_csv(f"{data_dir}/
    {ticker}_ohlc.csv", parse_dates=['Date'],
    index_col='Date')
44.     ohlc_df = ohlc_df[['Close','Volume']]
```

```
45.      ohlc_df.rename(columns={'Close': f"{ticker}_
    close", 'Volume': f"{ticker}_volume"},
    inplace=True)
46.
47.      # Update final DataFrame
48.      final_df = ohlc_df if final_df.empty else
    final_df.join(ohlc_df, how='outer')
49.
50. # Display the first 5 rows of the final DataFrame
    to get an overview of the data
51. print(final_df.head())
52. # Display the first 5 rows of columns containing
    'close' in their names (e.g., stock closing
    prices)
53. print(final_df.filter(like='close').head())
54. # Display the first 5 rows of columns containing
    'volume' in their names (e.g., stock trading
    volumes)
55. print(final_df.filter(like='volume').head())
56. # Display the first 5 rows of columns related to
    TSLA
57. print(final_df.filter(like='TSLA').head())
```

The results (truncated) of the code are:

```
          JNJ_div  JNJ_split  JNJ_close  JNJ_volume  AMZN_div  AMZN_split  \
Date
2022-01-01    NaN        NaN        NaN         NaN       NaN         NaN
2022-01-02    NaN        NaN        NaN         NaN       NaN         NaN
2022-01-03    0.0        0.0     171.54   6012777.0       0.0         0.0
2022-01-04    0.0        0.0     171.08   6748363.0       0.0         0.0
2022-01-05    0.0        0.0     172.22   7016099.0       0.0         0.0
```

```
(...)
2022-01-05    94537602.0      36851084859
```

Date	TSLA_div	TSLA_split	TSLA_close	TSLA_volume
2022-01-01	NaN	NaN	NaN	NaN
2022-01-02	NaN	NaN	NaN	NaN
2022-01-03	0.0	0.0	1199.78	34895349.0
2022-01-04	0.0	0.0	1149.59	33416086.0
2022-01-05	0.0	0.0	1088.12	26706599.0

This Python code example performs data manipulation tasks to create a DataFrame (`final_df`) containing exchange market information. It starts by setting the directory (`data_dir`) where the CSV files are stored. It then lists all files in the directory and filters them to get action and OHLC files. The tickers are extracted from these file names, and sets are created to identify tickers that are only found in OHLC files and ones that are found across all assets (JNJ, AMZN, ... TSLA). Two main loops populate `final_df`. The first loop (lines *26-38*) iterates through tickers common to action and OHLC files. It reads and filters the data, renames columns, and merges the DataFrames. The second loop (lines *41-48*) similarly processes tickers that are only present in OHLC files. Finally, the code prints the first five rows of `final_df` and subsets related to `'close'`, `'volume'`, and `'TSLA'` to provide an overview.

Elementary Data Clearing Patterns

The best way to understand essential data clearing patterns is through practical Python code examples. Execute the following code and take a look at the results:

```
1.  # ETL Pattern: Inspect the Data Frame
2.  # Display the data types and non-null counts for
    each column
3.  print("Initial DataFrame Info:")
4.  print(final_df.info())
```

```
 5.  # Display the number of rows and columns in the
     DataFrame
 6.  print("Initial DataFrame Shape (Rows, Columns):",
     final_df.shape)
 7.  # Display the first 5 rows of the DataFrame
 8.  print("First 5 Rows of Initial DataFrame:")
 9.  print(final_df.head())
10.  # Display the last 5 rows of the DataFrame
11.  print("Last 5 Rows of Initial DataFrame:")
12.  print(final_df.tail())
13.
14.  # ETL Pattern: Data Sorting
15.  # Sort the DataFrame by index (Date) in ascending
     order
16.  final_df.sort_index(inplace=True)
17.
18.  # ETL Pattern: Data Cleaning
19.  # Check for NaN values in each column and display
     the sum
20.  print("\nNumber of NaN Values in Each Column:")
21.  print(final_df.isna().sum())
22.  # Check for duplicate rows and display them
23.  print("Duplicate Rows in DataFrame:")
24.  print(final_df[final_df.duplicated()])
25.  # Drop all duplicate rows from the DataFrame
26.  final_df.drop_duplicates(inplace=True)
27.  # For Sunday and Monday (non-business days), use
     Friday's data
```

```
28.  # Forward-fill missing values for every day by
     the last valid observation
29.  final_df = final_df.ffill()
30.  # Drop remaining NaN values from the DataFrame
31.  final_df.dropna(inplace=True)
32.  # Confirm that there are no more NaN values
33.  print("Number of NaN Values After Cleaning:")
34.  print(final_df.isna().sum())
35.  # Identify columns to change data types
36.  volume_cols = [col for col in final_df.columns if
     '_volume' in col]
37.  close_cols = [col for col in final_df.columns if
     '_close' in col]
38.  split_cols = [col for col in final_df.columns if
     '_split' in col]
39.  # Change data types for volume columns to int64
     and close columns to float64
40.  final_df[volume_cols] = final_df[volume_cols].
     astype('int64')
41.  final_df[close_cols] = final_df[close_cols].
     astype('float64')
42.  final_df[split_cols] = final_df[split_cols].
     astype('int32')
43.
44.  # Inspect the DataFrame after all transformations
45.  print("\nFinal DataFrame Info:")
46.  print(final_df.info())
47.  # Display the first 5 rows of the final DataFrame
48.  print("\nFirst 5 Rows of Final DataFrame:")
49.  print(final_df.head())
```

The results (truncated) of the code are:

```
Initial DataFrame Info:
<class 'pandas.core.frame.DataFrame'>
DatetimeIndex: 660 entries, 2022-01-01 to 2023-10-22
Data columns (total 26 columns):
 #    Column          Non-Null Count   Dtype
---   ------          --------------   -----
 0    JNJ_div         453 non-null     float64
 1    JNJ_split       453 non-null     float64
 2    JNJ_close       453 non-null     float64
 3    JNJ_volume      453 non-null     float64 (…)
(...)
```

```
Final DataFrame Info:
<cla's 'pandas.core.frame.DataFr'me'>
DatetimeIndex: 658 entries, 2022-01-03 to 2023-10-22
Data columns (total 26 columns):
 #    Column          Non-Null Count   Dtype
---   ------          --------------   -----
 0    JNJ_div         658 non-null     float64
 1    JNJ_split       658 non-null     int32
 2    JNJ_close       658 non-null     float64
 3    JNJ_volume      658 non-null     int64
(...)
```

```
First 5 Rows of Final DataFrame:
            JNJ_div  JNJ_split  JNJ_close  JNJ_volume  AMZN_div  AMZN_split \
Date
2022-01-03    0.0        0       171.54    6012777       0.0         0
2022-01-04    0.0        0       171.08    6748363       0.0         0
2022-01-05    0.0        0       172.22    7016099       0.0         0
```

2022-01-06	0.0	0	171.63	7301633	0.0	0
2022-01-07	0.0	0	173.95	6986006	0.0	0
(...)						

Date	AAPL_close	AAPL_volume	BTC-USD_close	BTC-USD_volume
2022-01-03	182.01	104701220	46458.117188	33071628362
2022-01-04	179.70	99310438	45897.574219	42494677905
2022-01-05	174.92	94537602	43569.003906	36851084859
2022-01-06	172.00	96903955	43160.929688	30208048289
2022-01-07	172.17	86709147	41557.902344	84196607520

This Python code follows an ETL pattern to clean and transform a DataFrame (`final_df`) containing stock data. It starts by inspecting the initial DataFrame, displaying its data types, shape, and first and last five rows. It then sorts the DataFrame by date and checks for NaN values and duplicates, which it removes. The code also forward-fills missing values and changes data types for specific columns. Finally, this Python code inspects the cleaned DataFrame, confirming that there are no NaN values and displaying its updated data types and first five rows. The initial DataFrame had 660 entries with some NaN values, while the final DataFrame has 658 entries with no NaN values, indicating successful data cleaning.

Data Transformation and the Creation of New Features

Let us describe some Python code examples of data transformation and the creation of new feature techniques. For example, data transforming code may aggregate the RoR from daily to monthly averages. Execute the following code and analyze the results:

```
1.  # ETL Pattern: Data Transformation
2.  # Loop through each ticker to correct share price
    and volume for stock splits
3.  for ticker in common_tickers:
```

```
4.    # Create a new column to hold non-zero split
      values, replacing zeros with ones

5.    final_d"[f"{ticker}_spl"t1"] =
      final_d"[f"{ticker}_sp"it"]

6.    final_d"[f"{ticker}_spl"t1"].replace(0, 1,
      inplace=True)

7.    # Calculate the cumulative product of the split
      factor

8.    final_d"[f"{ticker}_spl"t1"] =
      final_d"[f"{ticker}_spl"t1"].cumprod()

9.    # Normalize the split factor

10.   final_d"[f"{ticker}_spl"t1"] = final_d"
      [f"{ticker}_spl"t1"].max() / final_d"
      [f"{ticker}_spl"t1"]

11.   # Correct the close price by dividing it by the
      normalized split factor

12.   final_d"[f"{ticker}_cl"se"] = final_d"
      [f"{ticker}_cl"se"] / final_d"[f"{ticker}_
      spl"t1"]

13.   # Correct the volume by multiplying it by the
      normalized split factor

14.   final_d"[f"{ticker}_vol"me"] = final_d"
      [f"{ticker}_vol"me"] * final_d"[f"{ticker}_
      spl"t1"]

15.   # Drop the temporary column used for split
      normalization

16.   final_df.dro"(f"{ticker}_spl"t1", axis=1,
      inplace=True)

17.   # Display the head and tail of the DataFrame
      filtered f'r 'A'ZN' as an example

18.   print(final_df.filter(li'e='A'ZN').head())

19.   print(final_df.filter(li'e='A'ZN').tail())
```

```
20.
21.  # Calculate the Rate of Return (RoR) for all
     tickers
22.  for ticker in all_tickers:
23.    final_d"[f"{ticker}_r"te"] =
       final_d"[f"{ticker}_cl"se"].pct_change()
24.  # Drop any rows with NaN values
25.  final_df.dropna(inplace=True)
26.  # Display the head of the DataFrame to inspect
     the first few rows
27.  print(final_df.head())
28.
29.  # ETL Pattern: Data Aggregation
30.  # Group by month
31.  df_pct_monthly = final_df.filter(li'e='r'te').
     resamp'e''M').apply(lambda x: x.mean() *
     x.count())
32.  # Assuming final_df has a DateTime index
33.  df_pct_monthly.index = df_pct_monthly.index.
     strfti'e('%Y'%m')
34.  print(df_pct_monthly.head())
```

The results (truncated) of the code are:

	AMZN_div	AMZN_split	AMZN_close	AMZN_volume
Date				
2022-01-03	0.0	0	170.4045	63869140.0
2022-01-04	0.0	0	167.5220	70725160.0
2022-01-05	0.0	0	164.3570	64302720.0

2022-01-06	0.0	0	163.2540	51957780.0
2022-01-07	0.0	0	162.5540	46605900.0

	AMZN_div	AMZN_split	AMZN_close	AMZN_volume
Date				
2023-10-18	0.0	0	128.13	42699479.0
2023-10-19	0.0	0	128.40	60961355.0
2023-10-20	0.0	0	125.17	56406410.0
2023-10-21	0.0	0	125.17	56406410.0
2023-10-22	0.0	0	125.17	56406410.0

Data with RoR values

(...)

	BTC-USD_close	BTC-USD_volume	BTC-USD_rate	JNJ_rate	AMZN_rate	\
Date						
2022-01-04	45897.574219	42494677905	-0.012066	-0.002682	-0.016916	
2022-01-05	43569.003906	36851084859	-0.050734	0.006664	-0.018893	
2022-01-06	43160.929688	30208048289	-0.009366	-0.003426	-0.006711	
2022-01-07	41557.902344	84196607520	-0.037141	0.013517	-0.004288	
2022-01-08	41733.941406	28066355845	0.004236	0.000000	0.000000	

	TSLA_rate	GS_rate	XOM_rate	AAPL_rate
Date				
2022-01-04	-0.041833	0.030734	0.037614	-0.012692
2022-01-05	-0.053471	-0.021719	0.012437	-0.026600
2022-01-06	-0.021523	-0.004265	0.023521	-0.016693
2022-01-07	-0.035447	0.001461	0.008197	0.000988
2022-01-08	0.000000	0.000000	0.000000	0.000000

```
Group by month data

          BTC-USD_rate  JNJ_rate  AMZN_rate  TSLA_rate   GS_rate  XOM_rate \
Date

2022-01     -0.176673  0.005265  -0.124930  -0.225129 -0.103653  0.181564

2022-02      0.142166 -0.043784   0.041404  -0.059767 -0.035976  0.035855

2022-03      0.068900  0.075528   0.067145   0.229130 -0.029531  0.060255

2022-04     -0.178505  0.019761  -0.253446  -0.196009 -0.073664  0.035199

2022-05     -0.144366 -0.004094  -0.019532  -0.106458  0.071233  0.125199


          AAPL_rate
Date

2022-01   -0.036327

2022-02   -0.054720

2022-03    0.060313

2022-04   -0.097564

2022-05   -0.047672
```

Those ETL patterns focus on data transformation and aggregation. The ETL process starts by correcting share prices and volumes for stock splits for each ticker in common_tickers. Then, the example calculates the RoR for all tickers and removes any rows with NaN values. Finally, the code aggregates the data by month, calculating each ticker's mean RoR. The code displays the head and tail of the DataFrame filtered for AMZN as an example and the first few rows of the DataFrame after RoR calculation. The results show that the DataFrame has been successfully transformed and aggregated and is ready for further analysis.

NOTE *Usually, the return on financial assets is represented by the daily increase in value. To make further comparisons, it may be necessary to recalculate the data for monthly or annual returns. Usually, 30 for a month and 360 (or 365) for a year are used as the multipliers for this recalculation. For financial exchanges that do not operate on weekends, however, the annual multiplier may be set at 250, the average number of working days per year.*

EDA ESSENTIALS FOR FINANCIAL ANALYSIS

After the preliminary data preparation in the ETL stage and before diving into modeling, forecasting, and investment decision-making, conducting additional substantive data analysis is crucial. This is done through EDA. Although we discuss EDA and ETL separately, they are closely integrated. For instance, handling missing data can involve simple imputation, transformation methods, and statistical measures such as median and mean. Moreover, we may need to revisit ETL tools for feature engineering and other adjustments after conducting EDA.

EDA for financial data involves common and specific financial patterns. These include descriptive statistics and statistical graphics such as boxplots, histograms, scatter plots, time-series data windows, and MA. These elements give a comprehensive view of analytical patterns and metrics in the financial datasets, revealing trends, volatilities, and potential investment opportunities. So, let us continue this analytical journey into the stock exchange data. The basic EDA data processing patterns can be described as follows:

- *Descriptive statistics* metrics give an overview of the financial dataset's central tendency, variation or volatility, and normality test.
- *Data visualization* techniques employ basic statistical graphics, for example, linear plots by time, boxplots, histograms, and scatter plots, to inspect data visually.
- *MA* and data windows are the fundamental financial time-series data metrics and can be utilized to understand trends and seasonality in financial and stock markets.
- *Correlation analysis* is assessing how different financial variables interact with each other.
- Candlestick charts, trend-following indicators, value-at-risk, regressions, and so on represent other *EDA financial metrics and methods*.

Now, let us dive deeper into each of these basic analytical patterns.

Descriptive Statistics

Descriptive statistics help for any data analysis, including financial data. They summarize the data's main aspects, offering a snapshot of its distribution, central tendency, and deviations. Now, we will discuss using descriptive statistics metrics for financial asset prices and the RoR as a profitability indicator:

    ▪   *Central tendency* is estimated by the mean, median, and mode metrics. The mean and median can be applied to quantitative data. The mode is useful for categorical data (such as the type of assets or trading region).

The *mean* price ($Mean_{Price}$) provides the average price ($Price_i$) of the stock (other assets over a specific period):

$$Mean_{Price} = \Sigma(Price_i) / n$$

Here, n is the number of observation units (days of market trades for these assets).

The $Mean_{Price}$ is the so-called simple average. The weighted average, however, is also used in financial calculations, in which the weighting indicator is considered separately. For the financial market, the weighting indicator is often the trading volume ($Volume_i$) of a given asset, namely:

$$Mean_{Price} = \Sigma(Price_i \cdot Volume_i) / \Sigma(Volume_i)$$

$Mean_{Price}$ and $MeanW_{Price}$ are the leading metrics of market trend detection. The same principle estimates the average level of financial asset outcomes by applying those central metrics to the RoR or logarithmic RoR.

The *median* is the second most important indicator for assessing the central values for stock prices and returns. The median value is often close to or the same as the mean. The median, however, is considered a stable estimate of the mean compared to the mean itself. The median price ($Median_{Price}$) is calculated as follows.

For an odd number of sorted observations:

$$Median_{Price} = Price_{(n+1)/2}$$

For an even number of sorted observations:

$$Median_{Price} = (Price_{n/2} + Price_{(n/2)+1}) / 2$$

As we see, the median is the center of the sorted observations array. The median is often used to fill in missing data or outliers in statistical data series (this will be covered later in this chapter).

NOTE   *The quartile is another type of central metric, but it does not significantly differ from the median. In fact, each quartile divides the sorted data array into half. The median is quartile 2 (Q2). Suppose we divide the observed dataset* *into two by the median and calculate the values of the middle (median-based method) of the series for the subset below and above the median. In that case, we will get quartile 1 (Q1) and quartile 3 (Q3).*

▨   *Deviation or volatility* is crucial for risk assessment and investment decision-making. The volatility is often estimated by the variation, *standard deviation (SD)*, and *coefficient of variation (CV)* metrics. These metrics show the *average* distance between the central metric and other observation data.

The variance of price (Var_{Price}) is expressed in terms of the square of the price deviation from $Mean_{Price}$. The squaring serves a specific purpose: it eliminates the sign, ensuring that all deviations from the mean are treated as positive values. This is crucial because when calculating variance, we are interested in the magnitude of the deviation from the mean, not its direction (whether it is above or below the mean):

$$Var_{Price} = \Sigma(Price_i - Mean_{Price})^2 / n$$

By squaring the deviations, we give more weight to extreme values, making variance sensitive to outliers. This is often desirable in financial analysis, where outliers represent risks or opportunities.

The SD is another measure of the stock's volatility and investment metric, which is the square root of the variance. The *standard deviation of price* (SD_{Price}) is estimated as follows:

$$SD_{Price} = \sqrt{Var_{Price}} = \sqrt{\sum_{i=1}^{n} \frac{\left(Price_i - Mean_{Price}\right)^2}{n}}$$

SD is a crucial metric in financial analysis. A higher SD indicates greater volatility, which may imply higher investment risk but often potential for higher returns. Conversely, a lower SD suggests less volatility and, typically, a less risky investment.

Both variance and SD are tied to units of measurement, price scales, currencies, and the like. The CV indicator does not have this limitation. *CV* is corrected on the *Mean* value and shows the scaled level of the deviation.

The CV for price (CV_{Price}) is estimated as follows:

$$CV_{Price} = (SD_{Price} / Mean_{Price}) \cdot 100$$

As we can see, the CV standardizes the risk per average unit of the share price, allowing for a comparison between different stocks.

We have discussed how the basic *descriptive statistics metrics* can be applied to financial asset prices. Still, it is important to note that similar metrics can be employed to evaluate investment efficiency, such as the RoR. Central tendency metrics (mean and median) of the RoR can provide insights into the typical return an investor might expect over a given period. Deviation metrics, such as the SD and CV, for the RoR offer a glimpse into the investment's volatility and risk. In summary, central tendency metrics for the RoR give us an idea of expected returns, while deviation metrics help us understand the risks involved. Both of these metrics offer a comprehensive view of the investment's performance, enabling financial investors to make informed decisions.

Consider an example of assessing descriptive statistics indicators for a data array prepared earlier in the ETL stages. Execute the following code and investigate the results:

```
1.  def generate_descriptive_stats(stat_data,
    w_data=None):
2.      # Initialize an empty DataFrame to store the
    results
3.      result_df = pd.DataFrame()
4.      # Calculate and store each statistic
5.      result_df['Mean'] = stat_data.mean()
6.      result_df['Median'] = stat_data.median()
7.      result_df['SD'] = stat_data.std()
8.      result_df['Var'] = stat_data.var()
9.      result_df['CV'] = (stat_data.std() / stat_
    data.mean()) * 100
10.     # Calculate the weighted means for all
    columns
11.     if w_data is not None:
12.         w_means = []
```

```
13.          for col in stat_data.columns:
14.              w_col = w_data.columns[stat_data.
     columns.get_loc(col)]
15.              w_mean = (stat_data[col] *
16.                     w_data[w_col]).sum() / w_
     data[w_col].sum()
17.              w_means.append(w_mean)
18.          result_df['Weighted_Mean'] = w_means
19.      return result_df
20.  # Filter data for 'close' and 'volume'
21.  stat_data_close = final_df.filter(like='close')
22.  w_data = final_df.filter(like='volume')
23.  # Generate descriptive statistics for asset
     prices
24.  result_close = generate_descriptive_stats(stat_
     data_close, w_data)
25.  # Display the results
26.  print("Descriptive Statistics for close
     prices:\n", result_close)
27.  # Generate descriptive statistics for RoR
28.  print("\nDescriptive Statistics for 'RoR':\n",
29.      generate_descriptive_stats(final_
     df.filter(like='rate')))
```

The results of the code are:

```
Descriptive Statistics for close prices:
                    Mean        Median         SD          Var  \
JNJ_close      167.962374    167.710000    8.046566  6.474723e+01
```

AMZN_close	121.359139	122.280000	21.400457	4.579796e+02
TSLA_close	239.846969	244.666667	57.278358	3.280810e+03
GS_close	334.381324	331.480000	23.985858	5.753214e+02
XOM_close	99.923546	104.160000	12.837336	1.647972e+02
AAPL_close	161.037139	162.410000	16.637431	2.768041e+02
BTC-USD_close	27336.538212	26664.550781	7829.313869	6.129816e+07

	CV	Weighted_Mean
JNJ_close	4.790696	168.123664
AMZN_close	17.633989	120.340881
TSLA_close	23.881210	226.746149
GS_close	7.173205	334.538805
XOM_close	12.847158	96.799949
AAPL_close	10.331425	159.019770
BTC-USD_close	28.640473	27129.027823

Descriptive Statistics for 'RoR':

	Mean	Median	SD	Var	CV
BTC-USD_rate	-0.000246	-0.000981	0.029051	0.000844	-11795.273031
JNJ_rate	-0.000134	0.000000	0.008967	0.000080	-6688.529736
AMZN_rate	-0.000209	0.000000	0.022842	0.000522	-10930.926477
TSLA_rate	-0.000441	0.000000	0.032298	0.001043	-7317.282534
GS_rate	-0.000320	0.000000	0.014115	0.000199	-4411.154162
XOM_rate	0.000986	0.000000	0.016464	0.000271	1669.679498
AAPL_rate	0.000045	0.000000	0.015738	0.000248	34896.523221

The code defines a function, generate_descriptive_stats(), that takes in a DataFrame, stat_data, and an optional DataFrame, w_data, for weighted calculations. The function calculates various descriptive statistics. The code example is applied to the filtered data (close prices and RoR) and prints the results.

The statistics results offer a lot of information. The SD for TSLA is 57.28, which is relatively high compared to other assets, such as JNJ (SD=8.04) and AAPL (SD=16.63). This indicates that TSLA's stock price has been more volatile, experiencing more significant fluctuations over the time analyzed. The coefficients of variation for the RoRs are incredibly high, even negative for some assets. This could be due to the mean RoR being very close to 0. The CV tends to inflate when the mean is near 0 because we divide by a small number, and the SD level is too high for daily values. Therefore, descriptive statistics is a universal, but not the only, method for analyzing investment risks.

Basic Statistical Data Visualization

Visualizing data is essential for exploratory data and investment analysis. It not only aids in understanding complex structures but also helps draw preliminary or even final decisions from the visualized information. Using plots and charts can reveal trends, patterns, and outliers that are not apparent through numerical summaries or descriptive statistics metrics. In financial data, particularly stock prices and RoR, only a few statistical and professional visualizations are commonly used. Let us describe three standard types of graphs:

- A *plot* (line or box) is commonly used for the first overview or inspection of time-series data. A plot demonstrates any obvious tendencies of data dynamics. It is crucial for the data in the observation dataset to have the same time details (same time of storage, no gaps, and so on). Based on these plots, we can evaluate the trend, outliers, and viable problems in the data and determine which data analysis methods can be used in the future.

- A *histogram* (frequency distribution plot, density plot) is a graphical representation of the distribution of a dataset. It shows the frequency of specific price or RoR values (or a range of values) in the observed dataset. By plotting the frequency of different return ranges, the histogram can reveal the data's central tendency and scale of variations. This is particularly useful for risk assessment, as a skewed histogram could indicate a higher probability of extreme values, either gains or losses. More details about risk estimations and probability distribution will be discussed in *Chapter 8, Risk Assessment and Volatility Modeling*.

- A *boxplot*, also known as a box and whisker plot, is a standardized way of displaying the dataset based on the following statistical metrics: the minimum, first quartile (Q1), median (Q2), third quartile (Q3), and maximum[1]. In financial analysis, a boxplot is a powerful tool for understanding the spread and skewness of data such as stock prices or RoR, detecting outliers, comparing RoRs, etc. The *box* in *boxplot* represents the *interquartile range (IQR)*, which gives us an idea of how spread out the middle 50% of values are. Usually, the whiskers extend to 1.5 times the IQR, providing a sense of the data's range. Data points outside the whiskers are generally outliers and could indicate volatility or anomalies in the asset's performance.

Execute the following code and try to interpret the resulting financial data visualization:

```
1.  import pandas as pd
2.  import matplotlib.pyplot as plt
3.  import seaborn as sns
4.
5.  # Filter data for 'close' and 'RoR' (Rate of
    Return)
6.  close_data = final_df.filter(like='close').
    drop(columns=['BTC-USD_close'])   # Excluding
    BTC-USD
7.  ror_data = final_df.filter(like='rate')
    # Assuming 'rate' is the RoR
8.  # Using Matplotlib plt
9.  # Line Plot for 'close'
10. plt.figure(figsize=(10, 6))
11. plt.plot(close_data)
12. plt.title('Line Plot for Close Prices
    (Matplotlib)')
13. plt.ylabel('Close Price')
```

---

[1]*A good description of constructing and interpreting a boxplot can be found through open Internet resources such as Wikipedia: https://en.wikipedia.org/wiki/Box_plot*

```
14. plt.xlabel('Date')
15. plt.legend(close_data.columns, loc='upper right')
16. plt.show()
17. # Using Seaborn sns
18. # Boxplot for 'close'
19. plt.figure(figsize=(12, 8))
20. sns.boxplot(data=close_data)
21. plt.title('Boxplot for Close Prices (Seaborn)')
22. plt.ylabel('Close Price')
23. plt.show()
24. # Using Pandas .hist()
25. # Histogram for comparison with the boxplot
    results
26. close_data.hist(bins=50, figsize=(12, 8),
    alpha=0.5)
27. plt.suptitle('Histogram for Close Prices')
28. plt.show()
29. # Histogram for 'RoR'
30. ror_data.hist(bins=50, figsize=(12, 8),
    alpha=0.5)
31. plt.suptitle('Histogram for Rate of Return
    (Pandas)')
32. plt.show()
33. # Performing outlier detection for BTC-USD using
    the boxplot
34. # Create a boxplot
35. btc_close = final_df.filter(like='BTC-USD')
    ['BTC-USD_close']
36. plt.figure(figsize=(10, 6))
37. plt.title('Boxplot for Close Prices of BTC-USD')
```

```
38. plt.boxplot(btc_close)
39. plt.xlabel('BTC-USD')
40. plt.ylabel('Close Price')
41. plt.show()
42. # Get the outliers
43. boxplot = plt.boxplot(btc_close)
44. outliers = boxplot['fliers'][0].get_data()[1]
45. print("\nOutliers from boxplot:", outliers)
46. # Identify outliers for BTC-USD_close manually
47. Q1 = btc_close.quantile(0.25)
48. Q3 = btc_close.quantile(0.75)
49. IQR = Q3 - Q1
50. outliers_manual = btc_close[(btc_close < (Q1 -
    1.5 * IQR)) | (btc_close > (Q3 + 1.5 * IQR))]
51. print("\nOutliers for BTC-USD_close (Manual):",
    outliers_manual)
```

The results (truncated) of the code are:

```
Outliers from boxplot: [45897.57421875 44118.4453125
44338.796875    44575.203125

 44354.63671875 44348.73046875 44500.828125
 46820.4921875

 47128.00390625 47465.73046875 47062.6640625
 45538.67578125

 46281.64453125 45868.94921875 46453.56640625
 46622.67578125

 45555.9921875 ]


Outliers for BTC-USD_close (Manual): Date
2022-01-04    45897.574219
2022-02-08    44118.445312
```

```
(...)
2022-04-04    46622.675781
2022-04-05    45555.992188
Name: BTC-USD_close, dtype: float64
```

The results of the visualization code are presented in *Figures 4.1, 4.2,* and *4.3:*

▣ Line Plot for Close Prices (Matplotlib)—see *Figure 4.1*—provides insight into the price trends over time for the securities in the dataset. The lines show the closing price movement, allowing you to identify periods of growth, decline, or stability visually:

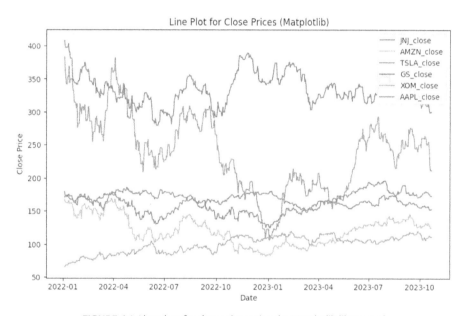

FIGURE 4.1 Line plots for close prices using the Matplotlib library tool

▣ Boxplots for Close Prices (Seaborn)—see *Figure 4.2*—summarizes the distribution of closing prices for each security. It highlights the median, the range (via the IQR), and any outliers that fall beyond the whiskers. These can be useful for comparing volatility and the spread of prices across different securities and can help with outlier detection. Also, in finance, boxplots are used to compare standardized values, such as various securities' RoRs:

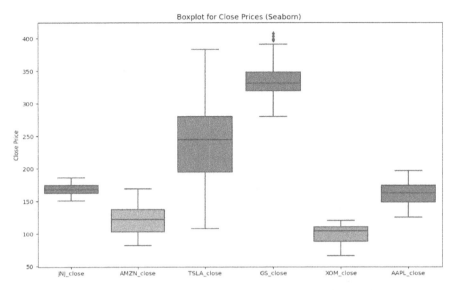

FIGURE 4.2 Boxplots for close prices using the Seaborn library tool

■ Histogram for Close Prices (see *Figure 4.3*), generated in pandas, reveals the frequency of the closing price distribution. This helps to understand the expected price spread around the average value and assess whether stock prices are skewed toward higher or lower values.

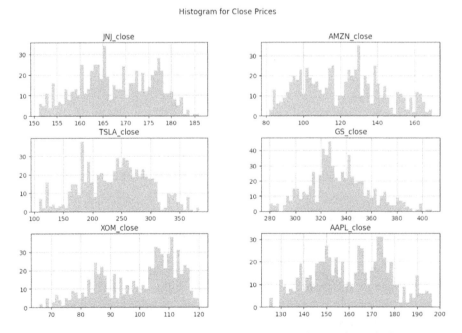

FIGURE 4.3 Histogram for closing prices using the built-in pandas method

The example Python code visualizes and analyzes financial data using the pandas, Matplotlib, and Seaborn libraries as replacement tools. The line plot for close prices was plotted using Matplotlib. The line plot was generated to visualize the trend of close prices over time for multiple assets. The boxplot for close prices was built with Seaborn library functions. It was employed to create a boxplot that summarizes the distribution of the close price values, including outliers. The histograms for close prices and RoR were based on the `.hist()` method. For outlier detection for BTC-USD (a figure with this plot was not provided, just the analytical results), a boxplot variable (object variable) for BTC-USD close prices was created using Matplotlib. The outliers were then identified using the `boxplot['fliers'][0].get_data()[1]` method, and manually calculated using the IQR method. The boxplot and histogram results are closely aligned, showing the same results but in different ways. We can get a high-level view (with a boxplot) and a low-level view (with a histogram) of the dataset, which adds new layers of understanding to analytical results.

Moving Averages in Financial Analysis

As we have already seen, timeline-based calculations are an essential part of financial analysis. After all, investment decisions are based precisely on forecasts of the futures of market states. Data windows become important structures for analysis and modeling. For example, we might look at stock prices for a particular company over a 30-day window. This *window* can slide over the time-series data to provide a rolling view of the behavior of the studied variable. Time-series windows are crucial for identifying seasonal patterns, trends, and anomalies in financial data. They also serve as the basis for various time-based calculations and transformations, such as MA and exponential smoothing.

MA is widely used in time-series analysis, particularly in financial markets, especially for stock price investigation, trend identification, smoothing out price action, and even prediction. It is calculated by taking the average of a set number of periods within a sliding window over the time-series data. There are various types of MA:

- The *simple moving average (SMA)*, similar to the simple mean for calculating the average price, is estimated with k previous data window points. There are $n-k+1$ number of SMAs available, as follows:

$$SMA_1 = (Price_1 + Price_2 + Price_3 + \dots + Price_k) / k$$

$$SMA_2 = (Price_2 + Price_3 + Price_4 + \dots + Price_{k+1}) / k$$

$$\dots$$

$$SMA_{n-k+1} = (Price_{n-k+1} + Price_{n+1-k+1} + Price_{n+2-k+1} + \dots + Price_n) / k$$

- The *cumulative moving average* (*CMA*), unlike the SMA and many other MAs, considers all the data points when calculating the average as a cumulative value. The CMA is calculated as follows:

$$CMA_1 = Price_1$$

$$CMA_2 = (Price_1 + Price_2) / 2$$

$$\dots$$

$$CMA_n = (Price_1 + Price_2 + Price_3 + \dots + Price_n) / n$$

- The *weighted moving average* (*WMA*) is a type of MA that gives different weights to different data points, unlike the SMA, where each data point has an equal weight. This makes it more responsive to a predefined range of price changes and a valuable tool for traders and analysts who want to understand unusual price movements. The standard formula for calculating the WMA for the stock prices dataset is:

$$WMA = \Sigma(w_i \cdot Price_{n-k-i}) / \Sigma w_i, \; \forall i \in [1, n]$$

- The *exponential moving average* (*EMA*) gives more weight to the recent prices and is calculated to react more quickly to price changes. The EMA benefits traders and financial analysts who want to capture the nuances of short-term price volatility. It is often used in conjunction with other types of MA to generate trading signals and identify trends in financial markets. The EMA is also commonly used in technical indicators such as the *moving average convergence divergence* (*MACD*). More details about applying the WMA and EMA will be described in *Chapter 5, Investment and Trading Strategies*. The standard calculation rule for the EMA is as follows:

$$EMA_t = (1 - \alpha) \cdot EMA_{t-1} + \alpha \cdot Price_t$$

Where:

- α is the smoothing factor determining the weight given to the most recent price (the value of α lies between 0 and 1, but $\alpha = 2/(k+1)$ is commonly used).
- $EMA_1 = SMA_1$, which is used to initialize the EMA calculation.

It is easier to understand MA in visualized form. It can be stated that the higher the value of k (bigger data window size), the smoother the time fluctuations in an MA graph. Usually, in financial analysis, we use data windows of 7 (week), 30 (month), 10 (decade), and so on. Execute the following code, and you will understand MA by viewing the resulting charts:

```
1.  # Select data for TSLA
2.  tsla_close = final_df['TSLA_close']
3.  # Window sizes
4.  windows = [30, 90]
5.  # Initialize an empty DataFrame to store the
    results
6.  tsla_ma = pd.DataFrame()
7.  tsla_ma['Actual Prices'] = tsla_close
8.  # Calculate and store SMA and CMA for each window
    size
9.  for window in windows:
10.     tsla_ma[f'SMA_{window}'] = tsla_close.
    rolling(window=window).mean()
11.     tsla_ma[f'CMA_{window}'] = tsla_close.
    expanding(min_periods=window).mean()
12. # Display the DataFrame
13. tsla_ma.plot(figsize=(12, 8))
```

The result of executing this code is shown in *Figure 4.4*:

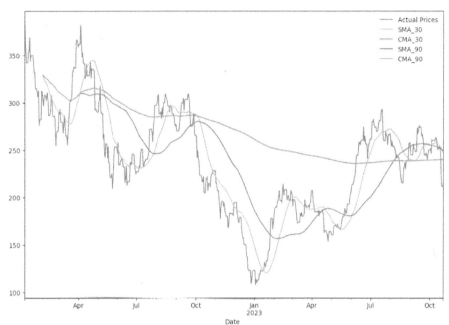

FIGURE 4.4 MA (SMA and CMA) with different TSLA closing price data levels

This Python code demonstrates MA analysis of Tesla's stock close prices using the SMA and CMA. It applies pandas tools for data manipulation and Matplotlib tools for visualization. Two window sizes, 30 and 90, are defined. The SMA and CMA are calculated and stored in the DataFrame for each window size. The SMA provides a simple average over a specific window, while the CMA gives the average from the start to each point in time. As shown in *Figure 4.4*, the larger the window size, the smoother the curve, reducing fluctuations and revealing long-term trends. For instance, SMA_90 and CMA_90 will be smoother than SMA_30 and CMA_30, making identifying general stock price movement trends easier. Thus, the MA tool provides powerful tools for making investment decisions and assessing market trends.

BASICS OF CORRELATION ANALYSIS

Although correlation analysis can be considered part of EDA, it receives much attention in subsequent financial analysis and modeling. We will look at correlation in detail in *Chapter 6, Asset Pricing and Portfolio Management*. Here, however, we will touch on the basics. All tools and indicators presented earlier in this chapter were applied to one variable (price, RoR, etc.). Correlation analysis and visualization tools such as scatter plots are used to study the mutual relationship of two variables.

A positive correlation indicates that the two variables move in the same direction, while a negative correlation means that they move in opposite directions. A correlation close to 0 suggests no linear relationship. The formula for calculating the *Pearson correlation coefficient* between two variables, *Price1* and *Price2*, is:

$$r_{12} = \frac{\sum_{i=1}^{n}\left(Price1_i - Mean_{Price1}\right) \cdot \sum_{i=1}^{n}\left(Price2_i - Mean_{Price2}\right)}{SD_{Price1} \cdot SD_{Price2}}$$

The correlation coefficient values range from −1 to 1. Close to 1 and −1 indicates a perfect positive and negative correlation, but 0 shows no correlation.

A visual representation of the relationship between two variables and the significance of the correlation can be obtained using scatter plot diagrams. The visual representation of the correlation coefficient is shown in *Figure 4.5*. Execute the following code to estimate the correlation matrix of Pearson coefficients for the close price and RoR and plot the basic scatter plots:

```
1.  # Correlation matrix for rates
2.  # This will print the correlation matrix for all
    columns that contain 'rate' in their names.
3.  print("Correlation Matrix for Rates:")
4.  print(final_df.filter(like='rate').corr())
5.  # Scatter plot for TSLA_rate and AAPL_rate
6.  # This will create a scatter plot to visualize
    the relationship between TSLA_rate and AAPL_rate.
7.  final_df.plot.scatter(x='TSLA_rate',
    y='AAPL_rate',
8.                          figsize=(12, 8), alpha=0.5)
9.  plt.title('Scatter Plot of TSLA_rate vs
    AAPL_rate')
```

```
10.  plt.xlabel('TSLA_rate')

11.  plt.ylabel('AAPL_rate')

12.  plt.grid(True)

13.  print("Displaying scatter plot for TSLA_rate vs
     AAPL_rate.")

14.  plt.show()

15.  # Correlation matrix for close prices

16.  # This will print the correlation matrix for all
     columns that contain 'close' in their names.

17.  print("Correlation Matrix for Close Prices:")

18.  print(final_df.filter(like='close').corr())

19.  # Create the pairplot

20.  # This will create a scatter plot matrix
     (pairplot) for each pair of 'close' columns in
     the DataFrame.

21.  g = sns.pairplot(final_df.filter(like='close'))

22.  g.figure.set_size_inches(12, 8)

23.  plt.suptitle('Scatter Plot Matrix of Close
     Prices')

24.  print("Displaying scatter plot matrix for Close
     Prices.")

25.  plt.show()
```

The results (truncated) of the code are:

```
Correlation Matrix for Rates:

              BTC-USD_rate  JNJ_rate  AMZN_rate  TSLA_rate   GS_rate  \
BTC-USD_rate    1.000000   0.080492   0.398333   0.367552   0.264479
JNJ_rate        0.080492   1.000000   0.161277   0.050447   0.258557
AMZN_rate       0.398333   0.161277   1.000000   0.523021   0.492348
TSLA_rate       0.367552   0.050447   0.523021   1.000000   0.349928
```

GS_rate	0.264479	0.258557	0.492348	0.349928	1.000000
XOM_rate	0.153500	0.095439	0.152478	0.087811	0.318666
AAPL_rate	0.379361	0.276900	0.623741	0.586555	0.508701

	XOM_rate	AAPL_rate
BTC-USD_rate	0.153500	0.379361
JNJ_rate	0.095439	0.276900
AMZN_rate	0.152478	0.623741
TSLA_rate	0.087811	0.586555
GS_rate	0.318666	0.508701
XOM_rate	1.000000	0.229913
AAPL_rate	0.229913	1.000000

(...)

The scatter plot (refer to *Figure 4.5*) demonstrates the relationship between Telsa Inc.'s RoR and Apple Inc.'s RoR on one chart in the form of intersection points for each date.

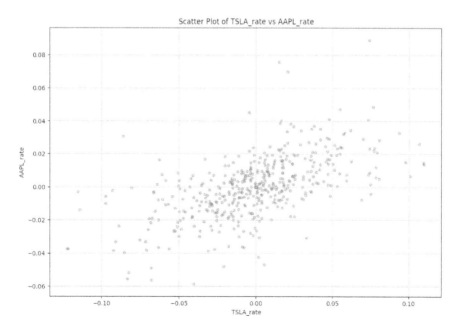

FIGURE 4.5 Scatterplot of TSLA_rate and AAPL_rate values

Figure 4.6 combines the scatter plots for the RoRs for the seven market assets on one canvas. This allows you to simultaneously see all paired dependencies and visualize the distribution histograms for each asset's RoR (along the main diagonal):

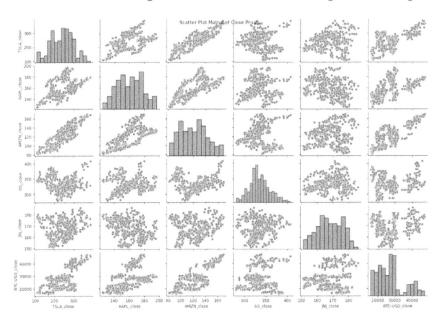

FIGURE 4.6 Seaborn pairplot visualization of the pair relationships for closing price data

This correlation matrix reveals varying degrees of relationships between the RoRs for different assets. Notably, TSLA and AAPL exhibit a strong positive correlation of 0.587, suggesting that they often move in the same direction. On the other hand, JNJ and TSLA have a very low correlation of 0.05, indicating that they are mainly independent regarding the RoR. As shown in *Figure 4.5*, a scatter plot can visualize linear correlations, outliers, and non-linear relationships. We can draw a line through the points to better understand these relationships. This line, in the future, can be used to analytically assess the results of regression analysis, but it is through creating visual representations such as the ones we've seen here that we can enable this visualization.

The pairplot from the Seaborn library offers advanced visualization capabilities for pairwise relationships. As seen in *Figure 4.6*, we can instantly assess the histogram distribution for each variable and their pairwise scatter plots. A pairplot helps identify significant relationships without using additional statistical methods. For example, it helps to distinguish the need for data segmentation into groups (as with the pair TSLA and BTC), detect non-linear relationships (as with the pair AMZN and GS), or detect the complete absence of a pairwise relationship (as with the pair AAPL and JNJ).

CONCLUSION

This chapter has highlighted the ETL patterns tailored explicitly for financial data. We explored the primary stages of data importing, cleaning, and structuring, which are crucial for setting the stage for any in-depth analysis. The *inspect*, *sort*, and *handle NaN and duplicates* stages are essential. Additionally, we discussed the importance of data transformation and the creation of new features, which can offer fresh perspectives and insights into the financial markets. These ETL processes are the start of any financial data analysis, ensuring that the data is reliable and structured in a way that is conducive to advanced analytical techniques.

EDA for financial data focuses on descriptive statistics and data visualization as the first line of financial investigations. Descriptive statistics metrics provide a snapshot of the data's central tendency, variability, and distribution, offering a quick yet insightful overview of what the data entails. We also delved into data visualization, discussing the utility of plots such as histograms and boxplots. These graphical representations are potent tools for visually inspecting data, identifying trends, spotting outliers, and suggesting areas that may warrant further investigation.

MA took center stage as we discussed its importance in trend analysis within financial markets. We covered various types of MA, including the SMA, WMA, and EMA. Each of these has its use cases, but they all serve the primary function of smoothing out price data to create a single flowing line, making it easier to identify the direction of the trend. Understanding these different types of MA and their applications can significantly enhance your toolkit for financial analysis.

Finally, we touched upon the basics of correlation analysis, emphasizing its role in understanding the relationships between different financial variables. We introduced the concept of the scatter plot as a visualization tool that can help identify the type and strength of the relationship between two variables. Correlation analysis is critical in portfolio management, risk assessment, and identifying investment opportunities by understanding how different assets are interrelated.

QUESTIONS

1. What are the differences between *extract, transform, and load* (ETL) and *exploratory data analysis* (EDA)?

2. What is the primary objective of EDA in the context of financial data?

3. Describe basic ETL patterns for financial data processing.

4. What additional ETL procedures do you know?

5. What are the essential problems when importing and structuring a DataFrame for financial analysis?

6. What are the key methods for creating new features in financial datasets?

7. What are descriptive statistics and why are they important in financial analysis?

8. Name three key metrics used to measure central tendency in a dataset.

9. What are the deviation metrics, and how are they used in assessing financial data?

10. What is the boxplot chart, and what information does it provide?

11. Explain the significance of basic statistical data visualization in EDA for finance.

12. What is a moving average and how is it used in financial analysis?

13. Describe the basics of correlation analysis.

14. How can scatter plots help with understanding the relationship between two variables?

KEY TERMS

- *Descriptive statistics* are summary statistics metrics that quantitatively describe or summarize features of a dataset. They typically offer a simple overview of the main quantitative aspects of the data, such as central tendency, deviation, range, type of variables, etc.

- *Central tendency metrics* describe the center position of a distribution for a dataset. The key metrics include the mean, median, and mode.

- *Deviation metrics* are measures that describe the spread or dispersion of a dataset. *Standard deviation (SD)*, *variance (Var)*, and *coefficient of variation (CV)* are commonly used deviation metrics.
- *Financial assets investment risk* for exchange market data refers to the potential for loss in the value of financial assets traded on stock exchanges. It is typically measured based on the deviation metrics for stock prices and indicates the potential volatility of the returns.
- A *boxplot* is a graphical representation of data that displays the distribution and spread of a dataset, as well as its quartiles and outliers.
- *Correlation* is a statistical measure that describes the extent to which two variables change together. A positive correlation indicates that as one variable increases, the other also increases.
- A *scatter plot* is the graphical representation of values for two variables as points on a two-dimensional plot. It is often used to determine a relationship between the two variables.

REFERENCES

- *Mukhiya, S. K. and Ahmed, U. (2020). Hands-On Exploratory Data Analysis with Python. Packt Publishing.*
- *Gupta, P. (2021). Practical Data Science with Jupyter [Paperback]. BPB Publications.*
- *Dixit, R. (2022). Data Analysis with Python. [Paperback]. BPB Publications.*

5

INVESTMENT AND TRADING STRATEGIES

INTRODUCTION

This chapter offers a general overview of investment and trading strategies. We will uncover some examples of technical, fundamental, and graphical analysis and their application to trading strategies. Our discussions on fundamental financial analysis are based on real-world applications and show insights mainly gained through practice. We will describe and dissect fundamental metrics such as *return on equity (ROE)*, *earnings per share (EPS)*, and the *price-to-earnings (P/E) ratio*. We will go through examples devoted to Python-powered visualization and unveil the techniques for bringing financial data to life. This chapter will show how financial market data can be represented and interpreted. With a hands-on introduction to *TA-Lib*, this chapter equips you with the theoretical knowledge and practical tools to test and refine your strategies. The chapter is peppered with real-life data (based on the tools presented in *Chapter 4, Exploratory Data Analysis for Finance*) behind investment strategies. All the examples give real-world information from stock and other financial markets, bridging the gap between theory and practice and ensuring you are ready for the dynamic world of trading.

In this chapter, we apply previously reviewed Python statistical and visualization tools to investigate investment asset prices and trends. You will learn how to use analytical tools to support investment decisions.

STRUCTURE

This chapter covers the following topics:

- Investment strategies in the financial assets markets
- Fundamental analysis
- Graphical analysis with Python
- Technical analysis metrics and tools

OBJECTIVES

By the end of this chapter, you will have learned a lot about investment and analytical and trading strategies, with the ability to integrate technical, fundamental, and graphical analysis into your trading strategy. You will have navigated the intricacies of core investment principles and metrics, receiving practical insights to improve your fundamental analysis skills. Armed with Python's visualization tools and advanced candlestick charts, you will be able to bring financial market data to life, identifying significant patterns and interpreting market indicators. Engaging with essential technical analysis tools will give you the practical experience to generate, test, and refine effective trading strategies. This chapter will use real-world market data to cement your understanding, ensuring you are well prepared to face the dynamic nature of trading, equipped with a thorough understanding of risk and return dynamics, and ready to make informed decisions using sophisticated analytical tools.

INVESTMENT STRATEGIES IN THE FINANCIAL ASSETS MARKETS

As we know from *Chapter 1, Getting Started with Python for Finance*, there are a lot of different financial assets. Therefore, investment strategies of profitability using these asset markets are both an art and a science, aiming to balance risk and reward. Every trader has their own collection of strategies and tools to achieve this goal and get enough profit alongside the associated risks. Each strategy involves a unique blend of financial instruments, allocation techniques, and analysis methods. The strategies, however, have one thing in common: processing a sufficiently large amount of information to justify investment decisions is necessary. Python's analytical tools can help investors achieve their objectives.

A generalized idea of the existing investment strategies for decision-making by traders in the capital market is presented in *Figure 5.1*. We have not listed every possible strategy; we have just shown many existing approaches classified into three groups that determine the features of strategic decision-making.

Investment strategies encompass the diverse approaches and methods investors employ to maximize the performance of their financial assets in the markets.

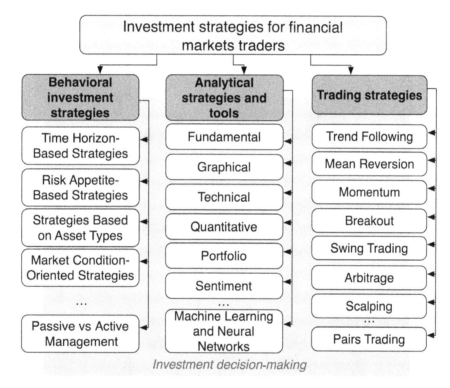

FIGURE 5.1 Classifications of the investment strategies for a financial market trader

As shown in *Figure 5.1*, investment strategies, chosen based on the personal preferences of traders and other decision-makers, include:

- *Time horizon-based strategies*:
  - *Short-term (intraday) trading*: Positions open and close within minutes of a single trading day, aligning with rapid market movements.
  - *Medium-term trading*: Trades span several days to weeks, bridging intraday's immediacy and the long-term strategy's patience.

- *Long-term trading*: Investments are nurtured over several months to years, often focused on fundamental value.

- *Risk appetite-based strategies*:
  - *Conservative*: Preferring lower-risk investments for steadier returns
  - *Balanced*: Combining risk and safety, typically by integrating equities and bonds
  - *Aggressive*: Pursuing higher-potential returns by accepting more significant risks, commonly through volatile assets

- *Strategies based on the type of assets*:
  - *Single asset class*: Specializing in one asset type, such as equities, bonds, or commodities
  - *Multi-asset class*: Diversifying across different asset classes to mitigate risk
  - *Currency pairs*: Concentrating solely on the foreign exchange market

- *Market condition-oriented strategies*:
  - *Bull market strategies*: Devised to appreciate market conditions
  - *Bear market strategies*: Crafted for depreciating market conditions
  - *Sideways market strategies*: Ideal for markets lacking a clear trend

- *Passive vs active management*:
  - *Passive investing*: Emulating market indices with minimal trading
  - *Active investing*: Actively managing a portfolio through rigorous research and strategy

Therefore, this behavioral *investment strategy* can be regarded as a multidimensional framework reflecting the investor's behavior, financial goals, risk tolerance, time commitment, market perspective, and other subjective feelings. These strategies provide a structured approach to navigating the complexities of the financial markets. Whether an investor is swayed by short-term market dynamics, aiming for medium-term growth, or settling in for the long game with a long-term investment horizon, their strategy is tailored to their investment profile.

The trading strategy is the second part of the investment strategy in the financial market. A trading strategy in the financial markets refers to a systematic plan formulated by traders to buy and sell financial instruments to generate predetermined outcomes. These strategies are predicated on various market analysis tools and investor behavioral preferences. Here is a brief overview of each strategy mentioned:

- *Trend following* involves identifying and riding the momentum of assets moving in a significant and sustained direction, capitalizing on existing trends.

- *Mean reversion* is a strategy based on the phenomenon that financial asset prices tend to return to their average, or mean, level after a deviation period.

- *Momentum's* strategy seeks to capitalize on assets exhibiting strong movement, entering trades toward momentum until they show reversal signals.

- *Breakout* refers to when the traders using this strategy enter the market when the price breaks through a predefined resistance or support level, often indicating a significant move away from the previous range.

- *Swing trading* involves attempting to capture gains by holding positions for a period ranging from overnight to several weeks, taking advantage of the swing in market prices.

- *Arbitrage* aims to profit from the price differences of the same financial asset in different markets or in various forms.

- *Scalping* is a high-volume trading strategy that aims to make numerous small profits on minor price changes. It typically involves holding for seconds or minutes.

- The *fundamental trading* strategy is based on making trading decisions around critical economic events and data releases and analyzing how they will affect asset prices.

- *Pairs trading* involves simultaneously buying and selling two correlating assets when their relationship deviates from the historical norm, expecting it to revert to the mean, allowing for profit on the divergence.

Therefore, a *trading strategy* is a customized approach designed to assist an investor in making decisions about buying and selling securities in the financial market. It combines various individual tactics to create a comprehensive plan for achieving the investment objectives.

The third facet of a comprehensive investment strategy is using various analytical methodologies and tools. Analytical investment strategies typically include:

- *Fundamental analysis*: This involves assessing an asset's intrinsic value by examining financial statements, economic indicators, company health, and other quantifiable factors.
- *Technical analysis*: This predicts future price movements by analyzing past market data, mainly price and volume.
- *Quantitative analysis*: This strategy employs complex mathematical models to detect trading opportunities, often utilizing statistical patterns.
- *Portfolio analysis*: This process aims to evaluate and adjust the composition and performance of an investment portfolio to maximize returns relative to risk.
- *Sentiment analysis*: This method assesses the market's mood by analyzing market commentary, news, and other qualitative indicators to gauge the trading behavior of market participants.
- *Machine learning (ML) and neural networks (NNs)*: These are cutting-edge computational methods used to discern intricate patterns and predict market trends, which can be beyond the capacity of traditional analysis.

There are a lot of other analytical tools that are arising. This is not an exhaustive list.

So, the analytical investment strategy is a systematic approach to making investment decisions using different analysis methods. These methods are the main tools for an investor. It is important to understand that various analytical investment strategies can be combined to fit an investor's goals, risk profile, and trading approach. These strategies work together to provide a strong framework for investors to navigate the complex and unpredictable financial markets.

The critical thread of rigorous analysis connects the complex strategies used in the financial market. This necessitates a robust foundation in managerial decision-making processes. Python emerges as a powerful ally to facilitate this, offering a spectrum of basic and advanced tools ranging from mathematical and statistical functions to graphical and specialized libraries. The subsequent chapters will interweave a comprehensive exploration of the analytical instruments outlined in *Figure 5.1*, enhancing your understanding and application of these tools. Specifically, *Chapter 6, Asset Pricing and Portfolio Management*, will be dedicated to the nuances of portfolio analysis, laying out strategies for balancing and optimizing various investments. *Chapter 7, Time-Series Analysis and Financial Data Forecasting*, and *Chapter 8, Risk Assessment and Volatility Modeling*, will venture into the quantitative methods of forecasting profitability and assessing risks, which are tools that are imperative for astute market engagement. Building on this foundation, *Chapters 9* and *10* will propel us into the forefront of financial technology, harnessing ML to sharpen profitability forecasting and risk estimations.

FUNDAMENTAL ANALYSIS

Fundamental analysis is a key tool in finance for making smart investment choices. It goes beyond just looking at prices and helps you understand the actual value of an asset. It is vital for long-term strategies and involves looking at various financial indicators and metrics. In the stock market, fundamental analysis often examines a company's financial statements, management effectiveness, industry health, and market conditions. Investors scrutinize earnings reports, balance sheets, cash flow statements, and other economic indicators. These metrics paint a detailed picture of the company's performance, growth potential, and stability.

When the fundamental analysis tools are applied to the forex market, it shifts focus on economic indicators, interest rates, monetary policies, and geopolitical events for each country and the world economy. Currency traders analyze economic data releases, central bank decisions, and political stability to forecast currency strength or weakness. This type of analysis may include examining GDP growth rates, employment statistics, trade balances, and inflation rates to determine the underlying value of a currency.

Fundamental analysis in the rapidly developing cryptocurrency world may show the central concept for the Bitcoin market, technical blockchain events, hackers' activity, and other metrics, such as the financial statements for the stock market. Analytical tools are manipulated with factors such as the coin's technology, the development team's track record, network activity, new technological developments, and overall market adoption. The aim is to ascertain a cryptocurrency's long-term viability and potential market penetration.

Acknowledging that fundamental analysis has no one-size-fits-all technique is crucial. Each market holds a unique set of variables and requires specialized methodologies. There are no specific Python tools for this, just the use of standard analytical tools such as pandas data manipulation, Seaborn visualization, and statistical methods application. For instance, universal Python tools and data libraries help to estimate essential metrics such as the P/E ratio, ROE, debt-to-equity ratio, and free cash flow. These metrics offer valuable insights into a company's profitability, debt levels, efficiency, and growth potential. Execute the following code to analyze the financial data of Tesla Inc. and Apple Inc.:

```
1.  # Fundamental Analysis Function by the ticker of
    Yahoo Finance
2.  # NOTE: yf.Ticker() stores data for the last 4
    years only.
3.  def calculate_fundamentals(ticker_symbol):
4.      # Fetching financials for the ticker
5.      ticker = yf.Ticker(ticker_symbol)
6.      financials = ticker.financials
7.      balance_sheet = ticker.balance_sheet
8.
9.      # Retrieving basic earnings per share (EPS)
10.     eps = financials.loc['Basic EPS']
11.
12.     # Calculating the Return on Equity (ROE)
13.     net_income = financials.loc['Net Income']
14.     stockholders_equity = balance_sheet.
    loc['Stockholders Equity']
15.     roe = ( net_income / stockholders_equity ).
    dropna()
16.
17.     # Fetching historical price data for the
    ticker
18.     start_date = eps.index[-1].strftime
    ('%Y-%m-%d')
19.     end_date = eps.index[0].strftime('%Y-%m-%d')
20.     history = ticker.history(start=start_date,
21.                              end=end_date,
22.                              interval='1d')
23.
```

```
24.      # Removing time zone information for ease of
    comparison
25.      eps.index = eps.index.tz_localize(None)
26.      roe.index = roe.index.tz_localize(None)
27.      history.index = history.index.
    tz_localize(None)
28.
29.      # Creating a date range that includes
    weekends
30.      full_date_range = pd.date_range(start=eps.
    index.min(),
31.                              end=eps.index.max(),
32.                                    freq='D')
33.
34.      # Reindexing the dataframe to include the
    full date range with weekends
35.      history_full = history.reindex(full_date_
    range,
36.                                 method='ffill')
37.
38.      # Fetching the closing prices from history
    that match # the dates in eps
39.      close_prices = history_full.loc[history_full.
    index.isin(eps.index),
40.                                    'Close']
41.
42.      # Calculating the Price to Earnings (P/E)
    ratio
43.      pe_ratio = close_prices / eps
```

```python
44.
45.    return {
46.        'ticker': ticker_symbol,
47.        'eps': eps,
48.        'roe': roe,
49.        'pe_ratio': pe_ratio
50.    }
51. #######################################
52. # Apply the function for AAPL and TSLA
53. aapl_financial_ratios = calculate_
    fundamentals('AAPL')
54. tsla_financial_ratios = calculate_
    fundamentals('TSLA')
55.
56. # Print the results for Apple
57. print(f"{aapl_financial_ratios['ticker']} Basic
    EPS:")
58. print(aapl_financial_ratios['eps'])
59. print(f"\n{aapl_financial_ratios['ticker']}
    Return on Equity (ROE):")
60. print(aapl_financial_ratios['roe'])
61. print(f"\n{aapl_financial_ratios['ticker']} P/E
    Ratio on EPS Dates:")
62. print(aapl_financial_ratios['pe_ratio'])
63.
64. # Print the results for Tesla
65. print(f"\n{tsla_financial_ratios['ticker']} Basic
    EPS:")
66. print(tsla_financial_ratios['eps'])
```

```
67.  print(f"\n{tsla_financial_ratios['ticker']}
     Return on Equity (ROE):")
68.  print(tsla_financial_ratios['roe'])
69.  print(f"\n{tsla_financial_ratios['ticker']} P/E
     Ratio on EPS Dates:")
70.  print(tsla_financial_ratios['pe_ratio'])
```

The results of the code are as follows:

```
AAPL Basic EPS:
2023-09-30     6.16
2022-09-30     6.15
2021-09-30     5.67
2020-09-30     3.31
Name: Basic EPS, dtype: object

AAPL Return on Equity (ROE):
2023-09-30     1.56076
2022-09-30     1.969589
2021-09-30     1.500713
2020-09-30     0.878664
dtype: object

AAPL P/E Ratio on EPS Dates:
2020-09-30     34.366723
2021-09-30     24.670486
2022-09-30     22.339021
2023-09-30     27.793832
Freq: A-SEP, dtype: object
```

```
TSLA Basic EPS:
2022-12-31          4.02
2021-12-31      1.866667
2020-12-31      0.246667
2019-12-31     -0.326667
Name: Basic EPS, dtype: object

TSLA Return on Equity (ROE):
2022-12-31      0.281474
2021-12-31      0.182815
2020-12-31      0.031046
2019-12-31     -0.130251
dtype: object

TSLA P/E Ratio on EPS Dates:
2019-12-31     -85.373381
2020-12-31     953.606796
2021-12-31     188.710686
2022-12-31      30.641791
Freq: A-DEC, dtype: object
```

The financial fundamentals shown for Apple Inc. and Tesla Inc. present essential metrics used by investors to assess a company's value and performance.

EPS directly measures a company's profitability. It is calculated by dividing the company's net income by the outstanding shares. A higher EPS indicates greater profitability. Looking at the AAPL data, the EPS has increased from 2020 to 2023, suggesting growth in profitability. For TSLA, there has been a notable increase in EPS over the years, moving from a negative value in 2019 (indicating a loss) to a positive value by 2022, showing profitability.

ROE is a financial performance measure calculated by dividing net income by shareholders' equity. It can be interpreted as the return a company generates on the money shareholders have invested. High ROE values typically indicate a company is efficient at generating profits from its equity. For AAPL, the

ROE has consistently been above 1, showing a robust return per dollar of equity. In contrast, TSLA's ROE shows a significant improvement from negative to positive, highlighting a turnaround in profitability.

The P/E ratio compares a company's share price to its EPS. It is a valuation metric that shows how much investors are willing to pay per dollar of earnings. A high P/E might suggest a company's stock is overvalued, or investors expect high future growth rates. AAPL's P/E ratios indicate that investors may have high expectations for the company's future growth, particularly when you notice a rise in the ratio from 2022 to 2023. TSLA's P/E ratio has experienced significant fluctuations, with an exceptionally high value in 2020, possibly indicating investors expected extraordinary growth.

NOTE *The code example attempts to reindex the history DataFrame using full_date_range, a date range without time zone information. An error may occur because the history still has time zone information attached to its index. Removing the time zone information from the indices is necessary to avoid those errors.*

These numbers show how the companies have been performing and how the market values them. It is essential to understand these figures in the context of the company's overall strategy, the economic environment, and the sector in which it operates. Remember, no single financial metric should be used to evaluate a company's financial health.

GRAPHICAL ANALYSIS WITH PYTHON

Graphical analysis of financial market data is the first step for any investor looking to gain a nuanced understanding of price dynamics. These visual representations are not just charts; they are the canvas where the market's story is told, capturing the sentiments, fluctuations, and trends that dictate the financial landscape. We already used universal statistical visualization tools for close price data in *Chapter 4, Exploratory Data Analysis for Finance*, but now we need to describe specific tools for stock and other exchange market datasets.

BASIC STOCK GRAPHICS TOOLS

Starting with the basics of stock graphics, we have two essential elements: bar charts and candlestick charts. These components concisely offer a lot of information. Bar charts are presented with simple vertical lines and horizontal ticks, providing details about the open and close prices within a specified time frame. On the other hand, candlestick charts add a visual dimension to this chart by vividly illustrating the interaction between buyers and sellers. The thick bodies of the candlesticks characterize the difference between the open and close prices (green, white, or empty if the market has risen; red or black if the market has fallen), and the wicks (high and low prices) provide a clear understanding of the emotional dynamics of the market, depicting the ongoing struggle between various market forces.

The following custom `ohlc_plot_candles()` function can be used to show candlestick charts by applying standard Matplotlib tools[1] (using `assets`, which is a dataset with OHLC data for the AAPL, TSLA, AMZN, JNJ, GS, and BTC-USD tickers. For details on the generation of this dataset, please look at the Python code for this chapter in the appendix):

```
1.  def ohlc_plot_candles(df, window,
2.                          figsize=(12, 6),
3.                          title='Candlestick Chart'):
4.      sample = df.iloc[-window:]
5.      plt.figure(figsize=figsize)
6.      plt.title(title)
7.      for i in range(len(sample)):
8.          # Plotting the wicks
9.          plt.vlines(x=i,
10.                     ymin=sample.iloc[i]['Low'],
11.                     ymax=sample.iloc[i]['High'],
12.                     color='black', linewidth=1)
13.
14.          # Plotting the candle's body (open to close)
```

[1]*The algorithm for this code is taken from the book Sofien Kaabar (2023) Mastering Financial Pattern Recognition: Finding and Back-Testing Candlestick Patterns with Python, 1st Edition. O'Reilly Media.*

```
15.          if sample.iloc[i]['Close'] > sample.
    iloc[i]['Open']:
16.                # Market rise (bullish)
17.              plt.vlines(x=i, ymin=sample.iloc[i]
    ['Open'],
18.                          ymax=sample.iloc[i]
    ['Close'],
19.                          color='green', linewidth=4)
20.        elif sample.iloc[i]['Close'] < sample.
    iloc[i]['Open']:
21.                # Market fall (bearish)
22.              plt.vlines(x=i, ymin=sample.iloc[i]
    ['Close'],
23.                          ymax=sample.iloc[i]['Open'],
24.                          color='red', linewidth=4)
25.        else:
26.                # No price movement (doji)
27.              plt.vlines(x=i, ymin=sample.iloc[i]
    ['Close'],
28.                          ymax=sample.iloc[i]
    ['Open'] + 0.00003,
29.                          color='black',
    linewidth=4)
30.    plt.grid()
31.    plt.show()
32.
33. #############################################
34. ohlc_plot_candles(asset, 100, title='TSLA')
```

This code provides a practical introduction to a candlestick, or Japanese candlestick, chart, with the outcome illustrated in *Figure 5.2*. The chart is constructed to provide a visual representation of price movements within a specific time frame. A candlestick in these charts is composed of a body and wicks. The *body's length* indicates the difference between the opening and closing prices, while the wicks show the highs and lows. The color of the candle body reflects market sentiment: green, white, or empty for bullish periods and red or black for bearish periods. The *wicks* or *shadows* portray the price extremes, with the top wick showing the highest and the bottom wick the lowest traded prices within the time frame:

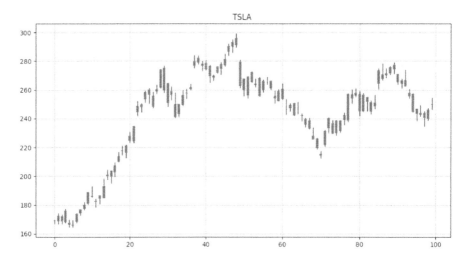

FIGURE 5.2 Candlestick charts for Telsa Inc. stocks over 100 days

A bar chart implements similar principles to the candlestick chart. A bar chart illustrates the price dynamics of assets using a series of vertical bars, each representing price movement within a given time frame. The top of each bar denotes the highest price on the timeline, while the bottom indicates the lowest price. A small horizontal line (tick) on the left side of the bar shows the opening price, and the tick on the right side shows the closing price. The function for creating bar charts (`ohlc_plot_candles_volumes()`) is detailed in the Python code for this chapter in the appendix. Since the construction logic and the volume of information for candles and bars are identical, the choice between these visual representations comes down to the investor's preference. Hereafter, the emphasis will be placed precisely on candlestick charts.

An essential enhancement to the functions of candlestick price analysis of financial instruments is the inclusion of *trade volumes*, which illustrate the strengthening or weakening of trends. Execute the following code to construct a candlestick chart with the indicated trading volumes:

```python
1.  def ohlc_plot_candles_volumes(df, window,
2.                                figsize=(12, 6),
3.                                title='Candlestick
    Chart with Volumes'):
4.      sample = df.iloc[-window:]
5.      fig, ax1 = plt.subplots(figsize=figsize)
6.      # Create a second y-axis to plot the volume
7.      ax2 = ax1.twinx()
8.      # Define the maximum volume to scale the
    y-axis of volume bars
9.      max_vol = sample['Volume'].max()
10.     for i in range(len(sample)):
11.         # Plotting the Candlechart
12.         ax1.vlines(x=i, ymin=sample.iloc[i]
    ['Low'],
13.                       ymax=sample.iloc[i]['High'],
14.                       color='black', linewidth=1)
15.         if sample.iloc[i]['Close'] > sample.
    iloc[i]['Open']:
16.             ax1.vlines(x=i, ymin=sample.iloc[i]
    ['Open'],
17.                           ymax=sample.iloc[i]
    ['Close'],
18.                           color='green', linewidth=4)
```

```
19.          elif sample.iloc[i]['Close'] < sample.
    iloc[i]['Open']:
20.              ax1.vlines(x=i, ymin=sample.iloc[i]
    ['Close'],
21.                      ymax=sample.iloc[i]
    ['Open'],
22.                      color='red', linewidth=4)
23.          else:
24.              ax1.vlines(x=i, ymin=sample.iloc[i]
    ['Close'],
25.                      ymax=sample.iloc[i]
    ['Open'] + 0.00003,
26.                      color='black',
    linewidth=4)
27.          # Plotting the Volume bars
28.          color = ('green' if sample.iloc[i]
    ['Close'] >
29.              sample.iloc[i]['Open'] else
    'red')
30.          ax2.bar(i, sample.iloc[i]['Volume'],
31.                  color=color, alpha=0.3)
32.      # Adjust the y limit of the second axis to
    fit the volume bars
33.      ax2.set_ylim(0, max_vol*5)
34.      ax2.set_ylabel("Volume")
35.      # Setting x-axis labels to the dates from
        # the DataFrame's index
36.      ax1.set_xticks(range(len(sample)))
37.      ax1.set_xticklabels([date.strftime('%Y-%m-%d')
38.                  for date in sample.
    index],
```

```
39.                                    rotation=90, ha='right')
40.      ax1.grid()
41.      ax1.set_title(title)
42.      plt.show()
43. #############################################
44. ohlc_plot_candles_volumes(asset, 50,
    title=ticker)
```

The code result for the TSLA ticker is shown in *Figure 5.3*.

As observed from *Figure 5.2*, over the 100 days considered, the price fluctuations of Tesla Inc. shares were distributed as follows: from period 0 to 50, a clear upward trend was evident (most candles are green), indicating a bullish trend. There were short-term reversals between periods 30 to 50; after that, from day 50, an intermediate bearish trend was formed. From day 70 to 90, bullish tendencies predominated once again. Referring to *Figure 5.3*, with detailed *dates* and *volumes*, we can also see that the trend of reversals on August 18-21 and September 11 was accompanied by modest increases in trading volumes. This typically signifies a strengthening of market trends. Psychological factors often support this inference; when a certain psychological threshold is crossed (such as a support or resistance level), more investors engage in trading:

FIGURE 5.3 Candlestick charts with volume data for Tesla Inc. stocks over 50 days

Regrettably, the mentioned conclusions can only be drawn from past periods. A prolonged period of stock market research, however, has facilitated the development of a comprehensive toolkit for forecasting trends, especially the moment of reversal. This includes using support and resistance lines, additional *moving averages (MAs)*, and other indicator lines on the chart; graphical analysis patterns; and so on.

Python's commonly used and specialized libraries are potent tools for graphical analysts and market researchers. One such specialized library is mplfinance, an extension of Matplotlib tailored specifically for financial data visualization. For those who wish to engage in hands-on experience and gain practical proficiency, a detailed exploration of mplfinance is highly recommended. The official repository and documentation provide in-depth insights and usage examples; they can be accessed from mplfinance's GitHub page: *https://github.com/matplotlib/mplfinance*. The installation process of this library has been covered previously in *Chapter 1, Getting Started with Python for Finance*. To illustrate the application of mplfinance and its capabilities, consider the following example, which generates a complex price chart for Tesla Inc. over 50 days:

```
1.  import mplfinance as mpf
2.  df = asset.iloc[-50:, 1:]
3.  # Rolling high/low for potential resistance/
    support
4.  rolling_max = df['High'].rolling(window=20,
5.                                   min_periods=1).
    max()
6.  rolling_min = df['Low'].rolling(window=20,
7.                                   min_periods=1).
    min()
8.  # Highest and lowest prices as resistance/support
9.  potential_resistance = np.max(rolling_max)
```

```
10.  potential_support = np.min(rolling_min)

11.  # Horizontal lines for resistance and support
     levels

12.  resistance_line = [potential_resistance] *
     len(df.index)

13.  support_line = [potential_support] * len(df.
     index)

14.  # Addplot for support and resistance lines

15.  apdict = [mpf.make_addplot(resistance_line,
     color='g',

16.                              linestyle='dashdot',
     width=2),

17.          mpf.make_addplot(support_line,
     color='r',

18.                              linestyle='dashdot',
     width=2)]

19.  # Plot with Moving Averages, volume, support, and
     resistance

20.  mpf.plot(df, type='candle', mav=(7, 14, 30),
     volume=True,

21.           figsize=(12, 6), addplot=apdict,

22.           title='Candlestick Chart - ' + ticker)

23.  # Display the plot

24.  plt.show()
```

The result of this code execution is shown in *Figure 5.4*:

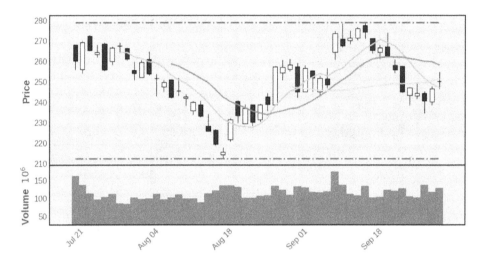

Candlestick Chart with Support/Resistance - TSLA

FIGURE 5.4 Candlestick chart with additional analytical tools applied to Tesla Inc. stocks over 50 days

The support and resistance lines in *Figure 5.4* clearly show additional confirmation of the trend reversal when they touch, which is a strong signal. Support levels act as a price floor where buying interest exceeds selling pressure. Resistance levels serve as a ceiling where selling pressure surpasses buying momentum. Identifying these levels is both an art and a science, offering traders crucial entry and exit points. Various MAs can signal reversals, aiding in executing specific trading strategies.

This example underscores the available power of mplfinance. By following these examples and experimenting with the library's features, you can improve your data visualization skills, paving the way for more advanced graphical analysis and research in financial markets.

GRAPHICAL ANALYSIS PATTERNS

Patterns within graphical analysis (or candlestick chart patterns) are like a visual dialect of market language. Classic patterns, such as head and shoulders, triangles, and double tops and bottoms, are the core signals of potential trend reversals or continuations. They are the lexicon through which seasoned traders anticipate and strategize. The following are some of the most well-known patterns to support trading strategies (the pattern charts are presented in the code appendix to this chapter):

- The *head and shoulders pattern* shows as a baseline with three peaks. The middle peak is the highest, and the two outside peaks are close in height. In the pattern, the price seems to rise to a peak and then decline, followed by a rise above the previous peak and then a decline again, and, finally, a rise that does not surpass the height of the second peak before declining again. This pattern is often interpreted as a reversal signal.

- The *inverse head and shoulders pattern* is the opposite of the head and shoulders pattern, typically signaling a downward trend reversal. It consists of a trough (head), with a peak on either side (shoulders), where the head is the lowest point. The pattern in the provided data shows a decline to a low point, a slight rise, followed by a decline to a lower point, and a rise again that goes higher than the first peak, suggesting a potential trend reversal to the upside.

- The *double top and double bottom patterns* are characterized by two consecutive peaks of approximately equal height with a moderate trough in between, suggesting an impending reversal from a bullish to a bearish market. On the other hand, the double bottom consists of two consecutive troughs approximately equal in depth, with a peak in between, indicating a potential reversal from a rising market to a falling market. This pattern shows these two peaks and troughs, suggesting critical points where the market sentiment could change.

- *Triangle patterns* indicate a continuation or a reversal and come in three forms. A horizontal top and an ascending lower line form the ascending triangle pattern. This pattern in the data suggests higher lows, but the highs remain consistent. It typically indicates accumulation and a potential bullish breakout. The descending triangle pattern has a horizontal bottom and a descending top line. The highs are getting lower, but the lows remain consistent. This may suggest selling pressure and a potential bearish breakout. The symmetrical triangle pattern describes the highs, and the lows converge to a point, creating a symmetrical triangle. It is a period of consolidation before the price breaks out.

- *Flags and pennants patterns* are short-term continuation patterns that mark a slight consolidation before continuing the previous move. The flag pattern resembles a rectangle sloped against the prevailing trend and is characterized by parallel trendlines that form a rectangular flag shape. The given data indicates a brief consolidation period after a sharp price movement. The pennant pattern is like the flag but has converging trendlines, forming a small symmetrical triangle resembling a pennant. In this pattern, the price consolidates narrowly after a significant move, suggesting continuation.

- The *cup and handle pattern* resembles the shape of a teacup with a handle on its right side. It signifies a period of consolidation followed by a breakout. In this pattern, the price gradually declines to form the cup, followed by a smaller bullish retracement, forming the handle, indicating a bullish continuation trend may follow.

These patterns are a shorthand traders use to predict future market behavior based on historical price movements. Visualizing them can provide valuable insights into market psychology and potential price movements. The visual details of these patterns are presented in the Python code for this chapter in the appendix.

TECHNICAL ANALYSIS METRICS AND TOOLS

Technical analysis is an important tool for investment and trading strategy support. It involves signal indicators and MA to predict future price movements. Now, we will delve into critical technical analysis indicators with Python. We will also cover visualization tools enabling traders to interpret data through graphical representations, improving the investment decision-making process.

There are many indicators that traders and analysts use to gain insights into past price movements and predict future ones. By analyzing and visualizing these indicators, you can more effectively recognize potential market trends and signals. Let us observe some of them:

- MA is a smoothing mechanism for stock price data, giving traders a clearer view of the trend's direction over different time frames. The different versions, such as short-term and long-term MAs, can signal impending bullish or bearish crossovers, often triggering strategic moves by traders (as in *Figure 5.4*).
- *Moving average convergence divergence (MACD)* is calculated by reducing the 26-period EMA on the 12-period EMA.

- *Bollinger Bands* consist of a middle band (an n-period SMA), an upper band, and a lower band at k times an n-period standard deviation above and below the middle band.

- *Volume* represents the number of financial asset units traded in the market during the period (*Figures 5.3* and *5.4*). It is used in conjunction with other indicators and analytical patterns.

- The *relative strength index (RSI)* is a momentum oscillator that shows the speed and change of price movements. The RSI is calculated using average price gains and losses over a specified period. The default time frame for comparing these averages is typically 14, with periods defined as anything from minutes to days, depending on the setup for the specific market being analyzed. The RSI oscillates between 0 and 100.

- The *stochastic oscillator* compares a particular closing price of the financial asset to a range of its prices over a certain period. The oscillator's sensitivity to market movements can be adjusted by changing the period or taking an MA of the result.

- *Fibonacci retracement* is derived from the mathematical Fibonacci sequence; these horizontal lines indicate potential support and resistance levels. They are created by drawing horizontal lines across a price chart at crucial Fibonacci levels (usually 23.6%, 38.2%, 50%, 61.8%, and 100%).

- *Ichimoku Cloud* provides more data points, which give a fuller picture of resistance, momentum, support, and trend direction. It uses five lines: Tenkan-sen, Kijun-sen, Senkou Span A, Senkou Span B, and Chikou Span.

NOTE *Remember, while these indicators provide insightful information about potential market movements, they should always be used with other tools and knowledge for trading decisions.*

MAs and their applications, such as Bollinger Bands, MACD, and RSI, are powerful tools in technical analysis. Let us explore them individually, backed by Python code examples using the NumPy, pandas, and mlpfinance libraries for data handling and visualization.

```
1. # Bollinger Bands plotting function
2. def plot_candlestick_with_bb(df, window=20,
3.                              no_of_std=2):
```

```
4.      # Calculate Bollinger Bands
5.      rolling_mean = df['Close'].
   rolling(window=window).mean()
6.      rolling_std = df['Close'].
   rolling(window=window).std()
7.      upper_band = rolling_mean + (rolling_std *
   no_of_std)
8.      lower_band = rolling_mean - (rolling_std *
   no_of_std)
9.      # Add Bollinger Bands to the DataFrame
10.     df['Upper Band'] = upper_band
11.     df['Lower Band'] = lower_band
12.     df['Middle Band'] = rolling_mean
13.     # Plot configuration
14.     apds = [mpf.make_addplot(df['Upper Band'].
   values,
15.                              color='green'),
16.             mpf.make_addplot(df['Middle Band'].
   values,
17.                              color='blue'), #
   MVA line
18.             mpf.make_addplot(df['Lower Band'].
   values,
19.                              color='red')]
20.     mpf.plot(df, type='candle', addplot=apds,
   volume=True,
21.             figsize=(12, 6), style='starsandstripes')
22. # MACD plotting function
23. def plot_candlestick_with_macd(df, span1=12,
```

```
24.                              span2=26,
25.                              signal_span=9):
26.     # Calculate MACD and Signal line
27.     exp1 = df['Close'].ewm(span=span1,
28.                         adjust=False).mean()
29.     exp2 = df['Close'].ewm(span=span2,
30.                         adjust=False).mean()
31.     macd_line = exp1 - exp2
32.     signal_line = macd_line.ewm(span=signal_span,
33.                         adjust=False).mean()
34.     # Plot configuration
35.     apds = [mpf.make_addplot(macd_line.values,
36.                     panel=1, color='fuchsia',
37.                         ylabel='MACD'),
38.             mpf.make_addplot(signal_line.values,
39.                         panel=1, color='b')]
40.     # Plot
41.     mpf.plot(df, type='candle', addplot=apds,
42.             volume=False, style='starsandstripes',
43.             panel_ratios=(6,3), figsize=(12, 6))
44. # RSI plotting function
45. def plot_candlestick_with_rsi(df, window=14):
46.     # Calculate RSI
47.     delta = df['Close'].diff()
48.     up = delta.clip(lower=0)
49.     down = -1 * delta.clip(upper=0)
50.     # Calculate the EMA of the UPs and DWONs
```

```
51.      roll_up = up.rolling(window=window).mean()
52.      roll_down = down.rolling(window=window).
    mean()
53.      # Calculate RS and RSI
54.      RS = roll_up / roll_down
55.      rsi_line = 100 - (100 / (1 + RS))
56.      # Create threshold lines
57.      overbought_line = [70] * len(df)
58.      oversold_line = [30] * len(df)
59.      # Plot configuration
60.      apds = [mpf.make_addplot(rsi_line.values,
61.                               panel=1,
62.                               color='purple',
63.                               ylabel='RSI'),
64.              mpf.make_addplot(overbought_line,
65.                               panel=1,
66.                               color='red',
67.                               alpha=0.5,
68.                               linestyle='dashed'),
69.              mpf.make_addplot(oversold_line,
70.                               panel=1,
71.                               color='green',
72.                               alpha=0.5,
73.                               linestyle='dashed')]
74.      # Ploting
75.      mpf.plot(df, type='candle',
76.              addplot=apds, volume=False,
77.              panel_ratios=(6,3),
```

```
78.                    figsize=(12, 6),
79.                    style='starsandstripes')
80.    ##############################
81.    df = asset.iloc[-100:, 1:]
82.    plot_candlestick_with_bb(df)
83.    plot_candlestick_with_macd(df)
84.    plot_candlestick_with_rsi(df)
```

The code results are presented in *Figures* 5.5, 5.6, and 5.7. Within these figures, the indicators reflect past price changes and can be utilized to refine future price predictions. For instance, from the onset of the study period until the end of June, there is a discernible bullish trend: closing prices graze and marginally breach the upper Bollinger Band, the MACD signal line (darker one) does not cross the MACD line, and the RSI oscillator consistently stays above 30 and even 70. A sell signal emerges at the end of June, marked by the MACD lines crossing and the RSI surpassing the 70 thresholds. The Bollinger Bands, however, do not indicate a shift to a bearish trend, which is only confirmed toward the end of July. An inverse pivot is noted between August 4 and September 1, where all considered indicators concurrently buy signal (close price lower than lower band, in *Figure* 5.5; MCAD lines intersect, in *Figure* 5.6; RSI line has inspected the oversold (green) line, in *Figure* 5.7):

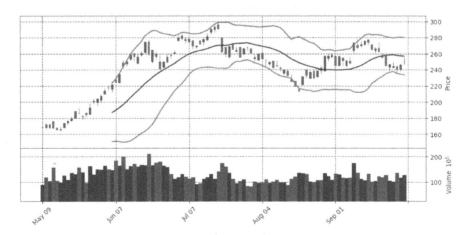

FIGURE 5.5 Bollinger Bands indicator for Telsa Inc. stocks over a 100-day period

In *Figure 5.5*, we see that Tesla Inc.'s stock prices have interacted with these bands in a manner indicative of the stock's volatility and the potential trading strategy that could be deployed. When prices approach the upper band, it often suggests that the stock is becoming overbought while approaching the lower band may indicate it is being oversold.

Figure 5.6 shows the momentum oscillator, which clarifies the direction and strength of the stock's trend. The MACD line crossing above the signal line can be considered bullish, while a cross below might suggest a bearish move.

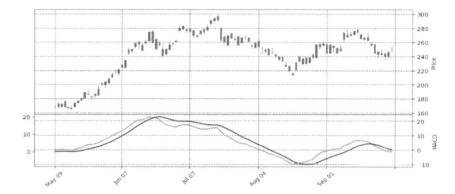

FIGURE 5.6 MCAD indicator for Telsa Inc. stocks over a 100-day period

Finally, in *Figure 5.7*, the RSI is analyzed over the same period. This momentum indicator varies between 0 and 100 and is typically used to identify overbought or oversold conditions. An RSI above 70 suggests that Tesla Inc. may be overbought and potentially due for a pullback. At the same time, an RSI below 30 could indicate an oversold condition and a possible reversal to the upside:

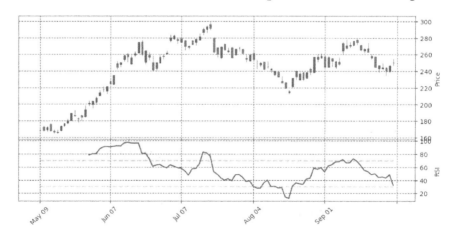

FIGURE 5.7 RSI indicator for Tesla Inc. stocks over a 100-day period

NOTE *There are a lot of different Python libraries for technical analysis automation. TA-Lib is one of them. It provides tools for computing technical indicators and trading analytics. It encapsulates the complexity of financial technical analysis calculations into straightforward function calls, enabling traders and analysts to focus more on strategy development than mathematical intricacies. You can find an example of TA-Lib on its official GitHub page, https://github.com/minggnim/ta-lib, but some of them are presented in the appendix with this chapter's Python code.*

Let us systemize the main approaches to interpreting Bollinger Bands charts:

- Bollinger Bands consist of three lines. The middle band is typically a 20-day SMA. The upper and lower bands are calculated based on the standard deviation of price from the SMA. The standard setting is 2 standard deviations above and below the middle band.

- When the price is closer to the upper band, the market may be considered overbought, and when it is near the lower band, it may be considered oversold.

- The distance between the upper and lower bands can indicate market volatility. Narrow bands indicate low volatility, while wide bands indicate high volatility.

- A Bollinger Band squeeze, when bands come very close together, may signal a period of low volatility and is often considered a potential indicator of future increased volatility and possible breakout.

- Prices breaking through the upper or lower band may signal a continuation of the current trend. To avoid false signals, however, this should be confirmed with other indicators.

- Patterns within the bands can be indicative of market behavior. A *W-bottom*, when the price makes a low, rises, and then falls back near the lower band, can be a sign of a potential upward move if the price breaks above the middle band. Similarly, an *M-top* suggests a potential downward movement if the price falls below the middle band after forming the pattern.

The main practical approaches for making investment decisions based on MACD interpretation can be summarized as follows:

- The MACD line is mainly calculated by subtracting the 26-period EMA from the 12-period EMA. When the MACD line crosses above the signal line (the blue or darker one), it may be a sign to buy, and when it crosses below, it may be a sign to sell.

- The 9-period EMA is typically used as the MACD signal line and helps to identify potential buy or sell signals based on where it crosses the MACD line.

- The MACD's crossing of the zero line can indicate a position's overall direction. If the MACD crosses above zero, it suggests upward momentum (bullish); if it crosses below zero, it is downward momentum (bearish).

- When the price of an asset is moving in the opposite direction of the MACD, it is known as divergence and can indicate a potential reversal. For example, if the price is making new highs but the MACD is not, it could suggest the uptrend is losing momentum.

The RSI analysis results can also be described as follows:

- RSI values range from 0 to 100, and the indicator typically uses thresholds of 70 and 30 to identify overbought or oversold conditions, respectively.

- When the RSI exceeds 70, the asset may be overbought and primed for a price pullback or trend reversal. Then, the RSI below 30 indicates an oversold condition, suggesting a potential upward price reversal.

- The RSI value 50 acts as a centerline between bullish and bearish trends. If the RSI crosses above 50, it is considered bullish; if it falls below 50, it is considered bearish.

- If the RSI moves in the opposite direction of the price (the price moves up while the RSI moves down, or vice versa), it is known as divergence and may indicate a potential price reversal.

- Swing rejections involve looking for situations where the RSI briefly moves into overbought or oversold territory and then reverses and exits these zones. This change can be a sign of a potential price reversal.

- RSI can be used to confirm the strength of a trend. During an uptrend, the RSI stays above 30 and frequently hits 70. During a downtrend, the indicator usually stays below 70 and frequently touches 30.

Remember, Bollinger Bands, MACD, RSI, and any other technical indicator should not be used in isolation. They are most effective only with other technical indicators, graphical patterns, or fundamental analysis to confirm trading signals.

CONCLUSION

To conclude our exploration of investment strategies within financial markets, we have encountered rich strategies, each with unique insights and outcomes. Investment strategies can be broadly categorized into behavioral, analytical, and trading strategies, each harnessing distinctive facets of market psychology, quantitative analysis, and tactical trade execution. Behavioral strategies delve into the general motivations of invertor and risk attitude, analytical strategies employ rigorous analysis methods and tools, and trading strategies focus on the timing and execution of trades to capitalize on market fluctuations.

When we pivot to the domain of fundamental analysis, we see its vital role in discerning the value of financial assets. Python's native tools do not directly support this analysis. It is excellent as a data-handling language; however, collecting financial data and calculating key investment metrics such as EPS, ROE, and P/E ratios. Those metrics are additional evidence in evaluating a company's financial health and growth potential and supporting informed investment decisions. They help with achieving support for an investment strategy goal. We can also collect and analyze other fundamental indicators for stock, currency, and cryptocurrency markets.

Graphical analysis enhances our visual interpretation of market data through candlesticks, bar plots, and volume analysis, complemented by pattern recognition. The Matplotlib and mplfinance Python libraries are powerful allies in this context, offering advanced and combined graphical representations that clarify market trends and patterns. These tools enable investors to decode the narrative of market dynamics visually.

Technical analysis is our compass in the vast ocean of market data, guiding us through various indicators and visualization techniques. Bollinger Bands, MACD, and RSI stand out as beacons among these indicators, each providing unique insights into market momentum, trends, and potential reversals. Integrating libraries such as TA-Lib and its variations facilitates the computation of these indicators, streamlining the analytical process for investors.

A synergistic approach combining fundamental, graphical, and technical analysis with Python's analytical power is key to creating and executing more informed, robust, and efficient investment strategies.

QUESTIONS

1. What different investment strategies do you know?

2. What are the critical differences between technical, fundamental, and graphical analysis in the context of trading strategies?

3. How can fundamental analysis be applied to enhance investment strategy?

4. Describe how Python can be utilized for financial market data analysis visualization techniques.

5. What are the advantages of using graphical analysis tools and patterns in trading?

6. How do volume trading data, support, and resistance lines in graphics inform trading decisions?

7. Discuss how technical analysis supports the development and refinement of trading strategies.

8. How does applying moving averages in technical analysis assist in making trading decisions?

9. In what manner do advanced candlestick charts aid in the interpretation of market data?

10. Describe a situation where technical analysis indicators may conflict with fundamental analysis findings.

KEY TERMS

- An *investment strategy* in the financial market is defined as a variety of approaches and methods used by investors to maximize the efficiency of realizing the potential of their financial assets.

- A *behavioral investment strategy* can be regarded as a multidimensional framework reflecting the investor's behaviors, financial goals, risk tolerance, time commitment, market perspective, and other subjective feelings.

- A *trading strategy* is a customized approach designed for investors to decide when buying and selling securities in the financial market.

- An *analytical investment strategy* is a systematic approach to making investment decisions based on various analysis methods.

REFERENCES

- *Kaabar, S. (2023). Mastering Financial Pattern Recognition: Finding and Back-Testing Candlestick Patterns with Python. 1st Edition. O'Reilly Media.*

- *Dixit, R. (2022). Data Analysis with Python. [Paperback]. BPB Publications.*

- *Hilpisch, Y. (2019). Python for Finance: Mastering Data-Driven Finance. 2nd Edition. O'Reilly Media.*

6

ASSET PRICING AND PORTFOLIO MANAGEMENT

INTRODUCTION

This chapter focuses on the crucial aspects of financial asset pricing and allocation and portfolio management. It provides a detailed exploration of different approaches to asset allocation, equipping readers with a broad perspective on portfolio construction. The chapter begins by looking at the *modern portfolio theory (MPT)* and models and presents a comprehensive framework for optimizing portfolios (with the *Markowitz* and *Sharpe ratio* optimization models). It dives into using simulations for portfolio strategy visualization and math optimization methods for decision-making. We will discuss the basic concepts, metrics of financial data statistics, and applications of *regression models*. We will also describe the basics of the *capital asset pricing model (CAPM)*. CAPM is implemented in Python as a regression model between the expected asset return rates and the market index growth rate.

By the end of this chapter, you will be able to apply Python tools to implement portfolio theory methods, CAPM, and regression models.

STRUCTURE

This chapter covers the following topics:

- Allocation of financial assets
- Portfolio theory with Python (simulations and optimization)
- Regression model essentials with Python

OBJECTIVES

By the end of this chapter, you will be familiar with Python tools for estimating stock portfolio parameters and the parameters of regression models. You will have mastered the basics of MPT to inform long-term investment strategies. This chapter will examine foundational portfolio theories, such as Markowitz's model and the Sharpe ratio criteria. Using statistical tools and regression models, you can quantify the risk-return ratio to make investment decisions. You will also become familiar with the power of Python's statistical libraries, such as *statsmodels* and *SciPy*, for regression analysis and finding the optimum solutions mathematically. These tools play an important role in analyzing complex relationships in financial datasets, providing accurate assessments of the performance of different portfolio models.

ALLOCATION OF FINANCIAL ASSETS AND CORE METRICS WITH PYTHON

As we know from *Chapter 5, Investment and Trading Strategies*, various investment strategies are available in the financial market. Each strategy has unique objectives, methods, and models designed to support informed investment decisions. Classical financial models are usually used for long-term capital investment strategies. They focus on owning or acquiring assets with the goal of future growth in their value. These models primarily cover portfolio theories, methods of optimal asset allocation, and regression relations. Such models provide a fundamental, structured approach to efficiently allocating investments across different assets. The goal of optimization is usually to balance risk and potential return growth, taking into account the current market dynamics.

If we have a certain amount of investment, we can use it to purchase either one type of financial asset or a group of assets in different proportions. In this situation, we face the concept of *asset allocation*. Asset allocation plays a pivotal role in stock market investment strategies. It involves distributing investments across various assets to balance risk and return according to an investor's time frame, risk tolerance, and investment objectives. In the context of the stock market, asset allocation is how an investor divides their investments into different categories, such as stocks, bonds, cryptocurrencies, and cash. This *diversification* helps in mitigating the risks associated with market volatility and sector-specific downturns.

The Python programming language and its special libraries and tools, discussed in previous chapters, enable us to explore the risk and returns of allocating different financial asset types. The approach of this chapter combines various allocation options, such as computer simulation, with user-controlled operations. We will begin by discussing the concept of a stock exchange index and listed securities, which demonstrate the ideology and strategy behind effective financial investments. We will conclude by going through the optimal asset allocation structure for the investment portfolio.

A stock market index is a statistical measure that reflects the weighted value of a selected group of securities. In fact, it is the weighted price of all related assets. The *NASDAQ composite* is a market capitalization-weighted index, meaning companies with larger market caps significantly impact the index's movement. The weights used in the index calculation are based on market capitalization and are adjusted periodically along with the divisor. The divisor is adjusted periodically to reflect changes such as stock splits, making it a dynamic measure. Therefore, the stock index helps to understand the overall trend and performance of a stock market. The crucial problem for the index estimation, however, is listed securities (the assets are used for the calculated index). NASDAQ is a notable example of a stock market index known primarily for listing technology and biotech companies. It tracks the performance of all stocks listed on the NASDAQ stock exchange[1]. This index is often used as a barometer for the overall performance of the tech sector. It is watched closely by investors for insights into the health of the technology and innovation-driven sectors of the economy.

The data for stock indexes is listed and published on official Web sites. For NASDAQ, the main components can be viewed on Yahoo Finance at the Yahoo Finance NASDAQ components page (*https://finance.yahoo.com/quote/%5EIXIC/components?p=%5EIXIC*). Use the following code to generate a `nasdaq_tickets` list and DataFrames with assets price (`df`) and NDX NASDAQ index (`index_data`) dynamics (the top 30 components may differ by the time you read this from those you see in the following code as the market is changing dynamically):

---

[1] *More details about NASDAQ methodology can be found on the official Web site: https://indexes.nasdaqomx.com/*

```python
1.  # Top assets of the NASDAQ Stock Exchange
2.  nasdaq_tickers = [
3.      'MRNA',   # Moderna, Inc.
4.      'DLTR',   # Dollar Tree, Inc.
5.      'ZS',     # Zscaler, Inc.
6.      'MCHP',   # Microchip Technology Incorporated
7.      'SBUX',   # Starbucks Corporation
8.      'HON',    # Honeywell International Inc.
9.      'JD',     # JD.com, Inc.
10.     'DDOG',   # Datadog, Inc.
11.     'AMAT',   # Applied Materials, Inc.
12.     'AAPL',   # Apple Inc.
13.     'AMGN',   # Amgen Inc.
14.     'INTU',   # Intuit Inc.
15.     'PCAR',   # PACCAR Inc
16.     'MDLZ',   # Mondelez International, Inc.
17.     'CSGP',   # CoStar Group, Inc.
18.     'FTNT',   # Fortinet, Inc.
19.     'KDP',    # Keurig Dr Pepper Inc.
20.     'META',   # Meta Platforms, Inc.
21.     'VRSK',   # Verisk Analytics, Inc.
22.     'MAR',    # Marriott International, Inc.
23.     'MRVL',   # Marvell Technology, Inc.
24.     'AZN',    # AstraZeneca PLC
25.     'ILMN',   # Illumina, Inc.
26.     'ENPH',   # Enphase Energy, Inc.
27.     'SIRI',   # Sirius XM Holdings Inc.
28.     'MELI',   # MercadoLibre, Inc.
```

```
29.        'ZM',      # Zoom Video Communications, Inc.
30.        'TSLA',    # Tesla, Inc.
31.        'BKR',     # Baker Hughes Company
32.        'URBN'     # Urban Outfitters, Inc.
33. ]
34. start='2021-01-01'
35. end='2023-10-01'
36. # Download data from the Yahoo Finance
37. df = yf.download(tickers=nasdaq_tickers,
38.                     start=start, end=end,
39.                     actions=False)
40. # Make a subset by the 'Adj Close' and 'Volume'
    columns
41. df = df.loc[:, ['Adj Close', 'Volume']]
42. df = df.sort_index()
43. # Creating a Multi-Level Column Structure for
    'RoR'
44. pct = df['Adj Close'].pct_change()
45. pct.columns = pd.MultiIndex.from_product
    ([['RoR'],
46.                                    pct.columns])
47. # Concatenating the new 'RoR' DataFrame with
48. # the original DataFrame
49. df = pd.concat([df, pct], axis=1)
50. df.dropna(inplace=True)
51. # Displaying the updated DataFrame
52. print(df.head())
53. # Save data into resulting files
54. df.to_excel('nasdaq_assets.xlsx')
```

```
55.  df.to_csv('nasdaq_assets.csv')
56.  # Fetching data for NASDAQ-100 index
57.  index_ticker = '^NDX'
58.  index_df = yf.download(index_ticker,
59.                                  start=start,
60.                                  end=end)
61.  index_df['RoR'] = index_df['Adj Close'].
     pct_change()
62.  index_df.dropna(inplace=True)
63.  print(index_df.head())
64.  index_df.to_excel('nasdaq_index.xlsx')
65.  index_df.to_csv('nasdaq_index.csv')
```

The DataFrames and files generated by executing the code will be utilized in this and other chapters to apply various financial models, regression analysis, forecasting, visualization techniques, portfolio allocation, etc. The metrics for this chapter's code examples (the *rate of returns (RoR)*, *logarithmic RoR*, and so on) are described in *Chapter 2, Python Tools for Data Analysis: Primer to pandas and NumPy*, and *Chapter 3, Financial Data Manipulation with Python*. They are frequently employed in graphical and technical analysis (see the previous chapter). Cumulative return and cumulative RoR are other crucial metrics for long-term strategies, particularly in portfolio management.

The *cumulative return* indicates the total amount of money gained or lost by an investment from the initial investment period. It provides a straightforward way to understand the overall performance of an investment from the start to the end of a specific period. This metric can be calculated in two ways, depending on whether you want to express it as total growth (including the original investment) or as net growth (only the gain or loss from the initial investment).

The *cumulative RoR* represents the cumulative return in rate terms. As a result, this is the same indicator as the cumulative return; the only difference is the calculation procedure. In this chapter, we will use these terms as synonyms.

The *cumulative return (total)* is estimated as follows:

Cumulative return (Total) = (Current value / Initial value) × 100

The *cumulative return (net)* is estimated as follows:

Cumulative return (net) = ((Current value / Initial value) – 1) × 100

Let us execute the following code to understand the cumulative return (total) for NASDAQ-listed securities:

```python
1.  # Calculate cumulative returns (total) for each
    stock
2.  cum_returns = (df['Adj Close'] /
3.                    df['Adj Close'].iloc[0])
4.  # Select the top and the bottom 5 performing
    stocks
5.  top = cum_returns.iloc[-1].sort_values(
6.      ascending=False)[:5].index
7.  bottom = cum_returns.iloc[-1].sort_values(
8.      ascending=False)[-5:].index
9.  # Plot the cumulative returns of
10. # the top and bottom 5 stocks
11. cum_returns[top].plot(figsize=(10, 5))
12. plt.legend(loc='upper left')
13. plt.show()
14. cum_returns[bottom].plot(figsize=(10, 5))
15. plt.legend(loc='upper left')
16. plt.show()
```

This code example is intended to calculate and visualize the cumulative RoR for NASDAQ-listed securities (stocks). Here are some notes on the code:

- Suppose all our investment is allocated to one financial asset. Therefore, each stock's cumulative RoR is calculated by dividing its adjusted closing price by its initial adjusted closing price.

- The tickers (as an index) are then ranked based on their final cumulative returns, and the top five and bottom five final investment results are defined.

Two plots are created (through the code execution) to visualize the cumulative returns (or RoR) of the five top (see *Figure 6.1*) and five bottom (see *Figure 6.2*) shares:

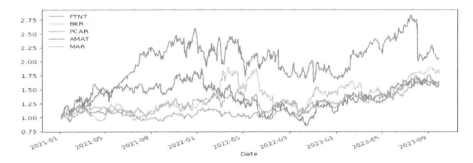

FIGURE 6.1 Dynamics of cumulative returns of top five securities

Figure 6.1 shows the most significant increase in the adjusted closing price relative to the initial price over the period is for the FTNT and BKR securities. The volatility of FTNT, however, is more significant than MELI. Suppose we bought Fortinet, Inc. stocks in January 2022 or May 2023. As a' result, we would have seen losses in the investment value in September 2023.

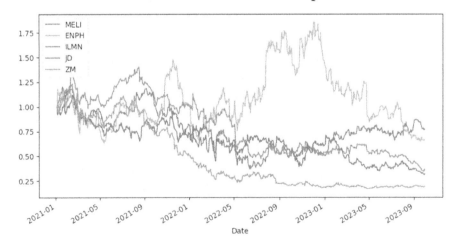

FIGURE 6.2 Dynamics of cumulative returns of bottom five securities

Figure 6.2 shows the cumulative returns of the bottom five performing stocks on NASDAQ. These stocks have shown the slightest increase, or potentially even a decrease, in their adjusted closing price relative to their initial price. If we had sold ENPH stocks in January 2023, however, we would have gained a profit in the growth of investment value.

Both plots are essential for investors as they visually represent both high and low performers in the market, which can inform decisions on asset allocation. Thus, each security on the stock market has its specific characteristics, which, within the framework of *assets allocation principles*, come down to risk assessments and return on investment when using them.

The core financial metrics of profitability and risk assessment can be estimated by executing the following code:

```
1.  RoR = df['RoR']
2.  # Calculate the mean, std, and mean/std ratio
    (yearly)
3.  mean_vals = RoR.mean() * 252
4.  std_vals = RoR.std() * np.sqrt(252)
5.  ratio_vals = mean_vals / std_vals
6.  # Create a figure and a set of subplots (2 plots)
7.  fig, (ax1, ax2) = plt.subplots(2, 1, figsize=(10,
    8),
8.                                  gridspec_kw={'height_
    ratios':
9.                                  [2, 1]})
10. # Plotting mean values as a bar plot in the first
    subplot
11. ax1.set_title('RoR and and Sharpe Ratio
    (yearly)')
12. ax1.bar(mean_vals.index, mean_vals,
    color='skyblue', label='RoR')
```

```
13.  # Plotting mean/std ratio as a line plot on the
     same axes
14.  ax1.plot(ratio_vals.index, ratio_vals,
     color='green',
15.          marker='o', linestyle='-', label='Sharpe
     Ratio')
16.  # Rotate x-axis labels for the first subplot
17.  ax1.tick_params(axis='x', rotation=90)
18.  ax1.legend()
19.  # Plotting std values as a bar plot in the second
     subplot
20.  ax2.set_title('Volatility (yearly)')
21.  ax2.bar(std_vals.index, std_vals,
22.          color='orange', label='Volatility')
23.  # Rotate x-axis labels for the second subplot
24.  ax2.tick_params(axis='x', rotation=90)
25.  ax2.legend()
26.  # Adjusting layout and showing the plot
27.  plt.tight_layout()
28.  plt.show()
```

The code calculates and visualizes key annual financial metrics for profitability and risk. Here are some notes on the code and financial metrics:

- `mean_vals` shows the annual average RoR for each security by multiplying the daily mean RoR by 252, the typical number of trading (working) days in a year.

- `std_vals` characterizes the annual standard deviation, a measure of volatility, by multiplying the daily standard deviation by the square root of 252. This transforms daily volatility into annual volatility.

- `ratio_vals` represents the Sharpe ratio, which is the `mean_vals` divided by `std_vals`. This ratio is used to understand the return on an investment compared to its risk.

- Two subplots are created based on these metrics, depicted in *Figure 6.3*.

Volatility is a statistical measure of the average gaps of returns for a given security or market index. In finance, volatility is often measured as the standard deviation of returns. Higher volatility indicates a higher risk of the investment. Annual volatility may be calculated by scaling up the daily standard deviation:

$$Annual\ volatility = (Number\ of\ trading\ days\ in\ a\ year)^{0.5} \times Daily\ volatility$$

The *Sharpe ratio*, developed by Nobel laureate *William F. Sharpe*, is a measure used to evaluate the risk-adjusted return of an investment portfolio or a single asset. It is defined as the investment's excess return minus the risk-free rate per unit of volatility or total risk. The Sharpe ratio is a way to quantify how much return an investor is receiving for the risk taken. The higher the Sharpe ratio, the better the risk-adjusted returns. When analyzing stocks, the Sharpe ratio can be used to determine how well the return of the stock compensates the investor for the risk taken. In this context, the Sharpe ratio of a stock is calculated using the stock's average return over a specified period minus the risk-free rate, all divided by the standard deviation of the stock's returns over that period:

$$Sharpe\ ratio = (Average\ rate\ of\ return) / Volatility$$

The visualization examples of those metrics for 30 securities of the NASDAQ stock market are represented in *Figure 6.3*:

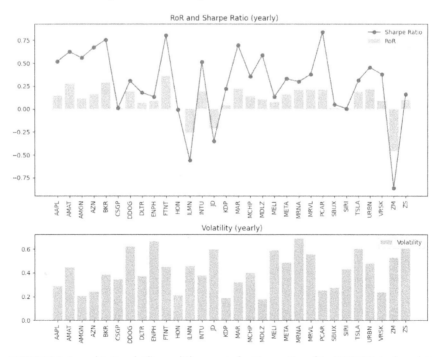

FIGURE 6.3 Annual RoR, volatility, and Sharpe rate for 30 securities of the NASDAQ stock market

Here, the upper plot (*Figure 6.3*) demonstrates both the RoR and the Sharpe ratio by showing blue bars for the RoR and a green line for the Sharpe ratio. Using bars and a line allows investors to assess the securities' absolute and risk-adjusted returns. The lower plot displays the volatility of each security as orange bars. This representation highlights the risk associated with each security based on the variability of their returns. For example, FTNT's stock shows the greatest level of annual RoR. It also has the highest Sharpe rate and volatility (see *Figure 6.1* for a better understanding of FTNT's cumulative RoR dynamics). The lowest volatility is shown for MDLZ, but its RoR is close to average. The Sharpe rate for Mondelez International, Inc. securities is high, too, however, because it shows both less RoR and less volatility.

PORTFOLIO THEORY AND DIVERSIFICATION

Despite the possibility of evaluating numerous financial metrics for market securities, putting all your eggs in one basket is not a good decision. In investment practice, financial asset allocation is diversified based on the value of crucial metrics. *Portfolio management* involves selecting a mix of investment assets to achieve financial goals. It aims to weigh risk and return through *diversification*. By spreading investments across various assets, investors reduce the impact of each poor-performance asset. This strategy enhances stability and growth potential.

The effect of *diversification* can be demonstrated by executing the following code:

```
1.  # Example of Portfolio Structures
2.  portfolio1_tickers = ['MELI','DLTR']
3.  portfolio2_tickers = ['TSLA','DDOG']
4.  # Calculate the cumulative return for a portfolio
    consisting
5.  # of 'MELI' and 'DLTR' with a 50% allocation to
    each
6.  portfiloi1_cum = 0.5 * cum_returns[portfolio1_
    tickers[0]] + \
```

```
7.                      0.5 * cum_returns[portfolio1_
     tickers[1]]

8.  # Plot the individual cumulative returns of
    'MELI' and 'DLTR'

9.  cum_returns[portfolio1_tickers].plot(figsize=(10, 5))

10. # Plot the cumulative return of the combined
    portfolio # ('MELI' and 'DLTR')

11. portfiloi1_cum.plot()

12. # Calculate the cumulative return for another
    portfolio # consisting of 'TSLA' and 'DDOG'

13. # with a 70% allocation to 'TSLA' and 30% to
    'DDOG'

14. portfolio2_cum = 0.7 * cum_returns[portfolio2_
    tickers[0]] + \

15.                      0.3 * cum_returns[portfolio2_
    tickers[1]]

16. # Plot the individual cumulative returns of
    'TSLA' and 'DDOG'

17. cum_returns[portfolio2_tickers].plot(figsize=(10, 5))

18. # Plot the cumulative return of the combined
    portfolio # ('TSLA' and 'DDOG')

19. portfolio2_cum.plot()
```

This code demonstrates how to structure and analyze two investment portfolios using cumulative returns for each stock. The resulting plot for a portfolio of MELI and DLRT stocks is depicted in *Figure 6.4*. The second plot and its Python code can be found in the appendix to this chapter:

FIGURE 6.4 The cumulative return dynamic for two shares and its proportional portfolio (the central line is the portfolio line)

As illustrated in *Figure 6.4*, the individual cumulative returns growth from two stocks exhibits significant fluctuations, particularly in mid-2022. *The volatility significantly decreases*, however, if we proportionally divide our investments (allocating 50% to each asset). Moreover, let us consider long-term investments (without monthly buying and selling). The cumulative returns remain roughly 50% (the central line in the last period is positioned midway between the blue (upper) and orange (bottom) lines). Therefore, this allocation achieves asset diversification.

Therefore, *financial asset diversification* means allocating investments across various assets to reduce the risk trends of any single asset. An important point is the dissimilarity of assets in their *behavior*. Thus, diversification is the strategy of spreading the investment across different assets to mitigate potential losses, as the return and performance of the assets are not directly correlated.

Execute the following code to assess the core financial metrics related to the diversification of different assets (in this example, the asset proportions are determined based on random number generation). As we know from *Chapter 5, Investment and Trading Strategies*, there are many different investment strategies.

```
1.  def calculate_portfolio_metrics(df, w):
2.      # Calculate log returns
3.      log_RoR = (df / df.shift(1)).apply(np.log).
    dropna()
4.      # Calculate portfolio return
5.      pRoR = np.sum(log_RoR.mean() * w) * 252
6.      # Calculate standard deviation (two methods)
7.      sd1 = np.sqrt(np.dot(w.T, np.dot(log_RoR.
    cov() * 252, w)))
8.      sd2 = (log_RoR.mul(w).sum(axis=1).std() *
9.                    np.sqrt(252))
10.     # Calculate Sharpe Ratio
11.     s_rate = pRoR / sd2
12.     return (pRoR, sd1, sd2, s_rate)
13. ####################################################
    ##########
14. # Define the portfolio tickers
15. portfolio3_tickers = ['FTNT', 'BKR', 'PCAR',
    'KDP', 'MDLZ']
16. # Allocaton Assets
17. np.random.seed(100)
18. for p in [portfolio1_tickers,
19.            portfolio2_tickers,
20.            portfolio3_tickers]:
21.     w = np.random.random(len(p))
22.     w /= np.sum(w)
23.     pm = calculate_portfolio_metrics(df['Adj
    Close'][p], w)
24.     print(f"Portfolio Assets: {p}")
```

```
25.     print(f"Portfolio weights: {w}")
26.     print(f"Rate of Return: {pm[0]}")
27.     print(f"Standard Deviation (Type 2): {pm[2]}")
28.     print(f"Sharpe Ratio: {pm[3]}")
```

The code's result is as follows:

```
Portfolio Assets: ['MELI', 'DLTR']

Portfolio weights: [0.66125811 0.33874189]

Rate of Return: -0.06459390136996225

Standard Deviation (Type 2): 0.43648406233426223

Sharpe Ratio: -0.14798684979360333


Portfolio Assets: ['TSLA', 'DDOG']

Portfolio weights: [0.33445182 0.66554818]

Rate of Return: -0.0025730388206032765

Standard Deviation (Type 2): 0.5358543707894354

Sharpe Ratio: -0.004801750178528179


Portfolio Assets: ['FTNT', 'BKR', 'PCAR', 'KDP', 'MDLZ']

Portfolio weights: [0.00268178 0.06908921 0.38119485
0.46934215 0.07769201]

Rate of Return: 0.10088858260039776

Standard Deviation (Type 2): 0.1681572353606613

Sharpe Ratio: 0.5999657545749568
```

NOTE *In the code, the np.random.random() function from NumPy is used. The function generates an array of random numbers from a uniform distribution over the interval (0, 1). np.random.seed(100) sets the seed for NumPy's random number generator. It means that Python can generate random values in the same sequence of random numbers every time you run the code.*

The code results showcase the calculated financial metrics for three different combinations of asset allocation. For the first portfolio, consisting of `MELI` and `DLTR`, the RoR is negative, with substantial volatility, resulting in a negative Sharpe ratio. The second portfolio, containing `TSLA` and `DDOG`, also shows a negative RoR, higher volatility, and a negative Sharpe ratio. The third portfolio, with a diversified mix of `FTNT`, `BKR`, `PCAR`, `KDP`, and `MDLZ`, presents a positive RoR, lower volatility, and the most favorable Sharpe ratio, indicating an efficient diversification.

Thus, to ensure the maximum effect of *diversification*, appropriate assets with varying market behaviors must be selected. This selection should be based on comprehensive analysis across the entire investment horizon, not solely on individual metrics.

Markowitz's Portfolio Theory and Its Modifications

Markowitz's portfolio theory, also known as the modern portfolio theory, or MPT, was introduced by *Harry Markowitz* in the 1950s. This groundbreaking concept revolutionized how investors construct an image portfolio, emphasizing the importance of diversification and the trade-off between risk and return[2]. According to MPT, more is needed beyond looking at the expected risk and return of one security; instead, you must consider how each asset's price movements are correlated with every other asset in the portfolio. This concept is essential for all investors, especially when implementing a long-term investment strategy. Approaches to its implementation, however, are constantly being improved.

Markowitz's portfolio theory suggests that an investor can construct a *frontier* of optimal portfolios offering the maximum expected return for a given level of risk. These are *efficient portfolios* and lie on the *efficient frontier*. The key is to find the balance where the portfolio's overall risk is minimized for a given level of expected return.

The classical Markowitz's portfolio theory optimization model and its variations are as follows.

---

[2]Markowitz, H. (1959). Portfolio Selection: Efficient Diversification of Investments. John Wiley & Sons

Model 6.1: Risk Minimization Strategy

The *portfolio variance* (Var_p) as an optimality criterion is represented by the sum of the product of weights and the covariance between the RoR of assets i and j, for all pairs of assets in the portfolio. In addition, the expected RoR for the portfolio ($E(RoR_p)$) should be greater than or equal to the minimum acceptable RoR (RoR_{min}):

$$Var_p = \sum \sum w_i \times w_j \times Cov(RoR_i, RoR_j) \rightarrow min$$

$$E(RoR_p) = \sum w_i \times E(RoR_i) \geq RoR_{min}$$

$$\sum w_i = 1; w_i \geq 0 \; for \; all \; i$$

Where:

- w_i is the weight of the asset i in the portfolio.
- $E(RoR_i)$ and $E(RoR_p)$ are the expected RoR of the asset i and the portfolio.
- RoR_{min} is the minimum expected RoR of the portfolio.
- Var_p is the variance of the portfolio's return.
- $Cov(RoR_i, RoR_j)$ is the covariance between the returns of assets i and j.

The classical *Model 6.1* operates under the premise that an investor minimizes the portfolio's risk by adjusting the asset weights (w_i) structure. Here, various indicators can measure risk, ranging from variance to standard deviation. In all optimization tasks, it is assumed that the asset structure cannot have negative asset weights, and the sum of all weights (w_i) always equals 1. Although these constraints may be relaxed in more advanced scenarios, they align with the asset allocation principles we will adhere to in our subsequent analysis.

In *Model 6.1*, it is possible to introduce an additional constraint on the portfolio's minimum expected RoR. This is because, in the pursuit of minimizing risk, the portfolio might exclude assets that, while reducing risk, could also significantly diminish the portfolio's returns, potentially to 0.

Model 6.2: RoR Maximization Strategy

This strategy is tailored to maximize the portfolio's expected return given a specific level of risk tolerance. Therefore, the expected RoR for the portfolio ($E(RoR_p)$) is maximized. On the other hand, the portfolio variance (Var_p), which represents the risk, is kept below a specified maximum variance (Var_{max}):

$$E(RoR_p) = \sum w_i \times E(RoR_i) \rightarrow max$$

$$Var_p \leq Var_{max}$$

$$\sum w_i = 1; w_i \geq 0 \text{ for all } I$$

Here, $- Var_{max}$ is the maximum variance of the portfolio's return acceptable to the investor.

Model 6.2 is the converse of *Model 6.1*, wherein the portfolio's RoR is maximized. This model may include a constraint on the maximum acceptable risk of the portfolio. Here, volatility constraints can be measured in terms of standard deviation or its square, which must be considered when formulating the optimization task.

Model 6.3: Sharpe Rate Maximization Strategy

The investment strategy is based on the Sharpe ratio of the portfolio ($SharpeRatio_p$), which is defined as the ratio of the expected return of the portfolio ($E(RoRp)$) divided by the portfolio's standard deviation ($SD_p = Var_p^{0.5}$):

$$SharpeRatio_p = E(RoR_p) / Var_p^{0.5} \rightarrow max$$

$$\sum w_i = 1; w_i \geq 0 \text{ for all } i,$$

A comprehensive solution is presented in *Model 6.3*, which aims to maximize the Sharpe ratio. This model effectively combines the multiple constraints of *Models 6.1* and *6.2* and is most frequently employed in investment calculations. It strikes a balance between seeking returns and managing risk, thereby aligning with the investment principle of not simply seeking the highest RoR or the lowest volatility in isolation but rather the most expected return for a given level of risk.

Modifications of the Original Markowitz's Portfolio Theory

Since the inception of MPT, several modifications and extensions have been proposed to address its limitations and apply it to a broader range of investment scenarios:

- The *post-modern portfolio theory* (*PMPT*) considers that investors prefer positive skewness and are more concerned about downside risk than variance (downside or upside). PMPT focuses on the probability of meeting or falling short of the desired return rather than on expected variance (see details here: *https://en.wikipedia.org/wiki/Post-modern_portfolio_theory*). The *Sortino ratio* is the typical metric within PMPT. It focuses only on downside volatility, which better reflects the risk of not meeting the investor's target return.

- The *Black-Litterman model* incorporates expected returns as a direct input, which allows the portfolio to include subjective views. It is a more advanced implementation that seeks to overcome some of the perceived limitations of MPT, particularly in asset allocation (see details here: *https://en.wikipedia.org/wiki/Black–Litterman_model*).

- The *behavioral portfolio theory* recognizes that investors may only sometimes act rationally; this model incorporates concepts from behavioral economics. It considers the psychological factors that can influence the investment decisions of individuals. These principles are challenging to illuminate with formal statistical data (see here: *https://breakingdownfinance.com/finance-topics/behavioural-finance/behavioral-portfolio-theory-bpt/*).

- The *risk parity* strategy modifies the traditional portfolio allocation to prioritize risk rather than capital. Each asset in the portfolio proportionally contributes to the overall risk, which can lead to a more stable performance across different market conditions (see details here: *https://www.investopedia.com/articles/active-trading/091715/how-create-risk-parity-portfolio.asp*).

- The *value at risk (VaR)* portfolio optimization metric is recognized to minimize the potential loss in value of a portfolio over a specified period for a given confidence interval. It helps with understanding extreme (not average) risks and sets risk limits. This method will be discussed in *Chapter 8, Risk Assessment and Volatility Modeling*.

As we delve deeper into the nuances of portfolio construction, it becomes clear that the process is both an art, in terms of understanding data, and a fundamental science. New approaches and practical examples appear almost every day. The following examples in this chapter will consider traditional modifications of MPT. Thus, understanding the principles of portfolio theory and their practical application, complemented by computational tools such as Python, will allow you to feel the connection between data and long-term investment strategy results.

Simulation Method for Estimated Optimal Asset Allocation

Asset allocation and its optimization are at the heart of portfolio management. The simulation method is an applied technique used to determine the optimal asset allocation with Python and other programming language tools. This approach allows us to estimate the potential returns and risks of different asset combinations, giving us insight into which mix might select the best balance of risks and returns.

The following code represents a sequence of procedures for simulating a set of estimates (2,000) for the distribution of assets in a portfolio for further search for the optimal weights within the selected optimization strategy. This method is commonly named Monte Carlo simulation (it will be discussed in detail in *Chapter 8, Risk Assessment and Volatility Modeling*).

Let us run the code and analyze the results:

```
1.  # Number of simulations to run
2.  simulation_numbers = 2000
3.  # Define the tickers for the portfolio
4.  portfolio_tickers = portfolio3_tickers
5.  # Generate random weights for all simulations
6.  weights = np.random.random((simulation_numbers,
7.                              len(portfolio_tickers)))
8.  weights /= weights.sum(axis=1)[:, np.newaxis]
9.  # Initialize arrays to store the results of the
    simulations
10. RoR_arr = np.zeros(simulation_numbers)
11. sd1_arr = np.zeros(simulation_numbers)
12. sd2_arr = np.zeros(simulation_numbers)
13. sharpe_arr = np.zeros(simulation_numbers)
14. # Run simulations to calculate portfolio metrics
15. for i in range(simulation_numbers):
```

```
16.     # Current set of weights
17.     w = weights[i]
18.     # Calculate portfolio metrics for the current
        weights
19.     portfolio_assets = df['Adj Close']
        [portfolio_tickers]
20.     m = calculate_portfolio_metrics(portfolio_
        assets, w)
21.     RoR_arr[i], sd1_arr[i], sd2_arr[i], sharpe_
        arr[i] = \
22.         m[0], m[1], m[2], m[3]
23. # Create a DataFrame to store the simulation
    results
24. portfolio_results = pd.DataFrame({
25.     'Weights': list(weights),
26.     'Rate of Return': RoR_arr,
27.     'Standard Deviation (Type 1)': sd1_arr,
28.     'Standard Deviation (Type 2)': sd2_arr,
29.     'Sharpe Ratio': sharpe_arr
30. })
31. # Scatter plot of the simulation results
32. plt.figure(figsize=(10, 5))
33. plt.scatter(portfolio_results['Standard Deviation
    (Type 2)'],
34.             portfolio_results['Rate of Return'],
35.             c=portfolio_results['Sharpe Ratio'],
36.             cmap='viridis')
37. plt.colorbar(label='Sharpe Ratio')
```

```
38.  plt.xlabel('Standard Deviation (Type 2)')

39.  plt.ylabel('Rate of Return')

40.  # Find the key points of the portfolios

41.  # Index of the portfolio with the max Sharpe
     Ratio

42.  max_sharpe_idx = portfolio_results['Sharpe
     Ratio'].idxmax()

43.  # Index of the portfolio with the min Standard
     Deviation

44.  min_std_idx = portfolio_results['Standard
     Deviation (Type 2)'].idxmin()

45.  # Index of the portfolio with the max Rate of
     Return

46.  max_ror_idx = portfolio_results['Rate of
     Return'].idxmax()

47.  # Highlight key points in the scatter plot

48.  plt.scatter(portfolio_results.loc[max_sharpe_idx,

49.                   'Standard Deviation (Type 2)'],

50.              portfolio_results.loc[max_sharpe_idx,
     'Rate of Return'],

51.              color='red', marker='*', s=100,

52.              label='Max Sharpe Ratio')

53.  plt.scatter(portfolio_results.loc[min_std_idx,

54.                   'Standard Deviation (Type 2)'],

55.              portfolio_results.loc[min_std_idx,
     'Rate of Return'],

56.              color='black', marker='*', s=100,

57.              label='Min Standard Deviation')

58.  plt.scatter(portfolio_results.loc[max_ror_idx,
```

```
59.                        'Standard Deviation (Type 2)'],
60.              portfolio_results.loc[max_ror_idx,
61.                                  'Rate of Return'],
62.              color='blue', marker='*', s=100,
63.              label='Max Rate of Return')
64. plt.legend()
65. plt.title('Portfolio Optimization')
66. plt.show()
```

The code uses the simulation approach to portfolio optimization. There are the estimation steps taken in the code:

1. *Initialize variables and constants for simulation experiments*: The constant `simulation_numbers = 2000` defines how many random portfolio compositions will be simulated. The variable `portfolio_tickers` holds the asset names included in the portfolios. An array of random weights is created for each asset in every simulated portfolio, ensuring that the sum of weights in each portfolio equals 1.

2. *Calculate portfolio metrics (simulations)*: The predefined portfolio metrics are used to calculate key financial metrics for each portfolio—RoR, two types of standard deviation, and the Sharpe ratio—using the `calculate_portfolio_metrics` function.

3. *Create a resulting DataFrame*: The calculated metrics for each simulation are compiled into a pandas DataFrame named `portfolio_results`. This structured data format is conducive to analysis and visualization.

4. *Visualize the simulation results*: A scatter plot is generated with the standard deviation on the x axis, RoR on the y axis, and point color representing the Sharpe ratio (*Figure 6.5*). Three key portfolios are identified and highlighted: one with the maximum Sharpe ratio, one with the minimum standard deviation, and one with the maximum RoR. These points are visually distinguished by color and marker style, providing clear indicators of optimal portfolio choices based on different investment objectives.

The code uses NumPy for numerical calculations, Matplotlib for plotting, and pandas for data manipulation (refer to *Figure 6.5*):

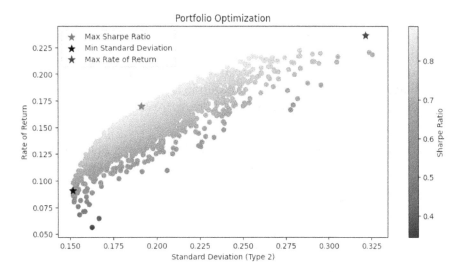

FIGURE 6.5 Visual analysis of asset allocation for the portfolio3_tickers utilizing the simulation method

Figure 6.5 illustrates the relationship between the RoR and volatility for various portfolio structures. The maximum points are marked with stars. This approach shows *Models 6.1* and *6.2* without secondary constraints, considering only the optimality criteria. The figure clearly shows, however, that optimization through the Sharpe ratio yields a more balanced value than the minimization of risk and the maximization of return without additional constraints. The output in *Figure 6.5* serves as a decision-making tool, allowing investors to visualize trade-offs between risk and return and to select portfolios that align with their investment strategies.

The simulation method is convenient and does not require a complex problem solution. It allows for a visual assessment of portfolio parameters. It has some drawbacks, however: it only sometimes leads to optimal values and it can be time-consuming, depending on the number of experiments and the complexity of the calculations (`simulation_numbers`).

Mathematical Optimization Method with Python

In addition to the well-understandable simulation method, optimization tasks can be solved using mathematical methods such as linear programming, quadratic programming, and non-linear optimization techniques. These methods strive to find a definitive extreme if one exists—by systematically searching through potential solutions. To avoid delving into the intricacies of mathematical optimization methods, we can turn to the SciPy library and its `minimize` function, a versatile tool for optimization tasks. You can find detailed guidance in the SciPy optimization manual here: *https://docs.scipy.org/doc/scipy/tutorial/optimize.html*.

The SciPy `minimize` tool is powerful for finding a mathematical function's local minimum. It includes several algorithms for optimization, and you can choose one based on the nature of your problem. Key components of SciPy `minimize` are:

- The *objective function* minimizes the decision variables as input and outputs the value to be underestimated.
- *Constraints* are conditions that the solution must satisfy. They can be equality constraints (e.g., the sum of weights equals 1 in portfolio optimization) or inequality constraints (e.g., weights must be non-negative).
- *Bounds* provide the lower and upper limits for the decision variables. In portfolio optimization, they can limit the proportion invested in each asset.

Execute the following code with SciPy minimization, then analyze and compare the results:

```
1.  from scipy.optimize import minimize
2.
3.  # Function to calculate portfolio return
4.  def portfolio_return(weights, log_returns):
5.      return np.sum(log_returns.mean() * weights) * 252
6.
7.  # Function to calculate portfolio volatility
```

```python
8.  def portfolio_volatility(weights, log_returns):
9.      return np.sqrt(np.dot(weights.T,
10.                           np.dot(log_returns.
    cov() * 252, weights)))
11.
12. # Function to maximize RoR (minimize negative
    return)
13. def minimize_negative_return(weights,
    log_returns):
14.     return -portfolio_return(weights,
    log_returns)
15.
16. # Function to minimize standard deviation
17. def minimize_volatility(weights, log_returns):
18.     return portfolio_volatility(weights,
    log_returns)
19.
20. # Function to maximize Sharpe Ratio (minimize
    negative Sharpe)
21. def minimize_negative_sharpe(weights,
    log_returns):
22.     return - (portfolio_return(weights, log_
    returns) /
23.              portfolio_volatility(weights,
    log_returns))
24.
25. # General function to optimize the portfolio
26. def optimize_portfolio(log_returns,
27.                        objective_function,
28.                        min_ror=None, max_vol=None):
```

```python
29.      # Number of assets in the portfolio
30.      num_assets = len(log_returns.columns)
31.      # Constraint: sum of weights equals 1
32.      constraints = [{'type': 'eq', 'fun': lambda
    x: np.sum(x) - 1}]
33.      # Add minimum RoR constraint if specified
34.      if min_ror is not None:
35.          constraints.append({'type': 'ineq',
    'fun': lambda x:
36.                               portfolio_return(x,
    log_returns) - min_ror})
37.      # Add maximum volatility constraint if
    specified
38.      if max_vol is not None:
39.          constraints.append({'type': 'ineq',
    'fun': lambda x:
40.                              max_vol - portfolio_
    volatility(x, log_returns)})
41.      # Bounds for each asset's weight (0% to 100%)
42.      bounds = tuple((0, 1) for _ in
    range(num_assets))
43.      # Initial guess for weights (even
    distribution)
44.      initial_guess = num_assets * [1. /
    num_assets,]
45.      # Minimize the objective function to find
    optimal weights
46.      opt_results = minimize(objective_function,
47.                              initial_guess,
48.                              args=(log_returns,),
49.                              method='SLSQP',
```

```
50.                              bounds=bounds,
51.
   constraints=constraints)
52.     # Print the optimal weights and metrics
53.     formatted_weights = [f"{weight:.2f}" for
   weight in opt_results.x]
54.     print("Optimal Weights: ", formatted_weights)
55.     print(f"RoR: {portfolio_return(opt_results.x,
   log_returns):.2f}")
56.     print(f"Volatility: {portfolio_
   volatility(opt_results.x, log_returns):.2f}")
57.     print()
58.     # Return the resulted object
59.     return opt_results
60.     ##################################################
   ################
61. # Example usage
62. log_returns = np.log(df['Adj Close'][portfolio_
   tickers] /
63.                       df['Adj Close'][portfolio_
   tickers].shift(1))
64. print(portfolio_tickers)
65.
66. print("Mathematical Optimization Results")
67. print("Optimize for maximum Sharpe Ratio:")
68. math_sharpe = optimize_portfolio(log_returns,
   minimize_negative_sharpe)
69. print("Optimize for maximum RoR:")
70. math_ror = optimize_portfolio(log_returns,
   minimize_negative_return)
71. print("Optimize for minimum Volatility:")
```

```
72. math_vol = optimize_portfolio(log_returns,
    minimize_volatility)
73.
74. print("Optimize for max RoR with max Volatility
    constraint of 0.4")
75. max_vol_constraint = 0.4   # Example maximum
    volatility
76. optimal_max_ror = optimize_portfolio(log_returns,
77.                         minimize_negative_return,
78.                       max_vol=max_vol_constraint)
79.
80. print("Optimize for min Volatility with min RoR
    constraint of 0.1")
81. min_ror_constraint = 0.1   # Example minimum rate
    of return
82. optimal_min_vol = optimize_portfolio(log_returns,
83.                             minimize_volatility,
84.                       min_ror=min_ror_constraint)
85.
86. # Simulation results
87. print("Simulation Optimal Results")
88. for w in [sim_weights_sharpe, sim_weights_ror,
    sim_weights_vol]:
89.     print("Weights: ", [f"{weight:.2f}" for
    weight in w])
90.     print(f"RoR: {portfolio_return(w,
    log_returns):.2f}")
91.     print(f"Volatility: {portfolio_volatility(w,
    log_returns):.2f}")
92.     print()
```

The results of the code are:

```
['FTNT', 'BKR', 'PCAR', 'KDP', 'MDLZ']
Mathematical Optimization Results
Optimize for maximum Sharpe Ratio:
Optimal Weights:  ['0.17', '0.19', '0.38', '0.00', '0.26']
RoR: 0.18
Volatility: 0.20


Optimize for maximum RoR:
Optimal Weights:  ['1.00', '0.00', '0.00', '0.00', '0.00']
RoR: 0.27
Volatility: 0.46


Optimize for minimum Volatility:
Optimal Weights:  ['0.00', '0.08', '0.12', '0.36', '0.44']
RoR: 0.09
Volatility: 0.15

Optimize for max RoR with max Volatility constraint of 0.4
Optimal Weights:  ['0.83', '0.17', '0.00', '0.00', '0.00']
RoR: 0.26
Volatility: 0.40

Optimize for min Volatility with min RoR constraint of 0.1
Optimal Weights:  ['0.02', '0.09', '0.15', '0.28', '0.45']
RoR: 0.10
Volatility: 0.15
```

```
Simulation Optimal Results
Weights:   ['0.12', '0.18', '0.47', '0.01', '0.22']
RoR: 0.17
Volatility: 0.20

Weights:   ['0.54', '0.24', '0.13', '0.01', '0.08']
RoR: 0.23
Volatility: 0.30

Weights:   ['0.02', '0.09', '0.15', '0.37', '0.38']
RoR: 0.09
Volatility: 0.15
```

This code is designed to implement MPT using the SciPy optimization library in Python. Essential functions and arguments and their role are as follows:

- `portfolio_return`: Calculates the portfolio's expected RoR based on the mean daily log returns scaled to an annual figure (multiplying by 252 trading days).
- `portfolio_volatility`: Computes the portfolio's volatility (standard deviation of returns) using the annualized covariance matrix of the asset returns.
- `minimize_negative_return`: Defines an objective function for minimization that represents the negative of the portfolio's RoR to facilitate the maximization of returns in the `minimize` SciPy function.
- `minimize_volatility`: Sets up an objective function to minimize the portfolio's volatility.
- `minimize_negative_sharpe`: Aims to maximize the Sharpe ratio by minimizing its reversed negative value.
- `optimize_portfolio`: A wrapper function that consolidates the optimization process. It sets up constraints (such as the weights summing to 1), bounds (limiting weights between 0 and 1, that is, no short selling), and so on.
- `minimize`: The core function from SciPy that performs the optimization. It takes the objective function, initial guesses for the weights, the bounds for these weights, and the constraints as arguments:

- Constraints are conditions placed on the solution. For this example, the portfolio's return must be above a minimum threshold, or the volatility must not exceed a certain level (see *Model 6.1* and *Model 6.2*).

- Bounds ensure each asset's weight is between 0 and 100 percent, preventing short selling and leveraging.

- `initial_guess` is the starting point for the optimization algorithm, for this code, set as an even distribution across all assets.

- `method('SLSQP')` refers to the sequential least squares programming optimization algorithm, a common choice for constrained optimization.

By calling `opt_results = minimize(...)`, the function finds the optimal set of weights that achieve the objective. The result of this optimization process will provide asset allocation weights (`opt_results.x`) that align with the specified investment strategy according to Markowitz's theory.

The code results demonstrate that the first three results are represented by simplified Markowitz models: that is, those shown with *Model 6.1*, *Model 6.2* (without constraints), and *Model 6.3*. Particularly, for the second model (maximizing RoR), we observe a degenerate portfolio structure, which we also see in *Figure 6.5*. This means that the optimization algorithm suggests placing all assets in the highest-yielding asset. Similar results can be seen for the risk minimization model without constraints on the RoR. Optimizing tasks 4 and 5 from the code results includes constraints, and as we can see, the portfolio structure is more dispersed, yet the RoR and volatility are constrained by the limits set. These problems are partly solved in the model with the Sharpe ratio optimality criterion, as evidenced in both *Figure 6.5* and the results of the code execution analysis. The code provides a comparison to compare the effectiveness of mathematical optimization methods and simulation. As we see, the values are nearly identical; however, the structure based on simulation does not reduce the model to a definitive minimum or maximum.

REGRESSIONS AND CAPITAL ASSET PRICING MODEL FUNDAMENTALS

Regression analysis is a statistical tool used to determine how the value of the dependent variable relates to one or more of the independent variables. This is not an entirely determined functional dependency but should be detected as a probability issue. One of the best-known regression models in finance is *CAPM*. This model describes the correlations between systematic risk and the expected RoR for assets. It serves as a method for assessing the risk and deriving the expected return on investment or RoR for financial assets.

The formula for the classical CAPM is:

$$E(RoR_i) = R_f + \beta_i\,(E(RoR_m - R_f))$$

Or:

$$E(RoR_i) - R_f = \beta_i\,(E(RoR_m - R_f))$$

Where:

- $E(RoR_i)$ is the expected return on the capital asset (RoR for asset i).
- R_f is the risk-free rate.
- β_i is the security beta.
- RoR_m is the expected market return (mainly portfolio based on stock market weights).

In essence, CAPM states that a security's expected RoR is equal to the risk-free profitability plus a risk premium based on the beta factor of the asset. The risk-free rate is the theoretical return of an investment with zero risk of financial loss. It is often represented by the yield on government bonds, such as U.S. Treasury bills. They are considered low-risk due to the government's financial stability and sovereign backing. Therefore, the investment's beta (β) measures its volatility about the expected market return. If the beta value is:

- 1: Implies that the asset's price will move with the market
- Greater than 1: Shows that the asset is more volatile than the market
- Less than 1: Means the asset is less volatile than the market
- Negative: Suggests that the asset moves opposite to the market

Beta is a crucial measure used to gauge the risk associated with security relative to the risk of the market as a whole.

When regression analysis is used to construct CAPM, the risk-free rate is typically omitted in a share-specific assessment equation. Therefore, the formula of the isolated CAPM for regression analysis is:

$$E(RoR_i) = \beta_i \cdot RoR_m + \alpha$$

Here, α represents the stock's excess return that cannot be explained by market movements, essentially capturing the unique, non-systematic risk of the stock. β reflects the same, the volatility of assets i in relation to the market (market-weighted portfolio). The equation focuses on the relationship between the asset and the market returns. The risk-free rate is implicit when analyzing the stock's alpha and beta since these metrics are usually derived from historical data where the risk-free rate effect is already included in the stock's return. The beta and alpha estimations in CAPM are based on regression methods, which measure the sensitivity of the security's returns to market movements.

Python Libraries for Regression Analysis

Regression analysis in Python is largely dominated by two powerful libraries: statsmodels and scipy.stats. These libraries provide comprehensive tools for statistical modeling and hypothesis testing. The statsmodels library, imported as sm, is particularly suited for building and analyzing various statistical models. It offers extensive algorithms and statistical tests, making it invaluable for econometrics, finance, and statistics (*https://www.statsmodels.org/dev/examples/notebooks/generated/ols.html*). The scipy.stats module is utilized for a broad spectrum of statistical functions, including probability distributions, summary and frequency statistics, correlation functions, and tests of significance, which you can read more about here: *https://docs.scipy.org/doc/scipy/reference/generated/scipy.stats.linregress.html*.

Let us execute the following code as an example of regression analysis with Python:

```
1.  import statsmodels.api as sm

2.  from scipy import stats

3.  reg_data = yf.download('TSLA', start=start,
    end=end)

4.  # Calculate the correlation matrix

5.  corr_matrix = reg_data.corr()

6.  print(corr_matrix)

7.  # Create a pair plot with regression lines

8.  sns.pairplot(reg_data[['Adj Close', 'Open',
    'Volume']],
```

```
 9.                   kind='reg',
     plot_kws={'line_kws':{'color':'black'}})
10. plt.show()
11. # Define the dependent variable (e.g., Adjusted
    Close Price)
12. y = reg_data['Adj Close']
13. # Prepare the independent variables
14. # Combine them into a single DataFrame
15. X = reg_data[['Open', 'Volume']]
16. # Add a constant to the independent variables
17. X = sm.add_constant(X)
18. # Create the OLS model
19. model = sm.OLS(y, X)
20. # Fit the model
21. results = model.fit()
22. # Print the summary of the regression
23. print(results.summary())
```

The results (truncated) of the code are:

```
             Open       High       Low       Close    Adj Close    Volume
Open       1.000000   0.996537   0.995061   0.989648   0.989648  -0.434236
High       0.996537   1.000000   0.995335   0.995291   0.995291  -0.412254
Low        0.995061   0.995335   1.000000   0.996040   0.996040  -0.456084
Close      0.989648   0.995291   0.996040   1.000000   1.000000  -0.430658
Adj Close  0.989648   0.995291   0.996040   1.000000   1.000000  -0.430658
Volume    -0.434236  -0.412254  -0.456084  -0.430658  -0.430658   1.000000


    OLS Regression Results
========================================================================
Dep. Variable:          Adj Close   R-squared:            0.979
Model:                        OLS   Adj. R-squared:       0.979
```

```
Method:                Least Squares   F-statistic:              1.633e+04
Date:             Wed, 03 Apr 2024   Prob (F-statistic):            0.00
Time:                     15:51:40   Log-Likelihood:             -2437.8
No. Observations:              690   AIC:                          4882.
Df Residuals:                  687   BIC:                          4895.
Df Model:                        2
Covariance Type:           nonrobust
==============================================================================
                 coef    std err          t      P>|t|      [0.025      0.975]
------------------------------------------------------------------------------
const          3.5983      2.020      1.781      0.075      -0.368       7.564
Open           0.9852      0.006    162.733      0.000       0.973       0.997
Volume     -1.508e-09   8.11e-09     -0.186      0.853   -1.74e-08     1.44e-08
==============================================================================
Omnibus:                      61.759   Durbin-Watson:               2.185
Prob(Omnibus):                 0.000   Jarque-Bera (JB):          227.073
Skew:                         -0.338   Prob(JB):                 4.92e-50
Kurtosis:                      5.728   Cond. No.                 6.99e+08
==============================================================================
```

The code example demonstrates how to employ statsmodels to perform regression analysis. It begins by downloading financial data for Tesla, computes the correlation matrix, and visualizes relationships between different variables with pairplots, including regression lines. Then, it defines an *ordinary least squares (OLS)* regression model to explore the relationship between the adjusted close price and other variables, such as Open and Volume, adding a constant to the model for the intercept. Finally, it fits the model and prints out a detailed summary of the regression results. This process is integral to financial analysis, where understanding the determinants of asset prices can inform investment strategies and risk management. The correlation matrix indicates that the variables Open and Adj Close exhibit a strong positive correlation (exceeding 0.98), while Volume has a negative correlation, albeit less than 0.5 in magnitude. This finding is visually corroborated by *Figure 6.6*, where the actual data points deviate significantly from the regression line in the Adj Close scatter plot against Volume.

The OLS regression results analysis confirms the significant influence of Open on Adj Close Price, with the model being:

$$Adj\ Close = 3.5983 + 0.9852 \times Open - 1.508e\text{-}09 \times Volume$$

The model's substantial efficacy is reinforced by detailed statsmodels outputs, such as an R-squared value of 0.979, a Prob (F-statistic) close to 0.00, and a p-value of 0.000 for the Open slope, affirming the model's robustness. The p-values for the Constant and Volume (0.075 and 0.853), however, indicate statistical insignificance (refer to the following figure):

NOTE   *The p-value in statistical theory measures the probability that an observed difference could have occurred just by random chance. It is a universal statistical metric used to determine the significance of the model results. Typically, a p-value less than 0.05 indicates that the result is statistically significant. We can use p-values to determine the whole model's reliability and some coefficients.*

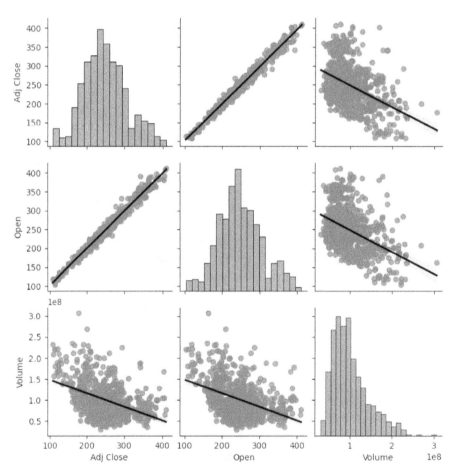

FIGURE 6.6 Pairs scatter plots for Adj Close, Open, and Volume of Tesla Inc.'s share

The scipy.stats module could be used for the same statistical tasks for one dependent variable and one independent variable (like for the CAPM issue), as we can see by executing the following code:

```
1.  from scipy import stats
2.  # Assuming 'reg_data' is your DataFrame with the
    necessary columns
3.  # Define the dependent variable (e.g., Adjusted
    Close Price)
4.  y = reg_data['Adj Close']
5.  # Prepare the independent variable (e.g., 'Open')
6.  X = reg_data['Open']
7.  # Perform linear regression using scipy
8.  slope, intercept, r_value, p_value, std_err =
    stats.linregress(X, y)
9.  # Print the results
10. print(f"y = {intercept:.3f} + {slope:.3f} * X")
11. print("Slope:", slope)
12. print("Intercept:", intercept)
13. print("R-squared:", r_value**2)
14. print("P-value:", p_value)
15. print("Standard Error:", std_err)
```

The results of the code are:

```
y = 3.326 + 0.986 * X
Slope: 0.9857115725185064
Intercept: 3.3255537096161447
R-squared: 0.9794025403403167
P-value: 0.0
Standard Error: 0.00544981617568275
```

The results of executing the provided code confirm that the procedures for estimating regression parameters are fully identical for the statsmodels and scipy.stats libraries. The robustness and related measures for scipy.stats, however, are significantly less. When implementing classical regression methods, we can use both libraries in the same way.

Python Tools for CAPM Assessment

In the context of what we have discussed in this chapter, we will introduce an example of using Python to calculate and analyze the expected returns of securities using an isolated CAPM formula. The `analyze_CAPM()` function within this section will demonstrate how to calculate percentage changes or returns and how to apply CAPM to assess the risk and expected return of individual stocks in relation to the market's performance. This function will incorporate beta and alpha values and plot the related scatter plot. *Figure 6.7* shows the level of correlation between the marker's RoR and the current share RoR. Moreover, the beta level is visible from the slope of the regression line (here, the asset is more volatile than the market).

Let us execute the code:

```
1.  def analyze_CAPM(stock_data, market_data,
2.                   prn = True, visualization = True):
3.      # Calculate percentage changes (returns)
4.      ShareRoR = stock_data.pct_change().dropna()
5.      ShareRoR.name = 'Share RoR'
6.      MarketRoR = market_data.pct_change().dropna()
7.      MarketRoR.name = 'Market RoR'
8.      # Perform linear regression to calculate beta
9.      beta, alpha, r_value, p_value, std_err = stats.linregress(x = MarketRoR,
10.                                     y = ShareRoR)
11.     if prn:
```

```
12.      # Print CAPM formula
13.          print(f"CAPM model: RoRi = {beta:.5f} *
     RoRm + {alpha:.5f} + errors")
14.          print(f"Beta: {beta:.5f}")
15.          print(f"Alpha: {alpha:.5f}")
16.          print(f"P-value: {p_value:.5f}")
17.          print(f"Standard Error: {std_err:.3f}")
18.          print(f"R-square: {r_value**2:.3f}")
19.      if visualization:
20.          # Scatter plot with regression line
21.          plt.figure(figsize=(10,5))
22.          sns.regplot(x=MarketRoR, y=ShareRoR,
23.                      line_kws={"color": "black"})
24.      return({'Beta': beta, 'Alpha': alpha})
25. # Example usage of the function
26. result = analyze_CAPM(df['Adj Close']['FTNT'],
                          index_data['Adj Close'])
27. print(result)
```

The textual results of the code are:

```
CAPM model: RoRi = 1.18329 * RoRm + 0.00109 + errors
Beta: 1.18329
Alpha: 0.00109
P-value: 0.00000
Standard Error: 0.053
R-square: 0.422
{'Beta': 1.1832898081893108, 'Alpha': 0.00108984641400661}
```

The graphical results in *Figure 6.7* clearly show the regression model line and the actual fluctuation of the stock's RoR and portfolio's RoR on real datasets.

The regression results indicate that the stock has a beta of 1.18329, suggesting it is more volatile than the market and can generate higher average returns. The alpha of 0.00109 implies a small positive performance over the market that is not accounted for by the market movements. The p-value near 0 signifies the statistical significance of the regression results, and the R-square value of 0.422 suggests that approximately 42.2% of the stock's movement can be explained by the market's movement.

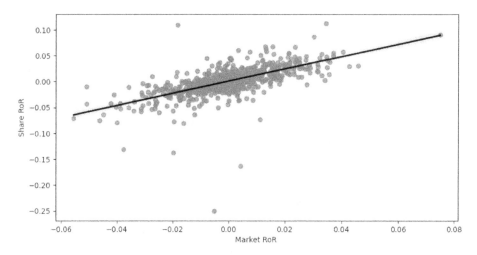

FIGURE 6.7 Scatter plot for market and share RoR with regression line

The scatter plot and regression line visually prove these relationships. In the evaluation, the error constant indicates the presence of noise and shows the absence of the dependency's complete determinacy. These noises are perceptible in *Figure 6.7* (some blue points are far from the black regression line) and confirmed by the determination coefficient (0.422). Overall, the graph and evaluations provide a comprehensive assessment of this asset and can form the basis for its inclusion in or exclusion from an individual investment portfolio.

CONCLUSION

We have discussed the essence of portfolio theory and the strategic allocation of financial assets utilizing Python analytical tools. We examined stock indices such as NASDAQ to understand market movements and explored cumulative return metrics to compare investment performance analysis over time. We also translated daily returns to annual figures, emphasizing the importance of asset allocation in shaping investment outcomes. We learned how to measure risk-adjusted returns using the Sharpe ratio, combining market insights and quantitative analysis.

The principles of MPT were also investigated. We dove into *diversification's* role in investment strategies, mainly through MPT. The chapter revealed that by employing the simulation (Monte Carlo) method and mathematical optimization, such as the methods found in *SciPy*, we can fine-tune our investment portfolios to achieve optimal goals. The real-world examples demonstrated that the Sharpe ratio is one of the best criteria for balancing risk against return, outperforming mere maximization of return or minimization of volatility. This chapter also underscored the importance of selecting a variety of assets that reflect a comprehensive market analysis rather than relying on individual metrics alone.

We discussed regression analysis and its application in finance, mainly through CAPM. We showed the fundamentals of *regression*, learning how it is a statistical cornerstone in predicting asset risk and performance. The chapter harnessed the analytical power of Python libraries, including statsmodels.api for OLS regression and scipy.stats for statistical analysis, to assess financial assets such as Tesla shares. Through the classical CAPM formula, we discovered the role of alpha and beta coefficients in understanding a security's market risk and calculating specific asset risk and expected return.

QUESTIONS

1. What is the primary insight of the modern portfolio theory?

2. How can financial asset allocation impact long-term investment strategies?

3. What does the Sharpe ratio indicate in portfolio optimization?

4. How do simulations contribute to portfolio strategy optimization?

5. How does Markowitz's portfolio theory weigh asset allocation?

6. In terms of asset allocation, what does diversification aim to achieve?

7. How do we apply the SciPy `minimize` function to portfolio optimization?

8. What do the alpha and beta in the CAPM formula mean?

9. How can the statsmodels.api and scipy.stats libraries be applied in regression analysis?

10. Why is it important to consider both return and volatility in portfolio management?

11. How can the historical performance of assets be visualized using Python?

12. Why might an investor prefer a portfolio with a higher Sharpe ratio?

13. How is optimal asset allocation determined using mathematical optimization?

14. Why is selecting a mix of assets crucial when constructing a portfolio?

KEY TERMS

- The *stock market index* is a complex indicator that represents the performance of a group of stocks, which gives a general idea of the behaviors of the stock market or a specific segment of it. It is commonly related to the stock exchange.

- *Capitalization* is the total cost of securities or shares of stock. It is calculated by multiplying the security price by its total volume in the market operations.

- The *cumulative rate of return* (*RoR*) is the total amount of money an investment has gained or lost over a certain period, expressed as a percentage of the initial investment period.

- *Asset allocation* is an investment strategy of dividing assets across various categories and their weights, such as stocks, bonds, and cash, to optimize the balance between risk and return.

- *Financial asset diversification* is allocating investments across various assets to reduce the risk trends of any single asset.

- A *portfolio* is a collection of diversified financial assets held by an investor.

- The *Sharpe ratio* is a measure to evaluate the risk-adjusted return of an investment portfolio and estimates by dividing the returns an investor receives by the volatility metric.

- The *capital asset pricing model* (*CAPM*) is a financial model that describes the correlation between systematic risk and expected return for assets, especially stocks.

- *Simulation* is modeling a real phenomenon with a set of random (computational) experiments. It simulates the behavior of markets or individual investors under various random scenarios.
- *Mathematic optimization* is a branch of applied mathematics that uses mathematical processes to find a function's maximum or minimum values, often used in various disciplines for decision-making.

REFERENCES

- *Markowitz, H. M. (1991). Portfolio Selection: Efficient Diversification of Investments. 2nd Edition. Wiley.*
- *Singh, H. (2021) Statistics For Machine Learning. [Paperback]. BPB Publications.*
- *Nunez-Iglesias, J., van der Walt, S., and Dashnow, H. (2017). Elegant SciPy: The Art of Scientific Python. O'Reilly Media.*

7

TIME-SERIES ANALYSIS AND FINANCIAL DATA FORECASTING

INTRODUCTION

This chapter explores the complicated world of *time-series analysis (TSA)*, an essential element in financial data forecasting. We will begin with explaining the core concepts of time-series data analysis and tools for transforming time-series data with Python, as well as understanding and manipulating financial time series. Then, we will cover the *moving average (MA)* and *Holt-Winters (HW)* models for financial forecasting tasks, explaining how these models capture trends and seasonality in financial time series. These models provide a practical starting point for forecasting.

As we progress, the principles of *autoregressive integrated moving average (ARIMA)* models are introduced. This allows the evaluation of a forecast based on past time-series data and errors in financial series. The chapter also delves into the decomposition of time series by breaking down a series into its core components—trend, seasonality, and residuals. This requires addressing issues such as stationarity, using various transformations to stabilize the data, and exploring the concepts of the *autocorrelation function (ACF)*, *partial autocorrelation function (PACF)*, and *cross-correlation*. We describe the power of the *pandas*, *statsmodels*, and *pmdarima* Python libraries. These help to identify the relationships within and between time-series datasets and guide the selection and calibration of forecasting models. The chapter will conclude by looking at advanced traditional models such as *seasonal ARIMA (SARIMA)* and *seasonal ARIMA with exogenous variables (SARIMAX)*. These models extend basic ARIMA principles to account for seasonality and the influence of external variables. Overall, the Python tools presented in this chapter help address complex financial forecasting challenges using standard statistical principles.

STRUCTURE

This chapter covers the following topics:

- TSA: Core principles and concepts
- Traditional forecasting methods and models
- Exponential smoothing and the HW model
- ARIMA approach: From MA to seasonality and external variables

OBJECTIVES

By the end of this chapter, you will be able to easily apply traditional TSA in financial forecasting and understand the core limitations of these models. As you explore various forecasting techniques, from *exponential smoothing* to advanced *SARIMAX* models, you will also discover the challenges these models face, particularly in volatile financial markets. Also, you will clearly understand why the *mean absolute percentage error (MAPE)* metric can sometimes show the best results with the actual variations in financial time-series data. This insight will be pivotal for applying more robust and adaptive forecasting techniques, such as machine learning.

TSA: CORE PRINCIPLES AND CONCEPTS

As we discovered in *Chapter 5, Investment and Trading Strategies*, time-series data is the central domain for preparing, supporting, and realizing investment strategies in the finance market. *Chapter 4, Exploratory Data Analysis for Finance*, introduced elementary toolkits for time-series data analysis through *data visualization* and *MA*. Forecasting financial indices is a more complicated problem, however. Therefore, the basic terms and principles of financial time-series data analysis are trends, volatility, seasonality, autocorrelation problems, and stationarity. Let us describe those essential concepts in detail.

Time-series data forecasting begins with an understanding of trends. A *trend* in a financial time series can indicate a persistent increase or decrease over time, offering insights into long-term market movements. As we know from *Chapter 4*, we can visualize the trend by using an MA plot (refer to *Figure 4.4*). Identifying and interpreting trends is only sometimes straightforward, however, due to the inherent volatility in financial data, which is characterized by rapid and unpredictable changes in its value. Volatility, or variation (as a statistical indicator), an intrinsic aspect of financial markets, presents both risks and opportunities. It is essential to quantify and understand volatility metrics and evaluate their impact on the forecasts' accuracy. In conjunction with volatility, seasonality plays a critical role. A particular type of trend and volatility combination is a seasonal pattern. *Seasonal* is a specific feature of time-series data observed at regular intervals, such as monthly or quarterly financial reports or annual shopping seasons that can significantly influence market behavior. All these characteristics are significant for forming an accurate forecast of the prices of financial assets, returns, etc.

Another core concept of time-series data is *stationarity*, a cornerstone application for TSA statistical methods. A stationary time series has properties that do not depend on the time the series is observed. The presence of a trend and seasonality determines a *non-stationary* time data series. Stationarity is usually associated with an RoR data series with 0 mean and constant time-independent variation. Transforming time-series data to be stationary is often a prerequisite for effective modeling, as most forecasting methods assume this property.

For example, let us execute the following code to visualize core time-series data concepts. First, we plot the lines of the 63-day and 252-day *exponential moving averages (EMAs)* according to the dynamics of absolute values of the NASDAQ index:

```
1.  # Calculate the Exponential Moving Average for
    different periods
2.  nasdaq_index_ac_df = pd.DataFrame({
3.      'Index': nasdaq_index_ac,
4.      'EMA_63': nasdaq_index_ac.ewm(span=63,
    adjust=False).mean(),
```

```
5.        'EMA_252': nasdaq_index_ac.ewm(span=252,
   adjust=False).mean()
6. })
7. # Plotting - NASDAQ Index with EMA trends
8. plt.figure(figsize=(10, 5))
9. plt.plot(nasdaq_index_ac_df['Index'],
   label='NASDAQ Index', color='blue')
10. plt.plot(nasdaq_index_ac_df['EMA_63'], label='63-
   day EMA', color='orange')
11. plt.plot(nasdaq_index_ac_df['EMA_252'],
   label='252-day EMA', color='purple')
12. plt.xlabel('Date')
13. plt.ylabel('Adjusted Close Value')
14. plt.legend()
15. plt.show()
```

The results are depicted in *Figure 7.1*:

FIGURE 7.1 EMAs for the NASDAQ index adjusted close values

Figure 7.1 visualizes the NASDAQ index adjusted close values alongside two EMAs: a 63-day EMA and a 252-day EMA. The 63-day EMA, shown by the sensitive and smooth line, represents a medium-term trend, smoothing the value fluctuations over roughly 2 months. The 252-day EMA (the flatter line) represents a long-term trend. Given the number of trading days a year, it is often considered an approximation of a yearly trend. The presence of these EMAs helps to identify the underlying trend in the index by dampening the daily volatility. The long-term EMA (252 days) is smoother and less reactive to daily value changes, providing a clearer view of the market's overall direction. The shorter-term EMA (63 days) is more responsive, reflecting intermediate trends and potential reversals. Therefore, it then shows the primary discretion of time-series data changes.

Next, let us plot the NASDAQ index percentage change to illustrate stationarity concepts in the time-series data by executing the following code:

```
1. # Plotting - The NASDAQ Index Percentage Change
   (Stationarity illustration)

2. plt.figure(figsize=(10, 5))

3. plt.plot(nasdaq_index_pc, label='NASDAQ Index Daily
   % Change', color='blue')

4. plt.xlabel('Date')

5. plt.ylabel('Percentage Change')

6. plt.legend()

7. plt.show()
```

The results are depicted in *Figure 7.2*:

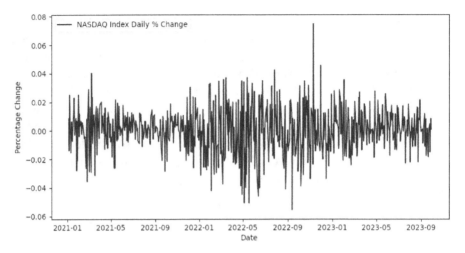

FIGURE 7.2 The NASDAQ index daily percentage change (RoR)

Figure 7.2 shows the NASDAQ index daily percentage change, a common way to illustrate stationarity in financial time-series data. By representing the data as daily returns rather than absolute values or prices, we typically observe a time series that fluctuates around a mean of 0 with an approximate constant variance. This plot is crucial for stationarity because in a stationary series, the mean and variance do not change over time, making it easier to model and predict. The percentage changes of the time-series data usually do not exhibit trends or seasonality, which are common causes of non-stationarity in absolute quantitative data. Another example of stationarity is the *growth metrics*, which are calculated as the difference between current and offset values. Therefore, the stationary series is freed from trend assessments, and the researcher can focus on predicting volatility indicators.

As we see in *Figure 7.1* and *Figure 7.2*, the trend cannot be predicted with absolute accuracy because it does not consider volatility. Thus, assessing volatility becomes the analyst's main problem.

Autocorrelation is the behavior of the time-series data when the observed values of a time series at a given time are correlated with its values at previous times. Autocorrelation poses unique challenges, particularly in distinguishing between true signals (trends) and noises. Execute this code to understand autocorrelation:

```
1.  # Autocorrelation matrix
2.  nasdaq_index_ac_autocorr = pd.DataFrame({
3.      'Shift_0': nasdaq_index_ac,
4.      'Shift_1': nasdaq_index_ac.shift(1),
5.      'Shift_2': nasdaq_index_ac.shift(2),
6.      'Shift_3': nasdaq_index_ac.shift(3),
7.      'Shift_4': nasdaq_index_ac.shift(4),
8.      'Shift_5': nasdaq_index_ac.shift(5)
9.  })
10. print(nasdaq_index_ac_autocorr.head(), '\n')
11. print(nasdaq_index_ac_autocorr.dropna().corr())
```

The code of the results is:

```
                Shift_0         Shift_1         Shift_2         Shift_3  \
Date
2021-01-05  12802.379883            NaN             NaN             NaN
2021-01-06  12623.349609  12802.379883             NaN             NaN
2021-01-07  12939.570312  12623.349609  12802.379883             NaN
2021-01-08  13105.200195  12939.570312  12623.349609  12802.379883
2021-01-11  12902.490234  13105.200195  12939.570312  12623.349609


                Shift_4  Shift_5
Date
2021-01-05          NaN      NaN
2021-01-06          NaN      NaN
2021-01-07          NaN      NaN
2021-01-08          NaN      NaN
2021-01-11  12802.379883      NaN
```

	Shift_0	Shift_1	Shift_2	Shift_3	Shift_4	Shift_5
Shift_0	1.000000	0.990797	0.982101	0.974073	0.966867	0.959630
Shift_1	0.990797	1.000000	0.990780	0.982100	0.974055	0.966854
Shift_2	0.982101	0.990780	1.000000	0.990772	0.982031	0.974017
Shift_3	0.974073	0.982100	0.990772	1.000000	0.990741	0.982032
Shift_4	0.966867	0.974055	0.982031	0.990741	1.000000	0.990746
Shift_5	0.959630	0.966854	0.974017	0.982032	0.990746	1.000000

The code provided calculates and displays the correlation matrix for the NASDAQ index adjusted close values with time shifts. The first part of the results shows the first five rows of the DataFrame, which contains the original time series (`Shift_0`) and its lagged versions (`Shift_1` to `Shift_5`). Each `Shift_n` column represents the NASDAQ index values shifted by n periods. The second part of the results is the correlation matrix derived from the autocorrelation. This matrix shows the Pearson correlation coefficients between the original and lagged series. As we see further from the diagonal (increasing the lag), the correlation coefficients generally decrease, suggesting that the relationship between current and past values diminishes over time. A high correlation coefficient close to 1 for the first few lags (such as `Shift_1`) indicates a robust positive autocorrelation, meaning that the index value on one day is highly predictive of its value on the following day. This is typical in financial time series, where the value of an index tends to follow a smooth trajectory over short intervals.

Therefore, autocorrelation indicates that past values contain information that can be used to predict future values. Distinguishing between true signals and noise can be challenging, however, especially with financial data that is often noisy. High autocorrelation in financial time series also raises concerns about the random walk hypothesis and market efficiency. High autocorrelation in financial time series also raises concerns about the random walk hypothesis and market efficiency. Thus, deeper analysis and modeling considerations are required.

Almost all traditional statistical forecasting models are built considering these fundamental concepts and metrics of time-series data, as shown later in this chapter.

Pandas Toolkits for Time-Series Data Analysis

Pandas provides extensive capabilities for handling and analyzing time-series data, especially its powerful date and time manipulation functionalities. A structured overview of the toolkit that pandas offers is provided in *Table 7.1*:

TABLE 7.1 The main functions of the pandas package for working with time-series data[1]

Task description	Example usage (function/method/attribute)
pandas functions	
Converts string formats to DateTime objects.	`pd.to_datetime(df['date_column'])`
Generates a range of DateTime indices with a specified frequency.	`pd.date_range(start='2023-01-01', periods=10, freq='D')`
Represents a time offset for arithmetic operations.	`pd.DateOffset(days=1)`
Represents a business day offset.	`pd.tseries.offsets.BDay()`
Customizes business day frequency considering holidays.	`pd.offsets.CustomBusinessDay(holidays=['2023-01-01', '2023-01-02'])`
Plots an autocorrection graphic for time-series data from the selected column.	`pandas.plotting.autocorrelation_plot(df['column'])`
pandas DataFrame methods	
Changes the frequency of the time-series data and calculates the average (`.mean()`) for values inside the range. `DateTimeIndex` is not changed.	`df['column'].resample('M').mean()`
Converts a `DateTimeIndex` to a `PeriodIndex`.	`df['column'].resample('M').mean().to_period('M')`
Provides rolling window calculations for the MVA calculation.	`df['column'].rolling(window=5).mean()`
Provides expanding window calculations for the CMA estimate.	`df['column'].expanding(min_periods=1).mean()`
Uses the EMA calculation.	`df['column'].ewm(span=63, adjust=False).mean()`
Shifts the index by a specified number of periods. `.shift(1)` means lagging by one period.	`df['column'].shift(1)`
Calculates the difference between an element and its predecessor. `.diff(2)` is the difference between the lagging of two periods.	`df['column'].diff(2)`
Calculates the percentage change from one element to another. `.pct_change(2)` is the calculation of percentage change between the lagging of two periods.	`df['column'].pct_change(2)`

(Continued)

---

[1] *For more details, see https://pandas.pydata.org/docs/user_guide/timeseries.html*

Task description	Example usage (function/method/attribute)
Sets the DataFrame index using one or more columns.	`df.set_index( pd.to_` `datetime(df['date']))`
pandas DataFrame attributes	
Returns the day of the month from the DataFrame index.	`df.index.day`
Returns the day number of the week from the DataFrame index.	`df.index.dayofweek`
Returns the day number of the year from the DataFrame index.	`df.index.dayofyear`
Returns the month of the date from the DataFrame index.	`df.index.month`
Returns the year of the date from the DataFrame index.	`df.index.year`
Returns the month number from the DateTime-like properties of the DataFrame column.	`df['date_column'].dt.month`

As we see in *Table 7.1*, data analysts can perform various time-series analyses by using core pandas functionalities, from basic data manipulations to more complex transformations and calculations tailored to the time-series data. The appendix with the program code for this chapter provides some additional examples of applying these functions.

TRADITIONAL FORECASTING METHODS AND MODELS

Traditional forecasting methods and models offer a blend of simplicity and effectiveness. Based on statistical theory, these methods form the foundation for understanding complex patterns in historical data, guiding predictions about future trends. The MA method, mentioned in *Chapter 4, Exploratory Data Analysis for Finance*, exponential smoothing, complex ARIMA models, and some others are used to capture subtler time-series aspects. Let us observe some of the traditional models[2].

Exponential smoothing is a time-series forecasting method that applies decreasing weights to past observations, giving more importance to recent data. *Chapter 4, Exploratory Data Analysis for Finance*, already covered a similar approach for calculating the EMA. It is especially effective in datasets with unclear trends or seasonality. Simple exponential smoothing uses a

[2]*For more details, see https://arxiv.org/pdf/2012.03854.pdf*

single smoothing factor (alpha) for weighting, which applies to data without a clear defining trend or seasonality. Double exponential smoothing includes a second smoothing factor to capture trends in the time series. Triple exponential smoothing (the HW model) adds a third smoothing factor to handle seasonality. The well-known HW model is a variation of the standard smoothing approach.

The smoothing components of the HW model are:

- *Level*: The average value in the time series
- *Trend*: The increasing or decreasing pattern in the series (trend capturing)
- *Seasonality*: The repeating short-term cycle (mainly seasonality)

This approach is the best for time series with a clear trend and seasonal pattern, which are commonly used in sales and stock market analysis.

ARIMA is a widely used forecasting model that combines autoregressive features with MA, incorporating differencing to achieve stationarity. This model uses an advanced regression method to estimate the dependence of the indicator on its values and model errors in previous periods.

The components of the ARIMA model are:

- *Autoregressive (AR)*: A part of the model based on the correlation between the time-series data values and several lagged observations.
- *Integrated (I)*: The differencing of the input data to make the time series stationary. For example, one-step lagged data may be stationarity, in which case *I = 1*.
- *Moving average (MA)*: A part of the model that uses the correlation between the time-series data values and a residual error from an MA model applied to lagged values.

These models are ideal for non-seasonal series with trends or cyclic patterns.

SARIMA extends the ARIMA method by adding seasonality components. It uses the same principles as ARIMA, but SARIMA focuses on modeling time-series data with seasonal fluctuations.

Essential components of the SARIMA model are:

- *Autoregressive (AR)*, *Integrated (I)*, and *Moving Average (MA)*: These are the same principles as the traditional ARIMA model.

- *Seasonal elements*: Models are often denoted as SARIMA (p, d, q)(P, D, Q)[S], where P, D, and Q are the seasonal orders for the AR, I, and MA components, respectively, and *[S]* is the size of the seasonal cycle component.

The SARIMA models use seasonal data, such as monthly or seasonal business indices, e.g., financial seasonality.

SARIMAX builds upon SARIMA by incorporating exogenous variables (external factors or regressors) into the model. This version of SARIMA is effective when external factors influence the time series in addition to trends and seasonality. This model is widely used in fields where external variables such as economics and environmental studies significantly impact the forecast.

Each of these models has specific application areas and is selected based on the characteristics of the data, such as *seasonality*, *trends*, *external factors*, and the need for *stationarity*.

Exponential smoothing methods and ARIMA-based models for forecasting time-series data have their scope and disadvantages. After careful parameter tuning, however, they can effectively analyze financial market data. Thus, understanding each model's nuances and appropriate application is crucial for effective forecasting in various domains.

The statsmodels Toolkits for TSA

The mathematical definitions of the HW, ARIMA, SARIMA, and SARIMAX models and methods for searching their parameters are complex and time-consuming. Still, the statsmodels Python library tools allow the implementation of traditional time-series forecasting models quickly and efficiently.

The statsmodels library's TSA module is a powerful tool for the statistical analysis of time-series data. Here is an overview of how statsmodels TSA can be applied to your tasks (refer to the following table):

TABLE 7.2 The main functions of statsmodels.tsa for working with traditional time-series models[3]

Instrument description	Function/ method name	Example/ key function
Functions of statsmodels.tsa		
Decomposes time series into trend, seasonality, and residuals.	`seasonal_decompose`	`from statsmodels.tsa. seasonal import seasonal_ decompose`
Tests for stationarity in time-series data.	`adfuller`	`from statsmodels.tsa. stattools import adfuller`
Calculates autocorrelation and partial autocorrelation.	`acf,pacf`	`from statsmodels.tsa. stattools import acf, pacf`
Visualizes time-series data and diagnostics autocorrelation and partial autocorrelation results.	Plotting `acf` and `pacf`	`from statsmodels.graphics. tsaplots import plot_acf, plot_pacf`
Measures the relationship between two time series.	Cross-correlations	`from statsmodels.tsa. stattools import ccf`
Exponential smoothing models for data with trend and seasonality.	Exponential smoothing and HW	`from statsmodels.tsa. holtwinters import ExponentialSmoothing`
Model for forecasting non-seasonal time-series data.	ARIMA	`from statsmodels.tsa.arima. model import ARIMA`
ARIMA model with seasonal support and exogenous variables.	SARIMAX	`from statsmodels.tsa. statespace.sarimax import SARIMAX`
Initialize the model object		
Initializes the HW exponential smoothing model.	Exponential smoothing and HW	`model = ExponentialSmoothing(data, seasonal='add')`
Initializes the ARIMA model for non-seasonal data.	ARIMA	`model = ARIMA(data, order=(p, d, q))`
Initializes the SARIMAX/ SARIMA model for seasonal data or with/no exogenous variables.	SARIMAX or SARIMA	`model = SARIMAX(data, exog = X, order=(p, d, q), seasonal_order=(P, D, Q, s))`
Methods of the model results object		
Fits (finds optimal parameters of the model) a time-series model to the data and returns a results object.	`.fit`	`model.fit()`
Provides a summary of the fitted model.	`.summary`	`model.summary()`
In-sample prediction and out-of-sample forecasting.	`.predict`	`model.predict()`

(Continued)

---

[3]*For more details, see https://www.statsmodels.org/stable/user-guide.html#time-series-analysis*

Instrument description	Function/ method name	Example/ key function
Forecasts future values.	`.forecast`	`model.forecast(steps=5)`
Predictions with confidence intervals.	`.get_prediction`	`model.get_prediction()`
Forecasts with confidence intervals.	`.get_forecast`	`model.get_forecast(steps=5)`
Confidence intervals for forecasts.	`.conf_int`	`model.conf_int()`

In the *Table 7.2* examples, `data` represents your time-series dataset, and p, d, q, P, D, Q, and s are the model parameters for ARIMA and SARIMAX. Thus, *Table 7.2* provides a structured overview of the tools offered by the statsmodels.tsa module for TSA, as follows:

- `seasonal_decompose()` is a function that breaks down time-series data into trend, seasonal, and residual components, discovering its underlying patterns.

- The `adfuller()` function, used for testing stationarity, is essential for determining whether a time series is suitable for ARIMA-type modeling without further differencing.

- The `acf()` and `pacf()` functions calculate the autocorrelation and partial autocorrelation of the data, which are pivotal in identifying ARIMA models' AR and MA components.

- The plotting utilities `plot_acf()` and `plot_pacf()` visually present autocorrelations and partial autocorrelations, aiding in model specification.

- Cross-correlations are measured using the `ccf()` function, which analyzes the relationship between two time series. This can inform about potential causality or lead-lag impacts.

- The `ExponentialSmoothing` class represents the HW model for data exhibiting trends and seasonality, providing mechanisms for forecasting in such contexts.

- The ARIMA and SARIMAX classes are central to the model's application. ARIMA applies to non-seasonal forecasting, and SARIMAX expands this to seasonal data and incorporates exogenous variables. For the SARIMA model, the argument used is `exog = None`.

- The `.fit()` method is used to estimate the model parameters from the data.

- Once fitted, the model object provides several methods, such as `.summary()`, `.predict()`, `.forecast()`, `.get_prediction()`, and

`.get_forecast()`, for summarizing the model, making predictions, and forecasting with confidence intervals.

- `.conf_int()` calculates confidence intervals, which are critical for visualizing and understanding forecast uncertainty.

In this chapter, we will also consider the application of tool data using specific data and models as an example.

Error Statistical Metrics: MAPE, MSE, and MAE

Each of the traditional statistical models has efficiency and robust indices. Still, universal metrics to estimate the accuracy of the forecast results are *mean squared error (MSE), mean absolute error (MAE)*, MAPE, and others. Unlike model-specific indices such as p-values, the *Akaike information criterion (AIC)*, and BIC, which provide information about the fit of a model to the historical data, these metrics directly evaluate the predictive performance. Explanations are as follows:

- The *MSE* quantifies the average squared discrepancy between the forecasted and actual values. It emphasizes more significant errors more than smaller ones because they are squared before they are averaged, which can be crucial when significant errors have more serious consequences:

$$MSE = \Sigma \, (ActualValue_i + PredictedValue_i)^2 \, / \, n, \, \forall \, i \in [1, n]$$

where n is the number of time-series data points and i is the current value index.

- The *MAE* shows the average errors by taking the absolute value. This metric can highlight whether the forecast consistently exceeds or underestimates the actual values:

$$MAE = (\Sigma \, |ActualValue_i + PredictedValue_i|) \, / \, n, \, \forall \, i \in [1, n]$$

- The *MAPE* measures the average of the errors in percentage terms, providing a straightforward interpretation of error size relative to the actual values. It is beneficial when comparing the accuracy of different models or when the scale of the data is essential:

$$MAPE = 100 \cdot (\Sigma \, |(ActualValue_i + PredictedValue_i) \, / \, ActualValue_i |) \, / \\ n, \, \forall \, i \in [1, n]$$

All of these metrics estimate the error of the predicted and actual values for the time-series data. The MSE and MAE, in absolute terms, and the MAPE, as a percentage, eliminate dimensionality's influence. The principles of using those metrics for the chosen model are:

- *Create subsets of time-series data of training and test samples.* The time-series data is typically split into two parts (for machine learning tasks, into three parts). The *training sample* is used to fit the model, and the *test sample* is applied to check predictive accuracy. These subsets help to ensure that the model's performance is assessed on unseen data, reflecting its potential real-world effectiveness.
- *Carry out model fitting* by estimating the model parameters. This best captures the patterns observed in the training time-series dataset.
- *Generate forecasts for the period covered by the test sample.* These are the model's predictions of the time-series values based on model-fitted results.
- *Statistical error metrics calculation* is necessary to evaluate the accuracy of the forecasts. They are assessed by calculating the MSE, MAE, MAPE, etc. The metrics apply to the actual observed values from the test sample and the forecasted values from the model.

Therefore, these error metrics are compared, often across multiple models or different sets of parameters within the same model. The model with the lowest error metrics is typically considered the best fit. By following these principles, analysts can systematically gauge the performance of the time-series models to deploy to forecast future values.

To estimate the MSE, MAE, and MAPE metrics, we can use user-defined functions or scikit-learn library tools, as follows:

```
1. from sklearn.metrics import mean_squared_error
2. from sklearn.metrics import mean_absolute_error
3. from sklearn.metrics import mean_absolute_
   percentage_error
```

Let us run the following code to estimate the MAPE metric based on a comparison of the actual and exponentially smoothed data:

```
1.  # Load dataset from seaborn library
2.  flights_df = sns.load_dataset('flights')
3.  # Extracting the 'passengers' column from the
    Flights dataset
4.  df = flights_df['passengers']
5.  print("MAPE for actual and 12-month EMA data")
6.  # Calculate Mean Absolute Percentage Error (MAPE)
    # between the actual data and its 12-month EWA
7.  mape = mean_absolute_percentage_error(df,
    df.ewm(span=12).mean())*100
8.  print("Mean Absolute Percentage Error (MAPE):",
    mape)
9.  # Calculate the metrics for the 3-month EMA
10. print("\nMAPE for actual and 3-month EMA data")
11. mape = mean_absolute_percentage_error(df,
    df.ewm(span=3).mean())*100
12. print("Mean Absolute Percentage Error (MAPE):",
    mape)
```

The results of the code are:

```
MAPE for actual and 12-month EMA data

Mean Absolute Percentage Error (MAPE): 9.725760321816695

MAPE for actual and 3-month EMA data

Mean Absolute Percentage Error (MAPE): 5.21703698803825
```

The code provided calculates the **MAPE** to evaluate the forecasting accuracy of exponential smoothing on the flight passengers time series. Two different exponential smoothing windows are used: a 12-month and a 3-month window.

NOTE   *The passengers dataset from the Seaborn library, commonly called the flights dataset, encapsulates monthly totals of international airline passengers from 1949 to 1960[4]. It is a classic dataset used frequently within the data science community to illustrate TSA and forecasting techniques. Each entry represents the number of passengers traveling each month, providing a clear example of seasonal patterns due to periodic peaks and troughs aligning with travel seasons and an overall upward trend. This dataset is valuable for learning time-series modeling tools and comparing the effectiveness of various methods.*

The results of the code execution are as follows:

- For the 12-month trend of EMA, the MAPE is approximately 9.73%. This indicates that, on average, the forecast is off by 9.73% from the actual variance of passenger numbers.

- For the 3-month EMA, the MAPE is approximately 5.22%. This suggests that using a shorter span for smoothing results in a more accurate forecast of the trend and variance, with the forecasts being off by 5.22% from the actual numbers on average.

EXPONENTIAL SMOOTHING AND THE HW MODEL

Exponential smoothing models and their application, the HW model, are well-known traditional methods in time-series forecasting. They offer a flexible framework to capture data trends and seasonality. The simplest model, *exponential smoothing*, is based on smoothing out noise and highlighting underlying patterns in a dataset. It applies to providing short-term forecasts. The *HW model*, an extension of the exponential smoothing approach, also handles datasets with both trends and seasonal variations. It refines predictions by updating estimates through three main equations:

- The *level equation* fine-tunes the baseline value of the series, adapting to changes in the mean level due to both trend and seasonality:

$$L'_t = \alpha(Y_t - S_{t-s}) + (1 - \alpha)(L'_{t-1} + T'_{t-1})$$

---

[4] *https://seaborn.pydata.org/tutorial/data_structure.html*

- The *trend equation* captures the direction and rate of the series' trend, adjusting over time as trends increase or decrease:

$$T'_t = \beta(L'_t - L'_{t-1}) + (1 - \beta) \, T'_{t-1}$$

- The *seasonal equation* highlights the repeating seasonal fluctuations, ensuring that the model accounts for regular patterns at fixed intervals:

$$S'_t = \gamma(Y_t - L'_t) + (1 - \gamma) \, S_{t-s}$$

- The *forecast equation* combines these elements to predict future observations:

$$Y'_{t+m} = (L'_t + mT'_t) + S'_{t-s+m}$$

Where:

- L'_t is the calculated level at time t.
- T'_t is the calculated trend at time t.
- S'_t is the calculated seasonal component at time t.
- Y'_{t+m} is the forecast for m periods ahead.
- Y_t is the actual value at time t.
- S_{t-s} is the seasonal component at time $t - s$.
- α, β, and γ are the smoothing coefficients for level, trend, and seasonality, respectively.
- m is the number of periods ahead for the forecast.
- s is the size of the seasonal cycle.

Let us run the following code to illustrate the results of using the HW model with Python:

```
1.  # Load ExponentialSmoothing initial class
2.  from statsmodels.tsa.holtwinters import
    ExponentialSmoothing
3.  # Load dataset from seaborn library
4.  flights_df = sns.load_dataset('flights')
```

```
5.   # Convert 'month' to its numeric representation

6.   flights_df['month'] = pd.to_datetime(flights_
     df['month'],
                              format='%b').dt.month

7.   # Create a combined 'year-month' column and
     convert it to the datetime

8.   flights_df['date'] = pd.to_datetime(flights_
     df['year'].astype(str) + \
     '-' + flights_df['month'].astype(str))

9.   # Set 'date' as an index and convert it to
     PeriodIndex

10.  flights_df.set_index('date', inplace=True)

11.  flights_df.index = flights_df.index.to_period('M')

12.  # Create training and test set

13.  test_period = 12

14.  df = flights_df['passengers']

15.  train_set = df.iloc[:-test_period]

16.  test_set = df.iloc[-test_period:]

17.  # Forecasting model

18.  model = ExponentialSmoothing(endog = train_set,

19.              trend = 'add',      # 'mul' or 'add'

20.              seasonal = 'add',   # 'mul' or 'add'

21.              seasonal_periods = 12).fit()

22.  # Predictions

23.  predictions_hw = model.forecast(steps = test_
     period).rename("Holt-Winters Forecast")

24.  predictions_hw.index = test_set.index

25.  predictions_hw.head()

26.  # Visualization
```

```
27.  df[-60:-1].plot(figsize = (10,5), legend = True)
28.  predictions_hw.plot(legend = True)
29.  # Displaying the MAPE value on the plot
30.  m_mape = mean_absolute_percentage_error(test_set,
     predictions_hw) * 100
31.  plt.text(0.45, 0.95, f'MAPE: {m_mape:.2f}%',
     transform=plt.gca().transAxes, fontsize=10,
     verticalalignment='top')
```

The results are depicted in *Figure 7.3*:

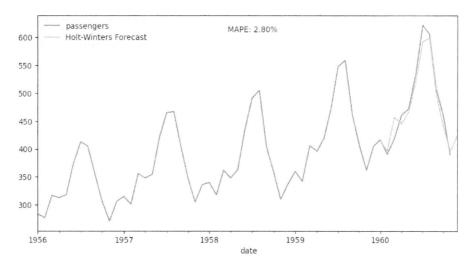

FIGURE 7.3 HW model forecasts of the flight passengers dataset

Based on the code provided, *Figure 7.3* shows how well the HW model, with its specified parameters, can capture the seasonal patterns and trends in the historical flight passengers dataset. It shows the forecast of the passenger numbers for the next 12 months and the MAPE value of 2.8%, providing insight into the percentage error of the model's forecasts. The lower the MAPE, the more accurate the model's predictions are. When it comes to financial data, however, the scenario often changes. Financial markets are characterized by their volatility, and the patterns the HW model excels in capturing may be less pronounced or even exist in a form that the model can utilize. Seasonality in financial data is only sometimes clear and consistent due to the many factors influencing market prices, including economic indicators, investor sentiment, geopolitical events, and market anomalies. Therefore, other specific tools are needed to identify trends and seasonality.

Seasonality Decomposition in Python

Seasonality decomposition is a crucial technique in TSA, allowing us to dissect complex data into fundamental components: trend, seasonality, and residual error. The following code shows an example of the use of the `seasonal_decompose()` function:

```
1.  # Use an additive model to decompose
2.  # Yt = Tt (Trend) + St (Seasonal) + Et (Residual
    (error))
3.  decomp = seasonal_decompose(flights['passengers'],
4.                                    period = 12,
5.                                    model = 'add')
6.  fig = plt.figure()
7.  fig = decomp.plot()
8.  fig.set_size_inches(10, 5)
9.  # Use a multiplicative model to decompose
10. # Yt = Tt (Trend) × St (Seasonal) × Et (Residual
    (error))
11. decomp = seasonal_decompose(flights['passengers'],
12.                                   period = 24,
13.                                   model = 'mul')
14. fig = plt.figure()
15. fig = decomp.plot()
16. fig.set_size_inches(10, 5)
```

The results for `period = 12` and the `model = 'add'` model are depicted in *Figure 7.4*.

The additive model is suitable for roughly constant seasonal variations (*Figure 7.4*). The multiplicative model (the figure is shown in the appendix with the program code) is used when seasonal variations change proportionally with the trend. Analysis of the data in *Figure 7.4* shows that the selected additive seasonality of 12 months for the dataset does not consider all periods. The figure shows residuals; fluctuations around 0 and dependence are visible. That is, additive seasonality is insufficient for the complete series data forecasting. Thus, even though the additive model provided the MAPE at the level of 2.20%, it is also necessary to consider the possibility of using the multiplicative form:

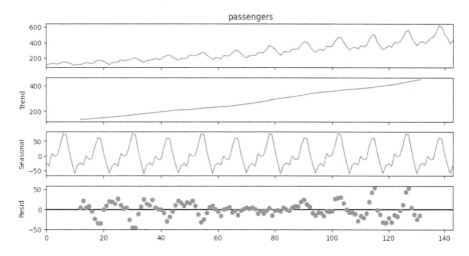

FIGURE 7.4 Seasonality decomposition of the flight passengers dataset (12 periods and additive model)

The HW Method: Multiplicative Trend and Seasonal Components

The HW method with multiplicative trend and seasonal components is a variation of the triple exponential smoothing technique, where both the trend and seasonal components are multiplied rather than added. Here are the equations for the HW method with a multiplicative trend and seasonal components:

▪ Level equation:

$$L'_t = \alpha \, (Y_t / S_{t-s}) + (1 - \alpha) \, (L'_{t-1} \times T'_{t-1})$$

▪ Trend equation:

$$T'_t = \beta \, (L'_t / L'_{t-1}) + (1 - \beta) \, T'_{t-1}$$

▪ Seasonal equation:

$$S'_t = \gamma \, (Y_t / L'_t) + (1 - \gamma) \, S_{t-s}$$

▪ Forecast equation:

$$Y'_{t+m} = (L'_t \times (T'_t)^m) \times S'_{t-s+m \, (mod \, s)}$$

where *mod(s)* is applied to the index of the seasonal component; other variables have the same meaning as for the additive version.

In this model, the multiplicative approach is beneficial when the seasonal variations change proportionally with the series level, and the trend evolves multiplicatively. Let us execute the following code to demonstrate the *multiplicative HW model* results:

```
1.  # Training and test set
2.  test_period = 12
3.  df = flights_df['passengers']
4.  train_set = df.iloc[:-test_period]
5.  test_set = df.iloc[-test_period:]
6.  # Forecasting model
7.  model = ExponentialSmoothing(endog = train_set,
8.                  trend = 'mul',       # 'mul' or 'add'
9.                  seasonal = 'mul',   # 'mul' or 'add'
10.                 seasonal_periods = 24).fit()
11. # Predictions
```

```
12.  predictions_hw = model.forecast(steps = test_
     period).rename("Holt-Winters Forecast")

13.  predictions_hw.index = test_set.index

14.  # Visualization

15.  df[-60:-1].plot(figsize = (10,5), legend = True)

16.  predictions_hw.plot(legend = True)

17.  # Displaying the MAPE value on the plot

18.  m_mape = mean_absolute_percentage_error(test_set,
     predictions_hw) * 100

19.  plt.text(0.45, 0.95, f'MAPE: {m_mape:.2f}%',
             transform=plt.gca().transAxes,
             fontsize=10, verticalalignment='top')
```

The results are depicted in *Figure 7.5*:

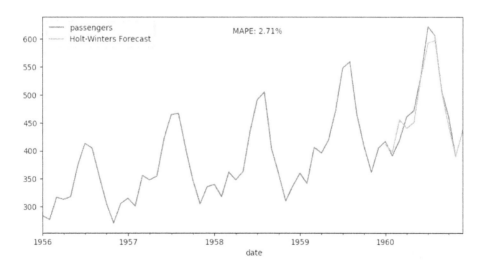

FIGURE 7.5 HW model forecasts of the flight passengers dataset (multiplicative trend and seasonal components)

As seen in *Figure 7.5*, the HW multiplicative model made it possible to reduce the MAPE to 2.71%. Despite their seeming simplicity, however, the HW models could be more applicable to the fundamental dynamics of the financial market. The appendix with the program code presents examples for the NASDAQ index, demonstrating this model's limitations.

ARIMA APPROACH: FROM MA TO SEASONALITY AND EXTERNAL VARIABLES

ARIMA time-series forecasting embodies the synthesis of autoregressive features with MA, all while incorporating the critical concept of integration to achieve stationarity. The following equations describe the ARIMA model:

▨ *Autoregressive (AR)* represents the correlation between an observation and a certain number of lagged observations:

$$Y_t = \phi_1 Y_{t-1} + \phi_2 Y_{t-2} + \ldots + \phi_p Y_{t-p} + \varepsilon_t$$

▨ *Integrated (I)* represents the differencing of observations to make the time series stationary:

$$Y_t' = (1 - B)^d Y_t$$

▨ *Moving average (MA)* represents the correlation between an observation and a certain number of lagged forecast errors:

$$Y_t = \theta_1 \varepsilon_{t-1} + \theta_2 \varepsilon_{t-2} + \ldots + \theta_q \varepsilon_{t-q} + \varepsilon_t$$

▨ Combining these, the ARIMA model can be written as:

$$Y_t' = c + \phi_1 Y_{t-1}' + \ldots + \phi_p Y_{t-p}' + \theta_1 \varepsilon_{t-1} + \ldots + \theta_q \varepsilon_{t-q} + \varepsilon_t$$

Where:

▨ Y_t is the value of the series at time t.
▨ Y_t' is the differenced series (if necessary).
▨ B is the backshift operator. It is used to shift the time-series data back by one period.
▨ $\phi_1 \ldots \phi_p$ c is a constant.

- $\phi_1...\phi_p$ are the parameters for the autoregressive part.
- $\theta_1...\theta_q$ are the parameters for the MA part.
- ε_t refers to the white noise error terms at time t.

To define the parameters of the ARIMA model, three essential tools are used. Stationarity tests are used to determine the level of differencing needed for the model (the I component). The ACF for the stationary series (calculated based on the differenced series with the order determined at the stationarity level—the I component) is used to evaluate the level of the MA component. The PACF is the basis for assessing the level of the AR component.

Stationarity Test

Transitioning to the main task of verifying stationarity, a prerequisite for the productive application of the ARIMA model, we employ the *augmented Dickey-Fuller (ADF)* test. This statistical test probes the time series for unit roots (the specific math indicator). By examining the ADF test results, we get conclusions about the temporal structure of the time series, ensuring that the foundational assumptions of the ARIMA model are met before proceeding with model estimation and forecasting. Execute the following code to provide the stationarity test of the passenger dataset:

```
1.  # Print the row results of the ADF test directly
2.  print(adfuller(flights_df['passengers']))
3.  # Define a function to interpret the ADF test
    results
4.  def describe_adfuller_results(series):
5.      # Perform ADF test
6.      result = adfuller(series)
7.      # Format the output
8.      adf_results = pd.Series(result[0:4], index=[
9.          'Test Statistic', 'p-value', '#Lags
    Used',
10.         'Number of Observations Used'])
11.     # Add critical values to the series
```

```
12.      for key, value in result[4].items():
13.          adf_results[f'Critical Value ({key})'] =
      value
14.      # Display the results
15.      print("\nResults of Dickey-Fuller Test:")
16.      print(adf_results)
17.      # Conditional statement for interpretation
18.      if adf_results['p-value'] < 0.05:
19.          print("The time series is stationary as
      the p-value is below 0.05.")
20.      else:
21.          print("The time series is not stationary
      as the p-value is above 0.05.")
22. # Example usage of the function
23. describe_adfuller_results(flights_df['passengers'])
24. describe_adfuller_results(flights_df['passengers'].
      diff(1).dropna())
25. describe_adfuller_results(flights_df['passengers'].
      diff(2).dropna())
```

The results (truncated) of the code are:

```
(0.8153688792060498, 0.991880243437641, 13, 130, {'1%':
-3.4816817173418295, '5%': -2.8840418343195267, '10%':
-2.578770059171598}, 996.692930839019)

Results of Dickey-Fuller Test:
Test Statistic              0.815369
p-value                     0.991880
(...)
```

The time series is not stationary as the p-value is above
0.05.

```
Results of Dickey-Fuller Test:

Test Statistic                        -2.829267

p-value                                0.054213

#Lags Used                            12.000000

Number of Observations Used     130.000000

Critical Value (1%)                   -3.481682

Critical Value (5%)                   -2.884042

Critical Value (10%)                  -2.578770

dtype: float64
```

The time series is not stationary as the p-value is above 0.05.

```
Results of Dickey-Fuller Test:

Test Statistic                        -2.961695

p-value                                0.038630

(...)
```

The time series is stationary as the p-value is below 0.05.

In TSA, the ADF test is used to check the stationarity of a dataset. A common criterion for stationarity is a p-value less than 0.05, indicating that the series is stationary. We get the p-value of 0.054213 for the first-differenced time series; it is slightly above the typical threshold for statistical significance. It is close to 0.05, however, which suggests that the series may be borderline stationary or that there is some evidence against the presence of a unit root, albeit not strong enough to meet the usual standard of statistical significance. Even if the p-value is slightly above 0.05, if other diagnostics (such as the ACF and PACF plots) indicate that the series does not exhibit significant autocorrelations and the time plot of the differenced series appears to fluctuate around a constant mean, it may still be reasonable to consider the series as sufficiently stationary for modeling, especially if further differencing could lead to over-differencing and introduce unnecessary complexity and variance. Therefore, it may be sufficient to set $I = 1$ for the passenger dataset for future modeling and forecasting.

Autocorrelation and Partial Autocorrelation Functions

The ACF and PACF are pivotal tools that provide insights into the temporal structure of the data. The ACF measures the correlation between observations in a time series separated by various lag lengths, which is instrumental in identifying an ARIMA model's MA component. The PACF offers a measure of correlation between observations at varying lags while accounting for the influence of shorter lags. This makes it particularly useful for identifying an ARIMA model's autoregressive component. It reveals the direct relationship between an observation and its lagged version, independent of other lagged observations.

The code provided illustrates how to generate plots for the ACF and PACF, including applying the ACF to a first-differenced series:

```
1.  # Plotting Autocorrelation Function (ACF)

2.  # ACF measures the correlation between time
    series observations at different lags

3.  # Useful for identifying the MA (Moving Average)
    component in ARIMA modelling

4.  fig_first = plot_acf(flights_df['passengers'])

5.  # Plotting Autocorrelation Function (ACF) for
    First-Differenced Series

6.  # This code subtracts each value in the
    series from the value that precedes it (first
    difference)

7.  # Plotting the ACF of the first-differenced
    series helps identify autocorrelation after
    removing the trend

8.  fig_first_shift = plot_acf((flights_
    df['passengers'].diff(1)).dropna())

9.  # Plotting Partial Autocorrelation Function
    (PACF)

10. # PACF measures the partial correlation between
    observations at different lags
```

```
11.  # Helps in identifying the AR (Autoregressive)
     component for ARIMA modeling
12.  fig_seasonal = plot_pacf(flights_df['passengers'])
```

The results are depicted in *Figure 7.6* and *Figure 7.7*:

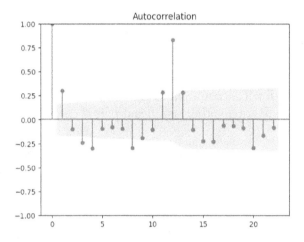

FIGURE 7.6 Autocorrelation function of the flight passengers dataset

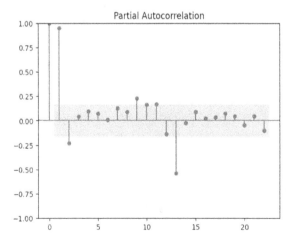

FIGURE 7.7 PACF of the flight passengers dataset

According to *Figures 7.6* and *Figure 7.7*, we can see two plots depicting the ACF and PACF for the passengers dataset. A few spikes outside the confidence interval (shaded area) suggest significant autocorrelation at those lags. The ACF is significant in periods 0 and 1. The autocorrelations at lags beyond the first few do not show a clear, systematic pattern of decay, which might have been expected in a purely MA process. Therefore, we expected MA(1), but it may be another. The PACF plot displays a significant positive spike at lag 1, indicating a potential AR(1) component where the current value has a strong linear relationship with its immediate previous value. In the second lag position, however, the level of the PACF is a significant negative spike. The subsequent lags fall within the confidence interval, which suggests that they are not significantly different from 0 when the direct effects of the intervening lags are accounted for. This could imply that an AR(1) or AR(2) model might be suitable, as there are no other significant partial autocorrelations at higher lags.

Custom ARIMA Model Estimation

Based on *Figure 7.6* and the ADF test alone, one might lean toward an ARIMA model with the parameters $p = 1$, $I = 1$, and $q = 1$ or 2. Yet, these plots and tests are merely a starting point; rigorous iterative testing and validation of the ARIMA model across different combinations of p and q values are crucial. Model fit statistics, residual analysis, and the MAPE should be assessed to confirm the model's suitability. After conducting several trial runs, explicitly evaluating the AIC and MAPE for the models ARIMA(1,1,1), ARIMA(1,2,1), ARIMA(2,2,2), and ARIMA(2,1,2), it was found that ARIMA(2,1,2) offers the lowest AIC and MAPE values. Let us present the corresponding code and execute it:

```
1.  from statsmodels.tsa.arima.model import ARIMA

2.  # Settings

3.  test_periods = 12   # Assuming you want to
    forecast the last 12 periods

4.  df = flights_df['passengers']

5.  # Splitting the dataset into training and test
    sets
```

```
 6.  train_set = df.iloc[:-test_periods]
 7.  test_set = df.iloc[-test_periods:]
 8.  # Define the ARIMA model with seasonal_order
 9.  model = ARIMA(train_set,
10.                 order=(2, 1, 2))
11.  results = model.fit()
12.  print(results.summary())
13.  # Forecast the next test periods
14.  forecast = results.get_forecast(steps=test_periods)
15.  predictions = pd.Series(forecast.predicted_mean)
16.  predictions.index = test_set.index
17.  # Visualization
18.  df[-60:].plot(figsize = (10,5), legend = True)
19.  predictions.plot(legend = True)
20.  # Displaying the MAPE value on the plot
21.  m_mape = mean_absolute_percentage_error(test_set,
     predictions)
22.  plt.text(0.45, 0.95, f'MAPE: {m_mape:.2f}%',
     transform=plt.gca().transAxes, fontsize=10,
     verticalalignment='top')
```

The results of the code are:

```
    SARIMAX Results

==============================================================================
Dep. Variable:          passengers   No. Observations:           132
Model:              ARIMA(2, 1, 2)   Log Likelihood          -607.782
Date:           Sun, 17 Dec 2023   AIC                     1225.563
Time:                   21:33:50   BIC                     1239.939
```

```
Sample:              01-31-1949   HQIC                1231.405
                   - 12-31-1959

Covariance Type:              opg

==================================================================
               coef    std err      z      P>|z|    [0.025    0.975]
------------------------------------------------------------------
ar.L1        1.6660     0.024   68.561    0.000    1.618     1.714
ar.L2       -0.9294     0.022  -41.536    0.000   -0.973    -0.886
ma.L1       -1.8324     0.032  -56.857    0.000   -1.896    -1.769
ma.L2        0.9581     0.032   29.998    0.000    0.895     1.021
sigma2     605.1587    73.622    8.220    0.000  460.863   749.454
==================================================================
Ljung-Box (L1) (Q):            0.45   Jarque-Bera (JB):       0.78
Prob(Q):                       0.50   Prob(JB):               0.68
Heteroskedasticity (H):        6.52   Skew:                   0.19
Prob(H) (two-sided):           0.00   Kurtosis:               3.01
```

The results are depicted in the following figure:

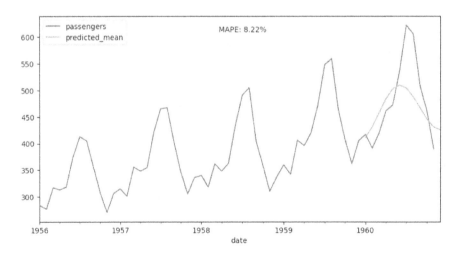

FIGURE 7.8 ARIMA(2, 1, 2) model forecasts of the flight passengers dataset

After executing the code for the ARIMA(2,1,2) assessment on the passengers dataset, we observe that all model coefficients are statistically significant (p-value < 0.005); the forecast error percentage over 12 months stands at an MAPE of 8.22%, and preliminary analysis based on the ADF test, ACF, and PACF did not yield a definitive result.

Thus, while ARIMA models are powerful forecasting tools, they may only sometimes be as accurate as simple exponential smoothing models. Another distinctive feature of these models is the ambiguity in parameter selection, necessitating the exploration of all possible ARIMA model variations and comparative evaluation of their performance indicators.

SARIMA and SARIMAX Models

The ARIMA model, while robust, may falter in the face of seasonality or when external variables play a significant role in the time-series dynamics. This is where SARIMA and SARIMAX come into play. The mathematical formulation of the SARIMA and SARIMAX models is quite complicated. You can view it on various public resources, for example, *https://www.statsmodels.org/stable/examples/notebooks/generated/statespace_sarimax_stata.html*. Therefore, we present only the main differences between the traditional ARIMA approach:

- The non-seasonal ARIMA component captures the relationship between a data point and its previous values, adjusting for trends and ensuring stationarity by differencing the data. This part does not consider any seasonal effects.

- The seasonal component of the SARIMA model accounts for patterns that repeat at regular intervals, such as monthly or quarterly cycles. It includes seasonal autoregressive and MA elements and seasonal differencing to model and remove seasonal effects, making the data stationary within each season.

- The SARIMAX model is an extension of SARIMA that introduces a new element-exogenous variable or variables, like traditional regression. We can potentially improve forecast accuracy by incorporating these variables into the model. It is important to note that those exogenous variables must be known over the entire forecast horizon.

Thus, SARIMA, which integrates seasonality into the ARIMA framework, allows for a more nuanced understanding and prediction of seasonal time-series data. The SARIMAX model incorporates exogenous variables, offering a multifaceted approach that accounts for additional factors influencing the series.

In the Python ecosystem, the pmdarima package provides the `auto_arima` function, a powerful tool that automates the process of ARIMA model selection. It intelligently iterates over various model parameters, including seasonal components, to find the best-fitting model according to specified information criteria. This function can streamline the typically laborious process of identifying the optimal parameters for the SARIMA and SARIMAX models, making it an invaluable asset for practitioners in TSA. With `auto_arima`, one can harness the power of automation to traverse the model space efficiently and uncover the most effective configuration for forecasting.

Let us explore how to estimate the parameters of SARIMAX models by using the `auto_arima` function. The following results demonstrate how to estimate the parameters of SARIMAX models for the AstraZeneca PLC stock price in 2023. This process involves decomposing the seasonal components of the data, generating date-related features, tuning the SARIMAX model, and predicting along with the confidence intervals. The results highlight the model's performance and accuracy, which are visually represented in *Figure 7.9*.

Execute the following code to explore the results:

```
1.  from pmdarima import auto_arima
2.  # Seasonality decompose
3.  data = nasdaq_assets_ac['AZN']['2023']
4.  decomp = seasonal_decompose(data,
5.                                  period = 5,
6.                                  model = 'add')
7.  fig = plt.figure()
8.  fig = decomp.plot()
9.  fig.set_size_inches(10, 5)
10. # SARIMAX model tuning
11. data = nasdaq_assets_ac['AZN']['2023']
```

```
12.  dataframe = pd.DataFrame({
13.      'y': data,
14.      'day': data.index.day,
15.      'month': data.index.month,
16.      'day_year': data.index.dayofyear})
17.  dataframe.dropna(inplace=True)
18.  # Split into train and test sets
19.  test_size = 5
20.  train_set = dataframe.iloc[:-test_size]
21.  test_set = dataframe.iloc[-test_size:]
22.  #forecasting model
23.  model = auto_arima(y = train_set['y'],
24.                     X = train_set[['month']],
25.                     d = 1,
26.                     m = 10,
27.                     n_jobs = -1,
28.                     seasonal = True,
29.                     stepwise = False)
30.  print(model.summary())
31.  # Generate predictions and confidence intervals
32.  forecast, conf_int = model.predict
     (n_periods=test_size,
33.                              X=test_set[['month']],
34.                              return_conf_int=True)
35.  # Convert forecast and confidence intervals to
     pandas Series for easier plotting
36.  predictions = pd.Series(forecast).
     rename("SARIMAX")
```

```python
37. predictions.index=test_set.index
38. m_mape = mean_absolute_percentage_error (test_
    set['y'], predictions) * 100
39. lower_conf = pd.Series(conf_int[:, 0],
40.                          index=test_set.index).
    rename("Lower CI")
41. upper_conf = pd.Series(conf_int[:, 1],
42.                          index=test_set.index).
    rename("Upper CI")
43. # Plotting the observed data, forecast, and
    confidence intervals
44. plt.figure(figsize=(15, 5))
45. dataframe[-30:]['y'].plot(legend=True,
46.                             title='SARIMAX Forecast
    with Confidence Intervals')
47. test_set['y'].rename('True y').plot(legend=True)
48. # Plotting the confidence intervals
49. predictions.plot(legend=True, color='red',
    linestyle='-')
50. # Plotting the confidence intervals
51. plt.fill_between(lower_conf.index, lower_conf,
                 upper_conf, color='k', alpha=0.15)
52. # Displaying the MAPE value on the plot
53. plt.text(0.75, 0.95, f'MAPE: {m_mape:.2f}%',
54.         transform=plt.gca().transAxes,
55.         fontsize=10, verticalalignment='top')
56. plt.xlabel('Date')
57. plt.ylabel('Price')
58. plt.legend(loc='upper left')
59. plt.show()
```

The results of the code are:

```
                          SARIMAX Results
================================================================================
Dep. Variable:                         y     No. Observations:
182
Model:          SARIMAX(1, 1, 0)x(1, 0, 0, 10)   Log Likelihood
-244.187
Date:                    Sun, 17 Dec 2023     AIC
498.374
Time:                          22:02:57     BIC
514.366
Sample:                               0     HQIC
504.857
                                     - 182
Covariance Type:                     opg
================================================================================
                 coef    std err         z      P>|z|     [0.025     0.975]
--------------------------------------------------------------------------------
intercept      0.0571      0.082     0.699      0.484     -0.103      0.217
month         -1.0084      0.245    -4.117      0.000     -1.488     -0.528
ar.L1         -0.1296      0.076    -1.699      0.089     -0.279      0.020
ar.S.L10      -0.1612      0.082    -1.955      0.051     -0.323      0.000
sigma2         0.8683      0.080    10.906      0.000      0.712      1.024
================================================================================
Ljung-Box (L1) (Q):                0.01   Jarque-Bera (JB):         155.49
Prob(Q):                           0.91   Prob(JB):                   0.00
Heteroskedasticity (H):            1.68   Skew:                      -0.64
Prob(H) (two-sided):               0.05   Kurtosis:                   7.36
================================================================================
```

The results of the code are shown in the following figure:

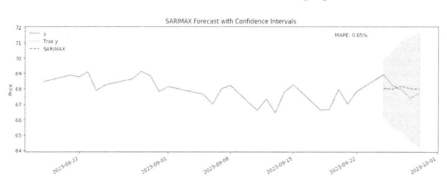

FIGURE 7.9 SARIMAX(0, 1, 3)x(0, 1, [], 12) model forecast of the AstraZeneca PLC stock price with month number as the exogenous variable

Here is what each `auto_arima()` parameter signifies in the given code snippet:

- *y*: The endogenous variable or the time series trying to model or predict. In this case, it is `train_set['y']`, a column from a DataFrame named `train_set`.

- *X*: Exogenous variables are external factors or predictors that might affect the endogenous variable. Here, `train_set[['month']]` indicates that the month may have some explanatory power over the target time series.

- *d*: The order of first differencing is needed to make the series stationary. Setting `d = 1` implies that the series should be differenced once.

- *m*: The seasonal period. This parameter is used to specify the number of steps in a seasonal period. Here, `m = 10` suggests 10 periods per season in the data.

- *n_jobs*: The number of CPUs to use during the model fitting process. A value of `-1` means that all available CPUs will be used.

- *seasonal*: A Boolean flag (`True` or `False`) indicating whether to apply the SARIMA model. Setting `seasonal = True` enables the function to consider seasonal components during model fitting.

- `stepwise`: A Boolean flag (`True` or `False`) that indicates whether the stepwise algorithm should be used to fit the model. Setting `stepwise = False` means that the function will use a brute-force approach, checking all possible model combinations, which can be more time-consuming but thorough.

The `auto_arima` function will iteratively explore different combinations of p, d, and q (for the non-seasonal part of the model) and P, D, Q, and s (for the seasonal part of the model) to find the best model that minimizes a given information criterion, typically the AIC.

The code also demonstrates how to split the dataset into training and testing sets, fit the SARIMAX model, generate predictions along with their confidence intervals, and visualize the results, including the MAPE metric, to assess forecast accuracy.

The SARIMAX model fitting results show that the model selected is a SARIMAX(1, 1, 0)x(1, 0, 0, 10). The reported MAPE of 0.68% indicates a relatively low average percentage error in the forecasts, which is promising. The p-values for the autoregressive terms at lag 1 and seasonal lags of 10 suggest that while the model captures some of the dynamics in the series, not all coefficients are statistically significant at conventional levels ($p < 0.05$). The output also includes other diagnostic statistics that provide insight into the model's fit. The model fitting and its subsequent evaluation, as depicted in *Figure 7.9*, underscore the utility of SARIMAX when accounting for both seasonal patterns and the impact of exogenous variables. The model's results are not fully valuable, however, which requires additional preliminary research, extensive data preparation, and high analytical proficiency. In addition, the linear nature of SARIMAX class models does not always correspond to practical issues.

CONCLUSION

TSA is an essential aspect of financial data forecasting, offering insights into trends, volatility, seasonality, and stationarity, which are critical for informed decision-making in the finance market. Python and its *pandas* and *statsmodels* libraries provide rich toolkits for manipulating and analyzing time-series data, enabling analysts to prepare, support, and realize investment strategies. Whether visualizing trends with MA, understanding the implications of volatility, dissecting seasonal patterns, or ensuring data stationarity for reliable modeling, the capacity to transform, visualize, and model time-series data using Python's functions and methods is invaluable.

We have explored the traditional models of TSA, which serve as fundamental tools in financial forecasting. These models, including exponential smoothing and ARIMA approaches, form the basis for understanding historical data trends, seasonality, and external factors influencing market movements. For example, the *HW exponential smoothing* method with multiplicative trends and seasonal components was explored as a flexible forecasting tool that can capture seasonal trends in time-series data. It is effective for short-term predictions, mainly when the data exhibits consistent seasonal patterns.

The ARIMA-based models are based on *autoregressive* and *MA features*. They can be used to solve complex financial problems, especially in combination with stationarity tests, autocorrelation, and PACF. The SARIMAX model further enhances classical ARIMA by considering *seasonal* patterns and the impact of *external variables*, making it suitable for complex scenarios where such factors significantly influence the time series. With tools such as the `auto_arima` function from the pmdarima package, parameter selection is automated, simplifying the typically strenuous model identification process. All of these time-series models are powerful yet require careful consideration of their parameters to ensure accurate forecasting, especially in fields influenced by seasonal and external factors.

All these standard time-series models are powerful, although they require careful estimation of their parameters to ensure accurate forecasting. The high complexity of financial time-series data, however, often does not allow the traditional statistical models to produce results with sufficient accuracy. Therefore, innovative tools, such as machine learning tools and neural network models, are now actively used, which will be discussed in subsequent chapters.

QUESTIONS

1. What are the main Python tools that can be used for time-series analysis and financial data forecasting?

2. What are the exponential smoothing models?

3. What is the HW model?

4. What is the ARIMA model?

5. What is the decomposition of a time series?

6. What is the stationarity of a time series?

7. How can the ACF and the PACF be used to identify the order of the ARIMA model?

8. How can the ARIMA model be used to forecast financial data?

9. What time-series data elements are considered by the SARIMA and SARIMAX models?

10. What are some of the complex financial forecasting challenges that the SARIMA and SARIMAX models can be used for?

11. What is the difference between the ARIMA and HW models?

12. What are some of the challenges of using the traditional time-series models?

KEY TERMS

- *Trend* refers to a time-series dataset's long-term movement or direction. It can be upward (increasing), downward (decreasing), or horizontal (stable).

- *Seasonality* describes the regular and predictable patterns or movements that recur over specific periods, such as annual seasons, days, weeks, months, and quarters. Factors such as the weather, holidays, or biological cycles may influence seasonality.

- *Stationarity* is the statistical properties that are constant over time. Stationarity, for example, can be defined as a time series without a trend, constant variance, stable autocorrelation, no periodic fluctuations, etc. This property is crucial for building stable forecasting models of the ARIMA types.

REFERENCES

- *Petropoulos, F. et al. (2022). Forecasting: theory and practice. https://arxiv.org/pdf/2012.03854.pdf.*

- *Peixeiro, M. (2022). Time Series Forecasting in Python. Manning Publications.*

- *pandas data analysis library. https://pandas.pydata.org.*

- *Time Series Analysis. Statsmodels User Guide. https://www.statsmodels.org/stable/user-guide.html#time-series-analysis.*

8

RISK ASSESSMENT AND VOLATILITY MODELING

INTRODUCTION

This chapter explores the essentials of the financial risk assessment and volatility modeling concepts. We will begin with an overview of the principles of probability theory and its applications in volatility analysis, highlighting the role of statistical distributions such as normal distribution. Then, we shift to practically implementing these concepts, using Python to calculate and analyze *value at risk (VaR)* and *average value at risk (aVaR)*. These metrics serve as vital indicators of potential financial loss, providing a quantitative framework for risk evaluation.

The chapter continues by laying out the theoretical framework for Monte Carlo simulations, which leverages randomness and statistical inference to support financial decisions. The application of this method is demonstrated through Python-based real-world examples, which include the computation of option prices and the estimation of VaR. In addition, you are introduced to practical examples of using Python code to obtain and analyze option pricing data.

Lastly, the section on the ARCH and GARCH models introduces you to advanced methods for predicting and understanding market volatility. The chapter provides a detailed guide on using these models to support financial decisions with practical Python applications.

STRUCTURE

This chapter covers the following topics:

- Probability theory basics
- VaR metric for risk assessment in finance
- Monte Carlo method in finance
- ARCH and GARCH models

OBJECTIVES

This chapter aims to empower you to seamlessly translate sophisticated principles of probability theory into executable Python code, culminating in a deep understanding of the principles of financial risk and volatility. By the end of this chapter, you will have acquired the proficiency to apply Python's computational capabilities to financial risk assessment and volatility modeling. You will also understand how to use Python tools with key probabilistic distributions through the computation of VaR and aVaR. Using the power of Monte Carlo simulations, you will be able to apply randomizing or stochastic methods to forecast the price of financial securities. By comprehensively exploring ARCH and GARCH models, you will be equipped with the foresight to anticipate and model financial volatility.

PROBABILITY THEORY BASICS

Previous chapters show that forecasting financial indices is fraught with uncertainty. Analysts and investors utilize various methodologies to predict market movements, from statistical and regression analysis to technical and graphical methods. Despite these efforts, we are perpetually confronted with the issue of discrepancies between our forecasts and actual data, manifested as errors. For instance, while we employed ARIMA models in *Chapter 7, Time-Series Analysis and Financial Data Forecasting*, our forecasts' *mean absolute percentage error (MAPE)* remained notably high. This persistent challenge is attributable mainly to financial markets' inherent variability or volatility.

Volatility, the statistical metric of the fluctuation of the price or the *rate of return (RoR)* for a given security or market index, is a multifaceted concept that captures the intensity of price deviation. We estimate it with the standard deviation or variation statistical metric. It is a central financial concept, serving as a key indicator of risk and uncertainty. Therefore, understanding the volatility is critical for optimizing financial investment portfolios, as discussed in *Chapter 6, Asset Pricing and Portfolio Management*, and other essential financial insights.

Risk and volatility are closely related concepts in the world of finance, but they are not identical. Volatility refers to a random variable's overall variability or fluctuation, encompassing upward and downward movements. It is a statistical measure that represents the degree to which the price of a security or a market index fluctuates over time. On the other hand, *risk* is typically associated with the potential for negative outcomes. An investment's actual return may differ from the expectation level. Moreover, the returns may be less than the amount invested. For instance, if an investment demonstrates high volatility, there is potential for both gains and losses. When the high volatility of an investment leads to greater-than-expected earnings, the positive outcome means that the risk, in this scenario, was not realized.

To comprehend volatility and risk, we must explore the fundamentals of probability theory, particularly the study of distributions, such as *normal* and *uniform*. The *normal distribution*, also known as the *Gaussian distribution*, is central to statistics and is often used in finance due to its natural occurrence in various random processes. The *uniform distribution*, by contrast, assumes equal probability for all values, providing a different perspective on randomness and its impact on financial instruments.

In financial practices, the concept of volatility is often encapsulated by the standard deviation, which measures the average absolute difference of a financial indicator from its mean value. While those metrics provide an insightful snapshot of past fluctuations, we cannot predict the exact deviation for a specific future observation. This uncertainty ushers in the concept of a random variable.

A *random variable* is a quantitative variable whose possible values are numerical results of a random phenomenon or process and often formalized by a quantity, depending on random events. In finance, a random variable could represent the future price of a stock, the RoR, or the change in an index value over a certain period. It is a cornerstone concept because it allows us to deal quantitatively with financial uncertainties.

When we refer to the behavior of a random variable, we discuss its tendency to assume different values, a pattern encapsulated by the *random variable distribution.* The distribution of a random variable is a mathematical function that describes the probability of the random variable taking on each possible value. It tells us how likely it is to observe each outcome associated with the variable. A *distribution function,* or *DF* (as a mathematical equation), *distribution table,* or *distribution plot* can represent the random variable distribution. For example, the normal distribution or the bell curve has a complicated mathematical function, but the graphical form is well understood. For more details and understanding of the features of random variables and the random variable distribution, you can refer to the specialized literature that is given at the end of this chapter or public open sources, such as the following: Massachusetts Institute of Technology courses (*https://ocw. mit.edu/courses/18-440-probability-and-random-variables-spring-2014/ pages/lecture-notes/*) and Statistics LibreTexts (*https://stats.libretexts.org/ Bookshelves*).

In addition to understanding the fundamental assessments of risk and volatility, it is essential to grasp the implications of two critical categories: population (or general population) and sample. A *sample* consists of datasets utilized to analyze information drawn from various sources. While it may appear that we have gathered all possible data about a market, stock, or price, invariably, some data still need to be accounted for. This oversight introduces the concept of a *general population* or *statistical population*, which, in this context, encompasses all potential values of an indicator that we did not consider.

For instance, in assessing price dynamics, the sample might comprise daily trading data (no gaps) from January 1, 2010, to January 1, 2024. Nevertheless, this sample is extracted from a broader general population that includes all price data across different periods or at varied time intervals and so on. These concepts are pivotal in probability theory because we infer estimates reflective of that sample's data when analyzing random variables based on a specific sample. The results could vary considerably, however, if we select a different sample from the general population for a distinct period.

This is where the concepts of confidence and prediction intervals come into play, previously encountered in *Chapter 6, Asset Pricing and Portfolio Management,* where we constructed forecast confidence intervals using SARIMA models. These statistical tools allow us to quantify the uncertainty of our predictions and provide a range within which we expect our estimates to fall with a given level of confidence.

Let us look at the details with practical Python examples.

Normal Distribution

Normal distribution[1] is a well-known distribution for random variables in finance. It is symmetric around the mean, showing that data near the mean is more frequent in occurrence than data farther from it. This distribution is characterized by two parameters: the average value (mean), located at the center of the distribution, and the standard deviation, which scales the spread of the distribution. For instance, financial analysts can calculate the likelihood that the RoR will exceed a certain threshold or determine the probability that the price of a security will fall within a particular range.

Please go ahead and execute the following code and analyze the results of the normal distribution principles:

```
1.  # Import of specific functions for generating
    indicators # of the Normal distribution

2.  from scipy.stats import norm

3.

4.  # Generate and plot 100 random samples from
    # a standard normal distribution

5.  np.random.seed(150)

6.  standard_normal = np.random.standard_normal(100)

7.  # Categorize the standard normal data into 10 bins

8.  categorized_data = pd.cut(standard_normal, 10)

9.  # Create a frequency table
    # (cross-tabulation) of the categorized data

10. frequency_table = pd.value_counts(categorized_
    data).sort_index()

11. df_frequency_table = pd.DataFrame({

12.     'Freq': frequency_table,

13.     'Weight': frequency_table / frequency_table.
    sum()
```

---

[1] *For more details, see https://en.wikipedia.org/wiki/Normal_distribution*

```
14.  }).reset_index().rename(columns={'index':
     'Interval'})
15.  # Calculate the PDF for the midpoint of each
     interval
16.  df_frequency_table['Midpoint'] = df_frequency_
     table['Interval'].apply(lambda x: x.mid)
17.  df_frequency_table['PDF'] = norm.
     pdf(df_frequency_table['Midpoint'])
18.  # Calculate the CDF for the upper bound of each
     interval
19.  df_frequency_table['CDF'] = norm.cdf(df_
     frequency_table['Interval'].apply(lambda x:
     x.right))
20.  print("Frequency Table of Standard Normal Data
     Categorized into 10 Bins:")
21.  print(df_frequency_table[['Interval', 'Freq',
                              'Weight', 'PDF', 'CDF']])
22.
23.  # Mean and standard deviation for
     # the Standard normal distribution
24.  mean = 0
25.  std = 1
26.  # Generate a range of x values from
     # the mean and standard deviation
27.  x_values = np.linspace(mean - 4*std, mean +
     4*std, 1000)
28.  # Calculate the PDF values for the x_values range
29.  pdf_values = norm.pdf(x_values, loc=mean,
     scale=std)
30.  # Create a combined plot
31.  plt.figure(figsize=(12, 6))
```

```
32.  # Histogram plot of the standard normal data with
     10 bins
33.  sns.histplot(standard_normal, bins=10, kde=False,
34.              stat='density', label='Sample
     Histogram')
35.  # Create a Kernel Density Estimate (KDE) plot
     # for the standard normal data
36.  sns.kdeplot(standard_normal, label='KDE of The
     Sample',
37.              color='black', linestyle='--')
38.  # Plot the theoretical PDF line
39.  plt.plot(x_values, pdf_values, color='red',
40.           label='Theoretical PDF - Standard
     Normal')
41.  # Ploting
42.  plt.title('Standard Normal Distribution with
     Sample Histogram and Theoretical PDF')
43.  plt.xlabel('Value')
44.  plt.ylabel('Density')
45.  plt.legend()
46.  plt.show()
```

Refer to the following text and *Figure 8.1* for the code results.

The frequency table of standard normal distributed data is categorized into 10 bins:

	Interval	Freq	Weight	PDF	CDF
0	(-2.68, -2.138]	3	0.03	0.021915	0.016258
1	(-2.138, -1.601]	7	0.07	0.069498	0.054688
2	(-1.601, -1.064]	9	0.09	0.164192	0.143664
3	(-1.064, -0.527]	16	0.16	0.290733	0.299097

4	(-0.527, 0.00931]	28	0.28	0.385799	0.503714
5	(0.00931, 0.546]	12	0.12	0.383857	0.707467
6	(0.546, 1.083]	11	0.11	0.286320	0.860596
7	(1.083, 1.619]	9	0.09	0.160167	0.947276
8	(1.619, 2.156]	4	0.04	0.067188	0.984458
9	(2.156, 2.693]	1	0.01	0.021109	0.996459

The following is an explanation of the code:

- The `norm` function from the scipy.stats module represents the normal (Gaussian) distribution, providing access to several important statistical functions, including the ability to calculate *probability density functions* (*PDFs*).

- `norm.pdf` calculates the PDF for the theoretical normal distribution of the general population. A PDF describes the likelihood of a random variable in the given value. The PDF plots the curve of the ideal normal distribution.

- `np.random.seed(150)` sets the seed for NumPy's random number generator, making the random numbers generated reproducible (will be the same on different platforms; the number 150 is arbitrary). This is crucial when you need to share reproducible results or debug code. In the real world, however, it should be a random variable, too, such as the current system time.

- `np.random.standard_normal(100)` generates 100 random samples from a standard normal distribution (mean=0 and sd=1). In general, the function `np.random.normal(loc=0, scale=1, size=100)` generates a normal distributed random variable, where n is the number of samples, `loc` is a mean (center) value, and `scale` is a standard deviation.

The resulting table is the most straightforward way to present the DF of a random variable. For instance, we observe a 10% probability (0.07 + 0.03 from `Weight`) that the historical values of the generated sample will be less than -1.601. The theoretical probability value for the midpoint of the interval (-2.68, -1.601) is 0,091413 (0.021915 + 0.069498 for the PDF column) or 0.054688 (for the CDF column). This discrepancy arises from the disproportionality between the sample ranges and the population (for the norm function results).

A more visible result is shown in *Figure 8.1*, which depicts the histogram of the generated sample, the KDE plot for the generated sample, and the theoretical PDF value for the general population. The graphical representation of the *standard normal distribution* demonstrates that the generated random variable differs from the standard distribution, even though the data was taken from the corresponding general population. This confirms the difference between these indicators.

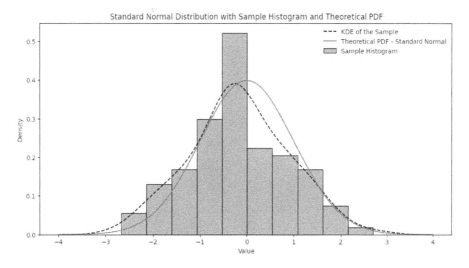

FIGURE 8.1 Histogram and KDE plots for the standard normal distributed random variable

NOTE *The PDF and the DF, often called the cumulative DF, are two fundamental concepts in statistics used to describe the distribution of a random variable. For a continuous random variable, the PDF shows the likelihood of the variable falling within a particular range of values (see Figure 8.1 and the PDF column in the results table). The area under the PDF curve for a given interval equals the probability that the variable falls within that interval. The CDF is a function that maps a value to its percentile rank or the probability that a random variable will take a value less than or equal to that value (see the CDF column in the results table). The CDF is integral to the PDF and provides the cumulative probability for the random variable from negative infinity up to a specific point. Both functions are used to interpret random variable behaviors.*

Next, we will consider an example related to the logRoR indicator value (see *Chapter 2, Python Tools for Data Analysis: Primer to Pandas and NumPy*) for the NASDAQ index's adjusted close prices.

Let us execute the following code:

```
1.  # Downloading historical data for the index
2.  index_data = yf.download(index_ticker,
    start=start, end=end)
3.  index_data['RoR'] = index_data['Adj Close'].
    pct_change()
4.  index_data['logRoR'] = np.log(index_data['Adj
    Close'] /
5.                                  index_data['Adj
    Close'].shift(1))
6.  index_data.dropna(inplace=True)
7.  mean = nasdaq_index['logRoR'].mean()
8.  std = nasdaq_index['logRoR'].std()
9.  # Create a BINS plot for NASDAQ's
    # Log Rate of Return (logRoR) density
10. plt.figure(figsize=(12, 6))
11. sns.histplot(nasdaq_index['logRoR'], kde=False,
12.              stat='density', bins=30, label='Log
    Rate of Return')
13. # Create a simulated KDE plot based on NASDAQ
    logRoR statistics
14. simulated_data = np.random.normal(mean, std, 10000)
15. sns.kdeplot(simulated_data, color = 'black',
16.             label = 'Simulated Normal KDE')
17. # Generate a range of x values for Theoretical PDF
18. x_values = np.linspace(mean - 4*std, mean +
    4*std, 1000)
19. # Calculate the PDF values for the x_values range
20. pdf_values = norm.pdf(x_values, loc=mean,
    scale=std)
```

```
21.  # Plot the theoretical PDF line
22.  plt.plot(x_values, pdf_values, color = 'red',
23.        linestyle = '--', label='Theoretical
     PDF')
24.  # Plotting
25.  plt.title('Theoretical PDF and Actual Data
     Distribution of NASDAQ logRoR')
26.  plt.xlabel('Log Rate of Return')
27.  plt.ylabel('Density')
28.  plt.legend()
29.
30.  # Create the Q-Q plot
31.  from statsmodels.graphics.api import qqplot
32.  qqplot_fig = qqplot(nasdaq_index['logRoR'],
     line='q', fit=True)
33.  qqplot_fig.set_size_inches(12, 6)
```

The code results are depicted in *Figure 8.2*:

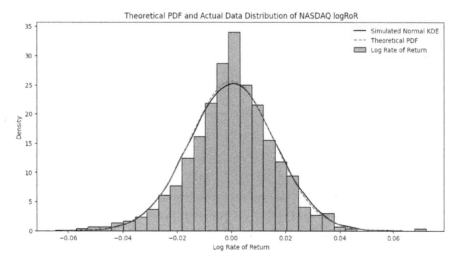

FIGURE 8.2 Histogram and KDE plots for NASDAQ logRoR and equivalent
normal distributed random variable

As observed from *Figure 8.2*, the actual logRoR values (represented by the histogram) significantly differ from the theoretical normal distribution with similar mean and standard deviation values (dashed line). In the example considered, however, the simulated normal KDE is represented by 10,000 random variables. In this case, the data from the general population is used to create the simulated data. This effect is associated with the fact that as the sample size increases, the statistical metrics of a random variable converge to the parameters of the general population.

Another interesting graph, presented in *Figure 8.3*, is the Q-Q plot. It shows the congruence between a random variable's theoretical and actual PDF values. The more the blue points on the graph differ from the red line, the further the given distribution is from the normal. A distribution such as the one shown in *Figure 8.3* corresponds to the case of *heavy (fat) tails*, meaning that the random variable's average values conform to the normal distribution, but the deviations that are far from the average do not. Heavy tails significantly increase the risk of losses from rare events, which is examined in more detail in the work of *Nassim Taleb* (see the *References* section of this chapter).

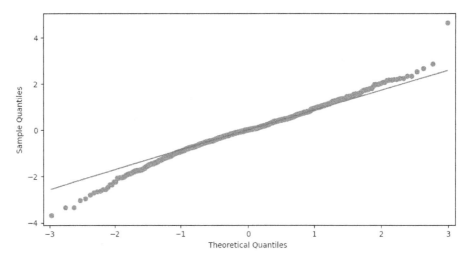

FIGURE 8.3 Q-Q plot for NASDAQ logRoR

Thus, the variation in the yield of securities should inherently correspond to the normal distribution; however, as the previous pre-action analysis showed, this is not always the case. There are both deviations from the heart and fat tails.

VaR METRIC FOR RISK ASSESSMENT IN FINANCE

As noted earlier in this chapter, the concept of risk in financial analysis embodies the potential for adverse movements within the market that could culminate in financial losses. Several quantitative methods have been developed to navigate this uncertainty. *VaR* is a preeminent metric that estimates the maximum potential loss over a specified time frame, given a certain confidence level. It is based on probability theory concepts and uses normal distribution features. The level of VaR is estimated as follows:

$$VaR = Z_{\alpha} \times \sigma + \mu$$

Where:

- Z_{α} is the Z-score (quartile for the theoretical normal distribution) with the level of confidence α.
- σ is the standard deviation of the random variable.
- μ is the mean of the random variable.

Therefore, this risk assessment tool considers the level of market volatility, which reflects the amplitude of asset price movements in a negative way. By focusing on the negative side of volatility, VaR emphasizes the potential for decline rather than the opportunity for gain. The metric captures the likelihood of a loss occurring within a predefined period and quantifies the potential losses that could exceed the VaR threshold.

Building on the VaR framework, which estimates maximum potential loss within a given confidence interval, the concept of *aVaR* extends this risk metric further. While VaR offers a threshold value, indicating that losses are not expected to exceed this point within a certain confidence level, aVaR delves deeper. It represents the expected loss, given that the VaR threshold has already been breached. Thus, the integral averages the VaR over the tail of the distribution beyond the confidence level α as follows:

$$aVaR = \frac{1}{(1-\alpha)} \int_{\alpha}^{1} VaR(u)\,du$$

As for discrete distributions:

$$aVaR = (\Sigma L_i) / N_{exceed}, \quad \forall\, i \in [1, N_{exceed}]$$

Where:

- α (alpha) is the confidence level (e.g., 0.95 for 95% confidence).
- $VaR(u)$ is the value at risk at confidence level u.
- N_{exceed} is the number of losses that exceed the VaR.
- L_i is the individual losses that exceed the VaR.

The aVaR is particularly useful because it gives a more comprehensive picture of the tail risk, which VaR alone might not fully capture. It is calculated as the average loss in the worst-case scenarios beyond the VaR limit, effectively quantifying the expected loss when the market movement is exceptionally adverse.

In essence, while VaR can be seen as the line in the sand that losses are not likely to cross on a given day, aVaR tells us about the expected severity of those rare but extreme events that cross that line. It is a vital tool in risk management because it accounts for the magnitude of extreme losses, thus helping institutions prepare for and mitigate the impact of potentially catastrophic financial events.

There are several methods to estimate VaR, including *historical, variance-covariance*, and *Monte Carlo simulation*. Let us look at examples for each:

- The *historical method* uses historical data to estimate the potential loss. It assumes that historical patterns will continue.

For example, suppose you have an index portfolio and have calculated its daily returns over the past year. To estimate the 5% VaR over one day:

- Sort these returns from the worst to the best.
- Find the 5th percentile (the point below which 5% of the observations fall).
- The return at this percentile is your 5% one-day VaR.

Execute the following code as an example:

```
1. def calculating_VaRs_hist(data, confidence_level
      = 0.95,

2.                        out_text = False, out_viz = False):

3.      # Sort the log returns
```

```
4.      data_sorted = data.sort_values()
5.      # Calculate the VaR
6.      historical_var = data_sorted.quantile(1 -
   confidence_level)
7.      # Calculate the aVaR
8.      avar = data_sorted[data_sorted <= historical_
   var].mean()
9.      # Print the Value at Risk (VaR) result
10.     if out_text:
11.         print('Historical Method.')
12.         print(f'With 95% confidence, the values
   will not exceed a loss of {-historical_var *
   100:.2f}%.')
13.         print(f'With 95% confidence, the values
   will not exceed a loss of {-avar * 100:.2f}%.')
14.
15.     if out_viz:
16.         # Plot the KDE of the log returns
17.         plt.figure(figsize=(10, 5))
18.         sns.kdeplot(data_sorted, fill=True)
19.         plt.axvline(historical_var, color='r',
   linestyle='--',
                    label=f'95% VaR level:
   {-historical_var * 100:.2f}%')
20.         plt.axvline(avar, color='b', linestyle=':',
                    label=f'95% aVaR level: {-avar
   * 100:.2f}%')
21.         plt.title('NASDAQ Log Return KDE with VaR')
22.         plt.xlabel('Log Rate of Return')
23.         plt.ylabel('Density')
```

```
24.        plt.legend()
25.        plt.show()
26.        # Plot the histogram of the log returns
    with 100 bins
27.        plt.figure(figsize=(10, 5))
28.        n, bins, patches = plt.hist(data_sorted,
    bins=100, alpha=0.7)
29.        for patch, rightside, leftside in
    zip(patches, bins[1:], bins[:-1]):
30.            if rightside <= historical_var:
31.                patch.set_facecolor('red')
32.            if leftside < historical_var <=
    rightside:
33.                fraction = ((historical_var -
    leftside) /
                            (rightside - leftside))
34.                patch.set_facecolor('red')
35.                patch.set_alpha(fraction)
36.        plt.axvline(historical_var, color='k',
    linestyle='--',
37.                    label=f'95% VaR level:
    {-historical_var * 100:.2f}%')
38.        plt.axvline(avar, color='b', linestyle=':',
39.                    label=f'95% aVaR level: {-avar
    * 100:.2f}%')
40.        plt.title('Histogram of Log Returns with
    VaR')
41.        plt.xlabel('Log Rate of Return')
42.        plt.ylabel('Frequency')
43.        plt.legend()
```

```
44.        plt.show()
45.
46.      # Return VaR and aVaR
47.      return({historical_var, avar})
48.
49.  # Input data: the nasdaq_index['logRoR'] Series is
     # sorted by values from the worst to the best.
50.  nasdaq_index_logRoR = nasdaq_index['logRoR'].
     sort_values()
51.  # Plot the KDE of the log returns
52.  plt.figure(figsize=(10, 5))
53.  sns.kdeplot(nasdaq_index_logRoR, fill=True)
54.  # Calculate the VaR and aVaR as previously
     described
55.  confidence_level = 0.95
56.  historical_var, avar =
     calculating_VaRs_hist(nasdaq_index_logRoR,
57.                    confidence_level =
     confidence_level,
58.                    out_text = True,
59.                    out_viz = True)
60.  # Print the Value at Risk (VaR) result
61.  print('Historical Method.')
62.  print(f'With 95% confidence, the daily logRoR
     will not exceed a loss of {-historical_var *
     100:.2f}%.')
63.  print(f'With 95% confidence, the average daily
     logRoR will not exceed a loss of {-avar *
     100:.2f}%.')
```

The code results are as follows and depicted in *Figure 8.4*:

```
Historical Method.
```

```
With 95% confidence, the daily logRoR will not exceed a
loss of 2.66%.
```

```
With 95% confidence, the average daily logRoR will not
exceed a loss of 3.52%.
```

The results of the historical method and data in *Figure 8.4* show that the VaR for logRoR of the NASNAQ index does not exceed 2.66%, and the average loss, if this excess occurred, is 3.52% with a 95% probability:

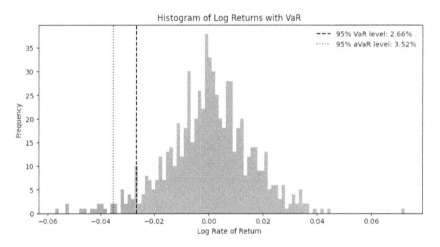

FIGURE 8.4 VaR(5%) for NASDAQ index logRoR visualization (historical method results)

- The *variance-covariance* (parametric) *method* assumes data is normally distributed (as in the general population) and uses the mean and standard deviation with the previously defined equations.

Example: For an index portfolio with an average daily return (mean) of μ and standard deviation σ, the VaR at a confidence level (e.g., 95%) can be calculated using the Z-score corresponding to that confidence level:

- Calculate the Z-score for 95% confidence (which is approximately 1.65).
- VaR is then $\mu - 1.65 \times \sigma$. If μ is close to 0, typically for daily logRoR, VaR simplifies to $1.65 \times \sigma$.

The following code provides an example of calculation using this method:

```
1.  from scipy.stats import norm
2.  # Input data: the nasdaq_index['logRoR'] Series is
    # sorted by values from the worst to the best.
3.  nasdaq_index_logRoR = nasdaq_index['logRoR'].
    sort_values()
4.  mean_return = nasdaq_index_logRoR.mean()
5.  std_return = nasdaq_index_logRoR.std()
6.  # Assuming normal distribution and 95% confidence
7.  confidence_level = 0.95
8.  z_score = stats.norm.ppf(confidence_level)
9.  variance_covar_var = mean_return - (std_return *
    z_score)
10. # Calculate the aVaR as previously described
11. avar = nasdaq_index_logRoR[nasdaq_index_logRoR <=
    historical_var].mean()
12. # Print the Value at Risk (VaR) result
13. print('Variance-Covariance Method.')
14. print(f'With 95% confidence, the daily logRoR
    will not exceed a loss of {-variance_covar_var *
    100:.2f}%.')
15. print(f'With 95% confidence, the average daily
    logRoR will not exceed a loss of {-avar *
    100:.2f}%.')
16. # Generate a range of x values from the
    # mean and standard deviation
17. x_values = np.linspace(mean_return - 4*std_
    return, mean_return + 4*std_return, 1000)
18. # Calculate the PDF values for the x_values range
```

```
19. pdf_values = norm.pdf(x_values, loc=mean_return,
    scale=std_return)
20. # Plot the normal distribution PDF
21. plt.figure(figsize=(10, 5))
22. plt.plot(x_values, pdf_values, label='Normal
    Distribution')
23. # Plot a vertical line for the VaR and aVaR on
    the PDF plot
24. plt.axvline(variance_covar_var, color='r',
    linestyle='--', label=f'95% VaR level:
    {-variance_covar_var * 100:.2f}%')
25. plt.axvline(avar, color='b', linestyle=':',
    label=f'95% aVaR level: {-avar * 100:.2f}%')
26. # Add labels and legend to the plot
27. plt.title('Normal Distribution of NASDAQ Log
    Returns with VaR and aVaR')
28. plt.xlabel('Log Rate of Return')
29. plt.ylabel('Density')
30. plt.legend()
31. # Show the plot
32. plt.show()
```

The code results are as follows (refer to *Figure 8.5*):

```
Variance-Covariance Method.

With 95% confidence, the daily logRoR will not exceed a
loss of 2.54%.

With 95% confidence, the average daily logRoR will not
exceed a loss of 3.52%.
```

The results of the variance-covariance method demonstrate VaR = 2.54% and aVaR = 3.52 with a confidence level of 0.95. It has the same differences with the results from the historical methods because the logRoR does not correspond to the normal distribution, or the sample taken is too small.

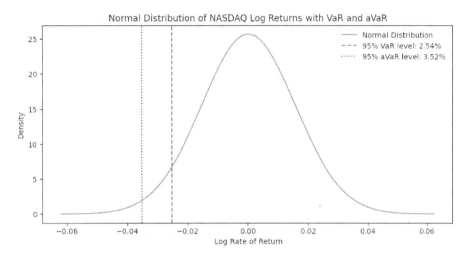

FIGURE 8.5 VaR(5%) for NASDAQ index logRoR visualization (variance-covariance method results)

▥ The *Monte Carlo simulation* uses simulated price paths based on statistical properties of asset returns to estimate the VaR. We will explain this method further in this chapter.

In a comparative analysis of risk and logarithmic RoR, we can use the VaR metrics to make decisions regarding investment in each type of asset. *Table 8.1* is the result of the code presented in the appendix to this chapter. The following table's data makes it possible to compare various assets by the metrics VaR and aVaR:

TABLE 8.1 VaR and aVaR values for the tickers of the NASDAQ market

Ticker	VaR	aVaR	Ticker	VaR	aVaR
MDLZ	1.75%	2.60%	BKR	4.10%	5.25%
KDP	1.81%	2.68%	MCHP	4.16%	5.38%
AMGN	1.97%	2.80%	META	4.22%	6.98%
HON	2.11%	3.10%	FTNT	4.31%	7.23%

(Continued)

Ticker	VaR	aVaR
VRSK	2.37%	3.56%
AZN	2.53%	3.56%
PCAR	2.58%	3.24%
DLTR	2.76%	5.53%
SBUX	2.80%	4.22%
CSGP	2.89%	4.91%
AAPL	3.08%	4.01%
MAR	3.21%	4.48%
SIRI	3.26%	5.46%
INTU	3.97%	5.40%
ILMN	4.03%	6.35%

Ticker	VaR	aVaR
AMAT	4.53%	6.06%
URBN	4.79%	6.33%
MRVL	5.25%	7.04%
ZM	5.54%	7.96%
JD	5.88%	7.97%
MELI	6.37%	8.45%
TSLA	6.56%	8.59%
DDOG	6.65%	8.55%
ENPH	6.67%	9.57%
MRNA	6.78%	9.56%
ZS	6.96%	9.00%

Table 8.1 provides a comparative risk landscape, as measured by the VaR and aVaR across a selection of NASDAQ-listed stocks. The metrics presented show a considerable range in the risk profiles of these assets. Lower VaR and aVaR values, as seen with MDLZ and KDP, suggest a relatively lower risk of loss, making them potentially more attractive to risk-averse investors. In contrast, stocks such as TSLA and ZS exhibit higher VaR and aVaR values, indicating a greater risk. This might appeal to risk-seeking investors looking for potentially higher returns in exchange for accepting increased risk. The aVaR values, being higher than the VaR for all listed assets, reflect the expected loss on days when the VaR threshold is exceeded. It provides additional insights into the risk of extreme losses. The differentiation in VaR and aVaR among these stocks also underscores the importance of portfolio diversification. By combining assets with varying levels of risk, investors can mitigate unexpected losses.

MONTE CARLO METHOD IN FINANCE

The Monte Carlo method, named after Monaco's famous *Monte Carlo Casino*, is an ingenious numerical technique that finds its roots in probability theory and sampling distributions. It was initially developed during the *Manhattan Project* in the 1940s, where it played a pivotal role in solving complex problems related to atomic bomb development[2]. Since then, it has found applications in many fields, including finance.

---

[2] *https://en.wikipedia.org/wiki/Monte_Carlo_method*

At its core, the Monte Carlo method is a simulation technique that harnesses the power of randomness. It allows us to model and analyze financial scenarios by generating random samples from various input distributions. We can estimate the probability distribution of possible outcomes by running these simulations repeatedly. This, in turn, empowers us to optimize strategies in an uncertain financial landscape.

For example, *Chapter 6, Asset Pricing and Portfolio Management,* describes portfolio optimization and visualization by using the random variable generation technique. In fact, this is the Monte Carlo method in action, and we utilized it for portfolio optimization and result visualization. Now, we venture further into financial analysis, employing this method to address an essential aspect of finance, which is *risk estimation*.

The Monte Carlo method in finance is particularly valuable because of its versatility. Key principles of the Monte Carlo method in financial analysis include:

- *Random sampling*, which is the generation of many random variables from specified probability distributions to simulate various scenarios.
- The *law of large numbers*, which, as noted earlier in this chapter, is if the number of simulations increases, the average of the results of the random samples converges to the expected value, offering a robust estimate that represents the true characteristics of the modeled financial system.
- *Statistical inference* to conclude future financial performance based on simulated data. It provides an opportunity to calculate the confidence intervals for forecasts, providing a probabilistic assessment of risks and returns.

The main directions for applying the Monte Carlo method in finance include:

- Monte Carlo simulations are extensively used to *estimate the risk* of financial instruments, particularly the VaR assessments and the tail (fat tail) risk associated with rare but consequential events.
- The method allows applying the *pricing of complex derivative instruments (options)*, including those without a closed-form analytical solution.
- It is used for *project valuation*, capital budgeting, and understanding the range of possible outcomes for investment decisions.
- The simulations help *optimize portfolios* by assessing the impact of different allocation strategies on the expected return and risk (as noted in *Chapter 6, Asset Pricing and Portfolio Management*) and so on.

Using practical examples, let us consider several main problems in the risk management theory and valuation of financial securities based on the Monte Carlo method.

Geometric Brownian Motion Method for Price Prediction

The *geometric Brownian motion (GBM)* method is the most popular Monte Carlo realization tool in the mathematical modeling of financial markets, particularly for price prediction. This stochastic process is widely utilized to model the trajectory of stock prices, currencies, and other financial instruments over time[3].

For financial asset pricing, the GBM assumes the existence of constant volatility rates, mirroring the natural lognormal distribution of asset prices over time. This reflects the compounded effect of many small, random fluctuations in the market. As a result, processes such as physical Brownian motion are observed in the financial market.

The stochastic differential equation defines the model for financial market data, as follows:

$$S_t = S_0 \cdot e^{(\mu + \sigma^2/2) \cdot t + \sigma \cdot St \cdot Wt}$$

Where:

- ex stands for the exponential function, which is the mathematical function ex.
- S_t is the asset price at the time t.
- S_0 is the initial asset price at the last known time.
- μ is the expected mean logarithmic RoR of the asset price (may consider dividend yield).
- σ is the volatility (standard deviation) of the logarithmic RoR of the asset price.
- W_t is the Brownian motion or Wiener process.

In the sphere of finance, the GBM model is heralded for its simplicity and the fact that it considers the randomness and unpredictability inherent to financial markets. It allows for the simulation of future price paths, providing a distribution of possible outcomes rather than a single, deterministic forecast.

---

[3] *https://en.wikipedia.org/wiki/Geometric_Brownian_motion*

This enables analysts to assess the likelihood of various price levels being reached and to evaluate the risk associated with an investment.

Let us look at a practical example of implementing the GDM model using the following code:

```python
1.  # Getting input Data
2.  log_returns = nasdaq_index['logRoR']
3.  data = nasdaq_index['Adj Close']
4.  # Estimate parameters
5.  mu = log_returns.mean()
6.  sigma = log_returns.std()
7.  # Time horizon in days for prediction
8.  T_pred = 30
9.  # Number of simulations
10. T_sim = 50
11. # Number of historical days to display
12. T_real = 30
13. # Number of intervals for simulation
14. N = T_pred
15. # Starting stock price (last available real data)
16. S0 = data[-1]
17. # Array to store simulation results
18. simulation_results = np.zeros((T_sim, N))
19. np.random.seed(11)
20. # Run multiple simulations
21. for i in range(T_sim):
22.     random_walk = np.random.standard_normal(size=N)
23.     # Assuming daily time steps
```

```
24.      brownian_motion = np.cumsum(random_walk) *
   np.sqrt(1.)
25.      simulation_results[i, :] = S0 * np.exp((mu -
   0.5 * sigma**2) *
26.                                np.linspace(0, T_
   pred, N) +
27.                                sigma *
   brownian_motion)
28. # Calculate the mean of simulations
29. mean_simulation = simulation_results.mean(axis=0)
30. # Historical dates and future dates
31. historical_dates = data.index[-T_real:]
32. future_dates = pd.date_range(start=data.
   index[-1],
33.                              periods=N+1,
   freq='D')[1:]
34. # Combine historical and future data for plotting
35. combined_dates = historical_dates.
   union(future_dates)
36. combined_prices = pd.concat([data[-T_real:],
37.                              pd.Series(mean_
   simulation,
38.
   index=future_dates)])
39. # Plotting
40. plt.figure(figsize=(10, 6))
41. plt.plot(combined_dates, combined_prices,
42.          label='Actual and Mean Simulated
   Prices')
43. plt.plot(future_dates, mean_simulation,
   color='red',
```

```
44.           label='Simulated Mean Future Prices',
     linestyle='-')
45. # Plot each simulation
46. for sim in simulation_results:
47.     plt.scatter(future_dates, sim,
     color='orange', alpha=0.2)
48. plt.title('Historical and Multiple Simulated
     Stock Prices')
49. plt.xlabel('Time')
50. plt.ylabel('Stock Price')
51. plt.legend()
52. plt.show()
```

The code result is depicted in *Figure 8.6*:

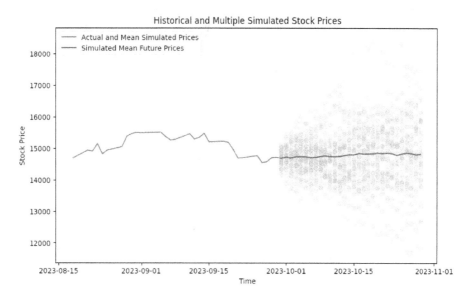

FIGURE 8.6 The results of the GBM simulated paths for the NASDAQ stock prices index

The code outlines a procedure to implement the GBM model, a common method for simulating the potential future for the NASDAQ stock prices index paths. By running multiple simulations (*T_sim* = *50* in this case), the code generates some of the possible future NASDAQ stock price index trajectories based on its historical log returns and volatility. The mean of these simulated paths (the red line) is calculated to provide a single representative trajectory.

The result in *Figure 8.6* shows that the mean trajectories of the possible future of the NASDAQ stock prices index are close to the last price value: *S0*. The cloud of dots, however, represents individual modeled trajectories of potential future index values, namely possible trajectories of its change or the confidence interval of the forecast. These simulations reflect the uncertainty and volatility expected in the future performance of the index value, with a wider spread of points indicating greater uncertainty. The dense cluster of orange dots around the red line suggests that most models predict an index value close to the simulation mean. The spread of dots from this mean, however, indicates that there is still considerable variability in the possible results. As seen in *Figure 8.6*, moving away from the last actual observation increases the confidence interval, meeting key statistical concepts. Since we move away from the last known values, the level of uncertainty increases.

Overall, the visualization conveys the probabilistic nature of predicting the value of specific asset prices, highlighting that while we can estimate an average future trajectory, the actual future price can be influenced by many factors, leading to different possible outcomes.

Based on the GBM model, we can also evaluate the indicators of VaR and aVaR. Please execute the following code and analyze its results:

```
1.  # Getting Input data
2.  log_returns = nasdaq_index['logRoR']
3.  data = nasdaq_index['Adj Close']
4.  # Estimate parameters
5.  mu = log_returns.mean()
6.  sigma = log_returns.std()
7.  # Time horizon in days for prediction
```

```
8.  T_pred = 10000
9.  # Number of intervals for simulation
10. N = T_pred
11. # Starting stock price (last available real data)
12. S0 = data[-1]
13. # Generate random Brownian Motion for prediction
14. np.random.seed(1)
15. random_walk = np.random.standard_normal(size=N)
16. brownian_motion = np.cumsum(random_walk) * np.sqrt(1.)
17. # Simulate future price path
18. future_prices = S0 * np.exp((mu - 0.5 * sigma**2) *
19.                       np.linspace(0, T_pred, N) +
20.                       sigma * brownian_motion)
21. # Combine historical and future data
22. historical_dates = data.index[-T_real:]
23. future_dates = pd.date_range(start=data.index[-1],
24.                          periods=N+1,
    freq='D')[1:]
25. # Estimation VaR and aVaR based on historical
    method
26. # calculating_VaRs_hist() function is defined in
    the code Appendix.
27. # The Function returns VaR and aVaR from
    pd.DataFame of the asset prices
28. x = pd.Series(future_prices)
29. logx = (np.log(x) - np.log(x).shift(1)).dropna()
30. var, avar = calculating_VaRs_hist(logx,
    confidence_level = 0.95,
31.                          out_text = True, out_
    viz = True)
```

The code results are given in the following text and *Figure 8.7*:

```
Historical Method.

With 95% confidence, the values will not exceed a loss of
2.51%.

With 95% confidence, the values will not exceed a loss of
3.17%.
```

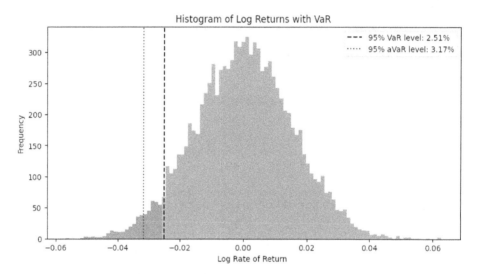

FIGURE 8.7 VaR(5%) for NASDAQ index logRoR visualization (Monte Carlo method results)

Comparing the results presented in *Figures 8.4, 8.5*, and *8.7*, it can be argued that, in general, all three methods for calculating the VaR and aVaR give approximately similar results, especially if the numbers of simulations are enormous.

Option Pricing: The Black-Scholes Formula

Another widespread application of the Monte Carlo method is forecasting option prices. Options are a type of *financial derivative* that derive their value from underlying assets. The essence of an option is a contractual agreement that provides the buyer the right, but not the obligation, to buy or sell the underlying asset at a predetermined price within a specified time frame.

There are two primary types of options—*put* options and *call* options:

- A *put option* gives the holder the right to sell the underlying asset at the strike price before the option expires. Investors may buy put options as a form of protection against a decrease in the asset's price, effectively setting a floor below which they choose not to bear losses.
- A *call option* gives the holder the right to buy the underlying asset at the strike price before the option expires. Call options are often purchased by investors who anticipate that the asset's price will increase, allowing them to secure a purchase price below the expected market value.

Options are used for various strategic purposes. They can be used as insurance to protect investments. They can also be used for speculation, allowing people to make money from predicting market movements without owning the underlying asset.

The Black-Scholes formula is a model that provides the theoretical estimates for the price of European-style options (they can be realized only on a predefined day). It assumes some factors, including that the underlying asset's prices follow a lognormal distribution and that the option can only be exercised at expiration. This formula has become a fundamental tool in the field of financial economics, helping to set the standard for the pricing of options in markets globally.

The following are the key elements of the Black-Scholes formula:

- The Black-Scholes formula for the call option price $C(S, t)$ at time t:

$$C(S,t) = S0 \cdot N(d1) - K \cdot N(d2) \cdot exp(-r \cdot (T{-}t))$$

The component $d1$ represents a measure of how many standard deviations the current stock price is above the strike price, adjusted for the time value of money and the expected volatility:

$$d1 = (1 / (\sigma \cdot sqrt(T{-}t))) \cdot [ln(S0 / K) + (r + (\sigma^2 / 2)) \cdot (T{-}t)]$$

The component $d2$ represents the same underlying factors as $d1$ but adjusted downward by the amount of expected volatility:

$$d2 = d1 - \sigma \cdot sqrt(T{-}t)$$

$$= (1 / (\sigma \cdot sqrt(T{-}t))) \cdot [ln(S0 / K) + (r - (\sigma^2 / 2)) \cdot (T{-}t)]$$

Where:

- *S0* is the current underlying asset price.
- *K* is the strike price of the option (fixed price at which an option can be exercised).
- *t* is the current time when we estimate the option price.
- *(T–t)* is the expiration time.
- *r* is the risk-free interest rate, for example, the rate of the Treasury bill or other state bonds.
- *σ* is the volatility of the stock (standard deviation).

N(x) is the cumulative DF of the standard normal distribution at *d*.

- The Black-Scholes formula for the put option price *P(S, t)* at time *t*:

$$P(S,t) = K \cdot N(-d2) \cdot exp(-r \cdot (T–t)) – S0 \cdot N(-d1)$$

The variables have the same meaning as the call option.

Thus, the models *C(s, t)* and *P(S,t)* provide closed-form solutions that estimate the theoretical price of these options based on several key variables: the current price of the underlying asset, the strike price, the risk-free interest rate, the time to expiration, and the volatility of the underlying asset. These models are relatively simple, but incorporating the critical market parameters and assuming the lognormal distribution of asset prices shows a robust framework for evaluating the fair value of the options.

Based on the theoretical equations, let us create a Python function, `black_scholes()`, to calculate the option's forecast price.

To do this, execute the following code:

```
1.  # Function to calculate Black-Scholes option
    price
2.  def black_scholes(S, K, T, r, sigma,
    option_type='call'):
3.      d1 = ((np.log(S / K) + (r + 0.5 * sigma ** 2)
    * T) /
            (sigma * np.sqrt(T)))
```

```
4.      d2 = d1 - sigma * np.sqrt(T)
5.      if option_type == 'call':
6.          price = (S * norm.cdf(d1) -
                    K * np.exp(-r * T) * norm.cdf(d2))
7.      elif option_type == 'put':
8.          price = (K * np.exp(-r * T) * norm.cdf(-d2) -
                    S * norm.cdf(-d1))
9.      return price
10. # Sample inputs - you'll need to replace these
    with real values
11. S = 150   # Current stock price
12. K = 100   # Strike price
13. T = 1     # Time to expiration in years or (T-t)
    in the BS formula
14. r = 0.01 # Risk-free rate
15. sigma = 0.25 # Volatility
16. # Calculate and print option price
17. call_price = black_scholes(S, K, T, r, sigma,
    'call')
18. put_price = black_scholes(S, K, T, r, sigma,
    'put')
19. print(f"Call Option Price: {call_price}")
20. print(f"Put Option Price: {put_price}")
```

The results are as follows:

```
Call Option Price: 51.60253352585224
Put Option Price: 0.6075169007690242
```

The code provided is a Python implementation of the Black-Scholes model, which is a practical template for further valuing European call and put options.

The function is used with sample inputs, a current stock price of $150, a strike price of $100, a time to expiration of 1 year, a risk-free rate of 1%, and a volatility of 25%. The call option price is approximately $51.60, and the put option price is approximately $0.61. These results suggest that the call option has a significant value with the given inputs, reflecting the probability that the stock price will exceed the strike price at expiration. Conversely, the put option has relatively little value, which indicates that the market does not expect the stock price to fall below the strike price by expiration.

Let us describe some real-world examples. As shown in *Chapter 3, Financial Data Manipulation with Python* (refer to *Figure 3.2*), data on options associated with the underlying financial assets can be obtained from the official page of *https://finance.yahoo.com*. Therefore, we can use the yfinance Python library and `Ticker()`.

```
1.  # Initialize a Ticker object
2.  ticker = yf.Ticker('AAPL')
3.  # Print the available expiration dates for
    options
4.  print(ticker.options)
5.  # Load current call options data
6.  e_date_c = ticker.options[0]
7.  calls = ticker.option_chain(e_date_c).calls
8.  calls.to_csv(f'calls_{e_date_c}.csv')
9.  # Load current put options data
10. e_date_p = ticker.options[3]
11. puts = ticker.option_chain(e_date_p).puts
12. puts.to_csv(f'puts_{e_date_p}.csv')
13. # Print the expiration date and the
    # first few rows of the call options data
14. print(f"Expiration date for calls: {e_date_c}")
15. print(calls.head())
```

```
16.  # Print the expiration date and the
     # first few rows of the put options data

17.  print(f"Expiration date for puts: {e_date_p}")

18.  print(puts.head())
```

The results (truncated) are as follows:

```
('2024-01-12', '2024-01-19', '2024-01-26', '2024-02-02',
'2024-02-09', '2024-02-16', '2024-03-15', '2024-04-19',
'2024-05-17', '2024-06-21', '2024-07-19', '2024-09-20',
'2024-12-20', '2025-01-17', '2025-06-20', '2025-09-19',
'2025-12-19', '2026-01-16')

Expiration date for calls: 2024-01-12
        contractSymbol           lastTradeDate  strike  lastPrice   bid \
0  AAPL240112C00060000 2023-12-21 16:40:40+00:00    60.0     134.90  120.35
(...)
4  AAPL240112C00130000 2024-01-05 18:22:07+00:00   130.0      51.69   50.70

     ask   change  percentChange  volume  openInterest  impliedVolatility \
0  122.10  0.000000       0.000000     NaN             2           2.953128
(...)
```

The code utilizes the yfinance Python library to interact with Yahoo Finance's API for fetching option chain data for Apple Inc. (AAPL) that is needed for the Black-Scholes model, as follows:

- The `Ticker()` object for the symbol AAPL serves as an interface to fetch various market data related to Apple Inc.
- `ticker.options` is a property of the `Ticker` object that returns a tuple of strings, each representing an available expiration date for the options of the specified ticker. This allows users to select an expiration date for which they want to analyze the option chain data.
- `.calls` retrieves all available call options for the specified expiration date.
- `.puts` retrieves all available put options for the specified expiration date.

The code is set up to fetch both call and put option data for specified expiration dates. The results make available the following data for the Black-Scholes model:

- The 'impliedVolatility' field in the data represents the market's estimate of the stock's future volatility over the option's life.
- The 'strike' field shows the strike price for the model, that is, the price at which an option holder can buy (the call option) or sell (the put option) the underlying asset or security upon exercising the option.

Based on the puts and calls DataFrames from the previous code and market data on Apple Inc.'s (AAPL) stocks, we will evaluate real call options in the following manner:

```python
1.  # Ticker symbol for asset
2.  ticker = yf.Ticker('AAPL')
3.  # Get data for call options
4.  expiration_date = pd.to_datetime(e_date_c,
    utc=True)
5.  now_day = expiration_date - 5 * pd.tseries.
    offsets.BDay()
6.  now_text = str(now_day).split(' ')[0]
7.  option = calls.iloc[10]
8.  # Get the current price of the basic asset
9.  current_price = ticker.history()['Close'].
    loc[now_text]
10. # Download the risk-free rate from a relevant
    U.S. Treasury yield
11. # ^IRX is the 13-week Treasury Bill
12. treasury_ticker = yf.Ticker("^IRX")
13. # Convert to a decimal
```

```
14.  risk_free_rate = treasury_ticker.history()
     ['Close'].loc[now_text] / 100
15.  # Get option contract data
16.  strike_price = option['strike']
17.  # Convert to a decimal
18.  implied_volatility = option['impliedVolatility']
     / 100
19.  # Calculate date for option expiration in years
     scale
20.  time_to_expiration = (expiration_date - now_day)
     .days / 365.0
21.  # Calculate Black-Scholes price
22.  bs_price = black_scholes(current_price,
     strike_price,
23.                           time_to_expiration,
     risk_free_rate,
24.                           implied_volatility,
     option_type='call')
25.  print(f'Option expiration date is {e_date_c}')
26.  print(f"Black-Scholes Call Option Price on {now_
     text} is {bs_price:.2f}")
27.  print('\n', option)
```

The results (truncated) are as follows:

```
Option expiration date is 2024-01-12
Black-Scholes Call Option Price on 2024-01-05 is 21.34
 Unnamed: 0                                        10
contractSymbol                    AAPL240112C00160000
```

```
lastTradeDate           2024-01-05 20:58:30+00:00

strike                                      160.0

lastPrice                                   21.36

bid                                         20.55

ask                                         22.15

(...)

impliedVolatility                        0.500005

(...)
```

The code outlines a process for calculating the Black-Scholes price for a specific call option on Apple Inc.'s stock. It operates with the `calls` DataFrame, uses the risk-free rate from the 13-week U.S. Treasury bill (identified by the ticker symbol "^IRX"), and converts it into a decimal form) and real AAPL stock price with the `yf.Ticker()` object. The Black-Scholes price for the call option is calculated using the predefined `black_scholes()` function.

The code results indicate that the predicted Black-Scholes price for the call option on January 5, 2024, is $21.34. This prediction is based on the provided inputs and is close to the last traded price of $21.36, within the bid-ask spread of $20.55 to $22.15. The closeness of the Black-Scholes price to the market price and its position within the bid-ask spread suggests that the model reasonably estimates the option's value based on the inputs used. This conclusion can be used to assess the option's market price's fairness or make informed trading decisions.

The following code estimates the forecast price of a put option. Execute it and analyze the results:

```python
1.  # Ticker symbol for asset
2.  ticker = yf.Ticker('AAPL')
3.  # Get data for call options
4.  expiration_date = pd.to_datetime(e_date_p,
    utc=True)
5.  now_day = expiration_date - 20 * pd.tseries.
    offsets.BDay()
```

```
 6.  now_text = str(now_day).split(' ')[0]

 7.  option = puts.iloc[-3]

 8.  # Get the current price of the basic asset

 9.  current_price = ticker.history()['Close']
     .loc[now_text]

10.  # Download the risk-free rate from a relevant
     U.S. Treasury yield

11.  # ^IRX is the 13-week Treasury Bill

12.  treasury_ticker = yf.Ticker("^IRX")

13.  # Convert to a decimal

14.  risk_free_rate = treasury_ticker.history()
     ['Close'].loc[now_text] / 100

15.  # Get option contract data

16.  strike_price = option['strike']

17.   # Convert to a decimal

18.  implied_volatility = option['impliedVolatility'] / 100

19.  # Calculate date for option expiration in years scale

20.  time_to_expiration = (expiration_date - now_day).
     days / 365.0

21.  # Calculate Black-Scholes price

22.  bs_price = black_scholes(current_price,
     strike_price,

23.                            time_to_expiration,
     risk_free_rate,

24.                            implied_volatility,
     option_type='put')

25.  print(f'Option expiration date is {e_date_p}')

26.  print(f"Black-Scholes Put Option Price on {now_
     text} is {bs_price:.2f}")

27.  print('\n', option)
```

The results (truncated) are as follows:

```
Option expiration date is 2024-02-02
Black-Scholes Put Option Price on 2024-01-05 is 27.98
 contractSymbol                 AAPL240202P00210000
lastTradeDate         2024-01-02 14:48:19+00:00
strike                                    210.0
lastPrice                                  23.4
bid                                        27.5
ask                                        30.3
(...)
impliedVolatility                      0.457037
(...)
```

The last code applies the Black-Scholes model to estimate the price of a put option for Apple Inc. stock. It operates with the same principles that do this for the call option: extracting necessary data from the `puts` DataFrame and retrieving the current stock price and the risk-free rate from U.S. Treasury bills from Yahoo Finance.

The results indicate that the predicted Black-Scholes price for the put option with a strike price of $210, expiring on February 2, 2024, is $27.98 when evaluated on January 5, 2024. This price is derived using the implied volatility of about 45.7%. This result is in the market bid-ask range from $27.50 to $30.30, but higher than the last traded price of $23.40. The calculated Black-Scholes price is slightly lower than the market ask price, suggesting that, according to the model, the option may be overvalued somewhat in the market. It is within the bid-ask spread, however, indicating that the model's output is reasonably aligned with market expectations given the inputs.

Therefore, these analyses can help traders and investors determine whether the market price for the call or put option is fair and make decisions accordingly. It demonstrates the usefulness of the Black-Scholes model as a tool for evaluating the theoretical price of options based on volatility and other market factors.

ARCH AND GARCH MODELS

The next step in exploring risk analysis is the study of the *Autoregressive Conditional Heteroskedasticity* (ARCH) and *Generalized Autoregressive Conditional Heteroskedasticity* (GARCH) models. These statistical models are used to forecast future volatility based on past data, considering the tendency for volatility to cluster over time[4].

In finance, the ARCH and GARCH models address an expected volatility characteristic of asset returns (RoR or percentage change, logRoR, and the same metrics): volatility clustering, where periods of high volatility are followed by high volatility and periods of low volatility follow low volatility. This is unlike traditional models, which often assume constant fluctuations.

ARCH models, introduced by *Robert Engle* in 1982, are used to model financial time series with time-varying volatility. The model allows for more accurate predictions by capturing the *volatility clustering* effect often observed in financial markets. An ARCH model expresses current volatility as a function of the sizes of previous periods' errors or shocks.

An ARCH(q) model can be defined as follows:

$$\varepsilon_t = \sigma_t \cdot z_t$$

$$\sigma_t^2 = \omega + \alpha_1 \cdot \varepsilon_{(t-1)}^2 + \alpha_2 \cdot \varepsilon_{(t-2)}^2 + \dots + \alpha_q \cdot \varepsilon_{(t-q)}^2$$

$$z_t \sim N(0,1)$$

Where:

- ε_t is the error term (residual) at time t.
- $\alpha_1, .., \alpha_q$ are the coefficients of the lagged squared error terms.
- σ_t is the conditional variance (volatility) at time.
- $\omega > 0$ and $\alpha_i \geq 0 \ \forall \ i=1,\dots,q$ are parameters to be estimated.
- z_t is a white noise error term with a standard normal distribution.

GARCH models, an extension of ARCH introduced by *Tim Bollerslev* in 1986, add a moving average component to the model, accounting for both short-term and long-term effects from past errors.

---

[4] *https://en.wikipedia.org/wiki/Autoregressive_conditional_heteroskedasticity*

A GARCH(p, q) model with an AR(k) mean for the logRoR metric can be defined as follows:

$$r_t = \varphi 0 + \sum \varphi_i \cdot r_{(t\text{-}i)} + \varepsilon_t, \ \forall\, i \in [1, k]$$

$$\varepsilon_t = \sigma_t \cdot zt$$

$$\sigma_t^2 = \omega + \sum \alpha_l \cdot \varepsilon_{(t\text{-}l)}^2 + \sum \beta_j \cdot \sigma_{(t\text{-}j)}^2, \ \forall\, l \in [1, q], \, , \ \forall\, j \in [1, p]$$

$$z_t \sim N(0,1)$$

Where:

- r_t is the asset return at time .
- ϕ_0 is the intercept term of the AR model.
- ϕ_i are the coefficients of the AR(k) model for lags $i = 1,\ldots,k$.
- $\beta_j \geq \forall\, j{=}1,\ldots,p$ are the GARCH parameters, respectively, to be estimated, and other variables have the same meaning as for the ARCH model.

NOTE *In practice, z_t may have a different distribution, such as Student's t-distribution, to capture excess kurtosis (fat tails) observed in financial returns.*

As can be seen from the formulas, the ARCH and GARCH models are regression analogs to ARIMA models, in which the dependent variable is volatility. In other words, the modeling outcome assesses the value of volatility, disregarding the sign, as a measure of dispersion. The GARCH model is, however, the most widely used volatility forecasting method because of its flexibility and ability to model different financial time-series data types. GARCH models are beneficial for risk management, option pricing, and financial market predictions, where understanding the variability of returns is crucial.

Financial modeling is complex and multifaceted, particularly when applying the GARCH model to assess volatility. It includes several stages: from initial data preparation to making informed forecasts and managerial decisions. Each stage builds upon the previous, integrating sophisticated statistical techniques to model and forecast financial market behaviors. The Python arch library is required to apply the ARCH/GARCH models for analysis and prediction. Let us move on, following this step-by-step algorithm:

1. *Data preparation* is crucial for any statistical modeling. For financial time-series data, this mainly involves the following:
   - Compute the RoR or the *logarithmic RoR* from the asset's price data. Log returns are typically used due to their desirable statistical properties.

- Perform the stationary check (e.g., the Dickey-Fuller test) to ensure the time-series data is stationary. Non-stationary data can lead to unreliable model estimations.
- Conduct a normality test (e.g., Jarque-Bera) on the RoR data or residuals of a fitted ARIMA model to assess the data distribution.

The following code demonstrates the crucial elements of *Stage 1*:

```python
1.  from scipy import stats
2.  # Stage 1: Data Preparation
3.  # Extract log returns and drop any missing values
4.  data = nasdaq_index['logRoR']['2023'].dropna().
    rename('NASDAQ')
5.  # Create a Q-Q (quantile-quantile) plot
6.  # to check the normality of the distribution
7.  qqplot_fig = qqplot(data, line='q', fit=True)
8.  qqplot_fig.set_size_inches(10, 5)
9.  plt.title('Q-Q Plot of NASDAQ Log Returns')
10. plt.show()
11. # Perform the Jarque-Bera test
12. # Null hypothesis (H0): The data is normally
    distributed
13. # If the p-value is less than
14. # the significance level (e.g., 0.05), we reject H0
15. jb_test_statistic, jb_p_value = stats.
    jarque_bera(data)
16. print(f"Jarque-Bera test statistic:
    {jb_test_statistic}")
17. print(f"p-value: {jb_p_value}")
18. is_normal = jb_p_value > 0.05
```

```
19.  print("The series is",
20.         f"{'normally distributed' if is_normal else
       'not normally distributed'}",
21.          "according to the Jarque-Bera test.")
22.  # Perform the Augmented Dickey-Fuller test to
       check the stationarity of the data
23.  adf_result = adfuller(data)
24.  print(f"ADF Statistic: {adf_result[0]}")
25.  print(f"p-value: {adf_result[1]}")
26.  is_stationary = adf_result[1] < 0.05
27.  print(f"The series is {'stationary' if is_
       stationary else 'non-stationary'}.")
```

The code results (text only) are as follows:

```
Jarque-Bera test statistic: 1.536940091045956

p-value: 0.4637219994058751

The series is normally distributed according to the
Jarque-Bera test.

ADF Statistic: -10.59929372978349

p-value: 6.231097281690702e-19

The series is stationary.
```

NOTE *The Jarque-Bera statistical test checks the null hypothesis that the data is normally distributed. It verifies whether sample data has skewness and kurtosis that match the normal distribution. Generally, if the p-value is less than the chosen significance level (often 0.05), the null hypothesis is rejected, and the data probably does not correspond to the normal distribution. Conversely, a larger p-value suggests the data does not significantly deviate from the normality distribution.*

2. *Model specification* means defining the structure of the GARCH model, which is essential for capturing the volatility clustering commonly observed in financial markets:

- Define a GARCH model object using the arch library. The typical GARCH(1,1) model is a good starting point.
- Configure the initial model parameters, including the order of the ARCH and GARCH terms (p and q), and any other parameters such as the mean model (constant, AR, etc.), distribution assumptions, etc.

Execute the following code to investigate the GARCH model parameters:

```
1.  # Stage 2: Model Specification
2.  from arch import arch_model
3.  # Show the arch_model() arguments:
4.  # see details here:
5.  # https://arch.readthedocs.io/en/latest/
    univariate/introduction.html
6.  help(arch_model)
7.  # Specify the GARCH model with an autoregressive
8.  # mean structure including one lag
9.  model = arch_model(y=data,
10.                     # Specify the volatility model
    to be GARCH
11.                    vol='GARCH',
12.                     # Specify the mean model to be
    autoregressive
13.                    mean='AR',
14.                     # Use one lag in the
    autoregressive model
15.                    lags=1,
16.                     # ARCH component order
```

```
17.                    p=1,
18.                    # GARCH component order
19.                    q=1,
20.                    # Do not automatically rescale
     data
21.                    rescale=False,
22.                    # Assume a normal distribution
     for the error term
23.                    dist='normal')
24. # Set a date to split the data into the in-sample
25. # for fitting and out-of-sample for forecasting
26. split_date = datetime(2023, 9, 1)
27. # Fit the model up to the split_date
28. # Frequency of output during estimation
29. model_fit = model.fit(update_freq=10,
30.                        last_obs=split_date)
31. # Print the model summary
32. model_fit.summary()
```

The code results (truncated) are as follows:

```
(...)
Parameters
    ----------

    y : ndarray, Series, None
        The dependent variable

    x : ndarray, DataFrame, optional
        Exogenous regressors.  Ignored if model does not
        permit exogenous regressors.
```

mean : str, optional

    Name of the mean model. Currently supported options are: 'Constant',

    'Zero', 'LS', 'AR', 'ARX', 'HAR' and 'HARX'

lags : int or list[int], optional

    Either a scalar integer value indicating lag length or a list of

    integers specifying lag locations.

 vol : str, optional

    Name of the volatility model. Currently supported options are:

    'GARCH' (default), 'ARCH', 'EGARCH', 'FIGARCH', 'APARCH' and 'HARCH'

   p : int, optional

    Lag order of the symmetric innovation

   o : int, optional

    Lag order of the asymmetric innovation

   q : int, optional

    Lag order of lagged volatility or equivalent

    power : float, optional

    Power to use with GARCH and related models

dist : int, optional

    Name of the error distribution. Currently supported options are:

     * Normal: 'normal', 'gaussian' (default)

     * Students's t: 't', 'studentst'

     * Skewed Student's t: 'skewstudent', 'skewt'

     * Generalized Error Distribution: 'ged', 'generalized error"

```
hold_back : int
                Number of observations at the start of the
                sample to exclude when

                estimating model parameters.  (...)
    rescale : bool
                Flag indicating whether to automatically
                rescale data if the scale

                of the data is likely to produce
                convergence issues when estimating

                model parameters. (...)


Optimization terminated successfully    (Exit mode 0)
            Current function value: -499.5965059794387
            Iterations: 8
            Function evaluations: 50
            Gradient evaluations: 4
AR - GARCH Model Results
Dep. Variable:  NASDAQ  R-squared:        0.000
Mean Model:     AR Adj. R-squared:        -0.006
Vol Model:      GARCH Log-Likelihood:     499.597
Distribution:   Normal AIC: -989.193
Method:         Maximum Likelihood BIC:   -973.633
No. Observations: 166
Date:  Sun, Jan 07 2024  Df Residuals: 164
Time:  11:15:26  Df Model:  2
```

```
Mean Model

coef      std err       t              P>|t|    95.0% Conf. Int.

Const     2.0123e-03   1.878e-04      10.714   8.724e-27  [1.644e-03,2.380e-03]

NASDAQ[1] 0.0164 6.565e-02            0.250 0.803         [ -0.112, 0.145]

Volatility Model

coef      std err      t     P>|t|    95.0% Conf. Int.

omega     2.9073e-06   3.432e-11     8.472e+04  0.000 [2.907e-06,2.907e-06]

alpha[1]          0.0100 2.303e-02   0.434  0.664 [-3.515e-02,5.515e-02]

beta[1]           0.9700 1.884e-02   51.490 0.000 [ 0.933, 1.007]
```

The code results show the volatility model, which assumes a normal error distribution and includes an autoregressive mean model (AR) and a GARCH model for volatility. The following parameters can be analyzed:

- The omega parameter (ω), which represents the long-run average variance, has a small value of $2.9073 \times 10{-6}$. P-value ≈ 0.000, however, and its significance is high.

- The alpha parameter ($\alpha[1]$), which measures the impact of the previous period's squared error on the current variance, has a coefficient of 0.0100. This is not statistically significant, as indicated by p-value ≈ 0.664.

- The beta parameter ($\beta[1]$), indicating the persistence of volatility shocks, has a high value of 0.9700 and is statistically significant with p-value ≈ 0.000, suggesting a high level of volatility persistence in the time series.

- The constant term in the mean model (const) has a value of 0.0020123 with a standard error of 0.0001878, which is statistically significant with a p-value much less than 0.05.

- The autoregressive term (NASDAQ[1] –), which represents the lagged value of the dependent variable, has a coefficient of 0.0164 with a standard error of 0.06565. This term, however, is not statistically significant, indicated by a high p-value, p-value ≈ 0.803.

These results provide insights into the dynamics of volatility in the NASDAQ index. The significant and high value of the beta coefficient suggests that volatility shocks are highly persistent. In contrast, the lack of significance in the alpha coefficient suggests that new shocks have a limited impact on future volatility. This could imply that the volatility tends to revert to its long-term mean slower. The AR part's lack of significance indicates that past returns do not predict future returns in this model.

Model Fitting and Diagnostic Checking

To carry out model fitting and diagnostic checking:

- Fit the GARCH model to the data and different model parameters.
- Examine the model summary for the significance of coefficients and the overall model fit.

The output from this stage helps validate the model's significance and the robustness of the model and its parameters.

Stage 3 involves a sequential iteration over the model parameters to fit the minimum values of the information criteria AIC and BIC and ensure that all model coefficients are significant, with p-value < 0.05. As a result of these iterative operations, the following parameters for the model from the previous code have been optimized:

```
1.  # Stage 3. Model Fitting and Diagnostic
2.  model = arch_model(data, vol='GARCH',
3.                     mean = 'Zero',
4.                     p = 1,
5.                     q = 1,
6.                     rescale=False,
7.                     dist='normal')
8.  split_date = dt.datetime(2023,9,1)
9.  model_fit = model.fit(update_freq=10,
10.                    last_obs=split_date)
11. model_fit.summary()
```

The code output is depicted in *Figure 8.8*:

```
Optimization terminated successfully    (Exit mode 0)
            Current function value: -500.2711007397694
            Iterations: 5
            Function evaluations: 4
            Gradient evaluations: 1
```

```
                   Zero Mean - GARCH Model Results
   Dep. Variable:              NASDAQ      R-squared:         0.000
    Mean Model:             Zero Mean   Adj. R-squared:       0.006
     Vol Model:                 GARCH   Log-Likelihood:     500.271
   Distribution:               Normal             AIC:     -994.542
        Method:   Maximum Likelihood             BIC:     -985.188
                                       No. Observations:        167
          Date:     Mon, May 20 2024    Df Residuals:           167
          Time:             10:15:37        Df Model:             0
                             Volatility Model
                  coef      std err        t      P>|t|      95.0% Conf. Int.
   omega    2.9864e-06     1.378e-10   2.167e+04    0.000   [2.986e-06,2.987e-06]
   alpha[1]     0.0100     1.685e-03      5.936   2.919e-09   [6.698e-03,1.330e-02]
   beta[1]      0.9700     4.008e-03    242.033      0.000   [ 0.962, 0.978]
```

FIGURE 8.8 The results of fitting the GARCH volatility model

Interpretation of the model results involves understanding the implications of each parameter and the model's overall fit:

- Interpret the *alpha coefficient(s)*, which measures past shocks' impact on current volatility.
- Interpret the *beta coefficient(s)*, which measure the persistence of past volatility.
- Get a *graphical* interpretation of the model results.

For example, a basic graphical analysis of the model can be represented as follows (refer to the following figure as well):

```
1.  # Stage 4: Interpretations
2.  # Generate a hedgehog plot of the volatility
    # forecast by the model
```

```
3.  model_fit.hedgehog_plot()

4.  plt.xticks(rotation=45)

5.  plt.title('NASDAQ Volatility Forecast Hedgehog
    Plot')

6.  plt.show()

7.  # Plot the conditional volatility from the model

8.  plt.figure(figsize=(10, 5))

9.  model_fit.conditional_volatility.plot()

10. plt.title('Conditional Volatility from GARCH
    Model')

11. plt.show()

12. # Plot the actual log returns alongside
    # the exponentially weighted moving average
    (EWMA)

13.

14. plt.figure(figsize=(10, 5))

15. data.plot(label='Log Returns')

16. data.ewm(span=60,
             adjust=False).mean().plot(label='60-day
    EWMA')

17. plt.title('Log Returns and EWMA Trend')

18. plt.legend()

19. plt.show()
```

Figure 8.9 illustrates multiple potential paths for future volatility as forecasted by the GARCH model. Each spike in the plot represents a different simulation of future volatility. This type of visualization helps understand the range of possible future volatility scenarios and the uncertainty inherent in the model's predictions:

FIGURE 8.9 Hedgehog plot for NASDAQ index logo 2023 GARCH model results

In *Figure 8.9*, you can observe a downward trend, indicating that the forecasted future volatility of NASDAQ is expected to decrease over time. The forecast, however, includes a range of outcomes, some higher and some lower than the mean, highlighting the inherent uncertainty in predicting future market conditions.

Predictions and Making Decisions

- Use the fitted GARCH model to forecast future volatility, calculate VaR for risk management purposes, and so on.
- Incorporate the GARCH model insights into investment strategies, such as option pricing, portfolio optimization, or hedging.

NOTE   *The GARCH model results should be interpreted in the context of current market conditions and economic indicators to improve decision-making results.*

```
1.  # Stage 5: Making Predictions
2.  # Forecast the future volatility over a horizon
    of 5 days,
```

```
 3.  # starting from the split date
 4.  test_forecast = model_fit.forecast(horizon=5,
 5.                                  start=split_date,
 6.                                  reindex=False)
 7.  # The forecast returns variance, so we take the
     square root
 8.  # to get the standard deviation, which represents
     volatility
 9.  predicted_volatility = np.sqrt(test_forecast.
     variance.dropna())
10.  # Printing the predicted volatility
11.  print("Predicted Volatility:")
12.  print(predicted_volatility)
```

The code results (truncated) are:

```
Predicted Volatility:
                 h.1       h.2       h.3       h.4       h.5
Date
2023-09-01  0.011824  0.011832  0.011840  0.011848  0.011855
(...)
2023-09-29  0.011632  0.011644  0.011656  0.011667  0.011678
```

This code will provide the predicted volatility for a 5-day horizon after the split_date, which is the out-of-sample period not used during model fitting. The predictions can be used for risk management, portfolio allocation, VaR and aVaR, trading strategies, performance attribution, stress testing, etc. Forecasts with the GARCH models provide valuable insights into future market conditions. It is still important to remember that all models have limitations, and forecasts are not guaranteed.

CONCLUSION

Applying probability theory and studying distributions such as the normal distribution helps quantify uncertainty. The market data, however, often shows fat tails, where extreme events are more common than predicted, requiring cautious risk assessment. Python examples illustrate how real-world data can diverge from theoretical models. The VaR and aVaR metrics are fundamental instruments of the tools for risk estimations. VaR shows the maximum expected loss within a confidence interval. Meanwhile, aVaR goes beyond this boundary, capturing the fat tails.

The Monte Carlo method and the GBM model are powerful tools in financial scenarios and managerial decision-making. The Monte Carlo method uses random samples to simulate various financial processes, providing each sample's risk and return assessment. The GBM model, based on Monte Carlo principles, simulates asset price trajectories, aiding in price and risk evaluation. These tools are not limited to these simulations and can also help calculate Black-Scholes prices for options, evaluations of VaR and AVaR metrics, forecasting behaviors of the market agents, etc.

The ARCH/GARCH models help with risk management and forecasting. The GARCH model captures errors of short-term and long-term effects. Although the mathematical formulation of these models is quite complex, analysts can use Python's arch library to systematically analyze data and perform diagnostic checks, integrating robust statistical foundations into financial decision-making.

In the next couple of chapters, you will explore machine learning techniques and the Facebook Prophet library for time-series data analysis and prediction, e.g., asset price prediction and risk assessment. They will cover preparing time-series data for machine learning purposes, building forecasting models, and interpreting results. As always, we will focus on practical applications and advanced forecasting techniques.

QUESTIONS

1. What does VaR stand for in financial risk analysis?

2. How does the Monte Carlo method help in financial risk analysis?

3. Why do analysts prefer to use the logarithmic RoR instead of the RoR when assessing risk?

4. What statistical test can be used to check the normality of a distribution in financial data?

5. What fundamental assumption about asset prices does the geometric Brownian motion model make?

6. What is the purpose of using the Black-Scholes formula in finance?

7. How do the ARCH and GARCH models differ from the ARIMA models?

8. Can you explain the basic difference between the ARCH and GARCH models?

9. In the context of GARCH models, what do the parameters mean?

10. What does the hedgehog plot represent in the context of GARCH model results?

11. How can the predictions from GARCH models be utilized in financial decision-making?

12. How do the concepts of VaR and aVaR relate to ARCH/GARCH models?

KEY TERMS

- *Volatility* refers to the degree of variation of a trading price or rate of return series over time as measured by the standard deviation.

- *Financial risk* involves losing money on an investment or business, e.g., due to high volatility.

- A *random variable* is a variable whose values depend on the outcomes of a random phenomenon. In finance, it is often used to model the rate of return, price changes, and other market variables.

- A *sample* (*statistical sample*) is a subset of the general population that is used to represent the entire group.

- *VaR* is a statistical measure used to quantify the level of financial risk of investment, portfolio, or position over a specific time frame. It represents the maximum expected loss with a given confidence level (e.g., 95%) under normal market conditions.

- An *option* (in the context of *financial securities*) is a contractual agreement that provides the buyer the right, but not the obligation, to buy or sell the underlying asset at a predetermined price within a specified time frame.

▪ The *probability density function (PDF)* and the *cumulative distribution function (CDF)* are two fundamental concepts in statistics used to describe the distribution of a random variable. The PDF shows the likelihood of the variable falling within a particular range of values. The CDF maps a value to its percentile rank or the probability that a random variable will take a value less than or equal to that value.

REFERENCES

▪ *Huang, C. and Petukhina, A. (2022). Applied Time Series Analysis and Forecasting with Python. Springer. https://doi.org/10.1007/978-3-031-13584-2.*

▪ *Takahashi, M., Omori, Y., and Watanabe, T. (2023). Stochastic Volatility and Realized Stochastic Volatility Models. SpringerBriefs in Statistics. Springer. https://doi.org/10.1007/978-981-99-0935-3.*

▪ *Taleb, N. N. (2022). Statistical Consequences of Fat Tails: Real World Preasymptotics, Epistemology, and Applications (Technical Incerto). Second Revised Edition. STEM Academic Press.*

9

Machine Learning and Deep Learning in Finance

INTRODUCTION

This chapter discusses *machine learning (ML)* by applying it to financial data. With their ability to process massive amounts of market data, ML algorithms become powerful tools for supporting decisions. We will delve into the foundational theories and the basis of ML tools. The chapter will guide us through the universal steps for creating ML models and allow us to harness the potential of this technology. We will explore the functionalities of the scikit-learn library, a powerful Python tool that leads the way in ML applications in finance. The library helps with practically understanding the theoretical underpinnings of ML tools and their application to financial analysis problems, offering solutions with clustering and regression models. We will also delve into using non-linear ML models with examples from the XGBoost library. We will unravel the principles of *artificial neural networks (ANNs)* and show examples of how they are adapted to financial datasets. A comparison of the results of the various ML models for predicting financial indicators will also be given.

STRUCTURE

This chapter covers the following topics:

- ML concepts
- Python ML libraries and tools
- ML models for financial data

OBJECTIVES

By the end of this chapter, you will have learned how to navigate the world of ML as it applies to the financial sector. You will be equipped with an understanding of the fundamental theories, models, and steps for applying ML and how they are applied to analyze and predict financial data. With a focus on the practical utility of the scikit-learn library, you will understand how to implement ML models such as clustering and regression and employ feature engineering to enhance model performance. You will also be able to evaluate ML models using appropriate metrics crucial for financial applications and try out the essentials of non-linear ML models through hands-on examples with XGBoost. Furthermore, you will have the skills to employ Python-based regression and clustering techniques while understanding the importance of cross-validation and executing hyperparameter tuning to improve model accuracy.

ML CONCEPTS

In previous chapters, we examined classical models and methods that assist financial investors and other market participants in making informed decisions. The contemporary directions for analytical decision support are also based on ML principles. On the one hand, ML is an extension of classical statistical methods; on the other, it has the ability to handle large volumes of data and the capabilities of modern computers. IT systems allow implementing models, such as the Monte Carlo method, to simulate financial processes and evaluate financial indices forecasts. This is a distinctive feature of ML methods and models. They leverage computational power and advanced algorithms to uncover patterns and insights that traditional methods may not detect due to their limitations in scale and complexity.

Thus, ML consists of using algorithms to parse data, learn from that data, and then decide or predict something relating to that data. Rather than following static program instructions, ML systems build a model based on sample data (training data subset) and validate the test and validation data results. They make predictions or decisions based on the universal analytical code. ML models are used in many training and validation processes on different datasets before being applied to real-world scenarios. This includes a range of models and techniques, from linear and logistic regressions to combinations of neural network models. Each ML tool has its own strengths and ideal use cases. The power of ML lies in its ability to analyze vast amounts of data. It can identify hidden structures in the data that might take time to be apparent or require extensive manual effort to uncover.

ML is iterative by nature, meaning models can learn, tune, and improve over time as new data becomes available. This aspect of continuous improvement is crucial in financial applications where market conditions can change rapidly and unpredictably. The interdisciplinary nature further enhances the adaptability (customizations) of ML. ML tools combine the concepts from computer science, statistics, mathematics, and specific knowledge, e.g., finance patterns. This enables innovative solutions tailored to the nuances of financial data and decision-making processes. Unfortunately, despite the stunning results compared to classical analysis methods, ML is not a *magic wand* that provides answers to all questions. Errors, although small, can be significant, and many learning problems fall on the researcher. This chapter will consider only a few classic examples without going deep into the details of ML, which would require a separate book and/or studying a series of books and practical examples.

Earlier chapters noted some keystone features of ML model implementation techniques. This includes a thorough discussion on the *extract, transform, and load (ETL)* process and *exploratory data analysis (EDA)*, both of which are instrumental in understanding and preparing our data (*Chapter 4, Exploratory Data Analysis for Finance*). We also touched on the importance of efficiency metrics, the role of test datasets and the parameter tunning process (*Chapter 7, Time-Series Analysis and Financial Data Forecasting*), the probability theory (*Chapter 8, Risk Assessment and Volatility Modeling*), and the necessity of feature cleaning to ensure the integrity of the models. Within the context of ML, however, integrated models and algorithms are not standalone entities but a decision support system. These integrated processes form a cohesive framework that supports the intricate workflow of ML, from initial data handling to the final stages of prediction and interpretation.

ML Models

In finance, ML models have revolutionized how we analyze data, assess risks, optimize portfolios, detect patterns, and so on. In addition, there are a lot of different ML models and their implementations now. Typically, we can use the following ML models and algorithms for various financial tasks[1]:

---

[1] *https://en.wikipedia.org/wiki/Machine_learning*

▪ *Basic ML models*:

  • *Regression models* are like classical regression, as described in *Chapters 6, Asset Pricing and Portfolio Management*, and *Chapter 7, Time-Series Analysis and Financial Data Forecasting*, but use another method for parameter estimation based on more than just statistical principles. Like the CAMP model, these models are widely used in finance based on quantitative analysis. They are used to assess the level of influence of external features on the dependent variable. They can be used to predict continuous outcomes such as stock prices and interest rates (*Chapter 7, Time-Series Analysis and Financial Data Forecasting*). Simple linear regression can reveal trends. A combination of simple regressions can help with understanding non-linear patterns. Varieties of ML regressions also include ridge and lasso regression—each can consider different aspects of financial data, such as multicollinearity or overfitting.

  • *Classification models* predict categorical outcomes and are used extensively in credit scoring, market movement prediction, and market signal detection (as described in *Chapter 5, Investment and Trading Strategies*). They can classify companies into creditworthy or high-risk categories based on financial indicators and predict categorical outcomes, such as whether financial assets will go up or down or a credit card transaction is fraudulent. They are often realized by logistic regression, which is widely used for simplification, but other algorithms and techniques can be used, too.

  • *Clustering models* or *unsupervised* classification is applied when we do not know how to make a classification; we have no "rules" for this. Clustering algorithms, such as k-means and agglomerative clustering, are pivotal in segmenting financial assets into homogeneous groups without predefined labels, aiding portfolio diversification and customer segmentation. These models identify structure in unlabeled data, uncovering relations that are only apparent after some time.

▪ Basic ML algorithms and techniques:

  • *Decision trees* and *random forest* methods are used for classification and regression tasks, such as predicting whether a stock or rates of return will increase in value or determining the probable default rates of loans or dividend payments. The essential advantage of those models is that they are interpretable, which is critical in financial applications where transparency in decision-making is crucial.

- The *gradient boosting* approach, which includes an ensemble of decision trees, is highly effective for classification and regression tasks. These models work by sequentially building trees, each of which corrects the errors of its predecessors. Therefore, the model's accuracy is continuously improving. In finance, gradient boosting models are used to handle non-linear complex predictive tasks, such as forecasting security prices, calculating rates of return, or determining risk levels.

- *Support vector machines* (*SVMs*) are supervised learning methods for detecting classification, regression, and outliers. They are mainly known for their ability to handle high-dimensional data and their effectiveness for tasks when the number of dimensions exceeds the number of data samples. In finance, the SVM methods may predict the direction of market movements or the security price. The kernel trick allows SVMs to capture complex relationships in financial data. SVMs can be part of models that assess the risk levels of specific investments or loan applicants.

- ANN methods are at the forefront of predicting complex non-linear patterns and are invaluable in algorithmic trading, market trend analysis, derivative pricing, and so on. They operate with vast amounts of data, like the biological brain. In this way, neural networks can analyze obvious and hidden relationships and structures that other models cannot capture. ANNs can operate different financial market data, both quantitative and categorical. They can assess and predict risks and process complex market data, including technical indicators and historical price patterns.

- Naive Bayes methods, *k-nearest neighbors* (*KNN*), *Adaptive Boosting* (*AdaBoost*), and many other algorithms and techniques can be applied to solve various decision-making problems. Every day, new solutions to existing problems emerge, requiring analysts to move forward continuously. Innovative approaches quickly become standardized and fail to provide significant added value.

As can be seen from the brief overview, ML methods and algorithms are universal and can be adapted for any financial task. Applying all these models, however, is a programming and analytical challenge in finance. The accuracy of financial predictions is often related to the quality of data, the correct selection of models, tuning hyperparameters, and the interpretation of the results. Therefore, combining ML with financial expertise helps solve complex problems. Finally, this will allow us to obtain more reliable forecasts than classical statistical methods can provide.

The Universal Algorithm of ML

ML models' training and application are characterized by a similar universal process (universal algorithm) comprised of a series of well-defined stages. These stages guide users from the initial conceptualization of the problem to the final evaluation of the model. Let us see each of these steps:

1. The *problem definition* is the starting point of any ML (and not only ML) project and is the precise definition of the problem. In finance, this could mean deciding whether to focus on predicting asset prices or rates of return, identifying volatility or risks, or solving other problems described in previous chapters.

2. *Data collection* involves gathering the data essential for training the model. This process, known as ETL, is followed by EDA, where the data is examined for patterns, anomalies, or trends. EDA provides valuable insights that form the basis for model design and feature selection (see *Chapter 4, Exploratory Data Analysis for Finance*).

3. *Feature engineering* is crucial and especially affects the accuracy of ML results. It involves creating new features from the existing data to improve model performance. This may also include encoding categorical variables, handling missing values, and more (as in the previous step). Data pre-processing as a part of feature engineering includes cleaning the data and transforming it into a format suitable for modeling, such as scaling or normalization. This is highly necessary for some types of models, such as ANNs.

4. *Models, algorithms, and Python tool selection* are pivotal for effective results. This decision is guided by the nature of the task, the nature of the data, and the desired outcomes. Python offers many libraries, such as *scikit-learn*, *XGBoost*, *LightGBM*, *TensorFlow*, and *PyTorch*, each with weaknesses and strengths. The selection of tools also depends on the model's complexity and the computational resources available.

5. *Model training and validation* involve feeding the pre-processed data into the learning model. The model trains and makes predictions or classifications based on the input data training subset. The input data is split into train, test, and validation subsets. The test subset is used to check the accuracy of the final model. The validation subset for cross-validation tests the model's performance on unseen data to ensure it generalizes well beyond the training dataset.

6. *Cross-validation* and *hyperparameter tuning* enhance the model's accuracy; cross-validation is used to test the model's effectiveness on different subsets (different splits) of the data. Most ML algorithms usually give

different results both on the same and different datasets. In fact, cross-validation averages the assessments of different results. Hyperparameter tuning involves adjusting the model's parameters to find the combination that yields the best performance. A simplified example of hyperparameter tuning was presented in *Chapter 7, Time-Series Analysis and Financial Data Forecasting*, where we used the `auto_arima()` function. For ANN models, the hyperparameters can be the number of layers of the neural network, etc.

7. The *final step* is evaluating the model's performance using appropriate metrics. In classification problems, this may include accuracy, precision, recall, and F1-score, whereas in regression, metrics such as *mean squared error (MSE)* or *mean absolute error (MAE)* are used. This phase assesses whether the model meets the initial objectives and how it might perform in real-world scenarios.

This step-based approach in ML is the basic principle for solving diverse and complex financial tasks. By adhering to these universal steps, we can apply many ML models, from conceptualizing the problem to deploying robust, effective, and valuable results.

PYTHON ML LIBRARIES AND TOOLS

While many ML libraries include classic models and algorithms and specific approaches to their implementation, the classic and time-tested libraries are scikit-learn, XGBoost, LightGBM, Keras, TensorFlow, and PyTorch. This book will observe the first three: scikit-learn, XGBoost, and LightGBM. You can, however, continually expand your horizons and skills based on the principles of working with these basic ML libraries.

Scikit-Learn Python Library

Scikit-learn is a widely known Python ML library. It is universal in application and relatively easy to use. Scikit-learn's tools were initially developed in 2007 as part of a *Google Summer of Code* project and later expanded with contributions from the analytical community. Scikit-learn is based on NumPy, SciPy, and Matplotlib and is designed to help users apply different ML models, algorithms, and techniques with one Python library[2].

---

[2] *https://en.wikipedia.org/wiki/Scikit-learn/*

At the time of writing this book, scikit-learn included the following main modules, each offering specific functionalities within the ML domain (*https://scikit-learn.org/stable/modules/classes.html*).

Functional modules for data preparation and results interpretation:

- `.impute` provides tools for handling missing data, including various imputation strategies.
- `.feature_extraction` provides tools for extracting features from data, which is particularly useful in processing text and images.
- `.feature_selection` offers methods for selecting the most informative features from the dataset to enhance model performance.
- `.preprocessing` provides data pre-processing utilities such as scaling and normalizing, which are critical for data preparation.
- `.metrics` provides metrics for evaluating model performance, which is essential for assessing ML models' effectiveness (level of errors).
- `.model_selection` includes model selection and validation tools such as train-test split and grid search.
- `.manifold` contains algorithms for non-linear dimensionality reduction and helps in uncovering underlying data structures.
- `.decomposition` offers matrix decomposition methods such as PCA and NMF for dimensionality reduction and feature extraction.
- `.utils` provides a collection of utility functions and classes, including methods for balancing datasets, creating synthetic samples, and other auxiliary functions.
- `.datasets` contains utilities for loading and generating datasets, which are helpful for testing algorithms and educational purposes.

Models and ML algorithm-based modules:

- `.cluster` offers clustering algorithms such as k-means and hierarchical clustering, which are suitable for unsupervised learning tasks.
- `.linear_model` encompasses linear models for regression and classification tasks, including logistic and linear regression.
- `.ensemble` includes ensemble methods such as random forest, AdaBoost, and gradient boosting for improved prediction accuracy.
- `.neural_network` offers models for multi-layer perceptron (neural networks) for complex, non-linear problems.

- ▦ `.gaussian_process` contains algorithms for regression and classification using Gaussian processes.
- ▦ `.neighbors` contains the KNN algorithm for classification and regression based on data proximity.
- ▦ `.semi_supervised` contains algorithms for semi-supervised learning when dealing with primarily unlabeled data.
- ▦ `.svm` offers SVM algorithm applications, including classification, regression, and outlier detection.
- ▦ `.tree` offers decision tree algorithms, which are widely used for their interpretability in classification and regression tasks.
- ▦ `.naive_bayes` contains the Naive Bayes algorithms, which are ideal for classification tasks, particularly in text analysis and situations where the independence assumption holds.

Therefore, each module of the scikit-learn library is designed to realize specific ML needs, making the library a comprehensive toolkit for data analysis. In *Table 9.1*, we systemize some of the crucial functions of scikit-learn for further application in finance.

TABLE 9.1 Comparing Python libraries for finance

Function/feature	Description	ML steps
Data collection and pre-processing functions		
`impute.KNNImputer` `impute.MissingIndicator`	Imputation transformer for completing missing values.	Step 2
`preprocessing.add_dummy_feature`	Augment dataset with an additional dummy feature.	Step 2, Step 3
`preprocessing.StandardScaler`	Standardize features by removing the mean and scaling to the variance.	Step 3, Step 4
`preprocessing.MinMaxScaler`	Transforms features by scaling each feature to a given range.	Step 3, Step 4
`preprocessing.OneHotEncoder`	Encode categorical integer features using a one-hot scheme.	Step 3, Step 4
Models and algorithm-based functions (regression, classification, and universal)		
`linear_model.LinearRegression`	Linear model for regression.	Step 4, Step 5
`linear_model.LogisticRegression`	Logistic model for binary classification.	Step 4, Step 5
`linear_model.SGDClassifier`	Linear classifiers (SVM, logistic regression, etc.) with SGD training.	Step 4, Step 5

(Continued)

Function/feature	Description	ML steps
`svm.SVR`	Support vector regression.	Step 4, Step 5
`ensemble.RandomForestClassifier`	Random forest for classification tasks.	Step 4, Step 5
`neural_network.MLPClassifier`	Multi-layer perceptron classifier.	Step 4, Step 5
`neural_network.MLPRegressor`	Multi-layer perceptron regressor.	Step 4, Step 5
`ensemble.RandomForestRegressor`	Random forest for regression tasks.	Step 4, Step 5
`ensemble.GradientBoostingClassifier`	Gradient boosting for classification.	Step 4, Step 5
`ensemble.GradientBoostingRegressor`	Gradient boosting for regression.	Step 4, Step 5
Models and algorithm-based functions with built-in cross-validation functions		
`linear_model.RidgeCV`	Ridge regression with built-in cross-validation.	Step 5, Step 6
`linear_model.LassoCV`	Lasso regression with built-in cross-validation.	Step 5, Step 6
`linear_model.ElasticNetCV`	Elastic net model with built-in cross-validation.	Step 5, Step 6
Models clustering		
`cluster.KMeans`	K-means clustering.	Step 5, Step 6
`cluster.AgglomerativeClustering`	Hierarchical clustering using a bottom-up approach.	Step 5, Step 6
Model evaluation and hyperparameter tuning		
`model_selection.train_test_split`	Split arrays or matrices into random train and test subsets.	Step 5, Step 6
`model_selection.TimeSeriesSplit`	Split arrays or matrices into random train and test subsets for time-series data cross-validation.	Step 6
`model_selection.GridSearchCV`	Exhaustive search over specified parameter values for an estimator.	Step 6
`model_selection.RandomizedSearchCV`	Randomized search on hyperparameters.	Step 6
`metrics.accuracy_score`	Accuracy classification score.	Step 7
`metrics.mean_squared_error`	MSE regression loss.	Step 4, Step 5, Step 7
`metrics.mean_squared_error`	MSE regression errors.	Step 4, Step 5, Step 7
`metrics.mean_absolute_percentage_error`	*Mean absolute percentage error (MAPE)* regression errors.	Step 7
`metrics.precision_score, metrics.recall_score, metrics.f1_score`	Precision, recall, and F1-score for classification tasks.	Step 7

XGBoost and LightGBM Libraries

The XGBoost and LightGBM libraries are highly regarded for their exceptional speed, superior performance, and ability to handle huge datasets, allowing them to be used in financial modeling and analysis. XGBoost is known for its robust and scalable gradient boosting implementation, making it one of the best choices for predictive tasks such as financial indices and algorithmic trading. A similar library, LightGBM, known for its lightning-fast processing speeds and efficiency in large-scale data handling, stands out without sacrificing accuracy in scenarios demanding rapid model training. Therefore, XGBoost and LightGBM represent cutting-edge ML techniques in finance, offering universal techniques to predict market trends and support strategic financial decisions. Let us briefly examine these libraries' syntax, methods, and main arguments.

As we have noted, XGBoost[3] is a powerful library optimized for boosting trees, widely utilized in finance for predictive analytics. Its syntax revolves around the `XGBRegressor` and `XGBClassifier` classes for regression and classification tasks like the scikit-learn syntax style. The main objects include the `.fit()` method to train the model, the `.predict()` method for making predictions, and the `.score()` method for model evaluation. XGBoost tools can handle various types of financial data, coupled with *speed* and applicable accuracy. The main advantages of XGBoost models are that they consider the dependence's non-linearity and require precise parameter tuning.

Initializing the XGBoost regressor object with a set of typical hyperparameters can be represented as in the following example:

```
1.  xgb_regressor = XGBRegressor(
2.      # Set maximum depth of each tree
3.      max_depth=3,
4.      # Set number of trees in the ensemble
5.      n_estimators=100,
6.      # Set learning rate for convergence
7.      learning_rate=0.1,
```

---

[3] *https://xgboost.readthedocs.io/en/stable/*

```
 8.        # Set subsampling rate of the training data
 9.        subsample=0.8,
10.        # Set subsampling rate of features for each tree
11.        colsample_bytree=0.8,
12.        # Set min loss reduction needed to make further
           splits
13.        gamma=0,
14.        # Set L1 regularization term on weights
15.        reg_alpha=0,
16.        # Set L2 regularization term on weights
17.        reg_lambda=1
18.    )
```

The primary hyperparameters for the XGBRegressor include:

- max_depth, which controls the depth of the tree. Higher values allow the model to capture more complex patterns but can lead to overfitting.
- The n_estimators parameter, which determines the number of trees in the ensemble. More trees can improve accuracy but may slow down the computation.
- learning_rate, which affects the contribution of each tree to the outcome. Lower values require more trees but can lead to better generalization.
- A subsample fraction of the training data sampled for building trees, which can help prevent overfitting.
- gamma, which specifies the minimum loss reduction required to make a split.
- The reg_alpha and reg_lambda parameters, which are the L1 and L2 regularization terms, respectively, on weights can help prevent overfitting by penalizing complex models.

It is crucial to perform hyperparameter tuning, such as cross-validation with GridSearchCV or RandomizedSearchCV, to find the best combination of these parameters for your dataset and regression task. Those tools operate with combinations to find the optimal settings for the specific dataset and classification task. For more details, see the official help: *https://scikit-learn.org/stable/modules/grid_search.html*.

Defining hyperparameters for the XGBoost classification model involves arguments that control the model's learning and complexity. Here is an example of how to set hyperparameters for XGBClassifier:

```
1.  xgb_classifier = XGBClassifier(
2.      # Set max depth for decision trees
3.      max_depth=3,
4.      # Define number of trees to build
5.      n_estimators=100,
6.      # Specify the learning rate for training
7.      learning_rate=0.1,
8.      # Set fraction of samples to train each tree
9.      subsample=0.8,
10.     # Set fraction of features for building trees
11.     colsample_bytree=0.8,
12.     # Minimum loss reduction needed to further split
13.     gamma=0,
14.     # L1 reg on weights, enhancing sparsity
15.     reg_alpha=0,
16.     # L2 reg on weights, reducing overfitting
17.     reg_lambda=1,
18.     # Objective function for binary classification
19.     objective='binary:logistic'
20. )
```

Thus, key hyperparameters for the `XGBClassifier` include:

- `max_depth`, which determines how deep each tree can grow during any boosting round.
- The `n_estimators` argument, which sets the number of trees to build.
- `learning_rate`, which shrinks the contribution of each tree to prevent overfitting.
- `subsample`, which controls the fraction of the training data to be used for each tree.
- `colsample_bytree`, which sets the subsample ratio of features to be used for each tree.
- `gamma`, which specifies the minimum loss reduction required to make a further partition.
- `reg_alpha` (L1 regularization) and `reg_lambda` (L2 regularization), which apply regularization to reduce overfitting.
- `objective`, which defines the loss function to be minimized. It can take the following values: '`binary:logistic`' for binary classification, '`multi:softmax`' for multiclass, and so on.

Hyperparameter tuning can also significantly affect and improve the performance of the `XGBClassifier` models by using the `GridSearchCV` and `RandomizedSearchCV` classes.

LightGBM[4] is one of the fastest libraries within the ML domain, and it is particularly favored for its performance in finance. This framework uses tree-based learning algorithms and is designed for speed and efficiency. LightGBM's core advantage is operating large datasets without compromising training speed or model accuracy. The main LightGBM classes are `LGBMRegressor()` for regression and `LGBMClassifier()` for classification tasks. These classes share a similar syntax, ensuring a smooth transition for those familiar with scikit-learn or XGBoost. LightGBM tools are commonly the same for financial modeling tasks as for XGBoost. This library, however, usually applies when the training speed is crucial.

To apply a LightGBM model to specific financial forecasting tasks, we can tune hyperparameters such as:

---

[4] *https://lightgbm.readthedocs.io/en/stable/*

- ▨ `num_leaves`, which refers to the number of leaves in one tree, corresponding to the model's complexity.
- ▨ `max_depth`, which is the maximum depth of the tree to control overfitting.
- ▨ `learning_rate`, which is the rate at which the model learns, affecting how quickly it adapts to the data.
- ▨ `n_estimators`, which is the number of boosted trees.
- ▨ `subsample`, which is the fraction of samples used per tree; a lower ratio prevents overfitting.

Hyperparameter tuning for LightGBM, as for other ML tools, is also crucial to maximize the model's predictive power.

ML MODELS FOR FINANCIAL DATA

ML methods can solve many different financial data analysis tasks. We discussed some of them in earlier chapters. Now, we will consider several typical financial tasks and their implementation using the previously presented ML libraries and algorithms.

Clustering Analysis of Financial Data

To generate an optimal portfolio in *Chapter 6, Asset Pricing and Portfolio Management*, we used the optimization method (from the SciPy library). We obtained the optimal structure of a portfolio from the top 30 financial assets of the NASDAQ exchange. Based on these results, we will conduct a clustering analysis of the same assets (see *Chapter 6* or the appendix with the corresponding software code for this chapter) based on the engineering of statistical metrics for *logRoR*. The corresponding code is presented here:

```
1. (...full version Chapter 6...)
2. # Display the DataFrame
3. print("Mathematical Optimization Results")
4. print("Optimize for maximum Sharpe Ratio:")
5. print(portfolio_df.transpose())
6. (...)
```

```
7.  # Features pre-processing for Clustering

8.  from scipy.stats import skew, kurtosis

9.  def sharpe_ratio(return_series):

10.     return np.mean(return_series) / np.std
    (return_series)

11. def moving_average(return_series, window):

12.     return return_series.rolling(window=window).
    mean()

13. # Initialize a DataFrame to store features

14. features = pd.DataFrame(index=nasdaq_assets
    ['logRoR'].columns)

15. # Generate the features

16. for column in nasdaq_assets['logRoR'].columns:

17.   returns = nasdaq_assets['logRoR'][column]

18.   features.loc[column, 'mean'] = returns.mean()

19.   features.loc[column, 'std'] = returns.std()

20.   features.loc[column, 'skewness'] = skew(returns)

21.   features.loc[column, 'kurtosis'] = kurtosis(returns)

22.   features.loc[column, 'Autocorrelation'] =
    returns.autocorr()

23.   features.loc[column, 'Sharpe Ratio'] = sharpe_
    ratio(returns)

24.   features.loc[column, 'Return 5th Percentile'] =
    np.percentile(returns, 5)

25.   features.loc[column, 'Return 95th Percentile'] =
    np.percentile(returns, 95)

26.   features.loc[column, '30-day MA'] = moving_
    average(returns, 21).iloc[-1]

27.

28. # Clustering
```

```python
29.  from sklearn.preprocessing import StandardScaler
30.  from sklearn.cluster import KMeans
31.  # Sciling Input Data
32.  scaler = StandardScaler()
33.  scaled_features = scaler.fit_transform(features)
34.  # Determine the optimal number of clusters
35.  k_optimal = 8
36.  # Perform K-Means Clustering
37.  kmeans = KMeans(n_clusters=k_optimal, random_
     state=42)
38.  cluster_labels = kmeans.fit_predict(scaled_features)
39.  # Add the cluster labels to your original DataFrame
40.  features['Cluster'] = cluster_labels
41.  # Merge with Sharpe Portfolio Wights
42.  sharpe_with_clusters = pd.concat([portfolio_df,
     features],
43.                                    axis = 1)
44.  print("\nSharpe Portfolio with Clusters:")
45.  print(sharpe_with_clusters.sort_values(
46.      ['Cluster'])[['Cluster', 'Weight',
47.                    'Sharpe Ratio', 'mean', 'std']])
48.  # Group by 'Cluster' and calculate the mean for
     each cluster
49.  cluster_centroids = features.groupby('Cluster').
     mean()
50.  # Show the results
51.  print("Cluster Centroids:")
52.  print(cluster_centroids[['Sharpe Ratio', 'mean',
     'std']])
```

The results of the code are as follows:

```
Sharpe Portfolio with Clusters:
```

	Cluster	Weight	Sharpe Ratio	mean	std
MRNA	0	0.00	-0.002633	-0.000114	0.043323
TSLA	0	0.00	0.001085	0.000041	0.037787
ZS	0	0.00	-0.008811	-0.000336	0.038138
MELI	0	0.00	-0.010074	-0.000374	0.037102
ENPH	0	0.00	-0.012462	-0.000523	0.041976
DDOG	0	0.00	-0.000057	-0.000002	0.039058
AZN	1	21.96	0.034604	0.000529	0.015301
KDP	1	0.00	0.007999	0.000094	0.011721
MDLZ	1	8.59	0.031310	0.000352	0.011266
CSGP	1	0.00	-0.010167	-0.000221	0.021737
DLTR	1	0.00	-0.000288	-0.000007	0.023187
SBUX	1	0.00	-0.005537	-0.000097	0.017499
HON	1	0.00	-0.007017	-0.000094	0.013445
AAPL	1	0.00	0.023847	0.000430	0.018034
URBN	2	0.00	0.013892	0.000416	0.029939
INTU	2	0.00	0.020531	0.000487	0.023717
AMAT	2	0.00	0.025408	0.000710	0.027981
MCHP	2	0.00	0.009883	0.000248	0.025141
MRVL	2	0.00	0.007047	0.000243	0.034539
SIRI	3	0.00	-0.013065	-0.000338	0.025921
AMGN	4	12.82	0.028793	0.000375	0.013023
BKR	4	14.07	0.035628	0.000863	0.024234
PCAR	4	28.65	0.045369	0.000716	0.015800
VRSK	4	0.00	0.016299	0.000247	0.015156

MAR	4	1.09	0.033856	0.000680	0.020103
ZM	5	0.00	-0.070788	-0.002378	0.033617
ILMN	6	0.00	-0.049928	-0.001430	0.028666
JD	6	0.00	-0.041195	-0.001519	0.036899
META	7	0.00	0.005120	0.000160	0.031200
FTNT	7	12.81	0.035020	0.001017	0.029072

Cluster Centroids:

Cluster	Sharpe Ratio	mean	std
0	-0.005492	-39564	
1	0.009344	0.000123	0.016524
2	0.015352	0.000421	0.028263
3	-0.013065	-0.000338	0.025921
4	0.031989	0.000576	0.017663
5	-0.070788	-0.002378	0.033617
6	-0.045561	-0.001475	0.032783
7	0.020070	0.000588	0.030136

The code calculates several statistical metrics and ratios that are commonly used for feature engineering in financial analysis:

- *Mean*: Average return of the asset
- *Standard deviation (std)*: Measures the variation or dispersion of returns
- *Skewness*: Indicates the asymmetry of the return distribution
- *Kurtosis*: Measures the "tails" of the return distribution
- *Autocorrelation*: Assesses the linear relationship between lagged values of returns
- *Sharpe ratio*: Represents the risk-adjusted return

- *Return percentiles (5th and 95th)*: Provide a sense of the possible distribution's tails
- *30-day moving average (MA)*: Smoothes out short-term fluctuations and defines longer-term return trends

In this example, the predefined optimal cluster equals 8. To define the optimal number of clusters for any clustering task, however, we can use various methods, such as:

- Plot the sum of squared distances from each point to its assigned center for a range of cluster numbers. The *elbow* points, where the rate of decrease sharply changes, can suggest the optimal number of clusters.
- Measure how similar an object is to its cluster compared to other clusters. The group score ranges from -1 to 1. The highest value shows that the object is well matched to this cluster and poorly matched to neighboring clusters and objects.
- Compare the total within intra-cluster variation with different numbers of clusters for the expected values under the null reference distribution of the data.

Regarding the portfolio optimization and clustering results, while clusters 1, 4, and 7 are consistent, cluster 2, despite having a centroid Sharpe ratio of 0.015352, is not included in the portfolio. This suggests that the clustering algorithm, which uses multiple features for clustering, offers a more sensitive approach to diversification than the optimizing model based on the Sharpe ratio alone. This can lead to more robust portfolios that provide better risk-adjusted returns. We can also use clustering for other financial tasks for unsupervised data classification.

Forecasting Stock Prices

In *Chapter 7, Time-Series Analysis and Financial Data Forecasting*, we applied the SARIMAX tool to predict the AstraZeneca PLC stock price in 2023. As you'll remember, the MAPE was 0.65% for the 5-day test data subset (see *Chapter 7* or the appendix with the corresponding software code for this chapter). We will use the same dataset to apply some ML regression models here.

First, the ML time-series model must understand the core principles for time-lagged feature generation. Look at *Figure 9.1*:

Date	y-actual		t_target	N_lag_X=0	N_lag_X=1	N_lag_X=2	N_lag_X=3	N_lag_X=4
2023-12-14	NaN		129,55	NaN	NaN	NaN	NaN	NaN
2023-12-15	129,55		198,06	129,55	NaN	NaN	NaN	NaN
2023-12-18	198,06		200,17	198,06	129,55	NaN	NaN	NaN
2023-12-19	200,17		182,18	200,17	198,06	129,55	NaN	NaN
2023-12-20	182,18		177,18	182,18	200,17	198,06	129,55	NaN
2023-12-21	177,18		159,47	177,18	182,18	200,17	198,06	129,55
2023-12-22	159,47		168,78	159,47	177,18	182,18	200,17	198,06
2023-12-27	168,78		165,48	168,78	159,47	177,18	182,18	200,17
2023-12-28	165,48		165,63	165,48	168,78	159,47	177,18	182,18
2023-12-29	165,63		NaN	165,63	165,48	168,78	159,47	177,18

t_target = y_actual.shift(-1)   X_lagged = y_actual.shift(0) … y_actual.shift(4)

FIGURE 9.1 Lagged features generation principles

Figure 9.1 illustrates the principle of generating lagged features for ML models that work with time-series data. The table describes how successful training of ML models requires creating a matrix of lagged dependent variables (the penultimate row of the table in *Figure 9.1*). As discussed in *Chapter 7, Time-Series Analysis and Financial Data Forecasting*, this is akin to the order of an *autoregressive (AR)* model. Suppose the variable y_actual represents the input data column. In that case, one must apply .shift(-1) to the dependent variable t_target (forecasts) and .shift(0) to .shift(n-1) for the lagged features X with a maximum delay of n periods. Execute the following code for the Python implementation of this principle:

```
1.  # Define the function of lagged feature creation
2.  def create_lagged_features(df, max_lag=5,
3.                            prediction_window=1,
4.                            seasonal = True):
5.
6.      lagged_df = pd.DataFrame(index=df.index)
7.      for col in df.columns:
8.
9.          # Create target column for prediction
```

```python
10.         if prediction_window > 0:
11.             lagged_df[f'{col}_target_plus_
    {prediction_window}d'] = \
12.                 df[col].shift(-prediction_window)
13.

14.

15.     # Create lagged features for each column
16.     for l in range(0, max_lag):
17.             lagged_df[f'{col}_lag_{l}'] = df[col].
    shift(l)
18.

19.     # Adding datetime (seasonality) features
20.     if seasonal:
21.         lagged_df['day'] = lagged_df.index.day
22.         lagged_df['dayofweek'] = lagged_df.index.
    dayofweek
23.         lagged_df['month'] = lagged_df.index.month
24.         lagged_df['dayofyear'] = lagged_df.index.
    dayofyear
25.     return lagged_df
26.

27. # AstraZeneca PLC Stock Price dataset
28. data = nasdaq_assets_ac['AZN']['2023']
29. # print the prepared data frame for AstraZeneca
    PLC Stock Price
30. print(create_lagged_features(pd.DataFrame(data)))
```

The results of the code are:

	AZN_target_plus_1d	AZN_lag_0	AZN_lag_1	AZN_lag_2	AZN_lag_3 \
Date					
2023-01-03	68.058800	67.892326	NaN	NaN	NaN
2023-01-04	68.362373	68.058800	67.892326	NaN	NaN
2023-01-05	69.331841	68.362373	68.058800	67.892326	NaN
2023-01-06	69.429771	69.331841	68.362373	68.058800	67.892326
2023-01-09	70.115250	69.429771	69.331841	68.362373	68.058800
...	...	...	...	...	...
2023-09-25	68.220001	68.940002	67.830002	67.019997	67.959999
2023-09-26	67.940002	68.220001	68.940002	67.830002	67.019997
2023-09-27	67.419998	67.940002	68.220001	68.940002	67.830002
2023-09-28	67.720001	67.419998	67.940002	68.220001	68.940002
2023-09-29	NaN	67.720001	67.419998	67.940002	68.220001

	AZN_lag_4	day	dayofweek	month	dayofyear
Date					
2023-01-03	NaN	3	1	1	3
2023-01-04	NaN	4	2	1	4
2023-01-05	NaN	5	3	1	5
2023-01-06	NaN	6	4	1	6
2023-01-09	67.892326	9	0	1	9
...	...	...	...	...	...
2023-09-25	66.669998	25	0	9	268
2023-09-26	67.959999	26	1	9	269
2023-09-27	67.019997	27	2	9	270
2023-09-28	67.830002	28	3	9	271
2023-09-29	68.940002	29	4	9	272

[187 rows x 10 columns]

In addition to generating the lagged features, the `create_lagged_fea-tures()` function extracts features based on date data—such as the day of the month, day of the week, and month. You are encouraged to experiment with this function to attain the most advantageous results for subsequent forecasting endeavors.

Moving forward, we will implement a forecast like the one presented at the end of *Chapter 7, Time-Series Analysis and Financial Data Forecasting*, for the AstraZeneca PLC stock price in 2023. Execute the following code and analyze the code results:

```
1.  from sklearn.linear_model import LinearRegression
2.  from sklearn.svm import SVR
3.  from sklearn.linear_model import ElasticNetCV
4.  from xgboost import XGBRegressor
5.  from sklearn.metrics import mean_absolute_
    percentage_error
6.  from sklearn.model_selection import train_test_
    split
7.  def train_and_evaluate_model(model,
8.                                  X_train, X_test,
9.                                  y_train, y_test):
10.     model.fit(X_train, y_train)
11.     predictions = model.predict(X_test)
12.     mape = mean_absolute_percentage_error(y_test,
    predictions)*100
13.     return mape, predictions, model
14. def plot_predictions(y_train, y_test, predictions,
15.                         mape=None, model_name=None,
16.                         observe=30, figsize=(12, 5)):
17.     plt.figure(figsize=figsize)
```

```
18.        plt.plot(y_train[-observe:].index,
19.                 y_train[-observe:],
20.                 label='Training Data')
21.        plt.plot(y_test.index, y_test,
22.                 label='Test Data', alpha=0.7)
23.        plt.plot(y_test.index, predictions,
24.                 label='Predictions', alpha=0.7)
25.        title = 'Training Data and Test Predictions'
26.        if model_name:
27.            title = f'Training Data and Test Predictions,
    {model_name}'
28.        if mape is not None:
29.            title += f' (MAPE: {mape:.2f}%)'
30.        plt.title(title)
31.        plt.xlabel('Date')
32.        plt.ylabel('Value')
33.        plt.legend()
34.        plt.show()
35. # Prepare the data
36. lagged_data = create_lagged_features(pd.DataFrame
    (data)).dropna()
37. X = lagged_data.iloc[:, 1:-1]
38. y = lagged_data.iloc[:, 0]
39. # split data to the train and the test subsets
40. # shuffle=False - for Time Series data
41. X_train, X_test, y_train, y_test = train_test_
    split(X, y,
42.                                    test_size=0.05,
```

```
43.                                        shuffle=False)
44. # Models set
45. models = {
46.     'LinearRegression': LinearRegression(),
47.     # xgb_regressor is the previously defined
    object
48.     'XGBoost': xgb_regressor,
49.     'SVR': SVR(),
50.     'ElasticNET': ElasticNetCV(cv=5, random_
    state=False)}
51. # DataFrame to store evaluation metrics for each
    ticker
52. evaluation_metrics = pd.DataFrame()
53. for model_name, model in models.items():
54.     mape, pred, _ = train_and_evaluate_model
    (model,
55.                                   X_train, X_test,
56.                                   y_train, y_test)
57.     evaluation_metrics.loc[model_name, 'MAPE'] =
    mape
58.     evaluation_metrics.loc[model_name,
    'Predictions'] = pred[-1]
59.     evaluation_metrics.loc[model_name, 'Actual']
    = y_test[-1]
60.     mape_5days = mean_absolute_percentage_
    error(pred[-5:],
61.                                   y_test[-5:]) * 100
62.     evaluation_metrics.loc[model_name, 'MAPE (5
    days)']=mape_5days
63. # Display the evaluation metrics DataFrame
```

```
64.  print(evaluation_metrics)
65.  # Find the best model based on MAPE
66.  best_model_name = evaluation_metrics['MAPE'].
     idxmin()
67.  best_model = models[best_model_name]
68.  best_mape, best_predictions, _ = \
69.      train_and_evaluate_model(best_model,
70.                    X_train, X_test, y_train, y_test)
71.  # Plot the results
72.  plot_predictions(y_train, y_test, predictions,
73.                    best_mape, best_model_name)
```

The results are given as follows (refer to *Figure 9.2*):

	MAPE	Predictions	Actual	MAPE (5 days)
LinearRegression	1.128706	66.240835	66.695198	0.885358
XGBoost	0.983265	66.909019	66.695198	0.579479
SVR	1.427638	67.676138	66.695198	1.173993
ElasticNET	1.067756	66.409969	66.695198	0.807304

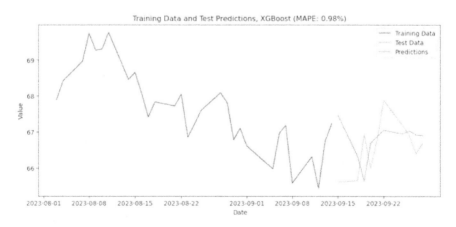

FIGURE 9.2 Forecasts of the AstraZeneca PLC stock price with the XGBoost model

Regrettably, the forecast based on the three ML models examined displayed an MAPE for the 5-day test data subset lower than it was for the SARIMAX model. There are a couple of crucial points to consider, however.

Firstly, when comparing *Figures 9.1* and *9.2*, it is evident that ML models may capture more non-linearity. This is precisely why some financial market indicators are better predicted using classic models, while others benefit from ML-based models.

Secondly, the complexity of financial indicators requires finer calibration of the ML models. Therefore, cross-validation and hyperparameter tuning are essential in effectively implementing ML models.

Cross-validation and hyperparameter tuning steps are also crucial for ANN models. The appendix to this chapter presents several implementations of the model `MLPRegressor(max_iter=500, random_state=42)`. By tuning the hyperparameters and optimizing the MAPE metric, we managed, for the parameter `hidden_layer_sizes = (100, 100)`, to reduce the forecast MAPE for the same dataset to 0.51% for the 5-day test data subset period, surpassing the results obtained with the SARIMAX model.

For a deeper understanding of the nuances of applying ML models, it is instructive to delve into the code parameters presented in the programmatic code for this chapter in the appendix. Specifically, you can use a large selection of models (refer to *Table 9.1* and the official scikit-learn documentation), modify and tune hyperparameters, adjust or engineer the features, and so on. Engaging with these principles will help you understand ML model characteristics comprehensively and unleash their potential in financial analysis and forecasting. This hands-on experimentation is not just an exercise but a pathway to practically mastering sophisticated analytical tools that can provide significant insights and advantages in the dynamic realm of finance.

CONCLUSION

ML enables advanced financial analysis, allowing for the extraction of insights from large datasets and improved decision-making. ML models require training on historical data to define model parameters and make future predictions, with techniques ranging from simple regressions to complex neural network models or their combinations. ML, however, also requires careful and professional model selection, feature preparation, cross-validation, hyperparameter tuning, and professional interpretation of the results. This helps fit models effectively, enabling them to adapt to new data and provide reliable financial insights.

The scikit-learn Python library is an essential tool within the ML community, providing modules to carry out ML comprehensively and with ease. It is the first choice for those applying financial models, providing various tools for data pre-processing, model selection, and evaluation. The scikit-learn modules and algorithms form a robust framework that can be used for multiple stages of ML, cross-validation, and hyperparameter tuning processes, which are crucial for finance tasks. The XGBoost and LightGBM libraries expand ML models' fitting functionality, especially in tasks where performance and speed are essential.

ML could enhance portfolio optimization and forecasting tasks, risk assumption processes, pattern detection in finance, and so on. Models such as regression, classification, and clustering offer diverse approaches to analyzing financial data. Decision trees provide interpretability for crucial decisions, while ensemble methods such as gradient boosting deliver powerful predictive capabilities. SVMs and neural networks (ANNs and others) realize complex, non-linear patterns, especially for tasks such as algorithmic trading.

QUESTIONS

1. What are the foundational principles of ML tools?

2. How do ML algorithms apply to financial data analysis?

3. What is the role of scikit-learn in ML applications for finance?

4. How does XGBoost handle non-linear financial modeling?

5. In what ways are LightGBM libraries advantageous for financial data processing?

6. Can you explain the concepts of training data, test data, and validation data in ML?

7. How do ML models improve over time with new data?

8. Why is cross-validation important in ML model development?

9. How does one implement the primary regression model using scikit-learn?

10. What is the significance of hyperparameter tuning in XGBoost and LightGBM?

11. What are the typical steps involved in the ML universal algorithm?

12. How does feature engineering impact ML results?

13. Why is data pre-processing critical for ANN models?

14. What measures are used to assess ML regression model performance?

15. How do clustering algorithms such as k-means function in unsupervised learning tasks?

16. What advantages do neural networks offer in algorithmic trading?

17. How can gradient boosting models be applied to forecast asset prices?

KEY TERMS

- *Train*, *validation*, and *test subsets* are core concepts of an efficient ML process. The input datasets are divided into three subsets for model training: train, validation, and test. The training subset is used to evaluate the ML model parameters for the known data. The validation subset is used to fine-tune the model parameters and perform robust model selection during training. The test subset is used to evaluate the final model's performance. The test subset is data that the model has never seen before and simulates new data for model applications.

- A *feature* is a property, characteristic, or external variable of discovered data. It is typically a column containing data that can help an ML model fit and make predictions.

- *Cross-validation* is a method used to estimate the robustness of ML models. Cross-validation divides the dataset into n subsets, and training the models is repeated k times in the different combinations. In each training loop, one of the n subsets is used as the test set (or the validation set), and the other $n-1$ subsets are gathered to form a training set. The error estimations are averaged over all n-loop results to get the total robustness and effectiveness of the model's learning algorithm. Cross-validation aims to protect against overfitting in the ML model.

- *Overfitting* occurs in model training when the model learns the parameters too well, including noise, on the training subset. Poor results (error metrics are significantly worse) on new data are due to poor generalization.

- *Hyperparameter tuning* is the process of optimizing the parameters that govern the training of an ML model. These parameters are not learned from the data but significantly impact the model's performance. Tuning involves finding the combination of hyperparameters that yields the best model performance.

- *Data scaling* is a pre-processing step in which the range of variables in a dataset is normalized or standardized. This process ensures that each feature contributes proportionally to the final prediction and prevents larger-scale features from dominating the model's learning. It is crucial for cluster analysis and applying ANN models.

- *Clustering* is an ML technique that groups different objects so that the objects in the same group (called a cluster) are more like each other than those in other groups. The critical difference in cluster analysis is that the grouping rule was unknown before clustering. Therefore, it is called unsupervised learning.

- An *artificial neural network (ANN)* is a computational model with a structure that functions or processes information similarly to the neural networks in a biological human brain. It comprises many interconnected processing nodes (*neurons*) that work in unison to solve specific problems.

REFERENCES

- Dixon, M. F., Halperin, I., and Bilokon, P. (2020). *Machine Learning in Finance From Theory to Practice.* Springer (eBook). https://doi.org/10.1007/978-3-030-41068-1.

- Inglese, L. (2023). *Python for Finance and Algorithmic Trading (2nd edition): Machine Learning, Deep Learning, Time Series Analysis, Risk and Portfolio Management for MetaTrader™5 Live Trading.*

- Grigorev, A. (2021). *Machine Learning Bookcamp: Build a Portfolio of Real-Life Projects.* Manning Publications. Shelter Island.

- Jansen, S. (2018). *Hands-On Machine Learning for Algorithmic Trading: Design and implement investment strategies based on smart algorithms that learn from data using Python.* Packt Publishing. Birmingham-Mumbai.

CHAPTER 10

TIME-SERIES ANALYSIS AND FORECASTING WITH THE *FB* PROPHET LIBRARY

INTRODUCTION

This chapter explores the domain of time-series analysis and forecasting within *Facebook's (FB's)* Prophet library, a valuable and easy forecasting tool. It begins by laying down foundational concepts of the Prophet library, tailored specifically for time-series analysis. The chapter then introduces and thoroughly discusses FB Prophet's simple and advanced functionalities, covering its development, primary objectives, and practical applications. We will guide you step by step through developing, evaluating, fine-tuning, cross-validating, and hyperparameter tuning the forecasting models using Prophet. This chapter is a crucial link, connecting earlier chapters' theoretical concepts and practical tools to real-world applications with FB's Prophet library tools.

By the end of this chapter, you will easily be able to apply FB's Prophet library to analyze and forecast time-series data, especially in a financial context.

STRUCTURE

This chapter covers the following topics:

- FB's Prophet essentials
- Functionalities with Prophet
- Additional resources
- Cross-validation and hyperparameter tuning

OBJECTIVES

This chapter will provide you with the expertise to harness the FB Prophet library for advanced time-series analysis and forecasting in finance. This chapter aims to provide a detailed understanding of Prophet's functionalities, from executing basic operations to exploiting its advanced features for more accurate forecasting. You will learn how to apply Prophet to various financial datasets. You will easily be able to forecast market trends, evaluate investment risks, and make well-informed financial decisions.

By the end of this chapter, you will have the tools to construct, assess, and refine complex forecasting models; employ cross-validation techniques; tune hyperparameters; and combine Prophet with ML methods to produce financial decisions.

PROPHET ESSENTIALS

Prophet from Meta (formerly Facebook) is a powerful, user-friendly analyzing and forecasting tool for time-series data that combines classical SARIMAX model principles and ML concepts. FB's Core Data Science[1] team developed it and it is widely adopted across various industries for forecasting. Prophet can analyze the complexities of daily, weekly, and yearly seasonal patterns and holiday effects, which are particularly common in business metrics. It is an open-source project in Python, making it accessible and integrated with other Python products and tools.

In previous chapters, we learned about traditional and advanced time-series analysis techniques, such as SARIMAX, which stands for seasonal autoregressive integrated moving averages with exogenous variables; GARCH for modeling financial time series volatility; and various ML models tailored for the prices of stock market forecasting. Each of these methodologies offers unique advantages and is suited for specific data and forecasting needs. They often, however, require a deep understanding of the statistical properties or careful adjusting and tuning of model parameters.

FB's Prophet simplifies forecasting by introducing an intuitive and powerful approach accessible to both novices and experts in data science, making it a versatile tool for various forecasting tasks. FB's Prophet was created to

---

[1] *https://facebook.github.io/prophet/*

democratize forecasting by making it more accessible. It helps to automate the model selection and evaluation process, allowing users to produce high-quality forecasts with minimal time and effort. Here are some core concepts that underpin FB's Prophet:

- *Ease of use and intuitive tools* make sophisticated forecasting tasks straightforward and accessible. With only a few lines of code, analysts can fit and visualize complex time-series models that automatically handle seasonality, trends, and holiday effects. This simplicity does not come at the expense of power or flexibility, making Prophet an attractive option for a broad spectrum of users, from data science beginners to seasoned analysts.

- Prophet excels at *automatically identifying and adjusting for seasonal patterns* in data, whether hourly, daily, weekly, or yearly (more advanced than SAIMA models). This automatic detection simplifies the forecasting process, especially for users unfamiliar with the nuances of seasonal adjustments in traditional time-series analysis.

- Prophet allows the incorporation of *additional regressors* (such as the SARIMAX model) into the forecasting model, enabling users to include other factors that might influence the target variable. This feature is invaluable for capturing the impact of external variables on stock prices, such as economic indicators or company-specific news.

- Another of the Prophet's strengths is considering *holidays or other special events*. It allows for explicitly modeling periods that can impact the forecasted indices, such as public holidays, promotional events, and custom ones.

- Prophet is well adjusted at modeling data with changing *trends*, accommodating linear and non-linear growth patterns over time. Its decomposable model structure—trend, seasonality, special events, etc.—offers a robust framework for capturing complex time-series dynamics.

- Detecting *changepoints*, the dots in the data where the underlying trend changes, is crucial for accurate forecasting. For example, this is highly helpful for practical technique analysis and stock price prediction. Prophet automatically identifies these changepoints and adjusts the model results accordingly, providing insights into when and how the trend in the data shifts. This capability is handy in financial markets, where sudden changes are expected.

- Prophet provides tools for *hyperparameter tuning* to optimize forecasting performance, such as seasonality and special event and regressor effects. *Cross-validation techniques* are integrated into Prophet's workflow, enabling model performance evaluation over different horizons and ensuring that the forecasts are accurate and reliable. Those tools have the same basis as ML models (as shown in the previous chapter).

The core forecasting model used by FB's Prophet is based on a decomposable time-series model with three main components: trend, seasonality, and special events, as follows:

$$y(t) = g(t) + s(t) + h(t) + r_i(t) + \varepsilon_t$$

Where:

- $y(t)$ is the predicted value at the time t.
- $g(t)$ is the trend component, which models non-periodic changes in the time-series value.
- $s(t)$ is the seasonality component, capturing periodic changes such as daily, weekly, or yearly seasonality.
- $h(t)$ is the effect of holidays or special events that could impact the time series.
- $r_i(t)$ is any additional regressors (as an optional feature).
- ε_t is the error term representing any idiosyncratic changes not captured by the model.

Each of these components can be explained as follows:

- The *trend component* $g(t)$ commonly offers two core options for modeling the trend: a linear trend model for data with a linear growth pattern and a logistic growth model for data with a saturating growth pattern, where the growth rate decreases over time.
- The *seasonality component* $s(t)$ uses the Fourier series to fit flexible seasonality patterns. Prophet automatically detects and includes yearly, weekly, and daily seasonality based on the frequency and span of the data.
- The *holiday component* $h(t)$ includes indicators for specified holidays and special events (such as dividends paid and stocks split) that could affect the time series. Users can define custom lists of holidays and special events, providing flexibility in capturing these effects.

▣ *Additional regressors, r(t)*, can be included in the model to consider other factors that may influence the forecast. For instance, we could use technical analysis indicators, the price of other assets, economic indicators, or other external variables as regressors in the model.

▣ Errors, ε_t, represent random errors not captured by the model, assumed to be normally distributed (as described in *Chapter 7, Time-Series Analysis and Financial Data Forecasting*, and *Chapter 8, Risk Assessment and Volatility Modeling*).

All additional libraries require prior installation (see *Chapter 1, Getting Started with Python for Finance*). Software errors, bugs, and compatibility problems sometimes, however, overshadow the benefits of an open-source software product. Unfortunately, conflicts may occasionally arise with new versions of core Python, NumPy, pandas, and other libraries. So, it is recommended that separate virtual environments are created for each of the different analytical tasks. For example, one called `PythonFinance` may be used with standard libraries, `ProphetFinance` for Prophet tasks, and `FinanceML` for ML tasks. This allows you to isolate the execution environments and avoids compatibility errors for already written code.

As mentioned earlier, Prophet gives meaningful results by executing simple code. Run the following example and examine its results:

```
1.  # nasdaq_index has information about NASDAQ index
       dynamics
2.  # Creating a DataFrame
3.  df = pd.DataFrame({
4.      'ds': nasdaq_index.index,
5.      'y': nasdaq_index['Adj Close']
6.  })
7.  # Initialize the Prophet model
8.  m = Prophet()
9.  # Fit the model
10. m.fit(df)
```

```
11.  # Make predictions
12.  forecast = m.predict(df[['ds']])
13.  # Plot the forecast using Plotly for an
     interactive plot.# Figure 10.1
14.  plot_plotly(m, forecast)
```

The results are depicted in *Figure 10.1*.

NOTE *As the code shows, the Prophet library requires the DataFrame to be in a specific format, with the column containing the timestamps named ds and the column containing the values you want to predict named y. This is to ensure that the Prophet library understands your data's structure when passed into the model for fitting and making predictions.*

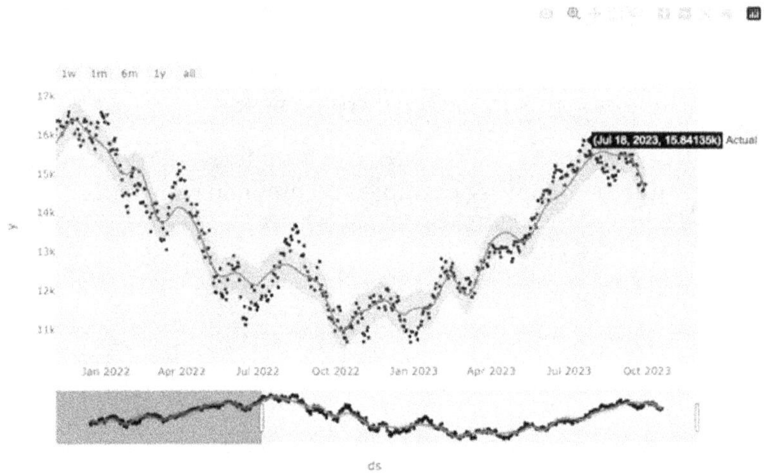

FIGURE 10.1 The results of the simple Prophet model for the NASDAQ index daily adjusted close

This short and simple code generates a well-fitted model for time-series data analysis and prediction. *Figure 10.1*, created with Plotly, illustrates the forecasting results from the Prophet model applied to the NASDAQ index data. The Plotly library (*https://plotly.com/python/*) facilitates interactive plotting capabilities, which enhance the visualization of time-series forecasts. The plots generated allow for dynamic and interactive exploration of the data.

The main plot displays the historical data points as black dots and overlays the predicted values with a blue line. The shaded area around the expected line represents the confidence interval, visually indicating the model's uncertainty. We can move the cursor to a point or line and see actual or predicted information and the date for the data point (as seen in the figure). The second subplot—the *interactive timeline feature*—allows operating with a timeline by zooming in and out of specific time ranges within the plot. For example, the gray timeline area in the bottom diagram is not depicted in the first plot. The interactive timeline is handy for examining the model's performance across different intervals and presenting a more detailed analysis of the forecast results.

A seasonality analysis, however, may expand the model presented in *Figure 10.1*. By executing the `m.plot_components(forecast)` Prophet object method, we can analyze default seasonality components:

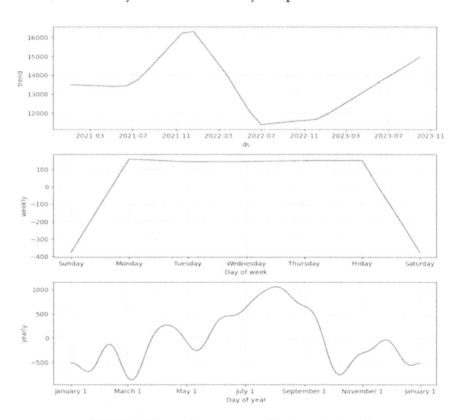

FIGURE 10.2 Seasonality components of Prophet's simple model

Figure 10.2 shows three components of visualizations (by default), as follows:

- The *trend component* (the top subplot) represents the overall trend of the time-series data over time. The *x* axis denotes time (ds), while the *y* axis represents the trend value. The plot shows fluctuations in the trend over different periods, indicating changes in the forecasted index values that are not attributed to seasonality or holidays. There is a noticeable trend change around July 2022, where the value sharply declines and then rises again, suggesting a significant event or shift in the underlying data.

- *Weekly seasonality* (the middle subplot) displays the weekly patterns or seasonality, with the *x* axis showing the days of the week and the *y* axis indicating the magnitude of each day's effect on the predicted value. The NASDAQ exchange operates only on weekdays, so it is logical for the trend to drop on Saturday and Sunday. We can, however, see a slight decline in the weekly activity on Tuesday.

- *Yearly seasonality* (the bottom subplot) illustrates the yearly seasonality (month by month), with the *x* axis representing the days, highlighting the months, of the year, and the *y* axis showing the seasonal effect on the forecasted value. The plot indicates a cyclical pattern within a year, with peaks and troughs corresponding to different times of the year. Peak annual activity occurs between July and September. This reflects yearly patterns in the data.

Thus, we can create a reasonably robust model for analyzing financial market data (dynamics of indices, prices, return levels, and volatility) by writing only 10 lines of code. For example, the model (depicted in *Figures 10.1* and *10.2*) has the MAPE metric of 2.09%. In *Chapter 7, Time-Series Analysis and Financial Data Forecasting*, we carried out some complicated SARIMA model-fitted code to produce the same results. The most significant advantage of the Prophet library, however, is the large number of automatic and custom forecasting tools.

FORECASTING WITH PROPHET

Prophet's ease of use is evident in its ability to produce highly accurate forecasts, as evidenced by the MAPE and other metrics. Prophet also benefits from a comprehensive set of automated and customizable forecasting tools that streamline the modeling process and extend it with various user-defined parameters to accommodate a wide range of data models and analyst preferences. Seasonality and trend are the two most pivotal parameters of Prophet's models. Let us look at them in more detail.

Seasonality Parameters of Prophet's Models

Seasonality refers to periodic fluctuations in time-series data that recur regularly due to human behavior, business cycles, or other features. Prophet models skillfully deal with seasonality through a set of parameters designed to match and predict these regular patterns. Moreover, Prophet uses the Fourier series to identify seasonal patterns by breaking down seasonal effects into sine and cosine components. Thus, Prophet can accurately model seasonal changes, accounting for both regular and irregular cycles. The main parameters of seasonality in Prophet's models relate to three cycles: annual, weekly, and daily. Each can be adapted to the dataset, allowing the model to adapt to its specific time dynamics.

To illustrate the application of these basic seasonality parameters, consider the following example code:

```
1.  test_period = 21
2.  df_train = df[:-test_period]
3.  df_test = df[-test_period:]
4.  # Initialize and Fit the Prophet model with
5.  # custom seasonality settings (Model 1)
6.  m = Prophet(
7.      seasonality_mode='multiplicative',
8.      daily_seasonality=False,
9.      weekly_seasonality=True,
10.     yearly_seasonality=4,
11.     seasonality_prior_scale=10.0
12. ).fit(df_train)
13. # Generate a DataFrame for future predictions
14. # covering 21 business days
15. future = m.make_future_dataframe(periods=21,
16.                                  freq='B')
```

```
17.  # Predict future values and plot the forecast
18.  forecast = m.predict(future)
19.  # Plot the forecast (Figure 10.3)
20.  fig1 = m.plot(forecast)
21.  # Re-initialize the Prophet model
22.  # with increased regularization
23.  # for seasonality (Model 2)
24.  m2 = Prophet(
25.      seasonality_mode='multiplicative',
26.      daily_seasonality=False,
27.      weekly_seasonality=False,
28.      yearly_seasonality=4,
29.      seasonality_prior_scale=0.001
30.  ).fit(df_train)
31.  # Make new predictions and plot the forecast
32.  # with increased regularization
33.  forecast2 = m2.predict(future)
34.  # Plot the new forecast (Figure 10.4)
35.  fig2 = m2.plot(forecast2)
```

The code provides predictions of future NASDAQ index values based on historical data. Here is what the different parts of the code mean:

- The `seasonality_mode` parameter determines how the model handles seasonality. The 'multiplicative' option means that the seasonal effect is multiplied by the trend to get the forecast (see *Chapter 7, Time-Series Analysis and Financial Data Forecasting*, specifically the information on the Holt-Winters model).
- `daily_seasonality`, `weekly_seasonality`, and `yearly_seasonality` control whether the model will fit daily, weekly, or yearly seasonality. Setting one of these to `True` tells Prophet to expect and model

seasonality patterns at that time scale. The `yearly_seasonality=4` setting uses four Fourier terms to capture yearly seasonality, which allows the model to fit more complex annual patterns.

▦ `seasonality_prior_scale` is a regularization parameter. A higher value (such as `10`) allows the model to fit more flexible seasonal effects. A lower value (such as `0.001`) applies stronger regularization to prevent overfitting by making the seasonality component smoother and less flexible.

▦ `m.make_future_dataframe(periods=21, freq='B')` is used to create a DataFrame containing future dates for which predictions are required. `periods=21` indicates the number of future points to predict, and `freq='B'` indicates that these points are business days, which excludes weekends and possibly holidays depending on the market considered.

The results of the code execution are depicted in *Figure 10.3* and *Figure 10.4*:

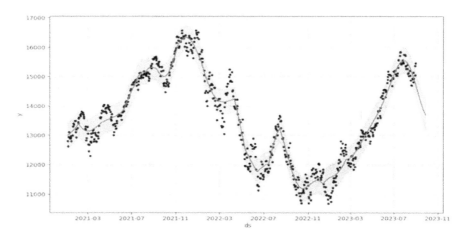

FIGURE 10.3 Prophet model forecast with basic seasonality settings

Seasonality modeling in Prophet hinges on two pivotal parameters: the *Fourier order*, which dictates the number of terms in the series to grasp the intricacies of fluctuations, and the `seasonality_prior_scale`, a regularization parameter that governs the model's flexibility. The Fourier terms or order parameter shapes the model's sensitivity to seasonal shifts. A higher Fourier order allows the model to detect more nuanced seasonal variations in the training dataset, as depicted in *Figure 10.3*:

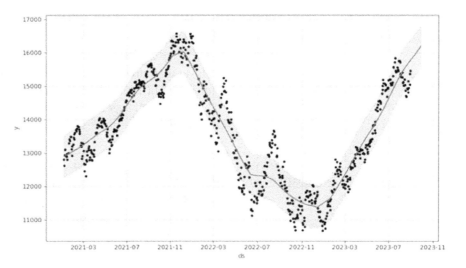

FIGURE 10.4 Prophet model forecast with increased regularization for seasonality

While this increased sensitivity helps capture complex patterns, it may carry the risk of overfitting—conversely, the `seasonality_prior_scale` parameter balances overfitting by adjusting the strength of the model's seasonal components. Setting a lower `seasonality_prior_scale` value limits the seasonal flexibility of the model, resulting in a more generalized and potentially more reliable forecast, as shown in *Figure 10.4*, where the trend is more significant in the forecast than seasonality.

In addition to the basic seasonality, Prophet adds custom seasonality through the `.add_seasonality()` method. This method is beneficial when the data exhibits non-standard seasonal patterns that do not align with the typical daily, weekly, or yearly cycles. Execute the following code to understand the custom seasonality example:

```
1.  # Re-initialize the Prophet model with custom
    seasonality
2.  # and Fourier terms (Model 3)
3.  m3 = Prophet(seasonality_mode='multiplicative',
4.              daily_seasonality=False,
```

```
 5.             weekly_seasonality=False,
 6.             yearly_seasonality=4
 7. ).add_seasonality(
 8.     name='monthly',
 9.     period=21,
10.     fourier_order=4,
11.     prior_scale=10
12. ).add_seasonality(
13.     name='weekly',
14.     period=5,
15.     fourier_order=5,
16.     prior_scale=10
17. ).fit(df_train)
18. future = m3.make_future_dataframe(periods=21,
    freq='B')
19. # Making and plotting predictions (Figure 10.5)
20. forecast3 = m3.predict(future)
21. Prophet.plot(m3, forecast3)
22. # Components Visualization (Figure 10.6)
23. m3.plot_components(forecast3)
24. # Print the last 2 forecast Components
25. print(forecast3.tail(2).transpose())
```

The results are depicted in *Figure 10.5* and *Figure 10.6*:

	687	688
ds	2023-09-27 00:00:00	2023-09-28 00:00:00
trend	1644.1684	1644.965134
yhat_lower	13652.134438	13648.101081
yhat_upper	14923.250511	14903.73936
trend_lower	1593.097457	1588.877566
trend_upper	1693.375513	1701.042052
monthly	-0.000921	-0.008026
monthly_lower	-0.000921	-0.008026
monthly_upper	-0.000921	-0.008026
multiplicative_terms	7.695638	7.685072
multiplicative_terms_lower	7.695638	7.685072
multiplicative_terms_upper	7.695638	7.685072
weekly	7.933842	7.935297
weekly_lower	7.933842	7.935297
weekly_upper	7.933842	7.935297
yearly	-0.237283	-0.242199
yearly_lower	-0.237283	-0.242199
yearly_upper	-0.237283	-0.242199
additive_terms	0.0	0.0
additive_terms_lower	0.0	0.0
additive_terms_upper	0.0	0.0
yhat	14297.09381	14286.640356

The code example uses the Prophet library to enhance a time-series forecasting model by incorporating custom seasonality. Each call to `.add_seasonality()` defines a new seasonal component with a specific name, period, Fourier order, and prior scale as used in the code:

- name is the title of the custom seasonality.
- period is the length of the seasonality cycle. For example, period=21 means the model expects the seasonality to repeat every 21 days.
- fourier_order is the number of Fourier terms to use when modeling this seasonality.
- prior_scale is a regularization parameter that adjusts the strength of this seasonality model.

The forecasted DataFrame, forecast3, is a valuable resource containing information about the trend and seasonal impact associated with each predicted data point. To better understand these insights, explore *Figures 10.5* and *10.6*:

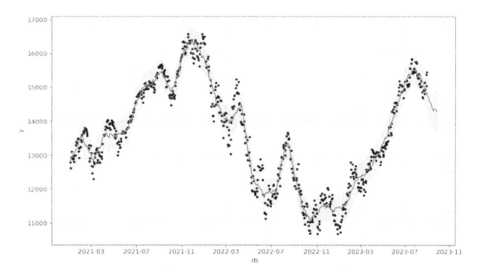

FIGURE 10.5 Monthly and weekly custom seasonality effects in a Prophet forecast

Figure 10.5 visualizes the modeling results based on the Prophet.plot(m3, forecast3) function. It provides essential information about the predicted value yhat, and the yhat_lower and yhat_upper, representing uncertainty intervals for the model's predictions. By default, the uncertainty interval is set to 0.8, equivalent to an 80% uncertainty interval for the predicted values:

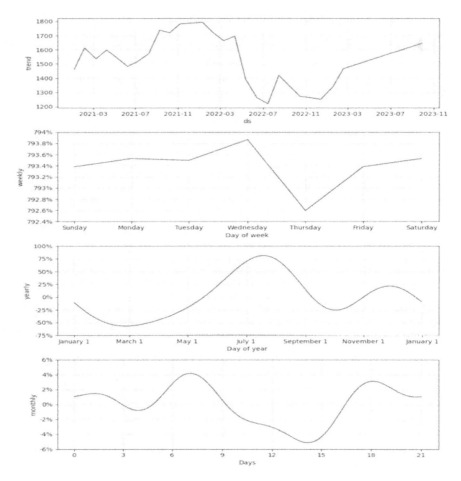

FIGURE 10.6 Components of Prophet's forecast with custom seasonality

The comparison of the weekly trend in *Figures 10.2* and *10.6* shows that the results vary significantly. The weekly seasonality figures are very similar, but *Figure 10.2* does not detect changes from Monday to Friday; otherwise, *Figure 10.6* demonstrates an increase in market activity on Wednesday and a fall on Thursday. Additionally, *Figure 10.6* allows us to analyze the monthly seasonality, which shows peaks around the 7th and 18th business days of each month.

Changepoints Adjusting

The second crucial feature of Prophet forecasting is the trend's changepoints. We considered similar problems in *Chapter 5, Investment and Trading Strategies,* within the technical and graphic analysis tasks framework.

Changepoints are pivotal moments where the data's trajectory shifts, indicating either a surge or a decline in the trend. Execute the following code to understand the changepoints and forecasted data trend impacts:

```
1.  from prophet.plot import add_changepoints_to_plot
2.  # Initialize Prophet with high sensitivity
3.  # to changepoints
4.  m = Prophet(changepoint_prior_scale=0.9)
5.  forecast = m.fit(df_train).predict(future)
6.  # Plot forecast with changepoint_prior_scale=0.9
7.  # (Figure 10.7)
8.  fig = m.plot(forecast)
9.  a = add_changepoints_to_plot(fig.gca(), m,
       forecast)
10. # Initialize Prophet with low sensitivity
11. # to changepoints
12. m = Prophet(changepoint_prior_scale=0.005)
13. forecast = m.fit(df_train).predict(future)
14. # Plot forecast with changepoint_prior_scale=0.005
15. # (Figure 10.8)
16. fig = m.plot(forecast)
17. a = add_changepoints_to_plot(fig.gca(), m, forecast)
18. # Prophet with manual changepoints and
19. # intermediate sensitivity
20. m = Prophet(
21.     changepoints=['2021-11-19',
22.                   '2022-10-14',
23.                   '2023-07-18']
```

```
24. )
25. forecast = m.fit(df_train).predict(future)
26. # Plot forecast with custom changepoints
27. # (Figure 10.9)
28. fig = m.plot(forecast)
29. a = add_changepoints_to_plot(fig.gca(), m, forecast)
30. # Prophet specifying a fixed number of
31. # changepoints without manual dates
32. m = Prophet(n_changepoints=5)
33. forecast = m.fit(df_train).predict(future)
34. # Plot forecast with n_changepoints=5
35. # (Figure 10.10)
36. fig = m.plot(forecast)
37. a = add_changepoints_to_plot(fig.gca(), m,
      forecast)
```

The results are depicted in *Figures 10.7–10.10*:

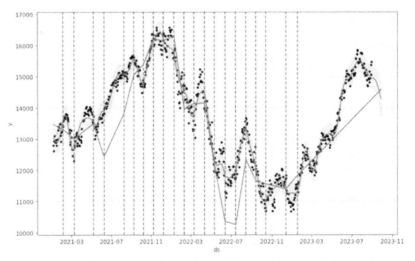

FIGURE 10.7 Visualization of the Prophet model's sensitivity to trend changepoints
(changepoint_prior_scale = 0.9)

Adjusting the `changepoint_prior_scale` in the Prophet model directly impacts its responsiveness to changepoints. A higher `changepoint_prior_scale` value, such as `0.9` (*Figure 10.7*), renders the model highly sensitive to such shifts, allowing it to detect more changepoints and react more swiftly to changes at the end of the trendline:

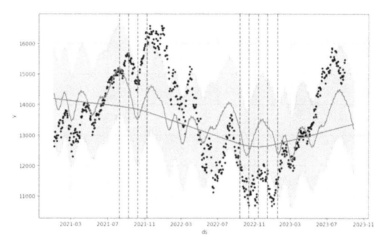

FIGURE 10.8 Visualization of the Prophet model's sensitivity to trend changepoints
(changepoint_prior_scale = 0.005)

A lower value, such as `0.005` (*Figure 10.8*), implies a more conservative approach, detecting fewer changepoints and resulting in a smoother overall trendline:

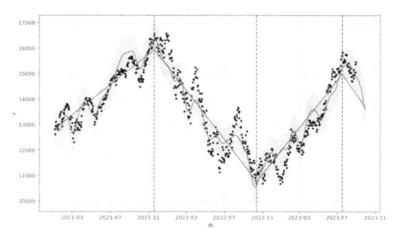

FIGURE 10.9 Visualization of the Prophet model's sensitivity to trend changepoints
(changepoints=['2021-11-19', '2022-10-14', '2023-07-18'])

Adjusting changepoints can be further done by specifying custom dates manually; see *Figure 10.8*, where we define `changepoints=['2021-11-19',` `'2022-10-14', '2023-07-18']`:

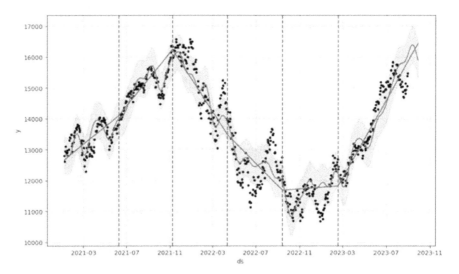

FIGURE 10.10 Visualization of the Prophet model's sensitivity to trend changepoints (n_changepoints=5)

The fixed number of changepoints can be automatically detected without manually specifying their dates (*Figure 10.9*). This allows you to determine the dates of trend changes more accurately.

This flexibility in the changepoint-defining tools allows the analyst to influence the model directly based on domain knowledge or rely on the model's algorithmic prowess to identify these pivotal moments. Thus, adjustments (manual or automatic) for seasonality and changepoints are crucial to refining model forecasts, as they allow the model to account for both regular patterns and significant shifts in trend. Seasonality adjustments capture repeated fluctuations, while changepoint adjustments help the model respond to structural breaks in the dataset.

ADDITIONAL REGRESSORS

Advanced time-series data analysis, which integrates *additional regressors* in the Prophet model, can be a good solution for achieving the best prediction accuracy. The regressors can include lagged indices or any other features that can be fully predicted and their impact on the target variable. Let us describe an example of the predicted Apple Inc. share price adjusted close with the influence of dividend pay-offs as the special events and one-day lagged high, low, and closed-open indicators.

```
1.  # Create the DataFrame for Prophet with lagged
    regressors
2.  data = nasdaq_assets.xs('AAPL', level=1, axis=1)
3.  df = pd.DataFrame({
4.      'ds': data.index,
5.      'y': data['Adj Close'],
6.      'High_lag1': data['High'].shift(1),
7.      'Low_lag1': data['Low'].shift(1),
8.      'tech1': (data['Close'].shift(1) > data
    ['Open'].shift(1))
9.  }).dropna()
10. # Split data into training and testing sets
11. df_train = df[:-21]
12. df_test = df[-21:]
13. # Define special events - dividends payouts as
    special events
14. dividends_events = pd.DataFrame({
15.     'holiday': 'dividend_event',
16.     'ds': data[data['Dividends'] != 0].index,
17.     'lower_window': -1,   # Day before dividend payout
18.     'upper_window': 1,    # Day after dividend payout
19. })
20. # Initialize Prophet model with multiplicative
    seasonality
```

```
21.  # and special events
22.  m = Prophet(seasonality_mode='multiplicative',
23.               holidays=dividends_events)
24.  # Add external regressors to the model
25.  m.add_regressor('High_lag1')
26.  m.add_regressor('Low_lag1')
27.  m.add_regressor('tech1')
28.  # Fit the model with training data
29.  m.fit(df_train)
30.  # Make predictions on both training and test
     datasets
31.  forecast = m.predict(df)
32.  # Plotting the forecast
33.  Prophet.plot(m, forecast)
34.  # Calculate and print the Mean Absolute
     Percentage Error (MAPE) on test data
35.  mape = mean_absolute_percentage_error(df_test['y'],
                          forecast['yhat'][-21:])*100
36.  print(f"MAPE for the test data: {mape:.2f}%")
```

The code results are depicted in *Figure 10.11*.

The example uses the Prophet forecasting library to create a predictive model with special considerations for additional regressors and events, as follows:

▪ A DataFrame was created on the NASDAQ assets data for the AAPL stock. The DataFrame includes the 'Adj Close' prices alongside lagged values of the 'High' and 'Low' prices, which are shifted by one day using the .shift(1) method. Additionally, it includes a technical indicator, 'tech1', which is a Boolean value indicating whether the 'Close' price was higher than the 'Open' price the previous day (similar to how analysis metrics work).

▪ *Holidays* and *special events* are based on the dividend event dates. This is done by creating a DataFrame (dividends_events) where each dividend event is marked by the day it occurs, with windows to capture the day before and after the event. The lower_window and upper_window parameters, set to -1 and 1, respectively, indicate that the model should consider the impact of the dividend payout one day before and after the dividend date.

▪ The .add_regressor() method includes the lagged 'High' and 'Low' prices and the 'tech1' indicator as additional regressors in the model. The full syntax is:

```
m.add_regressor(name, prior.scale = None, standardize =
"auto", mode = None)
```

  ◦ name is a string that specifies the name of the regressor.

  ◦ prior_scale is an optional argument that allows the scale (regularization) of the prior for this regressor to be set.

  ◦ The standardize argument dictates whether the regressor should be standardized in the standard normal distribution means (standardize='auto' or standardize=True) or not (standardize=False).

  ◦ mode is an optional argument, usually None, that can be set to 'additive' or 'multiplicative' to specify how the regressor will interact with the trend.

In the code context, the holidays parameter in the Prophet model initialization incorporates dividends as special events that could influence the stock price. The add_regressor() method allows for the integration of additional data series. By considering these additional factors, the model becomes more sophisticated.

The results of the code example are depicted in *Figure 10.11*:

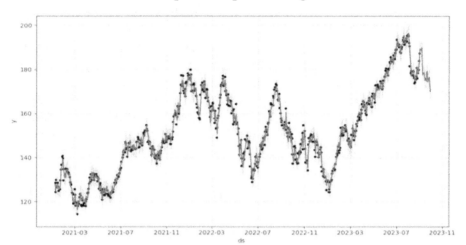

FIGURE 10.11 Enhanced forecast accuracy with additional regressors of the Prophet model

Figure 10.11 shows the Prophet model performance with these enhancements and the MAPE for test datasets. We can observe a significant increase in forecast accuracy. Furthermore, the MAPE for this model is equal to 1.13%.

CROSS-VALIDATION AND HYPERPARAMETER TUNING

Despite additional regressors, seasonality parameters, and trend changepoints making it easy to tune the Prophet model to high accuracy, problems may arise in overfitting or determining the best parameters of the model. These problems can also be solved using the Prophet library. Firstly, cross-validation functions can help avoid overfitting. Secondly, combining the parameters' loops and the cross-validation functions provides an application for hyperparameter tuning.

Cross-Validation and Preventing Overfitting

Cross-validation is critical in modeling and robust predictions, particularly when fine-tuning predictive Prophet models, to ensure they generalize well to new data. By systematically testing the model on different subsets of data, we can identify the model's performance and prevent overfitting when the model is too closely fitted to the training data and performs poorly on unseen data. The provided code illustrates how cross-validation is employed and how results are visualized within the Prophet framework:

```python
1.  from prophet.diagnostics import cross_validation,
    performance_metrics
2.  from prophet.plot import plot_cross_validation_metric
3.  # Load the data into a DataFrame 'df'
4.  data = nasdaq_assets.xs('AZN', level=1, axis=1)
5.  df = pd.DataFrame({
6.      'ds': data.index,
7.      'y': data['Adj Close']
8.  })
9.  test_period = 5
10. df_train = df[:-test_period]
11. df_test = df[-test_period:]
12. # Initialize and fit the Prophet model
13. m = Prophet()
14. m.fit(df_train)
15. # Perform cross-validation
16. df_cv = cross_validation(m, initial='504 days',
                period='126 days', horizon='5 days')
17. # Calculate performance metrics
18. df_p = performance_metrics(df_cv)
19. # Plot cross-validation metric
20. fig = plot_cross_validation_metric(df_cv, metric=
    'mape')
21. # Print Cross-Validation Table
22. print(df_p)
```

The code results are depicted in *Figure 10.12*, as follows:

```
   horizon       mse       rmse       mae      mape     mdape     smape   \

0   1 days  2.271056  1.507002  0.958291  0.014455  0.003739  0.014719

1   2 days  3.790078  1.946812  1.526941  0.024452  0.023193  0.024374

2   3 days  7.422492  2.724425  2.348240  0.036748  0.036590  0.036744

3   4 days  5.927198  2.434584  2.332173  0.036073  0.035725  0.035933

4   5 days  5.970388  2.443438  2.079578  0.031822  0.027852  0.032071

(...)
```

The highlights of cross-validation functions are:

- The `cross_validation` function is used to perform rolling forecast origin cross-validation on the time-series data, with the parameters `initial`, `period`, and `horizon` specifying the length of the training period, the spacing between cut-off dates, and the forecast horizon, respectively:
  - The `initial` parameter defines the size of the initial training period. In the case of 504 days, it indicates that the first 504 days of data from the beginning of the time series will be used to train the initial model before cross-validation begins.
  - The `period` parameter determines the spacing between cut-off dates in the cross-validation procedure. Here, 126 days suggests a new cross-validation fold will be started every 126 days. Each fold involves shifting the initial training period forward by this period and making predictions over the horizon.
  - `horizon` specifies the length of time for which predictions will be made during each fold of the cross-validation. After each new training period, the model will make predictions for the following 5 days.
- The `performance_metrics` function calculates metrics such as the MSE, RMSE, MAPE, and others that provide insights into the model's accuracy.
- The `plot_cross_validation_metric` function generates a visual representation of the model's performance using the MAPE, and the results are printed out for review.

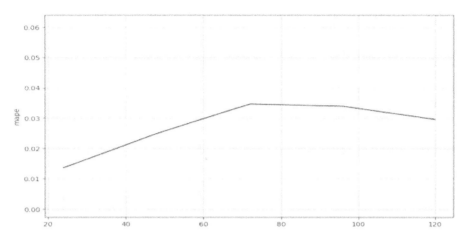

FIGURE 10.12 Dynamics of the cross-validated MAPE

The code results, derived from the code provided, present the performance of a Prophet forecasting model assessed through cross-validation. The MAPE values (by the resulting table values) presented per day (from *1 day* to *5 days*) suggest how the model's prediction accuracy changes over the consecutive days of the forecast horizon. *Figure 10.12* shows a graph of MAPE values for four cross-validation cycles. The chart shows that the average metric value is between 2.5% and 3%. In the cross-validated MAPE dynamics, we see a progression that typically informs adjustments to the model to balance the trade-off between capturing the data's trend and seasonality without overfitting.

Choosing parameters for the `cross_validation` function is paramount for forming a stable model. A minimal initial *period* will increase the forecast error due to cross-validation since there is a higher probability of a significant change in the data. Small period values lead to a substantial increase in the execution time of the cross-validation function. Most often, this does not lead to significant results. The research problem determines the forecasting horizon parameter, usually within a reasonable forecast timeline. Predicting daily prices for 21 business days based on 1 year of data will give too large an error or uncertainty interval.

Hyperparameter Tuning

Hyperparameter tuning with Prophet involves finding the perfect blend of parameters and adjusting for the best prediction accuracy on the test data, as for other ML models. It also involves iteratively experimenting with various sets of parameters. This process is crucial because there is a delicate balance to strike even with sophisticated relations, regressors, and seasonality adjustments.

Let us execute the following code to examine the hyperparameter tuning example:

```
1.  import itertools
2.  # Parameter grid for tuning
3.  param_grid = {
4.      'changepoint_prior_scale': [0.01, 0.5, 0.9],
5.      'seasonality_prior_scale': [0.01, 8.0, 10.0],
6.      'seasonality_mode': ['additive', 'multiplicative']
7.  }
8.  # Generate all combinations of parameters
9.  all_params = [dict(zip(param_grid.keys(), v)) for v in
               itertools.product(*param_grid.values())]
10. mapes = []   # Store the MAPEs for each params
11. # Use cross-validation to evaluate all parameters
12. for params in all_params:
13.     m = Prophet(**params).fit(df_train)
14.     df_cv = cross_validation(m, initial='504 days',
                period='126 days', horizon='5 days')
15.     df_p = performance_metrics(df_cv, rolling_
    window=1)
16.     mapes.append(df_p['mape'].values[0])
17. # Find the best parameters
18. tuning_results = pd.DataFrame(all_params)
19. tuning_results['mape'] = mapes
20. print(tuning_results.transpose())
21. best_params = all_params[np.argmin(mapes)]
```

```
22.  print(best_params)
23.  # Comparing the models
24.  # Initialize and fit the basic Prophet model
25.  m1 = Prophet().fit(df_train)
26.  # Predict on the test dataset
27.  forecast1 = m1.predict(df)
28.  # Calculate MAPE on the test dataset for the
     basic model
29.  mape1 = mean_absolute_percentage_
     error(forecast1['yhat'][-test_period:],
30.                               df_test['y']) * 100
31.  print(f"Basic model for test data: MAPE =
     {mape1:.2f}%")
32.  # Initialize and Fit the Prophet model with
     custom tunned parameters
33.  m2 = Prophet(
34.      changepoint_prior_scale=best_params
     ['changepoint_prior_scale'],
35.      seasonality_prior_scale=best_params
     ['seasonality_prior_scale'],
36.      seasonality_mode=best_params['seasonality_mode']
37.  ).fit(df_train)
38.  # Predict on the test dataset with the tuned model
39.  forecast2 = m2.predict(df)
40.  # Calculate MAPE on the test dataset for the
     tuned model
41.  mape2 = mean_absolute_percentage_error
     (forecast2['yhat'][-test_period:],
42.                               df_test['y']) * 100
43.  print(f"Tuned model for test data: MAPE =
     {mape2:.2f}%")
```

The code results (truncated) are:

```
(...)

                                0              1          2              3   \
changepoint_prior_scale      0.01           0.01       0.01            .01
seasonality_prior_scale      0.01           0.01        8.0            8.0
seasonality_mode         additive multiplicative   additive multiplicative
mape                     0.041357       0.040257   0.040865       0.040475

(...)

                               12             13         14             15   \
changepoint_prior_scale       0.9            0.9        0.9            0.9
seasonality_prior_scale      0.01           0.01        8.0            8.0
seasonality_mode         additive multiplicative   additive multiplicative
mape                     0.018522       0.016789   0.014944       0.010564


                               16             17
changepoint_prior_scale       0.9            0.9
seasonality_prior_scale      10.0           10.0
seasonality_mode         additive multiplicative
mape                     0.015737       0.013292

{'changepoint_prior_scale': 0.9, 'seasonality_prior_scale': 8.0,
'seasonality_mode': 'multiplicative'}

Basic model for test data: MAPE = 6.15%

Tuned model for test data: MAPE = 0.97%
```

As we can see, for the code results, it was possible to reduce the MAPE of forecast data on the test dataset from 16.15% to 0.97%. The presented example, however, is only a training example of using the *hyperparameter tuning* method. The `Prophet` class in the Prophet Python library has a lot of other parameters and methods that allow the tinning hyperparameters of the model to fit the forecasting model best. *Table 10.1* summarizes the key parameters, their default values, and their purpose:

TABLE 10.1 The essential parameters methods of the Prophet class for the model tuning

Parameter	Default value	Description
growth	'linear'	Specifies the trend model. Can be 'linear' for a linear trend model or 'logistic' for a model with a carrying capacity. The logistic model needs the 'cap' and 'floor' columns in the input DataFrame.
changepoints	None	Optionally specify the dates of potential changepoints. If not specified, Prophet will automatically select them.
n_changepoints	25	The number of automatically selected changepoints if changepoints is not specified.
changepoint_range	0.8	The proportion of the history where trend changepoints will be estimated. 0.8 means the first 80% of the time series are used.
yearly_seasonality, weekly_seasonality, daily_seasonality	'auto'	Fit yearly, weekly, and daily seasonality. Can be True, False, or 'auto', or specify the Fourier order of each seasonality type.
holidays	None	A DataFrame specifying holiday or special events dates to include in the model.
seasonality_mode	'additive'	Type of seasonality model. It can be 'additive' or 'multiplicative'.
seasonality_prior_scale, holidays_prior_scale	10.0 10.0	Strength or the *regularization level* of the seasonality model and holiday. Larger values allow the model to fit larger fluctuations; smaller values dampen the seasonality or special events.
changepoint_prior_scale	0.05	The flexibility of the automatic changepoint selection. Larger values allow for more flexible trend changes.
mcmc_samples	0	The number of MCMC samples to draw for the Bayesian estimation of uncertainty intervals. Setting this to a positive integer activates full Bayesian inference.
interval_width	0.8	The width of the uncertainty intervals provided for the forecast. A value of 0.8 means 80% uncertainty intervals.
uncertainty_samples	1000	The number of simulated draws used to estimate uncertainty intervals for the forecast.
.add_regressor()	None	Adds an additional regressor to the model. This regressor should be present in the DataFrame passed to the .fit method.
.add_seasonality()	None	Adds a custom seasonality to the model. It must specify the name, period, and Fourier order for the seasonality.
.add_country_holidays()	None	Incorporates holidays for the specified country into the model. The country code should be passed as a parameter.

Thus, continuous tuning and cross-validation create a new vision for the model results. They are crucial for all ML models and help optimize predictive accuracy. Even using a minimal set of selected parameters made it possible to significantly reduce the forecast error. All the parameters mentioned are in your hands; try to achieve even greater accuracy.

CONCLUSION

Prophet is an advanced library in time-series analysis and forecasting. It combines the advantages of classical ARIMA models and ML methods. Its intuitive interface and comprehensive analytic capabilities range from identifying trends and seasonal patterns to accounting for covariates and special events. Prophet's application in analyzing and forecasting time-series data makes it accessible and effective in predictive analytics, which can significantly improve decision-making in financial and related fields.

Cross-validation and hyperparameter tuning with Prophet demonstrate the tool's capabilities in refining time-series models for reliable forecasting. The cross-validation process guards against overfitting, making the model more effective. The application of hyperparameter tuning further highlights the powerful potential of Prophet, where different combinations of parameters are used to determine the most accurate prediction model. Using Prophet's basic and advanced parameters can provide relatively easy access to accurate and valuable results.

QUESTIONS

1. What is the primary benefit of using Prophet's seasonality parameters in time-series forecasting?

2. What does the 'multiplicative' option for the `seasonality_mode` parameter imply in the context of the Prophet model?

3. How can the Fourier series and `seasonality_prior_scale` parameters influence the model's tendency to overfit or underfit the data?

4. What is the impact of `changepoint_prior_scale` on the model's sensitivity to trend changes?

5. How do you add a regressor to the Prophet model, and what are the implications of its prior scale?

6. What is the purpose of including lagged values of other variables as additional regressors, and how do they affect the forecast?

7. Describe the process and purpose of cross-validation in the context of Prophet's forecasting model.

8. Explain how you would interpret the results of a hyperparameter tuning process in Prophet.

KEY TERMS

▪ *Regularization* is used to prevent overfitting in the context of Facebook's Prophet. This has an effect on time-series forecasting and reduces overfitting. Regularization introduces a penalty on the magnitude of the considered effects, encouraging the model to keep these effects small unless the data strongly suggests otherwise. It is like smoothing the time component, ensuring that the model captures only the most significant patterns and does not react too strongly to noise or minor fluctuations in the data.

▪ A *changepoint*, in the context of Facebook's Prophet, is a point in time where the time series experiences a significant shift in its trend. It represents the moment when the underlying growth rate of the time series changes.

▪ A *Fourier series* decomposes a function (e.g., the seasonality of a time series) into the sum of sinusoidal functions, each with different frequencies and amplitudes. Fourier series are used to assess complex seasonality with regular patterns and variations over time.

REFERENCES

▪ *Rafferty, G. (2023). Forecasting Time Series Data with Prophet: Build, improve, and optimize time series forecasting models using Meta's advanced forecasting tool, 2nd Edition, Packt Publishing.*

▪ *Prophet. Forecasting in Scale. Get Started in Python. Facebook Open Source (eBook). https://facebook.github.io/prophet/.*

PYTHON CODE EXAMPLES FOR FINANCE

CREATING A PYTHONFINANCE VIRTUAL ENVIRONMENT

Creating a `PythonFinance` virtual environment using `conda` involves specifying the environment's name and the packages you need (see *Chapter 1, Getting Started with Python for Finance*). However, we can easily use a `.yml` file to install the required libraries for the book's examples. Execute the following command in a Unix-based OS terminal or Windows CMD: `conda env create -f PythonFinanceConda.yml`. This command sets up the environment based on the configurations defined in the `.yml` file, including dependencies and channels, and often points to `conda-forge` for a more comprehensive package selection.

PythonFinanceConda.yml

```
name: PythonFinance
channels:
  - conda-forge
  - defaults
dependencies:
  - python=3.9
  - numpy
```

- pandas
- openpyxl
- matplotlib
- seaborn
- plotly
- bokeh
- scipy
- statsmodels
- scikit-learn
- ta-lib
- mplfinance
- lightgbm
- xgboost
- pandas-datareader
- quandl
- yfinance
- mplfinance
- arch-py
- prophet
- pmdarima
- beautifulsoup4
- requests
- jupyter
- jupyterlab
- ipykernel
- spyder
- spyder-kernels

The last four lines in `PythonFinanceConda.yml` are for installing optional packages to support the core offline IDEs: Jupiter Notebook and Spyder.

IMPORTING LIBRARIES

```
1.  # Import core analytical libraries
2.  import numpy as np
3.  import pandas as pd
4.  import matplotlib.pyplot as plt
5.  import itertools
6.
7.  # Import specific libraries for Finance
8.  import yfinance as yf
9.  import talib
10. import mplfinance as mpf
11. from pmdarima import auto_arima
12. from scipy.optimize import minimize
13. from prophet import Prophet
14. from prophet.diagnostics import cross_validation,
    performance_metrics
15. from arch import arch_model
16. from sklearn.metrics import mean_absolute_
    percentage_error
```

FETCHING STOCK PRICE DATA FROM YAHOO FINANCE

```
1.  # List of the selected NASDAQ tickers
2.  nasdaq_tickers = [
3.      'MRNA', 'DLTR', 'ZS', 'MCHP', 'SBUX', 'HON',
    'JD', 'DDOG',
```

```
4.      'AMAT', 'AAPL', 'AMGN', 'INTU', 'PCAR',
   'MDLZ', 'CSGP',

5.      'FTNT', 'KDP', 'META', 'VRSK', 'MAR', 'MRVL',
   'AZN',

6.      'ILMN', 'ENPH', 'SIRI', 'MELI', 'ZM', 'TSLA',
   'BKR', 'URBN'

7. ]

8.

9. # Fetching a DataFrame with a Single-Column Index

10. def fetch_yfinance_single_stock_data(ticker,
    start=None, end=None, actions=True):

11.     """

12.     Fetches historical stock prices for a given
    ticker and calculates RoR and LogRoR.

13.

14.     Parameters:

15.     - ticker: A single ticker symbol as a string
    or a list of ticker symbols.

16.     - start: Start date for fetching data. If
    None, fetches as much data as possible.

17.     - end: End date for fetching data. If None,
    defaults to the current date.

18.     - actions: Boolean flag to control the
    execution an aditional data fetching.

19.

20.     Returns:

21.     - DataFrame with stock prices and additional
    columns for RoR and LogRoR if actions is True.

22.     """

23.
```

```
24.      # Fetch historical data
25.      data = yf.download(ticker, start=start,
    end=end, actions=actions)
26.
27.      # Ensure data is a DataFrame (yf.download
    returns a DataFrame for multiple tickers or a
    Series for a single ticker)
28.      if isinstance(data, pd.Series):
29.          data = data.to_frame(name='Adj Close')
30.
31.      # Calculating daily percentage change (RoR)
    and Logarithmic Rate of Return (LogRoR)
32.      data['RoR'] = data['Adj Close'].pct_change()
33.      data['LogRoR'] = np.log(data['Adj Close'] /
    data['Adj Close'].shift(1))
34.
35.      return data
36.
37. # Initialize an empty DataFrame to store the
    concatenated data
38. nasdaq_assets_df = pd.DataFrame()
39.
40. # Iterate over each ticker and fetch its data
41. for ticker in nasdaq_tickers:
42.      ticker_data = fetch_yfinance_single_stock_
    data(ticker, actions=True)
43.
44.      # If data was fetched successfully, append it
    to the collective DataFrame
45.      if ticker_data is not None:
```

```
46.        # Adding a 'Ticker' column to identify
    the stock in the collective DataFrame

47.        ticker_data['Ticker'] = ticker

48.

49.        # Appending the data

50.        nasdaq_assets_df = pd.concat([nasdaq_
    assets_df, ticker_data])

51.

52. # Now, nasdaq_assets_df contains the historical
    stock prices, RoR, and LogRoR for all specified
    NASDAQ tickers

53. print(nasdaq_assets_df.head())

54.

55. # Fetching a DataFrame with a Multi-Column Index

56. def fetch_yfinance_stocks_data(tickers,

57.                        start=None,

58.                        end=None,

59.                        actions=True):

60.    """

61.    Fetches historical stock data, calculates
    percentage changes and logRoR,

62.    and creates a MultiIndex DataFrame.

63.

64.    Parameters:

65.    - tickers: List of ticker symbols.

66.    - start: Start date for fetching data.

67.    - end: End date for fetching data.

68.    - actions: Boolean flag to control the
    execution an aditional data fetching.
```

```python
69.

70.      Returns:

71.        - A MultiIndex DataFrame with 'Adj Close',
    'Volume', 'RoR', and 'logRoR'.

72.        """

73.

74.      # Download stock data

75.      df = yf.download(tickers=tickers,
    start=start, end=end, actions=actions)

76.

77.      # Calculate percentage change and logRoR for
    'Adj Close'

78.      pct_change = df['Adj Close'].pct_change()

79.      logRoR = np.log(df['Adj Close'] / df['Adj
    Close'].shift(1))

80.

81.      # Preparing the MultiIndex for new columns

82.      pct_change.columns = pd.MultiIndex.from_
    product([['RoR'], pct_change.columns])

83.      logRoR.columns = pd.MultiIndex.from_
    product([['logRoR'], logRoR.columns])

84.

85.      # Concatenating the new 'RoR' and 'logRoR'
    DataFrames with the original DataFrame

86.      df = pd.concat([df, pct_change, logRoR],
    axis=1)

87.      df.sort_index(inplace=True)

88.

89.      return df

90.
```

```
91.  # Fetching and processing stock data
92.  nasdaq_assets_df = fetch_yfinance_stocks_data
     (nasdaq_tickers)
93.  print(nasdaq_assets_df.dropna().head())
```

FETCHING OTHER DATA FROM YAHOO FINANCE

```
1.   # Fetching Options data for the selected ticker
2.   # Initialize a Ticker object
3.   apple = yf.Ticker(nasdaq_tickers[0])
4.   # Fetch options data (calls and puts) for the
     first available expiration date
5.   options_expiration_dates = apple.options   # Get
     all available options expiration dates
6.   first_expiration_date = options_expiration_
     dates[0]   # Select the first available expiration
     date
7.   options_data = apple.option_chain(first_
     expiration_date)   # Fetch options data for this
     date
8.   # Display the calls and puts data
9.   print("Calls for first expiration date:")
10.  print(options_data.calls.head())   # Display first
     few rows of call options data
11.  print("\nPuts for first expiration date:")
12.  print(options_data.puts.head())   # Display first
     few rows of put options data
13.
14.  # Fetching risk-free data
15.  # Initialize a Ticker object for the 13-week USA
     Treasury bill rate
```

```python
16.  irx = yf.Ticker("^IRX")
17.  # Fetch historical data for the 13-week Treasury
     bill rate
18.  irx_history = irx.history(period="1y")  #
     Example: Fetch data for the last year
19.  # Calculate the daily mean of the yearly
     percentage rate
20.  daily_mean_zero_rate = irx_history['Close'].
     mean()
21.  print("Mean Yearly Percentage Zero-Rate (13-week
     Treasury bill) over the last year:")
22.  print(f"{daily_mean_zero_rate:.2f}")
23.  print("Mean Daily Percentage Zero-Rate (13-week
     Treasury bill) over the last year:")
24.  print(f"{daily_mean_zero_rate / 252:.5f}")
25.
26.  # Fundamental analysis function for stock data
     from Yahoo Finance
27.  def calculate_fundamentals(ticker_symbol):
28.      # Fetching financial data for the selected
         ticker
29.      ticker = yf.Ticker(ticker_symbol)
30.      financials = ticker.financials
31.      balance_sheet = ticker.balance_sheet
32.      # Retrieving basic earnings per share (EPS)
         from the financials
33.      eps = financials.loc['Basic EPS']
34.      # Calculating the Return on Equity (ROE) by
         dividing Net Income by Stockholder's Equity
35.      roe = financials.loc['Net Income'] / balance_
         sheet.loc['Stockholders Equity']
```

```
36.      # Fetching historical price data for the
    ticker in the date range of the financial data
37.      history = ticker.history(start=eps.index[-1].
    strftime('%Y-%m-%d'),
38.              end=eps.index[0].strftime('%Y-%m-%d'),
39.                          interval='1d')
40.      # Removing time zone information for ease of
    comparison
41.      eps.index = eps.index.tz_localize(None)
42.      roe.index = roe.index.tz_localize(None)
43.      history.index = history.index.tz_localize(None)
44.      # Creating a date range that includes
    weekends
45.      full_date_range = pd.date_range(start=eps.
    index.min(),
46.                              end=eps.index.max(),
47.                                  freq='D')
48.      # Reindexing the dataframe to include the
    full date range with weekends
49.      history_full = history.reindex(full_date_
    range, method='ffill')
50.      # Fetching the closing prices from history
    that match the dates in eps
51.      close_prices_on_eps_dates = history_full.
    loc[history_full.index.isin(eps.index), 'Close']
52.      # Calculating the Price to Earnings (P/E)
    ratio by dividing the closing price by EPS
53.      pe_ratio_on_eps_dates = close_prices_on_eps_
    dates / eps
54.      return {
55.          'ticker': ticker_symbol,
```

```
56.          'eps': eps,
57.          'roe': roe,
58.          'pe_ratio': pe_ratio_on_eps_dates
59.      }
60.  # Apply the function for Stock1
61.  aapl_financial_ratios = calculate_fundamentals
     (nasdaq_tickers[0])
62.  # Print the results for Stock 1
63.  print(f"{aapl_financial_ratios['ticker']} Basic
     EPS:")
64.  print(aapl_financial_ratios['eps'])
65.  print(f"\n{aapl_financial_ratios['ticker']}
     Return on Equity (ROE):")
66.  print(aapl_financial_ratios['roe'])
67.  print(f"\n{aapl_financial_ratios['ticker']} P/E
     Ratio on EPS Dates:")
68.  print(aapl_financial_ratios['pe_ratio'])
```

TECHNIQUE ANALYSES INDICES (TA-LIB LIBRARY)

```
1.  # TA-lib for technical analysis indicator
    calculating
2.  #!pip install ta-lib-bin # uncomment to install
    library
3.  import talib
4.  ticker=nasdaq_tickers[9]
5.  df1 = fetch_yfinance_single_stock_data(ticker).
    copy()
6.  # Calculate Bollinger Bands
7.  df1['upper_band'], df1['middle_band'],
    df1['lower_band'] = talib.BBANDS(
```

```
8.       df1['Close'], timeperiod=20, nbdevup=2,
    nbdevdn=2, matype=0)

9.  # Calculate MACD

10. df1['macd'], df1['macdsignal'], df1['macdhist'] =
    talib.MACD(

11.      df1['Close'], fastperiod=12, slowperiod=26,
    signalperiod=9)

12. # Calculate RSI

13. df1['rsi'] = talib.RSI(df1['Close'],
    timeperiod=14)

14. # Display the head of the DataFrame to see the
    results

15. print(df1.tail())
```

GRAPHICAL ANALYSES (CORE LIBRARIES)

```
1.  # Candlestick chart within the core libraries

2.  def ohlc_plot_candles_volumes(df, window,
    figsize=(12, 6), title='Candlestick Chart with
    Volumes'):

3.      sample = df.iloc[-window:]

4.      fig, ax1 = plt.subplots(figsize=figsize)

5.      ax2 = ax1.twinx()   # Create a second y-axis
    to plot the volume

6.      # Define the maximum volume to scale the
    y-axis of volume bars

7.      max_vol = sample['Volume'].max()

8.      for i in range(len(sample)):

9.          # Plotting the high and low using black line

10.          ax1.vlines(x=i, ymin=sample.iloc[i]
    ['Low'], ymax=sample.iloc[i]['High'], color=
    'black', linewidth=1)
```

```
11.          # Determine the colour and position of
   the candle's body
12.          if sample.iloc[i]['Close'] > sample.
   iloc[i]['Open']:
13.              ax1.vlines(x=i, ymin=sample.
   iloc[i]['Open'], ymax=sample.iloc[i]['Close'],
   color='green', linewidth=4)
14.          elif sample.iloc[i]['Close'] < sample.
   iloc[i]['Open']:
15.              ax1.vlines(x=i, ymin=sample.
   iloc[i]['Close'], ymax=sample.iloc[i]['Open'],
   color='red', linewidth=4)
16.          else:
17.              ax1.vlines(x=i, ymin=sample.iloc[i]
   ['Close'], ymax=sample.iloc[i]['Open'] + 0.00003,
   color='black', linewidth=4)
18.          # Plotting the volume bars
19.          color = 'green' if sample.iloc[i]
   ['Close'] > sample.iloc[i]['Open'] else 'red'
20.          ax2.bar(i, sample.iloc[i]['Volume'],
   color=color, alpha=0.3)
21.      # Adjust the y limit of the second axis to
   fit the volume bars
22.      ax2.set_ylim(0, max_vol*5)
23.      ax2.set_ylabel("Volume")
24.      # Setting x-axis labels to the dates from the
   DataFrame's index
25.      ax1.set_xticks(range(len(sample)))
26.      ax1.set_xticklabels([date.strftime
   ('%Y-%m-%d') for date in sample.index],
   rotation=90, ha='right')
27.      ax1.grid()
28.      # Set the title for the plot
```

```
29.      ax1.set_title(title)

30.      plt.show()

31. ohlc_plot_candles_volumes(fetch_yfinance_single_
    stock_data(nasdaq_tickers[0]),

32.                      50, title=nasdaq_tickers[0])
```

GRAPHICAL ANALYSES (MPLFINANCE LIBRARY)

```
1. import mplfinance as mpf

2. # Bollinger Bands plotting function

3. def plot_candlestick_with_bb(df, ticker,
   window=20, no_of_std=2):

4.    # Calculate Bollinger Bands

5.    rolling_mean = df['Close'].rolling
   (window=window).mean()

6.    rolling_std = df['Close'].rolling
   (window=window).std()

7.    upper_band = rolling_mean + (rolling_std *
   no_of_std)

8.    lower_band = rolling_mean - (rolling_std *
   no_of_std)

9.    # Plot configuration for Bollinger Bands

10.    apds = [mpf.make_addplot(upper_band.values,
   color='green'),

11.           mpf.make_addplot(rolling_mean.values,
   color='blue'),  # MVA line

12.           mpf.make_addplot(lower_band.values,
   color='red')]

13.    # Plot with title

14.    mpf.plot(df, type='candle', addplot=apds,
   volume=True, title=f"{ticker} - Bollinger Bands",
```

```
15.                figsize=(12, 6), style='starsandstripes')
16. # MACD plotting function
17. def plot_candlestick_with_macd(df, ticker,
    span1=12, span2=26, signal_span=9):
18.     # Calculate MACD and Signal line
19.     exp1 = df['Close'].ewm(span=span1, adjust=
    False).mean()
20.     exp2 = df['Close'].ewm(span=span2, adjust=
    False).mean()
21.     macd_line = exp1 - exp2
22.     signal_line = macd_line.ewm(span=signal_span,
    adjust=False).mean()
23.     # Plot configuration for MACD
24.     apds = [mpf.make_addplot(macd_line.values,
    panel=1, color='fuchsia', ylabel='MACD'),
25.             mpf.make_addplot(signal_line.values,
    panel=1, color='b')]
26.     # Plot with title
27.     mpf.plot(df, type='candle', addplot=apds,
    volume=False, title=f"{ticker} - MACD",
28.             style='starsandstripes', panel_
    ratios=(6,3), figsize=(12, 6))
29. # RSI plotting function
30. def plot_candlestick_with_rsi(df, ticker,
    window=14):
31.     # Calculate RSI
32.     delta = df['Close'].diff()
33.     up = delta.clip(lower=0)
34.     down = -1 * delta.clip(upper=0)
35.     roll_up = up.rolling(window=window).mean()
```

```
36.        roll_down = down.rolling(window=window).mean()

37.        RS = roll_up / roll_down

38.        rsi_line = 100 - (100 / (1 + RS))

39.        # Plot configuration for RSI

40.        apds = [mpf.make_addplot(rsi_line.values,
       panel=1, color='purple', ylabel='RSI'),

41.              mpf.make_addplot([70] * len(df), panel=1,
       color='red', alpha=0.5, linestyle='dashed'),

42.              mpf.make_addplot([30] * len(df), panel=1,
       color='green', alpha=0.5, linestyle='dashed')]

43.        # Plot with title

44.        mpf.plot(df, type='candle', addplot=apds,
       volume=False, title=f"{ticker} - RSI",

45.              style='starsandstripes', panel_
       ratios=(6,3), figsize=(12, 6))

46. # Example usage with a single ticker from the
       NASDAQ list

47. ticker=nasdaq_tickers[9]

48. df = fetch_yfinance_single_stock_data(ticker).
       iloc[-126:].copy()

49. plot_candlestick_with_bb(df, ticker=ticker)

50. plot_candlestick_with_macd(df, ticker=ticker)

51. plot_candlestick_with_rsi(df, ticker=ticker)
```

PORTFOLIO OPTIMIZATION (SCIPY LIBRARY)

```
1. from scipy.optimize import minimize

2. def portfolio_performance(weights, log_returns,
       risk_free_rate=0.0):

3.        """
```

```
4.       Calculate expected portfolio performance
     metrics: return, volatility, and Sharpe ratio.
5.       Note: risk_free_rate is the annual rate, log
     returns are daily rates
6.       """
7.       expected_return = np.sum(log_returns.mean() *
     weights) * 252
8.       volatility = np.sqrt(np.dot(weights.T,
     np.dot(log_returns.cov() * 252, weights)))
9.       sharpe_ratio = (expected_return - risk_free_
     rate) / volatility
10.      return expected_return, volatility,
     sharpe_ratio
11. def minimize_negative_sharpe(weights, log_
     returns, risk_free_rate=0.0):
12.      """
13.      Objective function to minimize (negative
     Sharpe ratio).
14.      """
15.      return -portfolio_performance(weights, log_
     returns, risk_free_rate)[2]
16. def minimize_volatility(weights, log_returns,
     risk_free_rate=0.0):
17.      """
18.      Objective function to minimize portfolio
     volatility.
19.      """
20.      return portfolio_performance(weights, log_
     returns)[1]
21. def minimize_negative_return(weights,
     log_returns):
```

```
22.    """
23.    Objective function to minimize (negative
       return).
24.    """
25.    return -portfolio_performance(weights, log_
       returns)[0]
26. def optimize_portfolio(log_returns, objective_
       function, risk_free_rate=0.0,
27.                          min_ror=None, max_vol=None):
28.    """
29.    General optimization method.
30.    """
31.    num_assets = len(log_returns.columns)
32.    bounds = tuple((0, 1) for _ in range(num_assets))
33.    initial_guess = np.array([1. / num_assets] *
       num_assets)
34.    constraints = [{'type': 'eq', 'fun': lambda
       x: np.sum(x) - 1}]
35.    if min_ror is not None:
36.        constraints.append({'type': 'ineq',
       'fun': lambda x:
37.                           portfolio_
       performance(x, log_returns)[0] - min_ror})
38.    if max_vol is not None:
39.        constraints.append({'type': 'ineq',
       'fun': lambda x:
40.                           max_vol - portfolio_
       performance(x, log_returns)[1]})
41.    # Adjust the args passed to the minimize
       function based on the objective_function
```

```python
42.     if objective_function == minimize_negative_
    sharpe:
43.         args = (log_returns, risk_free_rate)
44.     else:
45.         args = (log_returns,)
46.
47.     opt_results = minimize(objective_function,
    initial_guess, args=args,
48.                             method='SLSQP',
    bounds=bounds, constraints=constraints)
49.     # Print portfolio results
50.     formatted_weights = [f"{weight:.2f}" for
    weight in opt_results.x]
51.     ret = portfolio_performance(opt_results.x,
    log_returns)[0]
52.     vol = portfolio_performance(opt_results.x,
    log_returns)[1]
53.     print("Optimal Weights: ", formatted_weights)
54.     print(f"Expected Annual Return: {ret:.2f}")
55.     print(f"Expected Volatility: {vol:.2f}")
56.     print()
57.     return opt_results.x
58. # Usage example for 2 years daily Returns
59. start_date = '2022-01-01'
60. end_date = '2023-12-31'
61. # Fetch historical data
62. df = fetch_yfinance_stocks_data(nasdaq_tickers,
63.                             start=start_date,
64.                         end=end_date)['Adj Close']
```

```
65.  # Annualy risk-free rate
66.  risk_free_rate = (yf.Ticker("^IRX").
     history(period="2y")['Close'].mean() / 100)
67.  log_returns = np.log(df / df.shift(1)).dropna()
68.  # Optimize results
69.  print("Mathematical Optimization Results")
70.  print("Optimize for maximum Sharpe Ratio:")
71.  sharpe = optimize_portfolio(log_returns,
72.                            minimize_negative_sharpe,
73.                               risk_free_rate)
```

STATSMODELS REGRESSION

```
1.  import statsmodels.api as sm
2.
3.  def capm_regression_and_visualization(index_returns,
4.                                        stock_returns,
5.                              risk_free_rate=0.0):
6.      """
7.      Performs CAPM regression analysis and
     visualization, incorporating the risk-free rate.
8.
9.      Parameters:
10.     - index_returns: Pandas Series of percentage
     changes for the market index.
11.     - stock_returns: Pandas Series of percentage
     changes for the stock.
12.     - risk_free_rate: The risk-free rate for
     calculating excess returns.
```

```
13.
14.     Returns:
15.     - A dictionary containing the regression
    results and model parameters.
16.     """
17.     # Ensure there are no NaN values
18.     index_returns = index_returns.dropna()
19.     stock_returns = stock_returns.dropna()
20.     # Adjust for risk-free rate to get excess
    returns
21.     excess_stock_return = stock_returns
    - risk_free_rate
22.     excess_market_return = index_returns
    - risk_free_rate
23.     # Add a constant to the independent variable
24.     X = sm.add_constant(excess_market_return)
25.     # Perform OLS regression
26.     model = sm.OLS(excess_stock_return, X)
27.     results = model.fit()
28.     # Extract regression parameters
29.     beta = results.params[1]
30.     alpha = results.params[0]
31.     r_value = results.rsquared ** 0.5
32.     p_value = results.pvalues[1]
33.     std_err = results.bse[1]
34.     # Return model results and parameters
35.     return {
36.         'beta': beta,
```

```
37.            'alpha': alpha,
38.            'correlation_coefficient': r_value,
39.            'p_value': p_value,
40.            'standard_error': std_err,
41.            'regression_summary': results.summary()
42.        }
```

TIME-SERIES DATA FEATURING

```
1.  # Define the function of lagged feature creation
2.  def create_lagged_features(df, max_lag=5,
    prediction_window=1,
3.                             seasonal = True):
4.      '''
5.      Create a DataFrame with lagged features and
    datetime features.
6.
7.      Parameters:
8.      df (pd.DataFrame): Input DataFrame with each
    column being a time series.
9.      max_lag (int): Maximum lag to create lagged
    features.
10.     prediction_window (int): The number of steps
    to predict.
11.     seasonal(bool): If is True, the datetime
    features are applied.
12.
13.     Returns:
14.     pd.DataFrame: DataFrame with the first column
    as the target and others
```

```
15.            as lagged features and datetime features.
16.      '''
17.      lagged_df = pd.DataFrame(index=df.index)
18.      for col in df.columns:
19.          # Create 'target' column for prediction
20.          if prediction_window > 0:
21.              lagged_df[f'{col}_target_plus_{prediction_
     window}d'] = df[col].shift(-prediction_window)
22.          # Create lagged features for each column
23.          for l in range(0, max_lag):
24.              lagged_df[f'{col}_lag_{l}'] = df[col].
     shift(l)
25.      # Adding datetime (seasonality) features
26.      if seasonal:
27.          lagged_df['day'] = lagged_df.index.day
28.          lagged_df['dayofweek'] = lagged_df.index.
     dayofweek
29.          lagged_df['month'] = lagged_df.index.month
30.          lagged_df['dayofyear'] = lagged_df.index.
     dayofyear
31.      return lagged_df
32. # Fetching data and features preparation
33. data = fetch_yfinance_single_stock_data(['AZN']).
     loc['2022':'2023']
34. features =
     create_lagged_features(data[['Volume']],
35.                                  max_lag=1,
36.                                  prediction_window=1,
37.                                  seasonal = True)
```

```
38. dataframe = pd.concat([data, features], axis=1)
39. dataframe.dropna(inplace=True)
40. print(dataframe.head())
```

PMDARIMA PARAMETERS TUNING (PMDARIMA LIBRARY)

```
1.  from pmdarima import auto_arima
2.  from sklearn.metrics import mean_absolute_
    percentage_error
3.
4.  def tune_forecast_sarimax(dataframe, target_col,
    exog_cols=None,
5.                            test_size=21, d=1,
    m=10, seasonal=True):
6.      """
7.      Auto-tune and forecast using SARIMAX model.
8.
9.      Parameters:
10.     - dataframe: pd.DataFrame containing the time
    series and exogenous variables.
11.     - target_col: str, name of the target
    variable column.
12.     - exog_cols: list of str, names of the
    exogenous variable columns.
13.     - test_size: int, the number of observations
    to use for the test set.
14.     - d: int, order of differencing.
15.     - m: int, seasonal periodicity.
16.
17.     Returns:
```

```
18.        - None, displays a plot of the actual vs
    predicted values with confidence intervals.
19.        """
20.        # Split into train and test sets
21.        train_set = dataframe.iloc[:-test_size]
22.        test_set = dataframe.iloc[-test_size:]
23.        # Prepare exogenous variables if provided
24.        X_train = train_set[exog_cols] if exog_cols
    else None
25.        X_test = test_set[exog_cols] if exog_cols
    else None
26.        # SARIMAX model tuning
27.        model = auto_arima(y=train_set[target_col],
28.                            X=X_train, d=d, m=m,
29.                            n_jobs=-1,
30.                            seasonal=seasonal,
31.                            stepwise=False)
32.        print(model.summary())
33.        # Generate predictions and confidence intervals
34.        forecast, conf_int = model.predict(n_
    periods=test_size, X=X_test, return_conf_int=True)
35.        # Convert forecast and confidence intervals
    to pandas Series for easier plotting
36.        predictions = pd.Series(forecast).rename
    ("SARIMAX")
37.        predictions.index = test_set.index
38.        lower_conf = pd.Series(conf_int[:, 0],
    index=test_set.index).rename("Lower CI")
39.        upper_conf = pd.Series(conf_int[:, 1],
    index=test_set.index).rename("Upper CI")
```

```
40.      # Calculate MAPE
41.      m_mape = mean_absolute_percentage_error(test_
    set[target_col], predictions) * 100
42.      # Plotting the results
43.      plt.figure(figsize=(15, 5))
44.      dataframe[-60:][target_col].plot(legend=True,
45.                                      title=f'SARIMAX
    Results with MAPE={m_mape:.2f}%')
46.      plt.fill_between(lower_conf.index, lower_
    conf, upper_conf, color='k', alpha=0.15)
47.      test_set[target_col].rename('True y').
    plot(legend=True)
48.      predictions.plot(legend=True, color='red',
    linestyle='--')
49.      plt.xlabel('Date')
50.      plt.ylabel('Price')
51.      plt.legend(loc='upper left')
52.      plt.show()
53.      return model
54.  # Example usage
55.  tune_forecast_sarimax(dataframe=dataframe,
56.                      target_col='Close',
57.                      # exog_cols=['month',
    'Volume_lag_1'],
58.                      test_size=10,
59.                      d=1,
60.                      m=12)
```

VAR

```
1.   # Calculate and plot VAR and aVAR
2.   def calculating_VaRs_hist(data, confidence_level
     = 0.95,
3.                              out_text = False, out_
     viz = False):
4.       # Sort the log returns
5.       data_sorted = data.sort_values()
6.       # Calculate the VaR
7.       historical_var = data_sorted.quantile(1
     - confidence_level)
8.       # Calculate the aVaR
9.       avar = data_sorted[data_sorted <= historical_
     var].mean()
10.      # Print the Value at Risk (VaR) result
11.      if out_text:
12.          print('Historical Method.')
13.          print(f'With 95% confidence, the values
     will not exceed a loss of {-historical_var *
     100:.2f}%.')
14.          print(f'With 95% confidence, the values
     will not exceed a loss of {-avar * 100:.2f}%.')
15.      if out_viz:
16.          # Plot the histogram with 100 bins
17.          plt.figure(figsize=(10, 5))
18.          n, bins, patches = plt.hist(data_sorted,
     bins=100, alpha=0.7)
19.          for patch, rightside, leftside in
     zip(patches, bins[1:], bins[:-1]):
```

```
20.            if rightside <= historical_var:
21.                patch.set_facecolor('red')
22.            if leftside < historical_var <= rightside:
23.                fraction = (historical_var -
     leftside) / (rightside - leftside)
24.                patch.set_facecolor('red')
25.                patch.set_alpha(fraction)
26.        plt.axvline(historical_var, color='k',
     linestyle='--',
27.                label=f'95% VaR level:
     {-historical_var * 100:.2f}%')
28.        plt.axvline(avar, color='b', linestyle=':',
29.                label=f'95% aVaR level: {-avar
     * 100:.2f}%')
30.        plt.title('Histogram with VaR')
31.        plt.xlabel('Return')
32.        plt.ylabel('Frequency')
33.        plt.legend()
34.        plt.show()
35.    # Return VaR and aVaR
36.    return({historical_var, avar})
37.
38. calculating_VaRs_hist(log_returns['AAPL'], out_
     viz=True, out_text=True)
```

GARCH MODELS (ARCH LIBRARY)

```
1. from arch import arch_model
2. import itertools
3.
```

```python
4.  def auto_tune_garch(data, param_dict,
    dist='normal',
5.                      information_criterion='aic',
6.                      pvalues = 0.05):
7.      """
8.      Automatically tune GARCH model parameters.
9.
10.     Parameters:
11.     - data: pd.Series, the time series data.
12.     - param_dict: dict, dictionary where keys are
    parameter names ('p', 'q', etc.)
13.         and values are lists of parameter values to
    iterate over.
14.     - dist: str, the distribution assumption
    ('normal', 't', etc.).
15.     - information_criterion: str, criterion to
    select the best model ('aic' or 'bic').
16.
17.     Returns:
18.     - Best model fit based on the specified
    information criterion.
19.     """
20.     best_ic = np.inf
21.     best_model = None
22.     best_params = {}
23.     # Create a list of all parameter combinations
    to iterate over
24.     param_names = sorted(param_dict)
25.     param_combinations = itertools.product(*(param_
    dict[name] for name in param_names))
```

```
26.      for params in param_combinations:
27.          try:
28.              # Unpack parameters for the current
    combination
29.              model_params = dict(zip(param_names,
    params))
30.              # Specify and fit the model
31.              model = arch_model(data, dist=dist,
    **model_params)
32.              model_fit = model.fit(disp='off')
33.              # Select the best model based on the
    specified information criterion
34.              if information_criterion == 'aic':
35.                  current_ic = model_fit.aic
36.              else:
37.                  current_ic = model_fit.bic
38.
39.              if (current_ic < best_ic):
40.                  if np.sum(model_fit.pvalues >
    pvalues) == 0:
41.                      best_ic = current_ic
42.                      best_model = model_fit
43.                      best_params = model_params
44.          except Exception as e:
45.              print(f"Error with parameters
    {params}: {e}")
46.              continue
47.      print(f"Best Model: {best_params} with
    {information_criterion.upper()}={best_ic}")
```

```
48.      if best_model is not None:
49.          print(best_model.summary())
50.      return best_model
51. # Example usage:
52. param_dict = {
53.     'p': range(1, 5),   # Example range for p
54.     'q': range(1, 5),   # Example range for q
55.     'mean': ['Zero', 'Constant', 'AR']
56. }
57. best_model = auto_tune_garch(log_returns['AAPL'],
58.                         param_dict, dist='normal',
59.                     information_criterion='aic',
60.                             pvalues=0.1)
```

PROPHET LIBRARY: MODEL PARAMETERS DEFINITION AND HYPERPARAMETERS TUNING WITH CROSS-VALIDATION

```
1. from prophet import Prophet
2. from prophet.diagnostics import cross_validation,
   performance_metrics
3. import itertools
4. from sklearn.metrics import mean_absolute_
   percentage_error
5.
6. def tune_prophet_model(df_train, df_test, param_
   grid, regressors=None,
7.                     cv_initial='504 days', cv_
   period='126 days', cv_horizon='5 days'):
8.      """
```

```
9.      Tune Prophet model parameters including
   optional regressors.

10.

11.     Parameters:

12.     - df_train: DataFrame with columns ds, y, and
   optionally additional regressors for training.

13.      - df_test: DataFrame with columns ds, y, and
   optionally additional regressors for testing.

14.      - param_grid: Dictionary with parameter names
   as keys and lists of parameter settings to try as
   values.

15.      - regressors: List of strings, names of
   additional regressor columns in df_train and
   df_test.

16.      - cv_initial: String, initial period size for
   cross-validation.

17.       - cv_period: String, period size for
   cross-validation.

18.      - cv_horizon: String, horizon size for
   cross-validation.

19.

20.     Returns:

21.     - best_params: Best parameters based on
   cross-validation MAPE.

22.     - model: Fitted Prophet model with best
   parameters.

23.     """

24.     if regressors is None:

25.         regressors = []

26.     all_params = [dict(zip(param_grid.keys(), v))
   for v in itertools.product(*param_grid.values())]
```

```python
27.     mapes = []  # Store the MAPEs for each
   parameter set here
28.     for params in all_params:
29.         m = Prophet(**params)
30.         # Add regressors if specified
31.         for regressor in regressors:
32.             m.add_regressor(regressor)
33.         m.fit(df_train)  # Fit model with given params
34.         df_cv = cross_validation(m, initial=cv_
   initial, period=cv_period, horizon=cv_horizon)
35.         df_p = performance_metrics(df_cv,
   rolling_window=1)
36.         mapes.append(df_p['mape'].values[0])  #
   Collect MAPE
37.     # Find the best parameters
38.     tuning_results = pd.DataFrame(all_params)
39.     tuning_results['mape'] = mapes
40.     best_params = all_params[np.argmin(mapes)]
41.     print("Tuning results:\n", tuning_results)
42.     print("\nBest parameters:\n", best_params)
43.     # Fit the best model
44.     m_best = Prophet(**best_params)
45.     for regressor in regressors:
46.         m_best.add_regressor(regressor)
47.     m_best.fit(df_train)
48.     # Model evaluation
49.     forecast = m_best.predict(df_test)
50.     mape = mean_absolute_percentage_error(df_
   test['y'], forecast['yhat']) * 100
```

```
51.        print(f"\nTuned model for test data: MAPE =
    {mape:.2f}%")
52.    return best_params, m_best
53. # Example usage:
54. param_grid = {
55.     'changepoint_prior_scale': [0.01, 0.5, 0.9],
56.     'seasonality_prior_scale': [0.01, 8.0, 10.0],
57.     'seasonality_mode': ['additive', 'multiplicative']
58. }
59. # Defining df_train and df_test for Prophet
60. data = fetch_yfinance_single_stock_data('AZN',
61.                             start='2021-01-01',
62.                  end='2023-12-31', actions=False)
63. df = pd.DataFrame({
64.     'ds': pd.to_datetime(data.index),
65.     'y': data['Close']
66. })
67. test_period = 5
68. df_train = df[:-test_period]
69. df_test = df[-test_period:]
70. best_params, model = tune_prophet_model(df_train,
    df_test, param_grid)
```

B

GLOSSARY

- An *analytical investment strategy* is a systematic approach to making investment decisions based on various analysis methods.

- An *application programming interface* (*API*) is a set of rules and protocols that enable different applications to communicate using the same language. In the finance industry, APIs are used to retrieve data, access real-time information, and even automate trading processes.

- An *artificial neural network* (*ANN*) is a computational model with a structure that functions or processes information similarly to the biological human brain neural networks. It comprises many interconnected processing nodes (*neurons*) that work in unison to solve specific problems. Due to their adaptive learning abilities, ANNs can carry out ML and pattern recognition.

- *Asset allocation* is an investment strategy that divides assets across various categories and their weights, such as stocks, bonds, and cash, to optimize the balance between risk and return.

- A *behavioral investment strategy* can be regarded as a multidimensional framework reflecting the investor's behaviors, financial goals, risk tolerance, time commitment, market perspective, and other subjective feelings.

- A *boxplot* is a graphical representation of data that displays the distribution and spread of a dataset, as well as its quartiles and outliers.

- A *candlestick chart* is a visual plot of price movements in financial markets. It uses candles to show the open, high, low, and close prices for a given period.

- *Capitalization* is the total cost of securities or shares of stock. It is calculated by multiplying the security price by its total volume in the market operations.

- The *capital asset pricing model (CAPM)* is a financial model that describes the correlation between systematic risk and expected return for assets, especially stocks.

- *Central tendency metrics* describe the center position of a distribution for a dataset. The key metrics include the *mean, median,* and *mode.*

- A *changepoint,* in the context of Facebook's Prophet, is a point in time when the time series experiences a significant shift in its trend. It represents a moment when the underlying growth rate of the time series changes.

- *Clustering* is an ML technique that groups different objects so that objects in the same group (called a cluster) are more like each other than those in other groups. A critical feature of cluster analysis is that the grouping rule was unknown before clustering. Therefore, it is called unsupervised learning.

- *Correlation* is a statistical measure that describes the extent to which two variables change together.

- *Cross-validation* is a method for estimating the robustness of ML models and protecting against overfitting in predictive models.

- *Comma-separated values (CSV)* is a commonly used file format for large amounts of tabular data (numbers and text) in plain text. Each file line is a data row (record) with several fields separated by commas.

- The *cumulative rate of return* is the total amount of money an investment has gained or lost over a certain period, expressed as a percentage of the initial investment period.

- *Data* is usually understood as raw, unorganized facts and figures collected from various sources for analysis, computation, interpretation, or other purposes. Data may seem random and meaningless in its raw form, but once processed and interpreted, it gains context and becomes useful information.

- *Data manipulation* is the process of adjusting, organizing, and restructuring data to make it more suitable for analysis. This includes operations such as sorting, filtering, merging, grouping, and reshaping data, which are fundamental in data analysis tasks.

- *Data scaling* is a pre-processing step in which the range of variables in a dataset is normalized or standardized.

- A *DataFrame* is a two-dimensional, size-mutable, potentially heterogeneous tabular data structure with labeled axes (rows and columns). In Python, it is supported by the pandas library functionality (Python class).

- *Descriptive statistics* are summary statistics metrics that quantitatively describe or summarize features of a dataset. They typically offer a simple overview of the main quantitative aspects of the data, such as central tendency, deviation, range, and type of variables.

- *Deviation metrics* are measures that describe the spread or dispersion of a dataset. The *standard deviation* (*SD*), *variance* (*Var*), and *coefficient of variation* (*CV*) are commonly used deviation metrics.

- *Diversification* is an investment strategy that reduces risk by allocating funds to various financial instruments, industries, and other groups.

- An *extract, transform, and load* (*ETL*) process involves collecting data from various sources, converting it into a format suitable for further analysis, and cleaning it. ETL processes are the first and most time-consuming stage in preparing large datasets for analytical tasks in financial data analysis.

- The *exploratory data analysis* (*EDA*) process is an approach in statistics and machine learning that analytically and visually examines datasets to understand their underlying characteristics, features, and other crucial dependencies.

- A *feature* is a property or characteristic of a discovered sample. In an ML dataset, a feature is typically a column containing data that can help an ML model make predictions.

- *Financial assets* are any resources that provide value and produce income (income potential) through interest, dividends, capital gains, or other outcomes. These assets range from stocks and bonds to derivatives and cryptocurrencies. Acquiring financial assets means preserving and accumulating wealth over time.

- *Financial asset diversification* is allocating investments across various assets to reduce the risk trends of any single asset.

- *Financial assets investment risk* for exchange market data refers to the potential for loss in the value of financial assets traded on stock exchanges. It is typically measured based on the deviation metrics for stock prices and indicates the potential volatility of the returns.

- *Financial information* often refers to processed data used to make informed decisions, such as investments. The information is usually derived from raw financial data, such as stock price, market volumes, returns and rate of returns, and risk estimation.

- *Financial instruments* are assets that can be traded or used for investment purposes. They represent a legal agreement that may hold monetary value, including the potential for price fluctuations, and can also have other financial benefits.

- A *financial investor* is an individual or institution that invests primarily in financial assets.

- A *financial portfolio* is a collection of financial assets held by an investor.

- Financial risk involves losing money on an investment or business uncertainly, e.g., due to high volatility.

- A *Fourier series*, in the context of Facebook's Prophet, decomposes a function (e.g., the seasonality of a time series) into a sum of sinusoidal functions, each with different frequencies and amplitudes. Fourier series are used to assess complex seasonality with regular patterns and variations over time.

- *Geometric Brownian motion (GBM)* is a mathematical model used to predict the future prices of financial instruments. It assumes that price changes follow a continuous random path.

- *Hyperparameter tuning* is the process of optimizing the parameters that govern the training of an ML model.

- An *investment strategy* in the financial market is defined as a variety of approaches and methods used by investors to maximize the efficiency of realizing the potential of their financial assets.

- An *investment portfolio* (portfolio of financial assets—for financial investors) combines various assets the investor owns. It is usually designed to balance returns and risk according to the investor's financial goals. Investment is using an asset's potential to make a profit in the future. Thus, investing aims to increase short-term or long-term wealth and achieve other specific financial goals over time.

- The *logarithmic rate of return (RoR)* is a method to assess investment performance, emphasizing the continuous effect. It is derived by finding the natural logarithm of the price growth rate—the division of the asset's current price by its previous price. The logarithmic RoR is approximately equal to RoR and is used as one of their values.

▦ *Mathematic optimization* is a branch of applied mathematics that uses mathematical processes to find a function's maximum or minimum values. It is often used in various disciplines for decision-making.

▦ *Monte Carlo simulation* is a computational algorithm that uses repeated random computing sampling to get numerical results.

▦ *NumPy* is a Python library for numerical computations and advanced mathematical operations. It allows the operation of large, multidimensional arrays and matrices and a collection of mathematical functions.

▦ *Open data sources* are publicly available datasets that anyone can freely use, modify, and share. This source offers not only free access but also easy access to well-structured data.

▦ *Overfitting* occurs in model training when the model learns the parameters too well, including noise, on the training subset. Poor results (error metrics are significantly worse) on new data are due to poor generalization.

▦ *Pandas* is a Python library for data manipulation and analysis. It offers data structures such as a DataFrame and Series for tabular data (similar to Excel data sheets), time-series analysis functions, and other tools for data manipulation, such as merging, reshaping, sorting, filtering, selecting, and data cleaning.

▦ The *percentage change* (*pct change*) of income is a mathematical expression of the return indicator. It is calculated as the relative increase in income or by dividing profit or loss by the value of the investment in the previous or base (initial) period.

▦ The *probability density function* (*PDF*) and the *cumulative distribution function* (*CDF*) are two fundamental concepts in statistics used to describe the distribution of a random variable. The PDF shows the likelihood of the variable falling within a particular range of values. The CDF maps a value to its percentile rank or the probability that a random variable will take a value less than or equal to that value.

▦ *Quantitative finance* applies mathematical models and large datasets to analyze financial markets and securities. Python's libraries, such as NumPy, SciPy, and pandas, are extensively used in quantitative finance for data analysis, modeling, and simulation.

▦ A *random variable* is a value that depends on a random phenomenon. In finance, it is often used to model rates of return, price changes, and other market variables.

- The *rate of return* (*RoR*) is a financial metric that measures the investment's returns (profits or losses) or performance changes over a certain period. It is calculated by dividing the asset's current price by its previous price minus 1 or 100%. The result, usually expressed as a percentage, illustrates the overall gain or loss experienced by the investor. Mathematically, these are the percentage changes in the price of an asset.

- *Regularization* is used to prevent overfitting in the context of Facebook's Prophet. This has an effect on time-series forecasting and reduces overfitting.

- The *return*, or outcome, refers to the profits or losses generated by an investment over a specified period, usually expressed as a percentage of the asset's original cost.

- *Risk*, in terms of *investment risk*, refers to the degree of uncertainty associated with future losses from an investment or the possibility of suffering losses greater than the predicted results. Financial losses are monetary reductions that occur when an investment performs negatively. Risk goes hand in hand with the possibility of loss, and understanding both is critical to making informed financial decisions. Risk assessment usually involves calculating the probability of losses exceeding a certain level.

- The *risk-free rate* is the theoretical return of an investment with zero risk, often represented by the yield on government securities such as *Treasury bills*.

- *Stocks*, also known as *shares* or *equities*, are financial instruments that confirm the right to a part (share) of a company's property, including the potential to receive profits in the form of dividends or equity growth.

- *Securities* are financial instruments, in the broader sense, that encompass a range of tradable assets, including stocks, bonds, and derivatives. Securities can produce income through interests, dividends, capital gains, and so on.

- A *statistical sample* is a subset of the general population that represents the entire group.

- A *scatter plot* is a graphical representation of values for two variables as points on a two-dimensional plot. It is often used to determine the relationship between the two variables.

- *Seasonality* describes regular and predictable patterns or movements that recur over specific periods, such as annual seasons, in particular, days, weeks, months, and quarters. Factors such as the weather, holidays, and biological cycles may influence seasonality.

▪ *Series* are one-dimensional arrays with flexible indices in the pandas package (a Python class). They represent a single column of tabular data in a DataFrame.

▪ The *Sharpe ratio* is a measure to evaluate the risk-adjusted return of an investment portfolio and estimates by dividing the returns an investor receives by the volatility metric.

▪ *Simulation* is modeling a real phenomenon with a set of random (computational) experiments. It simulates the behavior of markets or individual investors under various random scenarios.

▪ *Stationarity* describes regular and predictable patterns or movements that recur over specific periods, such as annual seasons, days, weeks, months, and quarters. Factors such as the weather, holidays, and biological cycles influence seasonality.

▪ The *stock market index* represents the performance of a group of stocks. It gives a general idea of the behaviors of the stock market or a specific segment of it.

▪ *Support and resistance levels* are the price levels on charts that indicate where the prices of securities have historically faced upward or downward pressure, acting as barriers to price movements.

▪ A *trading strategy* is a customized approach designed for investors to help them decide when buying and selling securities in the financial market.

▪ *Train, validation,* and *test subsets* are crucial elements of an efficient machine learning process. The training subset is the most significant portion of the dataset and is used to build and train the machine learning model. The validation subset is used to fine-tune the model parameters and perform model selection. The test subset is used to evaluate the final model's performance, ensuring that the evaluation of the model's predictive power is unbiased.

▪ *Trend* refers to a time-series dataset's long-term movement or direction. It can be upward (increasing), downward (decreasing), or horizontal (stable).

▪ *Value at risk (VaR)* is a statistical measure used to quantify the level of financial risk of an investment, portfolio, or position over a specific time frame. It represents the maximum expected loss with a given confidence level (e.g., 95%) under normal market conditions.

▪ *Volatility* refers to the degree of variation of the price or rate-of-return series over time as measured by the standard deviation.

- *Volume analysis* examines the volume of traded securities or contracts to make investment decisions and is used alongside price movement analysis to determine future market movements.

- *Web scraping* is the process of extracting data, commonly raw data, from the Internet. This technique is used to gather data programmatically from the Web.

- *yfinance* is a Python library that allows users to access the open financial data available on Yahoo Finance, including historical market data, financial statements, and stock metadata.

VALUABLE RESOURCES

- *Kaggle* is a well-known platform for data science competitions, real-world dataset analysis, and Jupiter Notebook-like code applications. It often hosts competitions with financial and other datasets and provides a playground for testing and improving Python data analysis skills.

  URL: *https://www.kaggle.com*

  Financial analysts can access a wide range of real-world datasets related to the financial market, analyze them using Python, and apply data analysis techniques, financial models, machine learning algorithms, etc. Kaggle notebooks offer a cloud-based environment for practicing and sharing insights with a global community. Junior programmer analysts can both analyze their code and submit their analytical programs to the community.

  The widespread free use of well-known algorithms, however, means it is not possible to earn income from unique strategies in the financial market.

- *GitHub* is a code hosting platform for version control and collaboration. It offers repositories of Python and other software engineering projects related to vast tasks, e.g., finance, including data collection and clearing, exploratory data analysis, algorithmic trading, financial data analysis, machine learning models, and even graphical application development.

  URL: *https://github.com*

  Anyone can explore real-world projects, collaborate on open-source finance projects, and share the programming code. This is the best resource for seeing practical applications of Python in finance and learning from the community's code examples and task solutions.

Most of the projects posted, however, need to be completed or debugged. Looking at somebody else's projects and implementing tasks takes a lot of time.

▪ *Stack Overflow* is a question-and-answer site for programmers. It's a universal resource for solving coding problems and discovering best practices for any software engineering task, e.g., Python or finance programming.

URL: *https://stackoverflow.com*

The resource helps Python learners and developers overcome programming challenges, learn from the community's solutions, and stay updated with the latest Python trends and best practices in finance. The solutions presented on Stack Overflow are more focused on universal software engineering problems than on analytical problems in the world of finance.

▪ *AI-based chat interfaces* (such as ChatGPT, Copilot, etc.) can understand and generate text and code based on input requests based on human language words. While it is not a direct Python learning resource, it can greatly help analysts and amateur programmers.

URLs: *https://chat.openai.com, https://copilot.microsoft.com, https://gemini.google.com*

It can be used by finance analysts to quickly answer Python queries, fix code errors, explain complex financial models, or generate code snippets. This is like having an AI tutor who can guide you through learning Python and its applications in finance. If you rely heavily on the model GPT results, however, you avoid falling into the trap of overfitting or fake results. That is why these GPT language models must only be considered a powerful advisor at this stage. There is no substitute for the work of a market decision-maker.

INDEX

To my beloved wife, Darya

www.ingramcontent.com/pod-product-compliance
Lightning Source LLC
Chambersburg PA
CBHW080134060326
40689CB00018B/3778